THIS YEAR I'M GOING TO GO SEE *YU-GI-OH!* IN AMERICA!

高橋和希

YU-GI-OH! IS FINISHED IN THE MAGAZINE, AND I THINK I'VE MANAGED TO CONVEY THE THEMES I WANTED TO. THE CARDS PLAYED A BIG ROLE IN THE STORY, BUT MORE IMPORTANTLY, THE CHARACTERS' HEARTS SWUNG LIKE A PENDULUM BETWEEN THE TWO SIDES WHICH EXIST IN EVERYONE...LIGHT AND DARK, GOOD AND EVIL, KINDNESS AND ANGER. THE CARDS EXPRESSED THE PAIN AND SORROW OF THIS BACK-AND-FORTH CONFLICT, IN THE FORM OF DUELS.

BUT WHEN A PENDULUM SWINGS ALL THE WAY AROUND, IT DRAWS A CIRCLE, AND THAT IS THE STRENGTH OF THE MAIN CHARACTER.

—KAZUKI TAKAHASHI, 2004

Artist/author Kazuki Takahashi first tried to break into the manga business in 1982, but success eluded him until **Yu-Gi-Oh!** debuted in the Japanese **Weekly Shonen Jump** magazine in 1996. **Yu-Gi-Oh!**'s themes of friendship and fighting, together with Takahashi's weird and wonderful art, soon became enormously successful, spawning a real-world card game, video games, and two anime series. A lifelong gamer, Takahashi enjoys Shogi (Japanese chess), Mahjong, card games, and tabletop RPGs, among other games.

YU-GI-OH!: MILLENNIUM WORLD VOL. 6
The SHONEN JUMP Manga Edition

STORY AND ART BY
KAZUKI TAKAHASHI

Translation & English Adaptation/Anita Sengupta
Touch-up Art & Lettering/Kelle Han
Design/Sean Lee
Editor/Jason Thompson

Editor in Chief, Books/Alvin Lu
Editor in Chief, Magazines/Marc Weidenbaum
VP of Publishing Licensing/Rika Inouye
VP of Sales/Gonzalo Ferreyra
Sr. VP of Marketing/Liza Coppola
Publisher/Hyoe Narita

In the original Japanese edition, YU-GI-OH!, YU-GI-OH!: DUELIST and YU-GI-OH!:
MILLENNIUM WORLD are known collectively as YU-GI-OH!. The English YU-GI-OH!:
MILLENNIUM WORLD was originally volumes 32-38 of the Japanese YU-GI-OH!.

Printed in the U.S.A.

Published by VIZ Media, LLC
P.O. Box 77010
San Francisco, CA 94107

SHONEN JUMP Manga Edition
10 9 8 7 6 5 4 3 2 1
First printing, October 2007

www.viz.com

THE WORLD'S
MOST POPULAR MANGA

www.shonenjump.com

SHONEN JUMP MANGA

Millennium World

Vol. 6

THE NAME OF THE PHARAOH

STORY AND ART BY

KAZUKI TAKAHASHI

THE MAIN CHARACTERS

KATSUYA JONOUCHI

HASAN   ANZU MAZAKI   HIROTO HONDA

YUGI MUTOU

THE STORY SO FAR...

Shy 10th-grader Yugi spent most of his time alone playing games...until he solved the Millennium Puzzle, a mysterious Egyptian artifact. Possessed by the puzzle, Yugi developed an alter ego: Yu-Gi-Oh, the King of Games, the soul of a pharaoh from ancient Egypt! Using the three Egyptian God Cards, Yu-Gi-Oh traveled into the "world of memories" of his own life 3,000 years ago. There, he found himself on the throne, served by six priests who used the Millennium Items, which had been created 15 years ago to save Egypt from invaders.

But unbeknownst even to the pharaoh, the Millennium Items were stained with blood. Created by the high priest Akhenaden, the Millennium Items were powered by human souls—the souls of the village of Kul Elna, which had been ritually slaughtered by troops under Akhenaden's command! Bakura, the sole survivor of Kul Elna, grew up into a revenge-obsessed madman. His goal: to gather the seven Millennium Items and summon the dark god Zorc Necrophades!

After many battles, the pharaoh's forces pursued Bakura to a shrine beneath the village of Kul Elna. But just when the Ancient Egyptian Bakura was defeated, the modern-day Bakura suddenly appeared. Bakura told Yu-Gi-Oh the shocking truth: he really hadn't gone back in time. The "world of memories" is a simulation, a shadow role-playing game based on Yugi's memories of the past. And if Bakura wins the game, then the soul of Zorc Necrophades will be reborn in the modern world!

Before Yu-Gi-Oh's eyes, the corrupt priest Akhenaden switches sides and summons the dark god, Zorc Necrophades. Now the only thing that can save Yu-Gi-Oh is his friends—Yugi, Honda, Anzu and Jonouchi—who have followed him into the "world of memories." As Yu-Gi-Oh fights the last battle, his friends explore the pharaoh's tomb to find the most powerful magic in the "world of memories": the pharaoh's forgotten name!

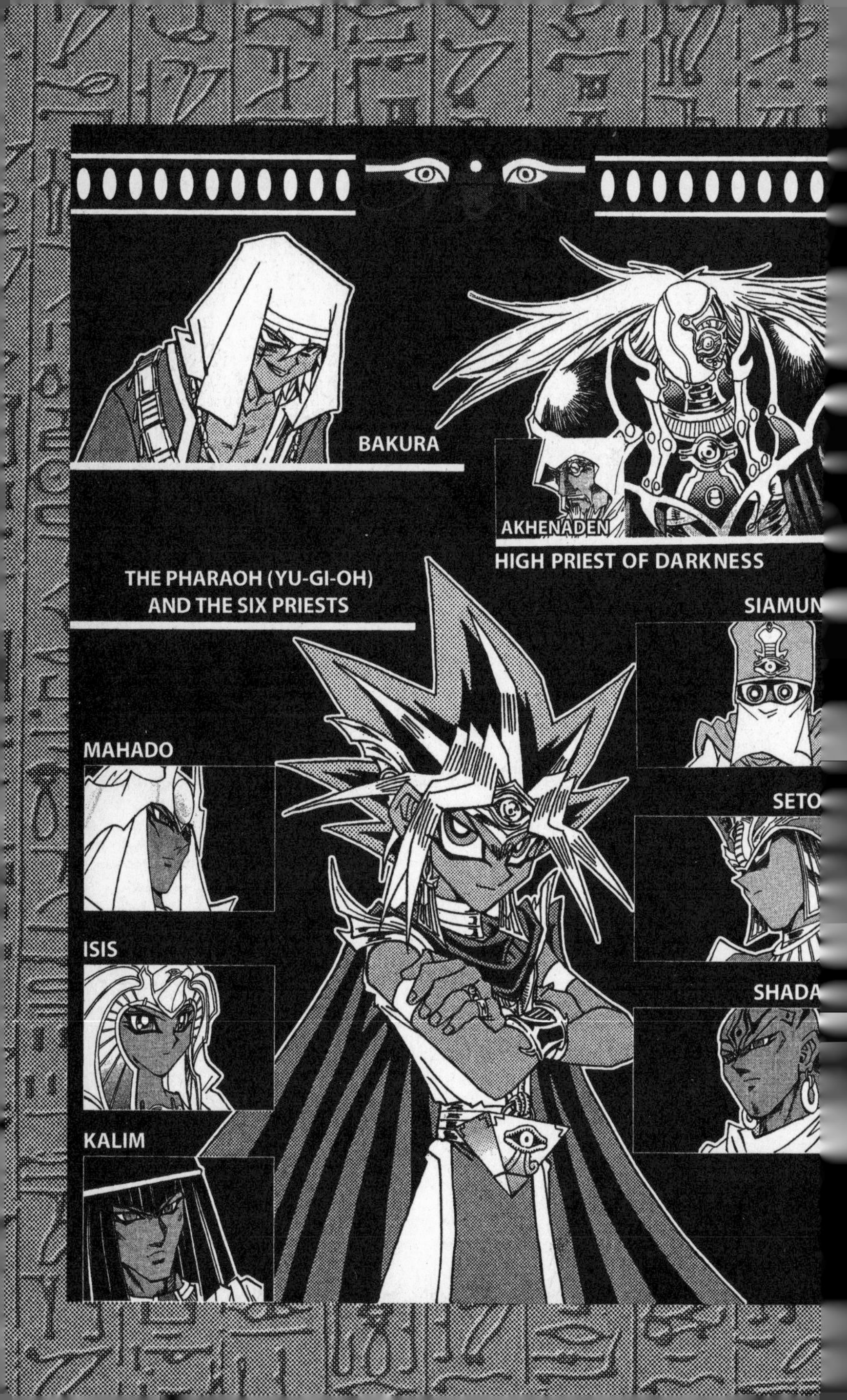
BAKURA
AKHENADEN
HIGH PRIEST OF DARKNESS
THE PHARAOH (YU-GI-OH)
AND THE SIX PRIESTS
SIAMUN
MAHADO
SETO
ISIS
SHADA
KALIM

Vol. 6

CONTENTS

Duel 46	Battle in the Shrine!	7
Duel 47	The Silent Duelist!!	27
Duel 48	Gather, Ghosts!	47
Duel 49	I Won't Give Up!!	67
Duel 50	The End of the World!!	87
Duel 51	Until Our *Ba* Runs Out!	107
Duel 52	The Guardian God!	127
Duel 53	The Light of the Soul!	147
Duel 54	The Stone Slabs of the Modern World!	165
Duel 55	In the Name of the Pharaoh	183
Previews		200

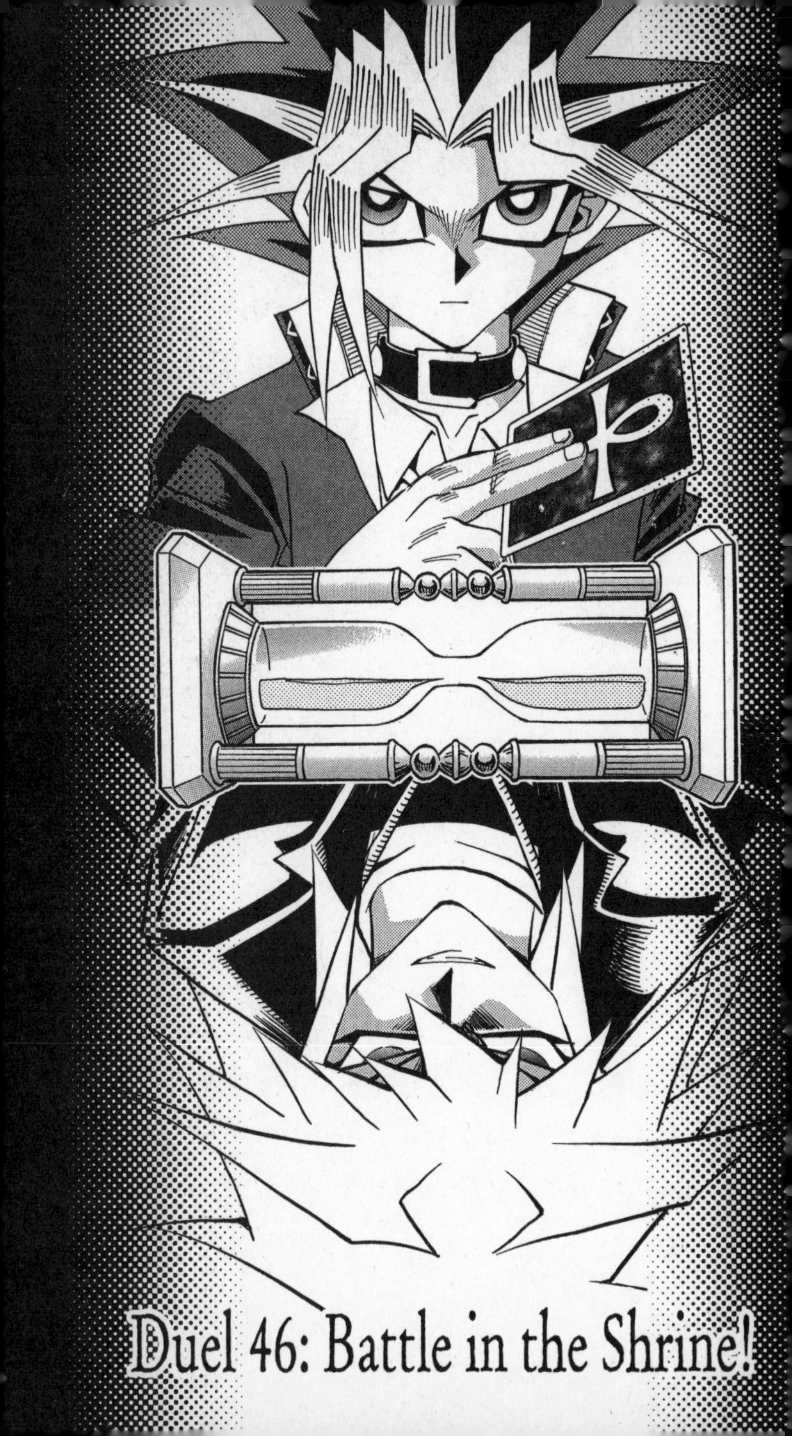
Duel 46: Battle in the Shrine!

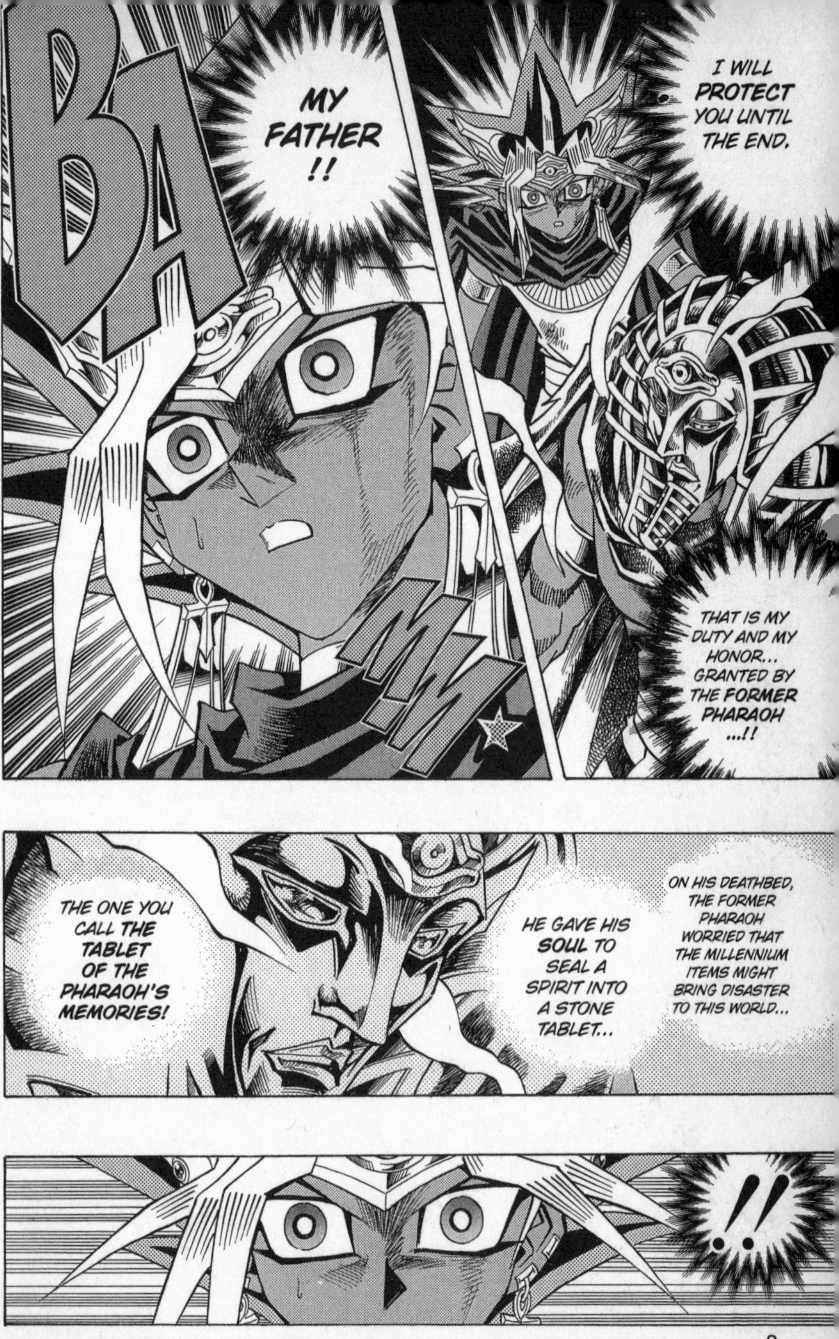
I WILL PROTECT YOU UNTIL THE END.
THAT IS MY DUTY AND MY HONOR... GRANTED BY THE FORMER PHARAOH ...!!
MY FATHER !!
BA
MM
ON HIS DEATHBED, THE FORMER PHARAOH WORRIED THAT THE MILLENNIUM ITEMS MIGHT BRING DISASTER TO THIS WORLD...
HE GAVE HIS SOUL TO SEAL A SPIRIT INTO A STONE TABLET...
THE ONE YOU CALL THE TABLET OF THE PHARAOH'S MEMORIES!
!!

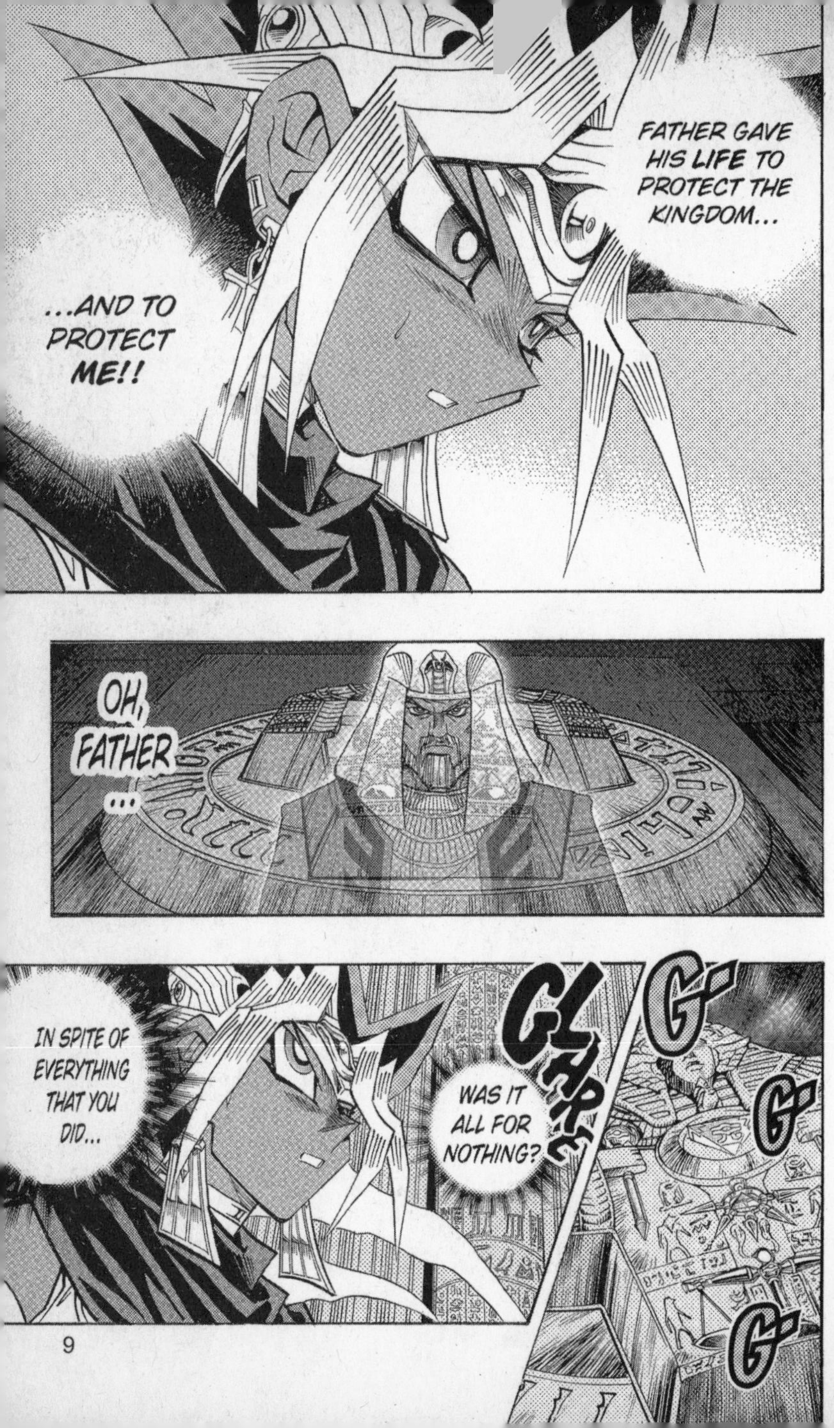
FATHER GAVE HIS LIFE TO PROTECT THE KINGDOM...
...AND TO PROTECT ME!!
OH, FATHER...
G G G
GLARE
IN SPITE OF EVERYTHING THAT YOU DID...
WAS IT ALL FOR NOTHING?

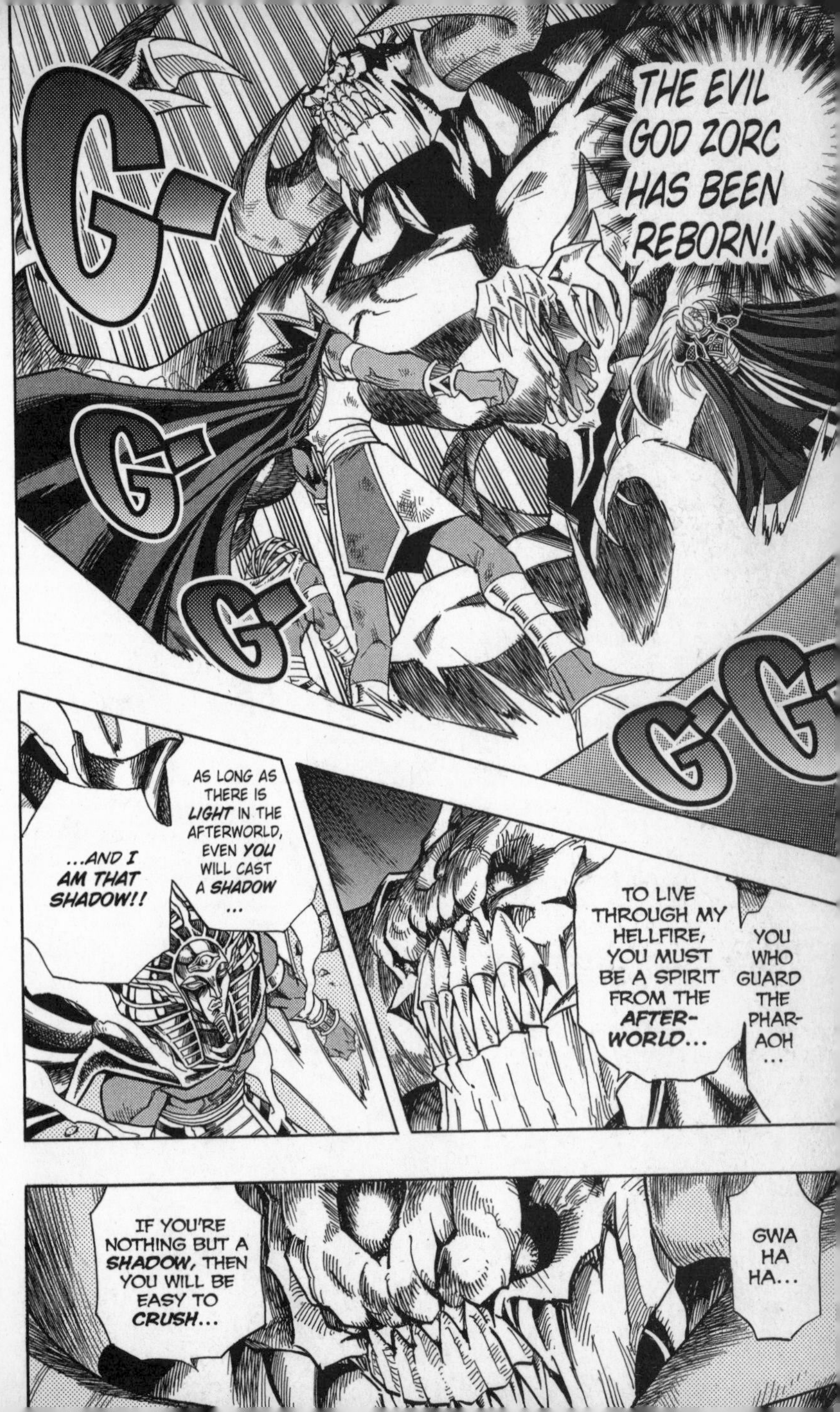
THE EVIL GOD ZORC HAS BEEN REBORN!
G-
G-
G-
G-G-
YOU WHO GUARD THE PHARAOH...
TO LIVE THROUGH MY HELLFIRE, YOU MUST BE A SPIRIT FROM THE AFTERWORLD...
AS LONG AS THERE IS LIGHT IN THE AFTERWORLD, EVEN YOU WILL CAST A SHADOW...
...AND I AM THAT SHADOW!!
GWA HA HA...
IF YOU'RE NOTHING BUT A SHADOW, THEN YOU WILL BE EASY TO CRUSH...

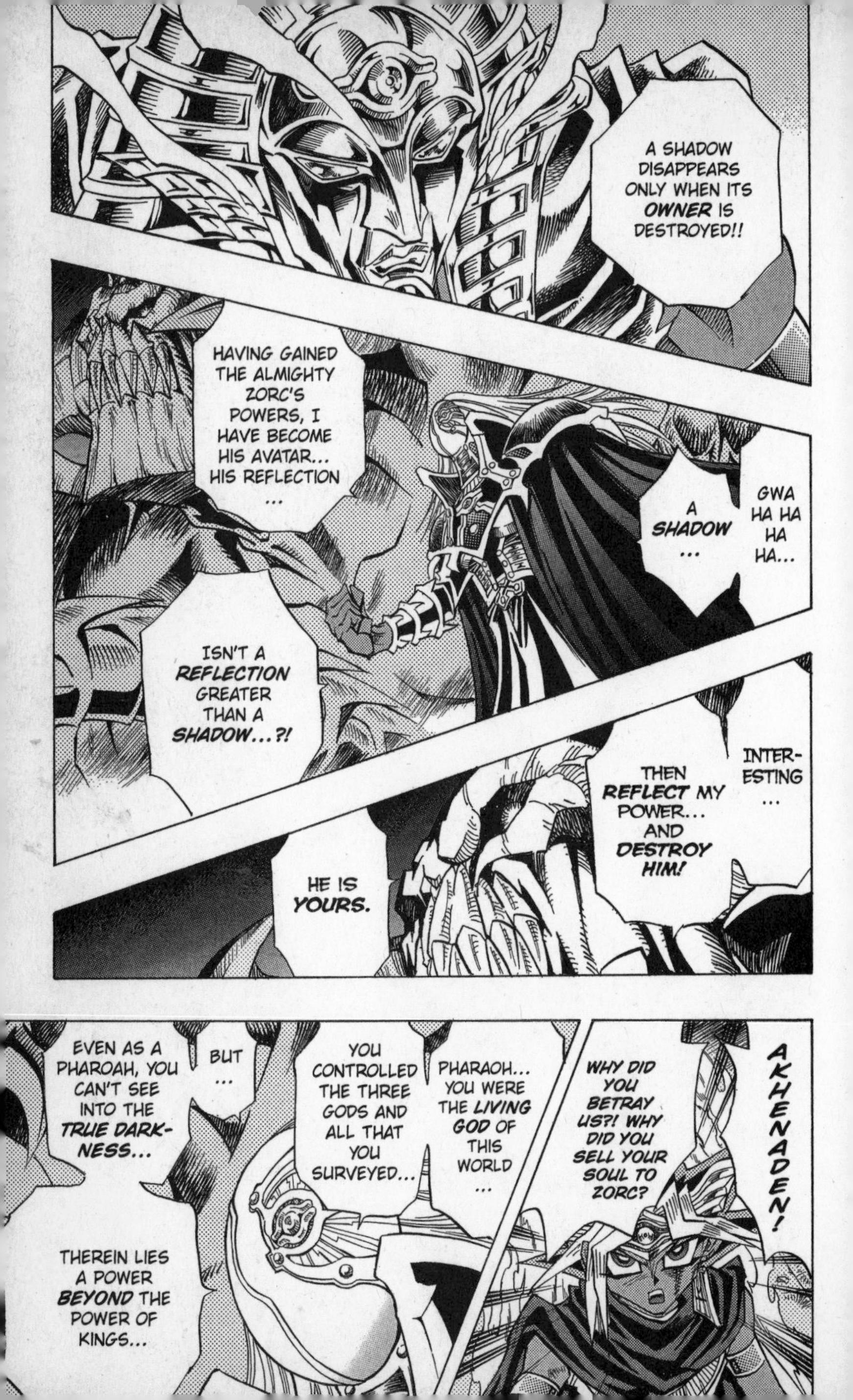

A SHADOW DISAPPEARS ONLY WHEN ITS OWNER IS DESTROYED!!
GWA HA HA HA HA...
A SHADOW...
HAVING GAINED THE ALMIGHTY ZORC'S POWERS, I HAVE BECOME HIS AVATAR... HIS REFLECTION...
ISN'T A REFLECTION GREATER THAN A SHADOW...?!
INTER-ESTING...
THEN REFLECT MY POWER... AND DESTROY HIM!
HE IS YOURS.
AKHENADEN!
WHY DID YOU BETRAY US?! WHY DID YOU SELL YOUR SOUL TO ZORC?
PHARAOH... YOU WERE THE LIVING GOD OF THIS WORLD...
YOU CONTROLLED THE THREE GODS AND ALL THAT YOU SURVEYED...
BUT...
EVEN AS A PHAROAH, YOU CAN'T SEE INTO THE TRUE DARK-NESS...
THEREIN LIES A POWER BEYOND THE POWER OF KINGS...

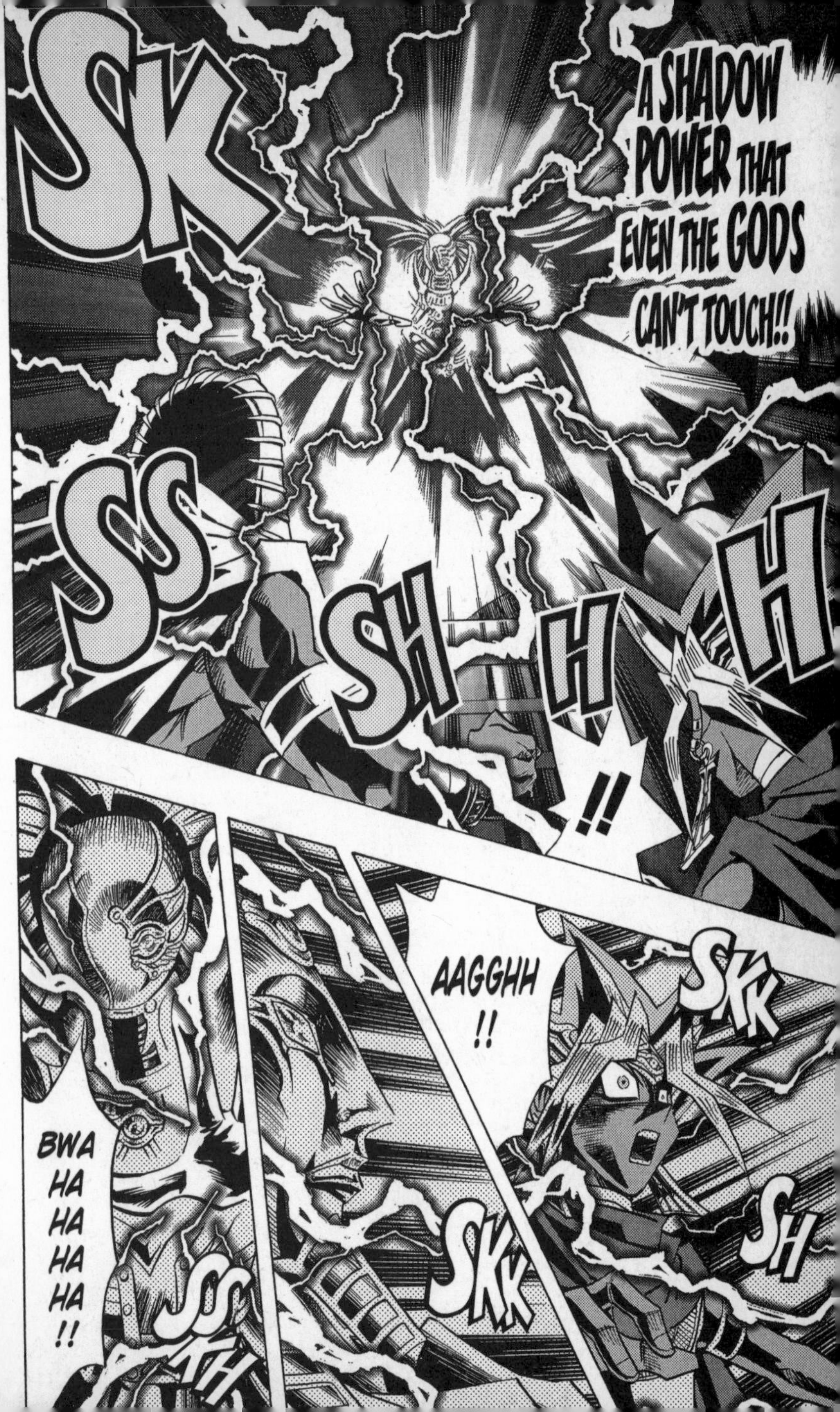
A SHADOW POWER THAT EVEN THE GODS CAN'T TOUCH!!
SK
H
H
SH
SS
!!
SKK
AAGGHH!!
SH
SKK
BWA HA HA HA HA!!
SS

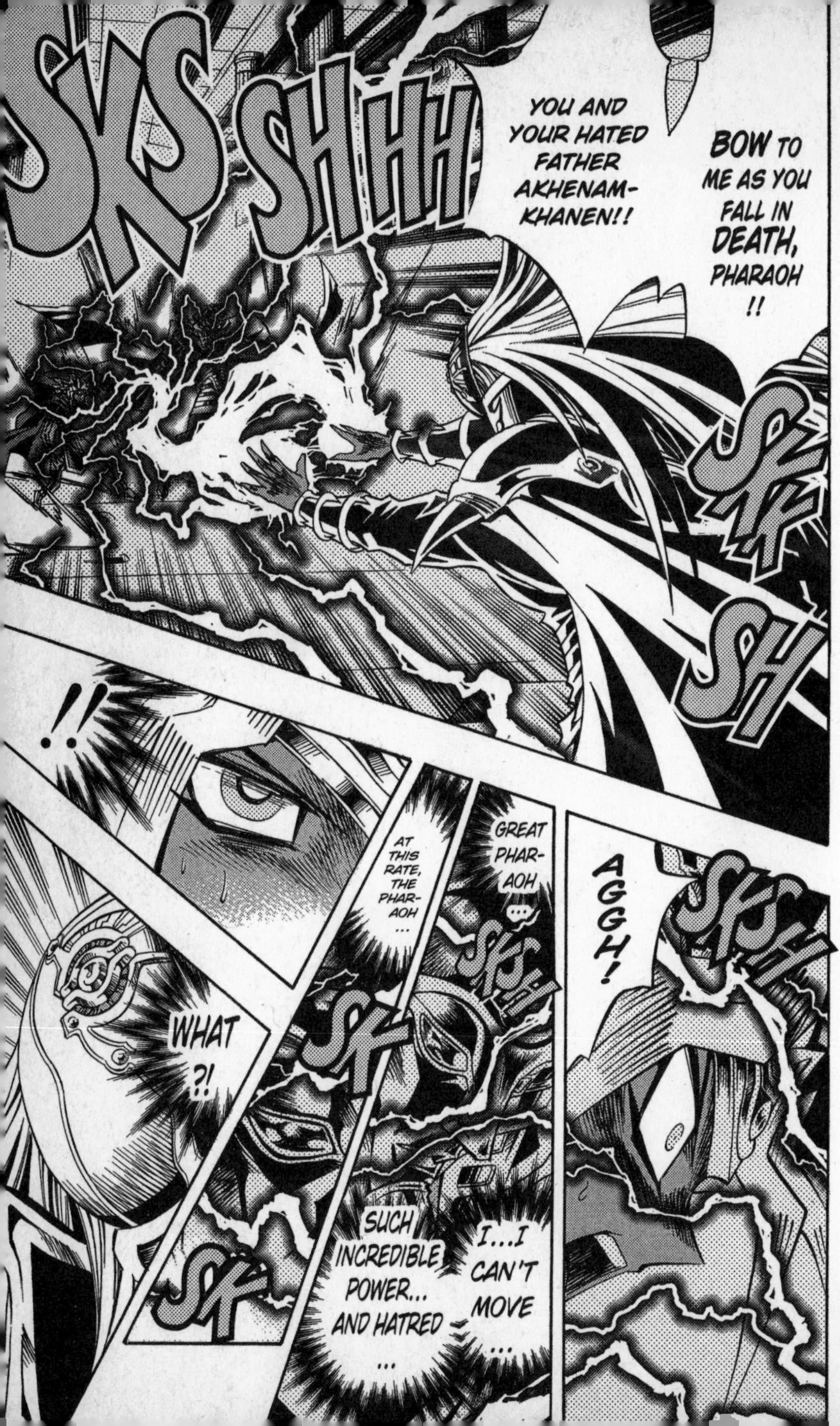
BOW TO ME AS YOU FALL IN DEATH, PHARAOH !!
YOU AND YOUR HATED FATHER AKHENAM-KHANEN!!
SHHH
SKS
SKK
SH
!!
SKSH
AGGH!
GREAT PHAR-AOH ...
AT THIS RATE, THE PHAR-AOH ...
SKSH
SK
I...I CAN'T MOVE ...
SUCH INCREDIBLE POWER... AND HATRED ...
SK
WHAT ?!

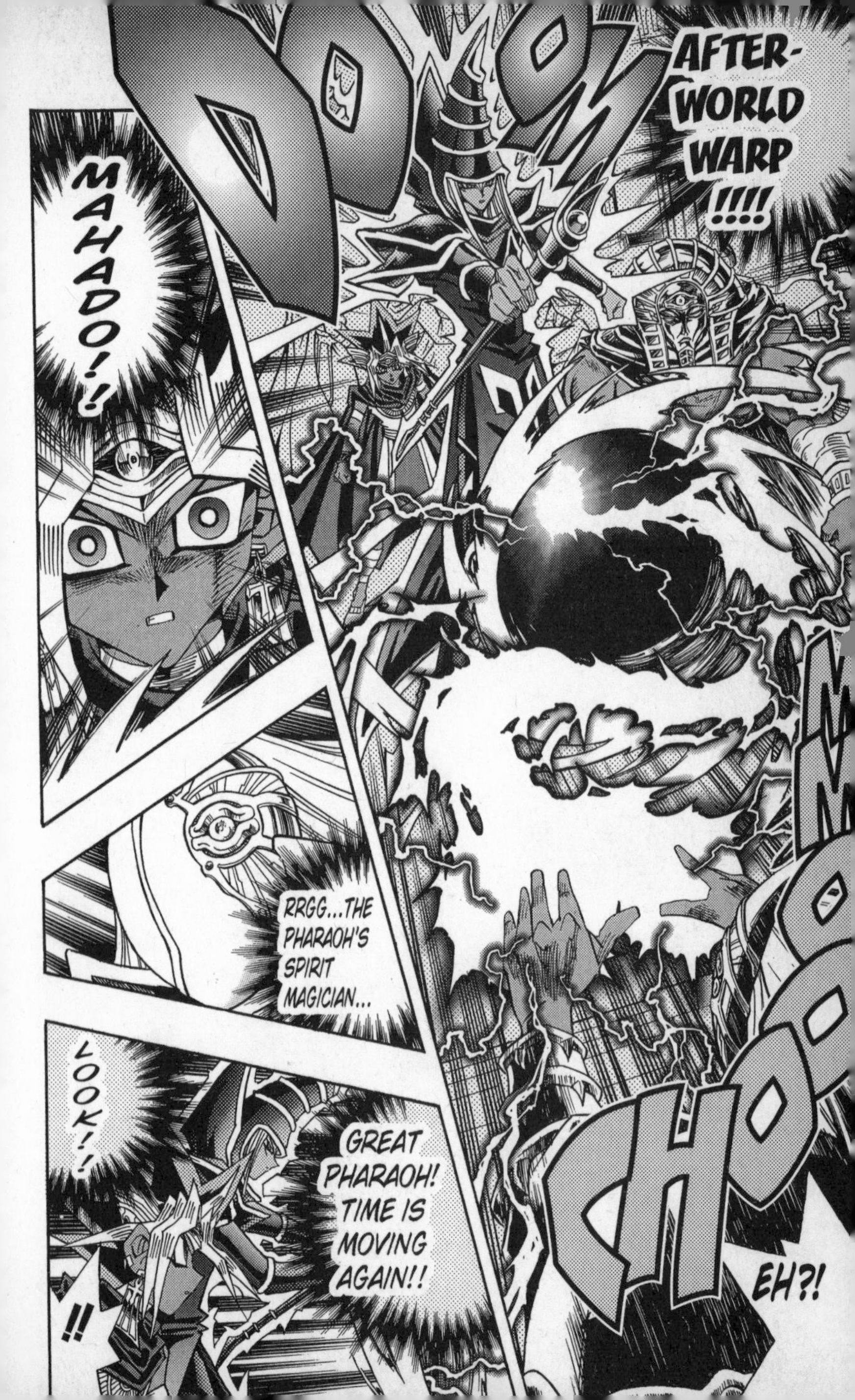
AFTER-WORLD WARP !!!!
EH?!
MAHADO!!
RRGG...THE PHARAOH'S SPIRIT MAGICIAN...
LOOK!!
GREAT PHARAOH! TIME IS MOVING AGAIN!!
!!

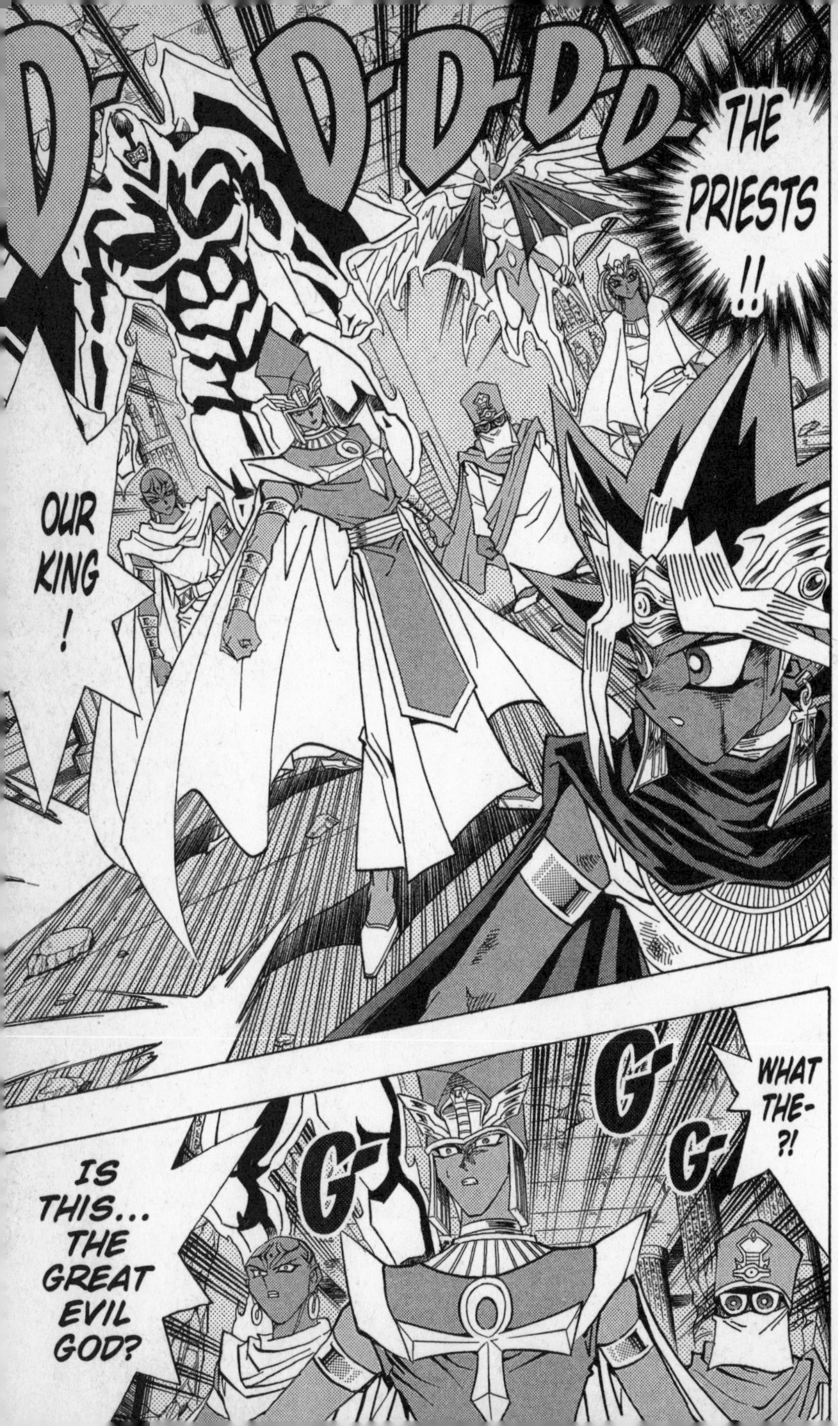
D-D-D-D-D
THE PRIESTS !!
OUR KING !
WHAT THE- ?!
G-G-G
IS THIS... THE GREAT EVIL GOD?

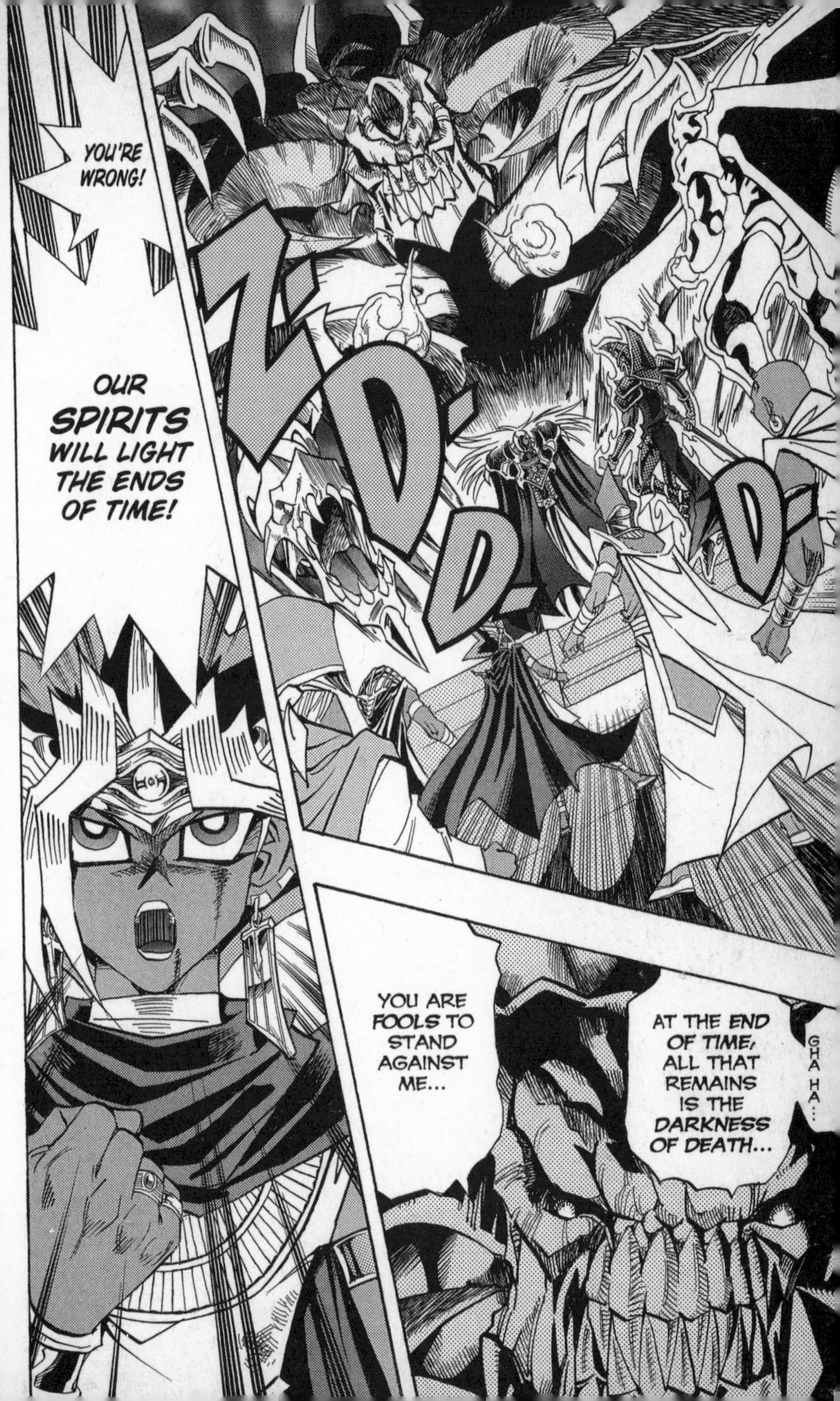
ZDDD
GHA HA...
AT THE END OF TIME, ALL THAT REMAINS IS THE DARKNESS OF DEATH...
YOU ARE FOOLS TO STAND AGAINST ME...
YOU'RE WRONG!
OUR SPIRITS WILL LIGHT THE ENDS OF TIME!

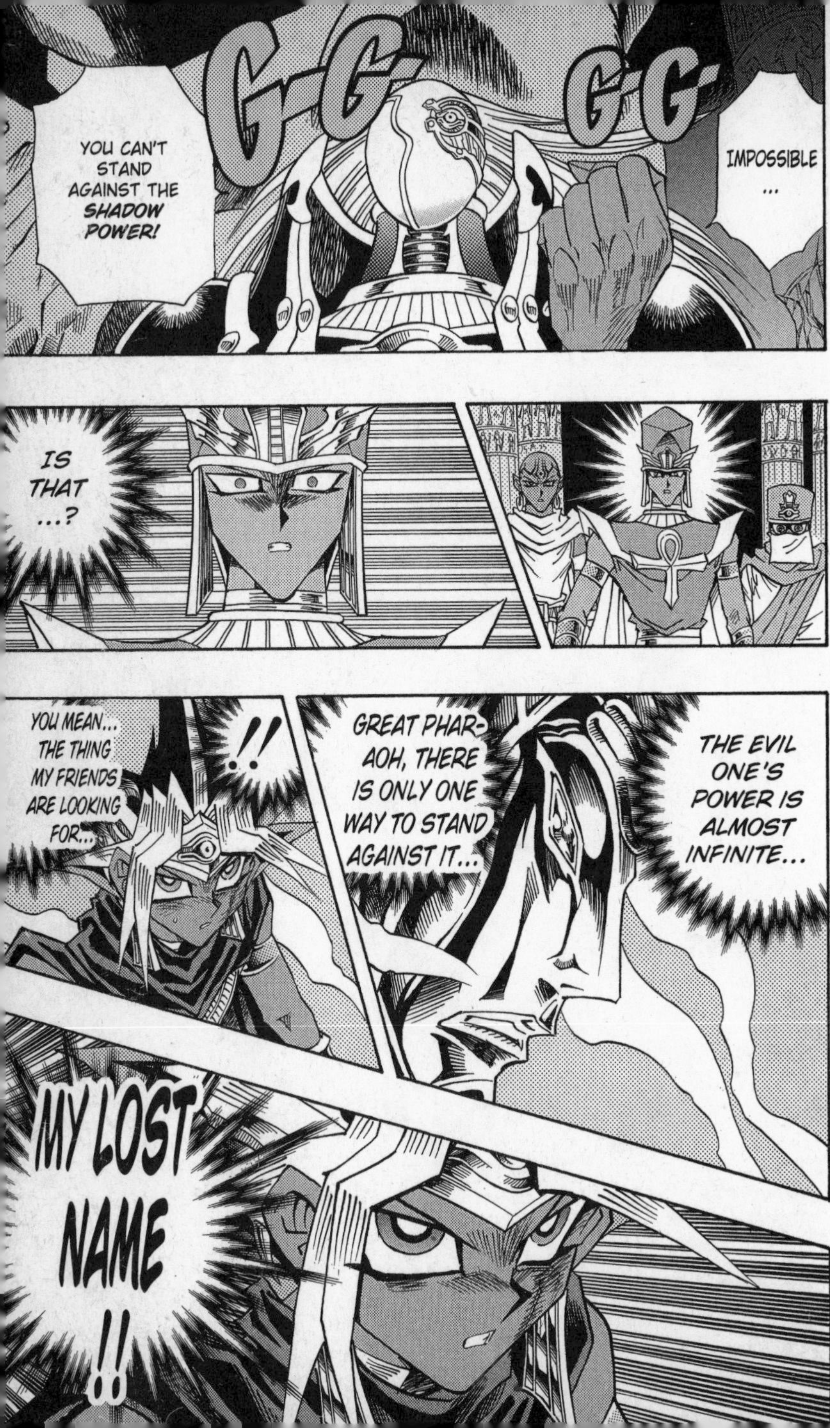
IMPOSSIBLE ...
G-G
G-G
YOU CAN'T STAND AGAINST THE SHADOW POWER!
IS THAT ...?
THE EVIL ONE'S POWER IS ALMOST INFINITE...
GREAT PHARAOH, THERE IS ONLY ONE WAY TO STAND AGAINST IT...
!!
YOU MEAN... THE THING MY FRIENDS ARE LOOKING FOR...
MY LOST NAME !!

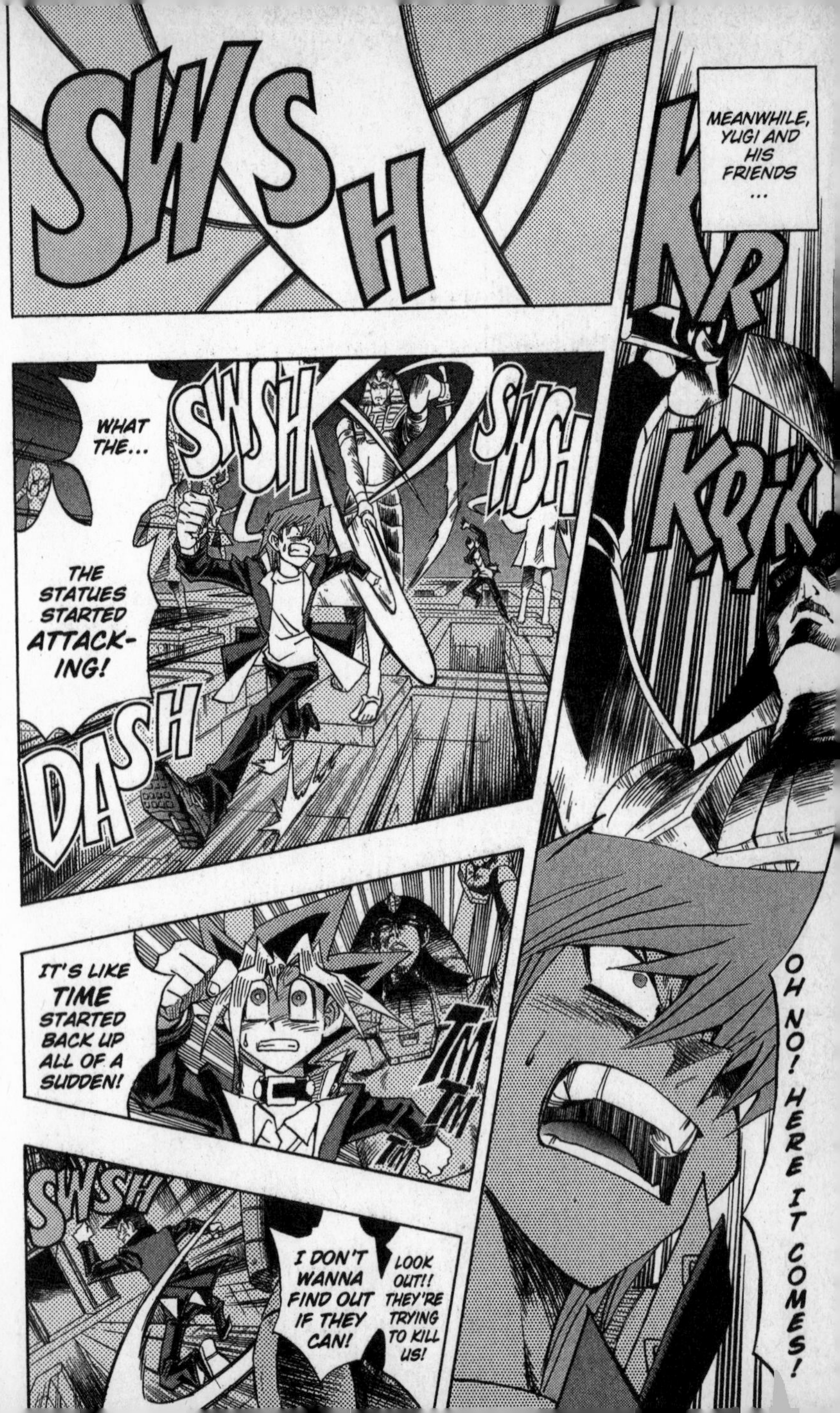
MEANWHILE, YUGI AND HIS FRIENDS ...
KR
KRIK
OH NO! HERE IT COMES!
SWSH
SWSH
SWSH
WHAT THE...
THE STATUES STARTED ATTACKING!
DASH
TM TM TM
IT'S LIKE TIME STARTED BACK UP ALL OF A SUDDEN!
LOOK OUT!! THEY'RE TRYING TO KILL US!
I DON'T WANNA FIND OUT IF THEY CAN!
SWSH

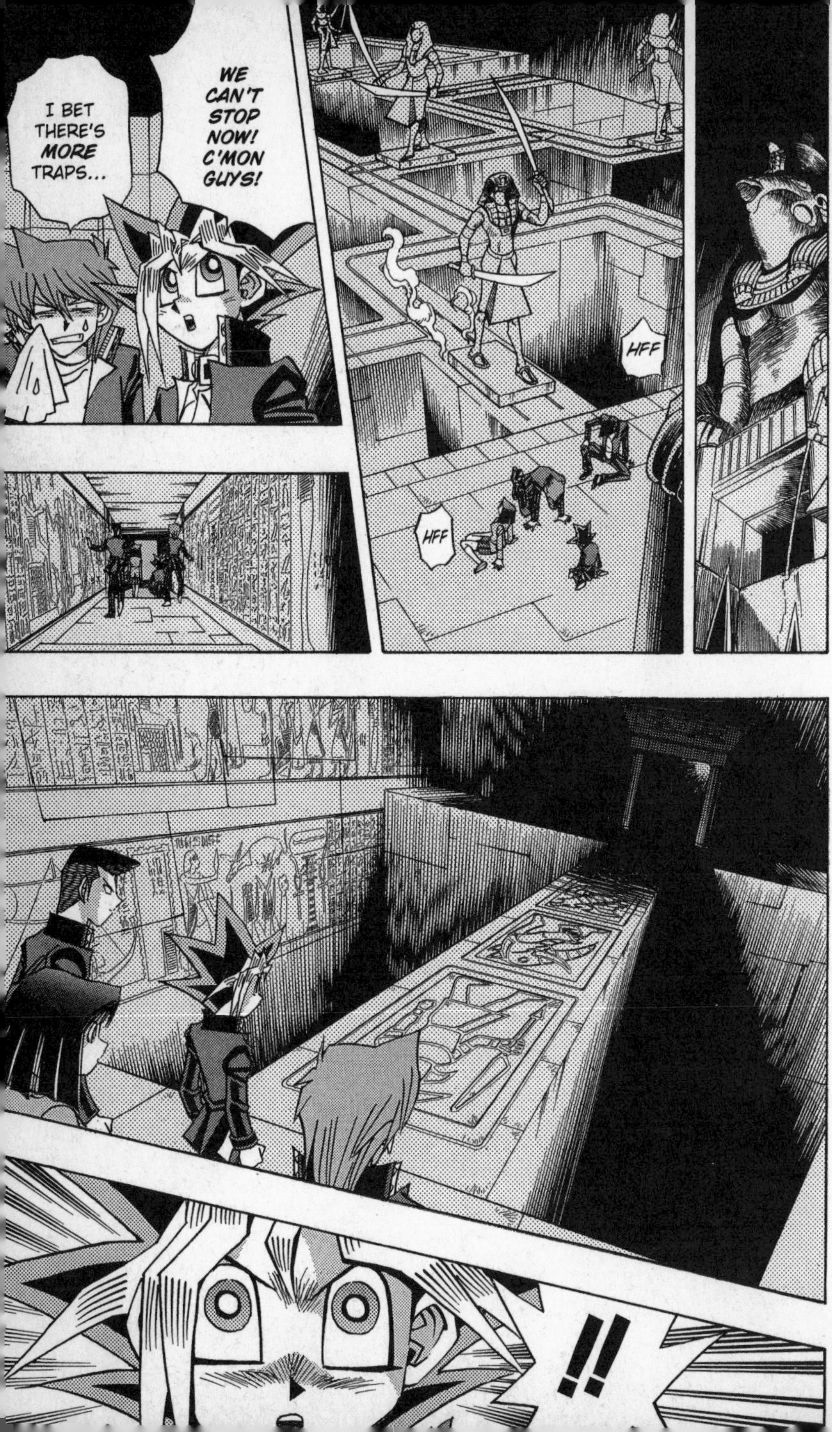
HFF
HFF
WE CAN'T STOP NOW! C'MON GUYS!
I BET THERE'S MORE TRAPS...
!!

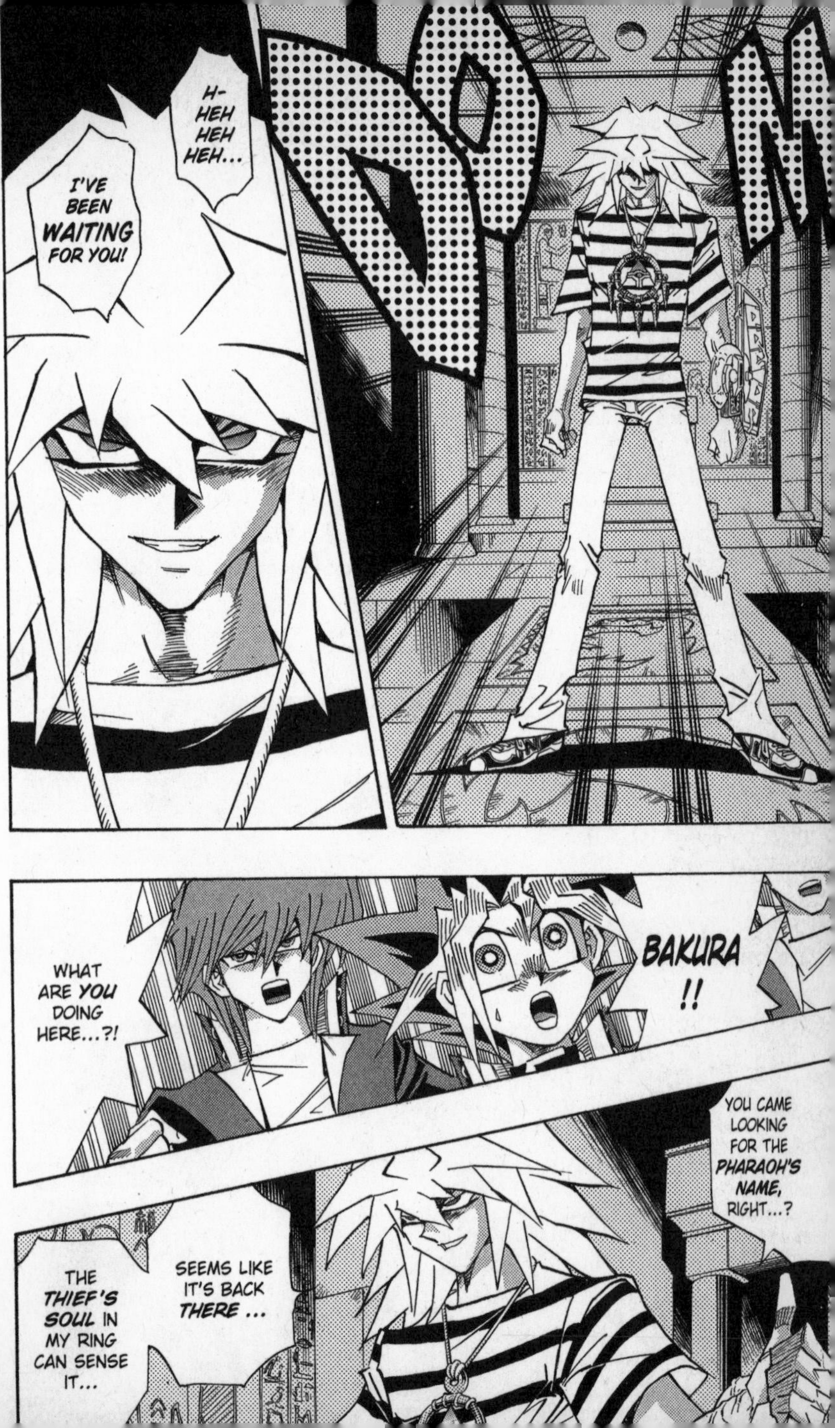
H-HEH HEH HEH...
I'VE BEEN WAITING FOR YOU!
BAKURA !!
WHAT ARE YOU DOING HERE...?!
YOU CAME LOOKING FOR THE PHARAOH'S NAME, RIGHT...?
SEEMS LIKE IT'S BACK THERE ...
THE THIEF'S SOUL IN MY RING CAN SENSE IT...

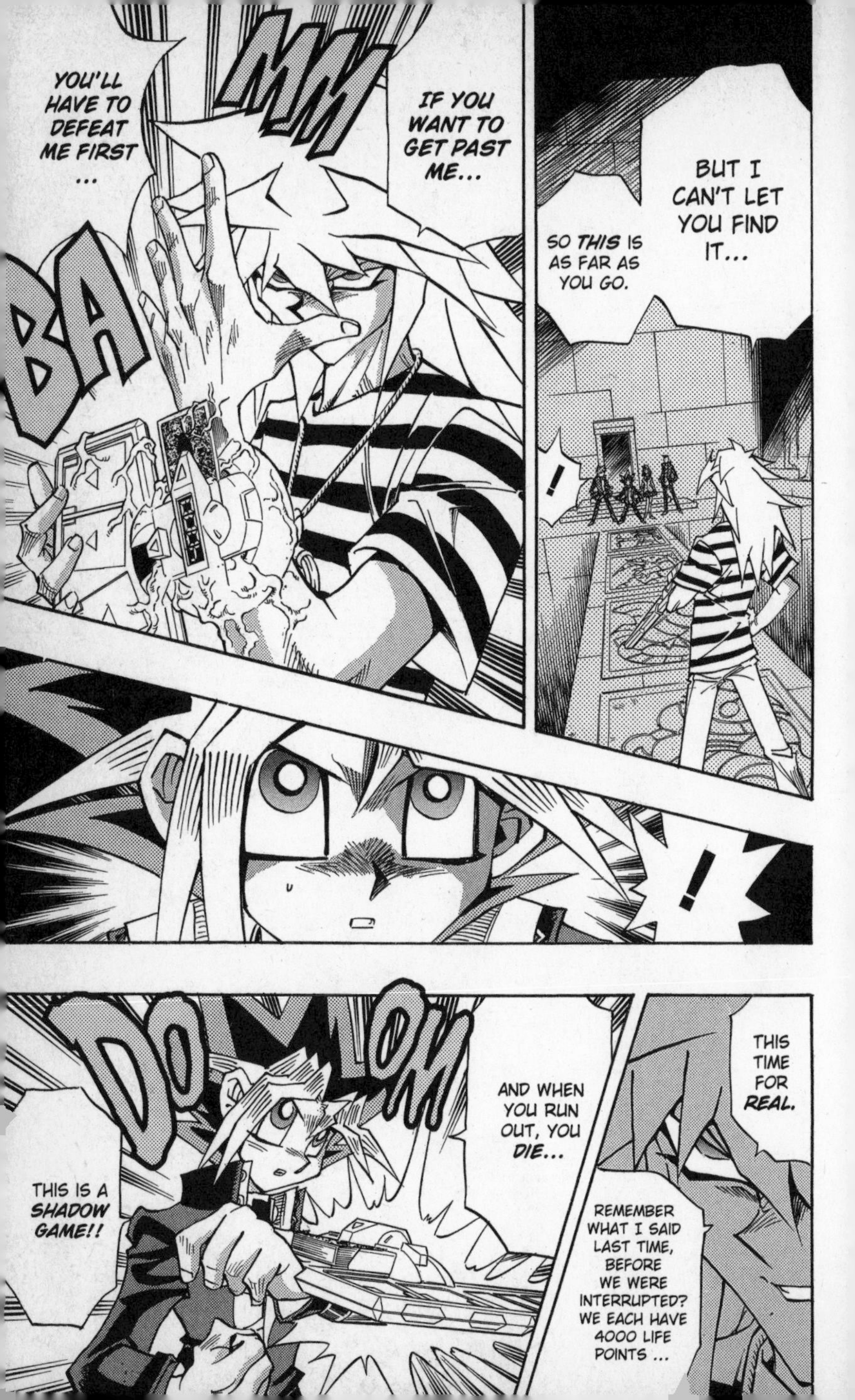

BUT I CAN'T LET YOU FIND IT...
SO THIS IS AS FAR AS YOU GO.
!
MM
IF YOU WANT TO GET PAST ME...
YOU'LL HAVE TO DEFEAT ME FIRST...
BA
!
THIS TIME FOR REAL.
REMEMBER WHAT I SAID LAST TIME, BEFORE WE WERE INTERRUPTED? WE EACH HAVE 4000 LIFE POINTS...
AND WHEN YOU RUN OUT, YOU DIE...
THIS IS A SHADOW GAME!!

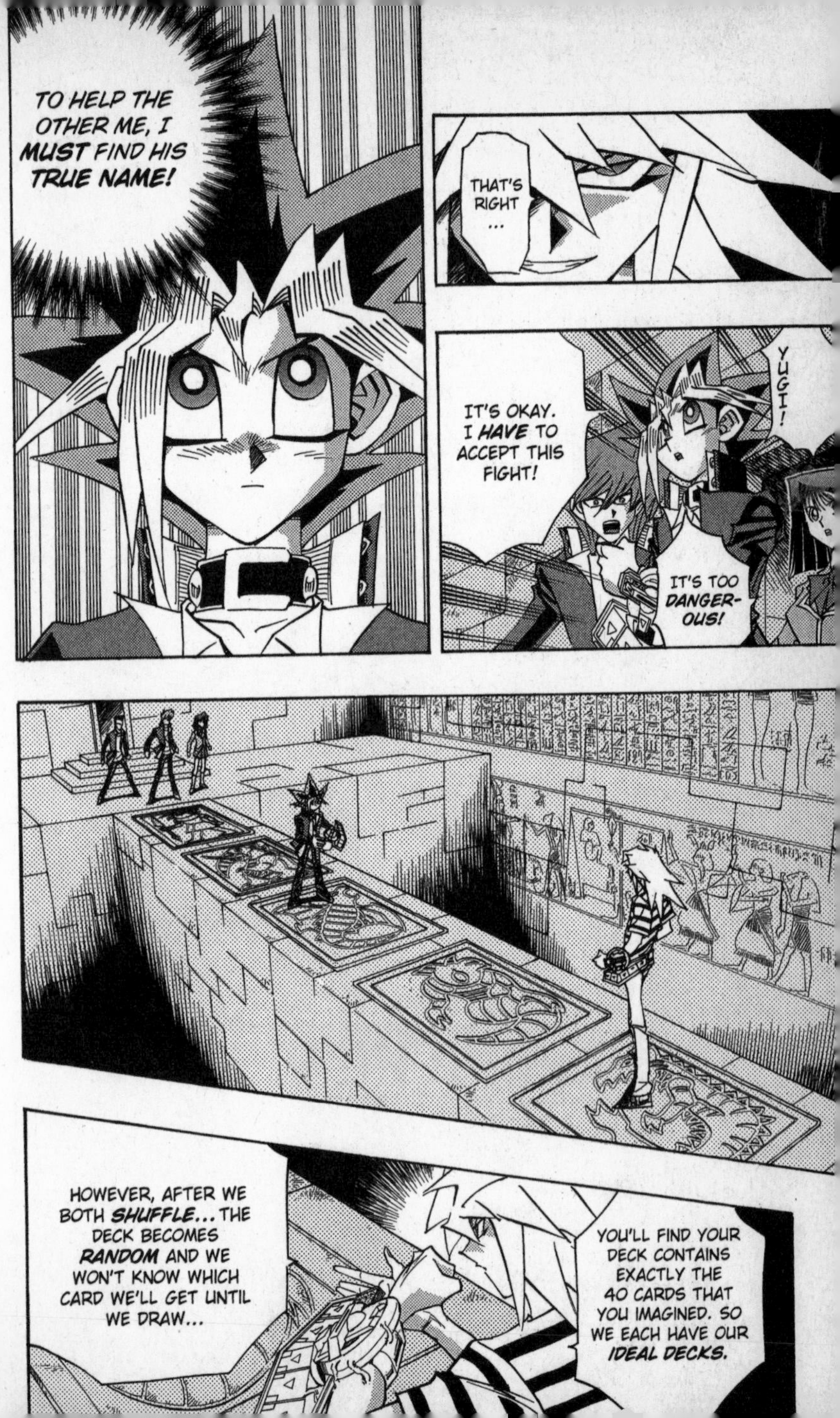

THAT'S RIGHT ...
YUGI!
IT'S OKAY. I HAVE TO ACCEPT THIS FIGHT!
IT'S TOO DANGEROUS!
TO HELP THE OTHER ME, I MUST FIND HIS TRUE NAME!
YOU'LL FIND YOUR DECK CONTAINS EXACTLY THE 40 CARDS THAT YOU IMAGINED. SO WE EACH HAVE OUR IDEAL DECKS.
HOWEVER, AFTER WE BOTH SHUFFLE... THE DECK BECOMES RANDOM AND WE WON'T KNOW WHICH CARD WE'LL GET UNTIL WE DRAW...

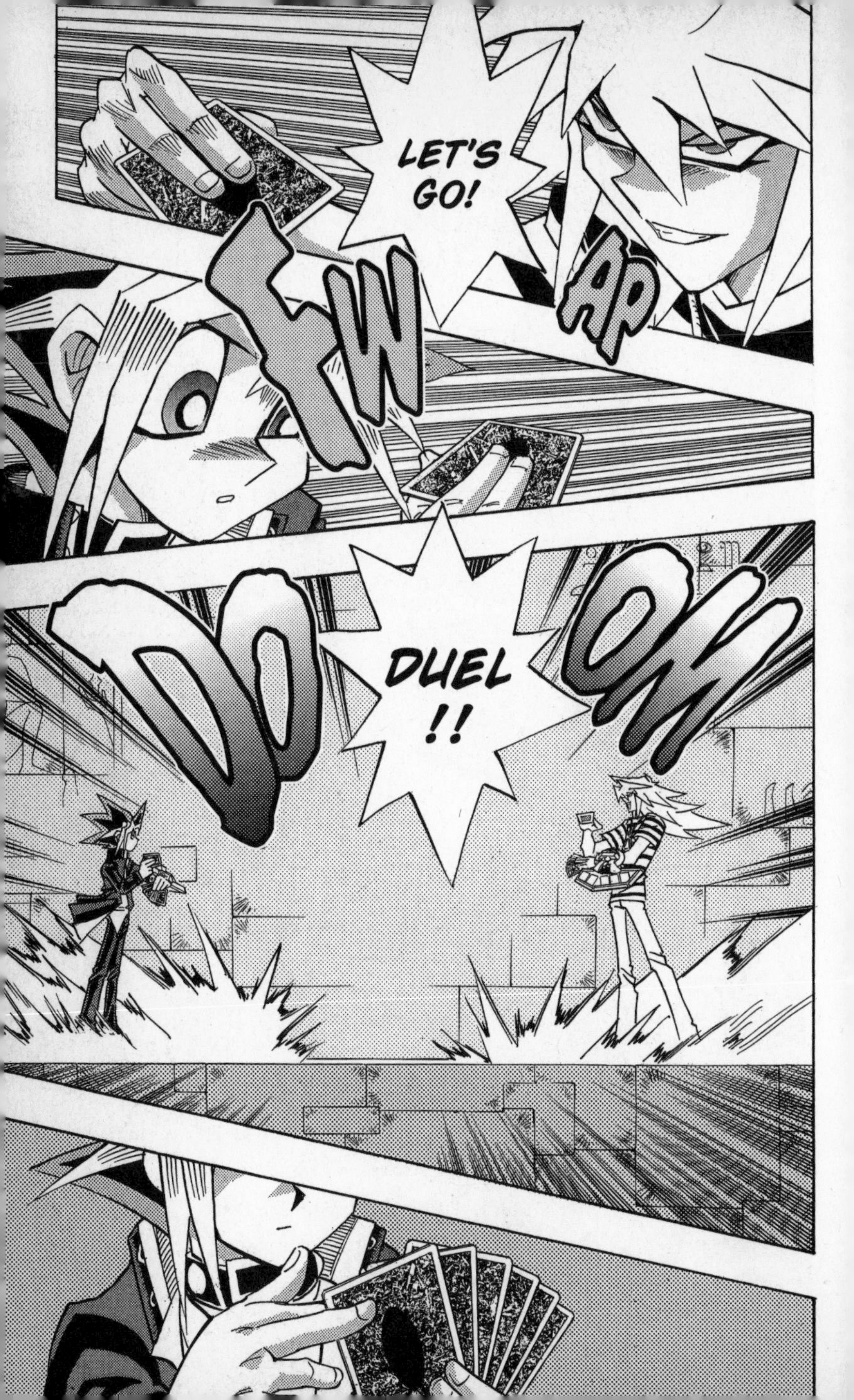
LET'S GO!
SWAP
DUEL!!
DOOM

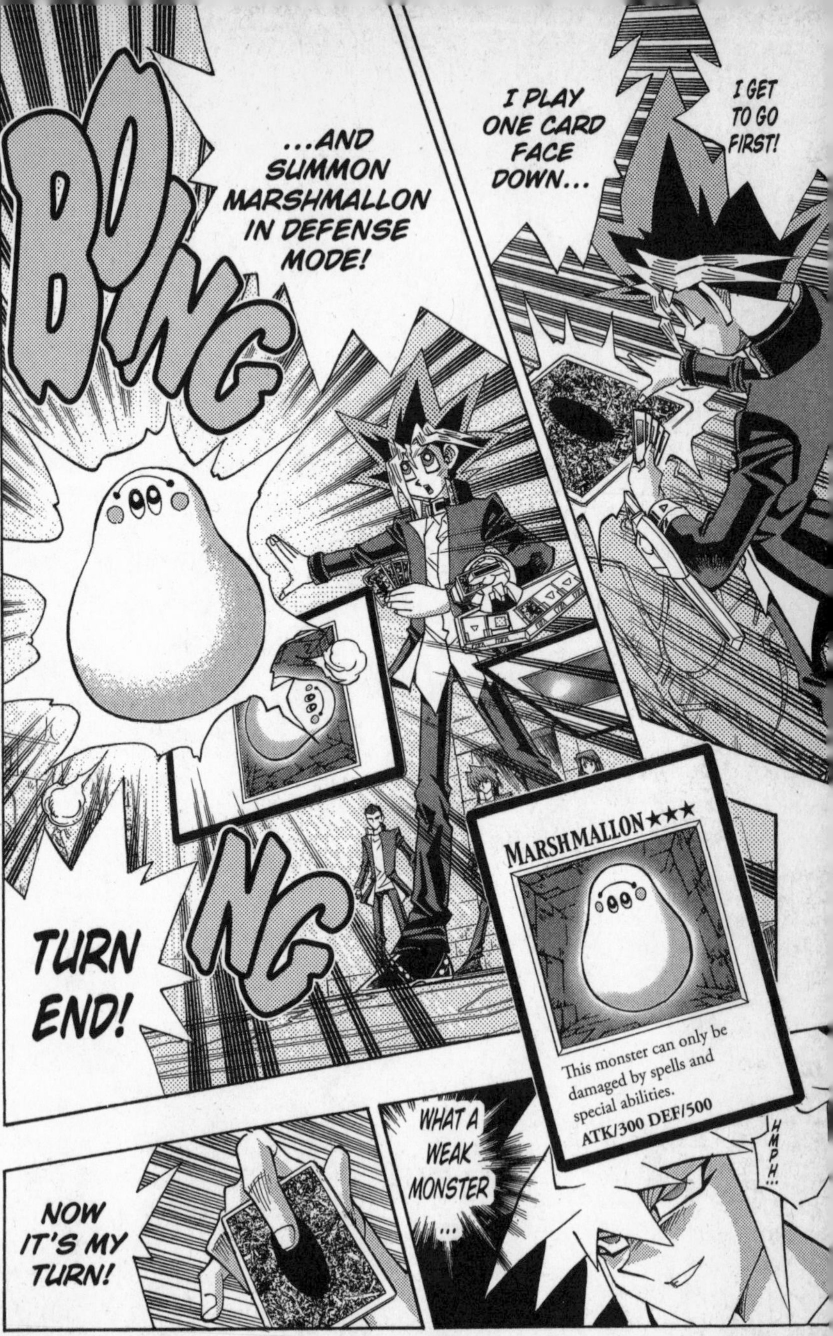
I GET TO GO FIRST!
I PLAY ONE CARD FACE DOWN...
...AND SUMMON MARSHMALLON IN DEFENSE MODE!
BOING
NG
TURN END!
MARSHMALLON★★★
This monster can only be damaged by spells and special abilities.
ATK/300 DEF/500
HMPH..!!
WHAT A WEAK MONSTER...
NOW IT'S MY TURN!

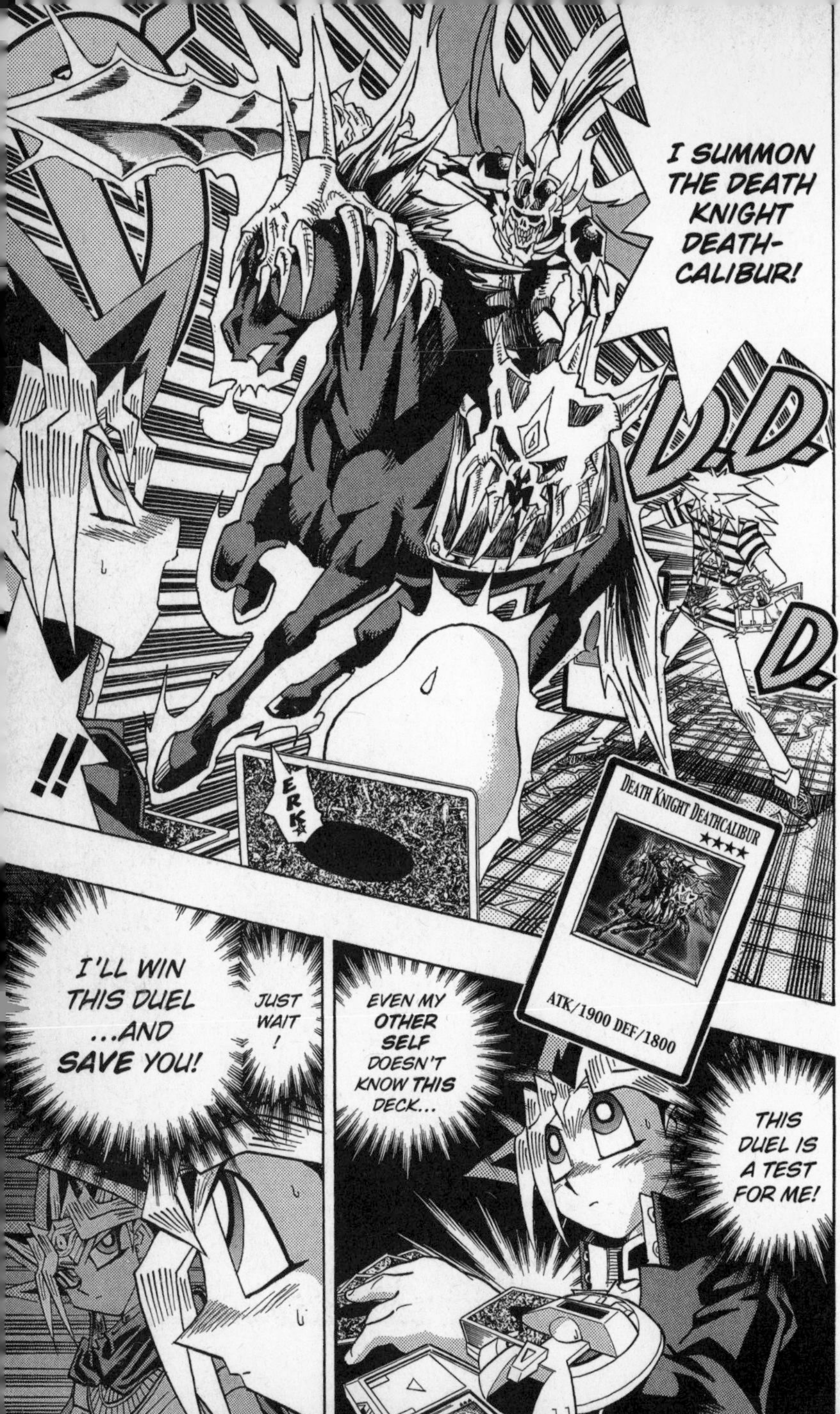
I SUMMON THE DEATH KNIGHT DEATH-CALIBUR!
D.D. D.
DEATH KNIGHT DEATHCALIBUR
ATK/1900 DEF/1800
ERK
!!
THIS DUEL IS A TEST FOR ME!
EVEN MY OTHER SELF DOESN'T KNOW THIS DECK...
JUST WAIT!
I'LL WIN THIS DUEL ...AND SAVE YOU!

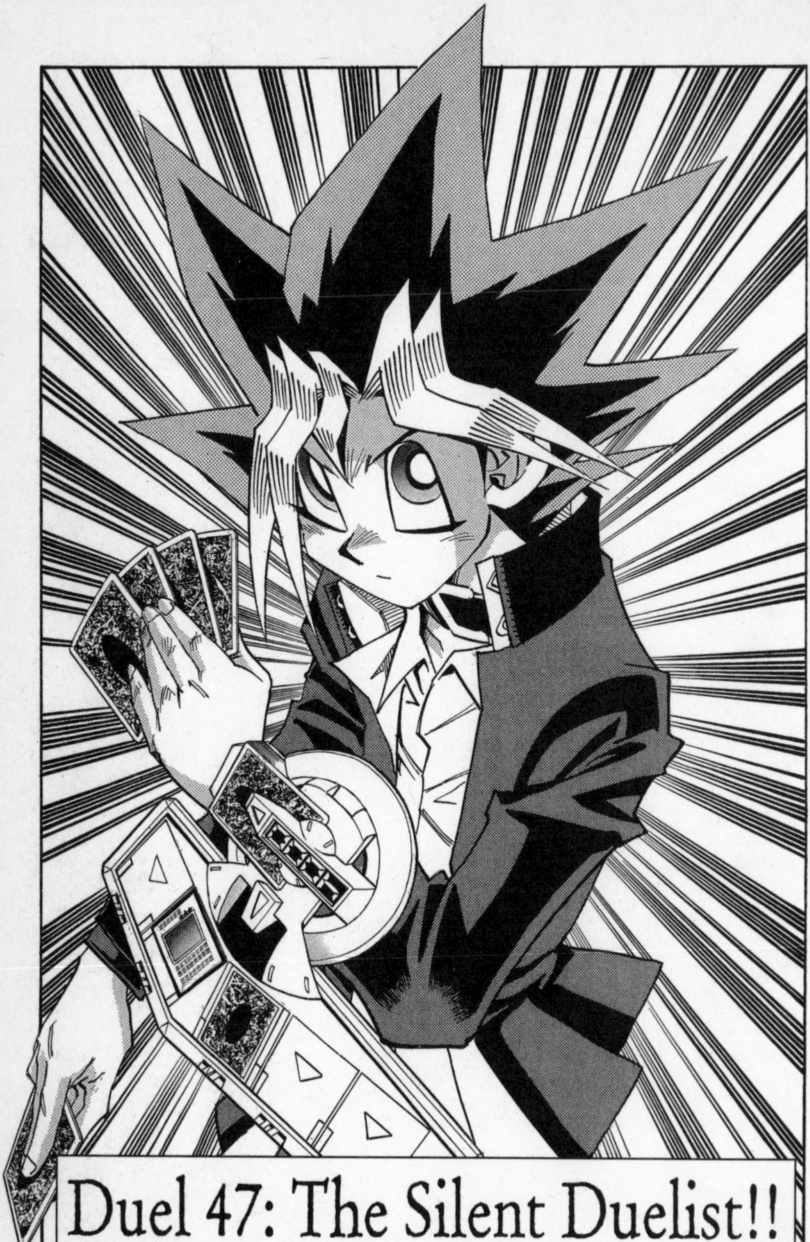
Duel 47: The Silent Duelist!!

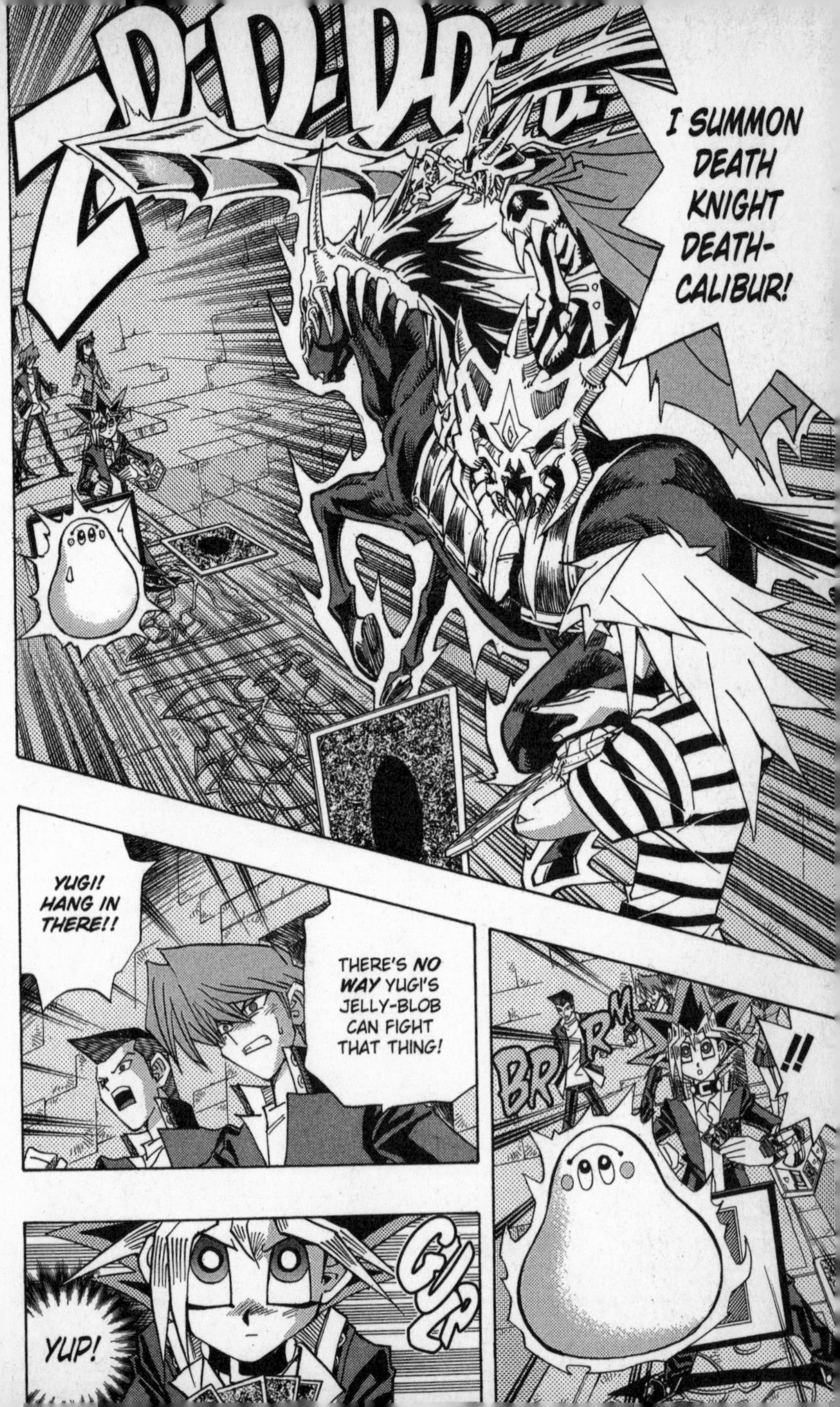
I SUMMON DEATH KNIGHT DEATH-CALIBUR!
!!
YUGI! HANG IN THERE!!
THERE'S **NO WAY** YUGI'S JELLY-BLOB CAN FIGHT THAT THING!
YUP!

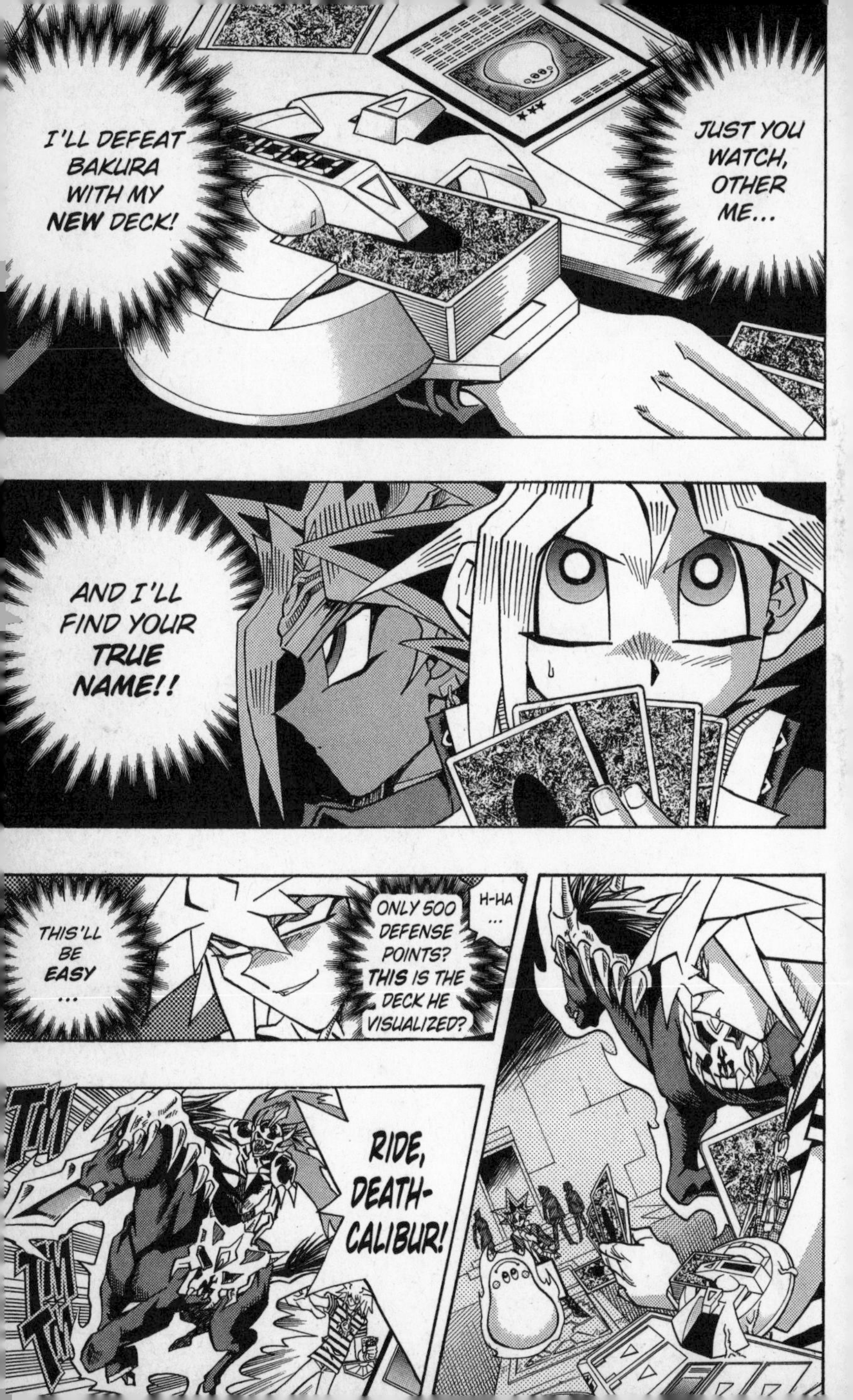
JUST YOU WATCH, OTHER ME...
I'LL DEFEAT BAKURA WITH MY **NEW** DECK!
AND I'LL FIND YOUR **TRUE NAME!!**
H-HA ...
ONLY 500 DEFENSE POINTS? **THIS** IS THE DECK HE VISUALIZED?
THIS'LL BE **EASY** ...
RIDE, DEATH-CALIBUR!

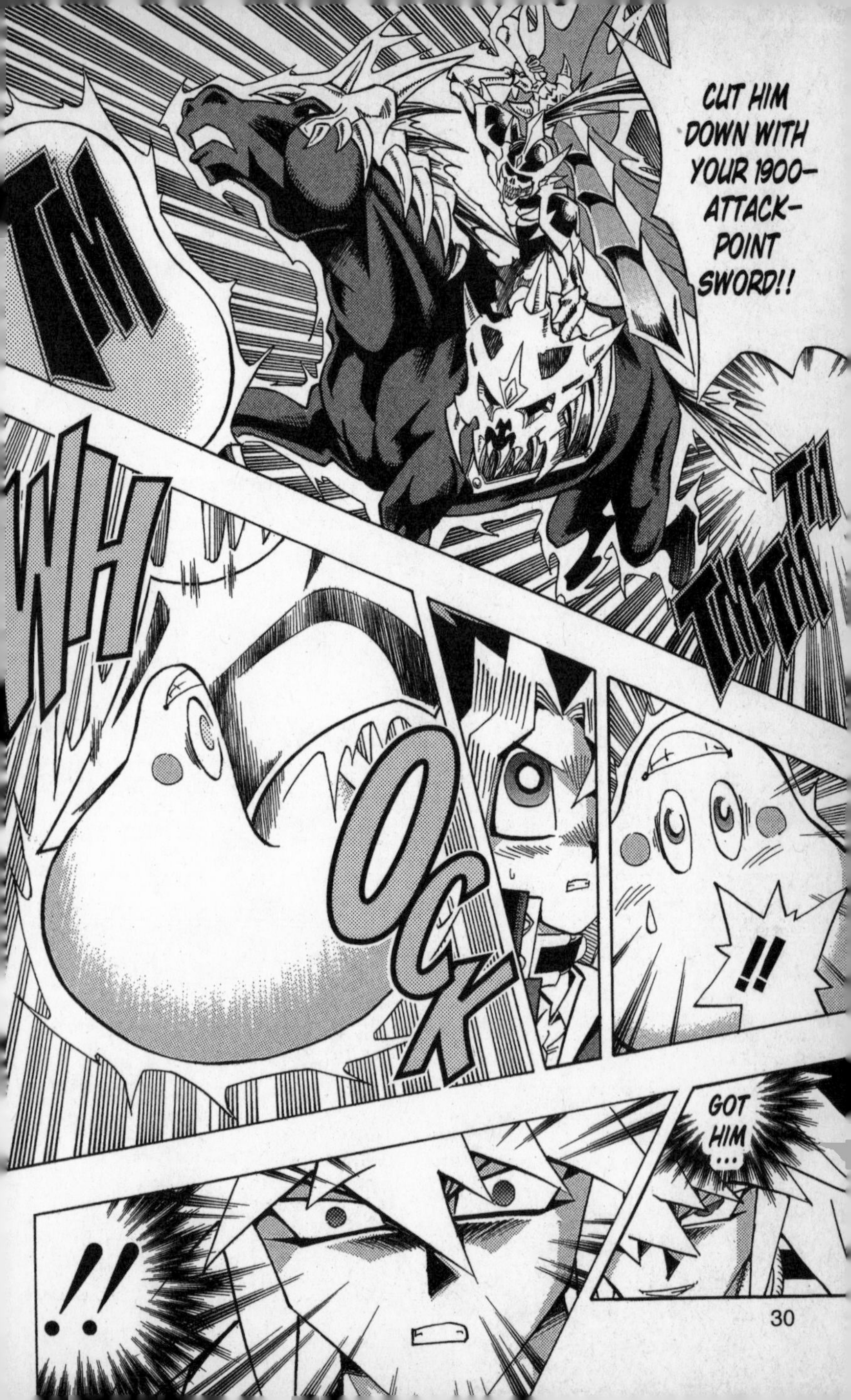
CUT HIM DOWN WITH YOUR 1900-ATTACK-POINT SWORD!!
TM
TMTMTM
!!
WH
OOCK
GOT HIM...
!!

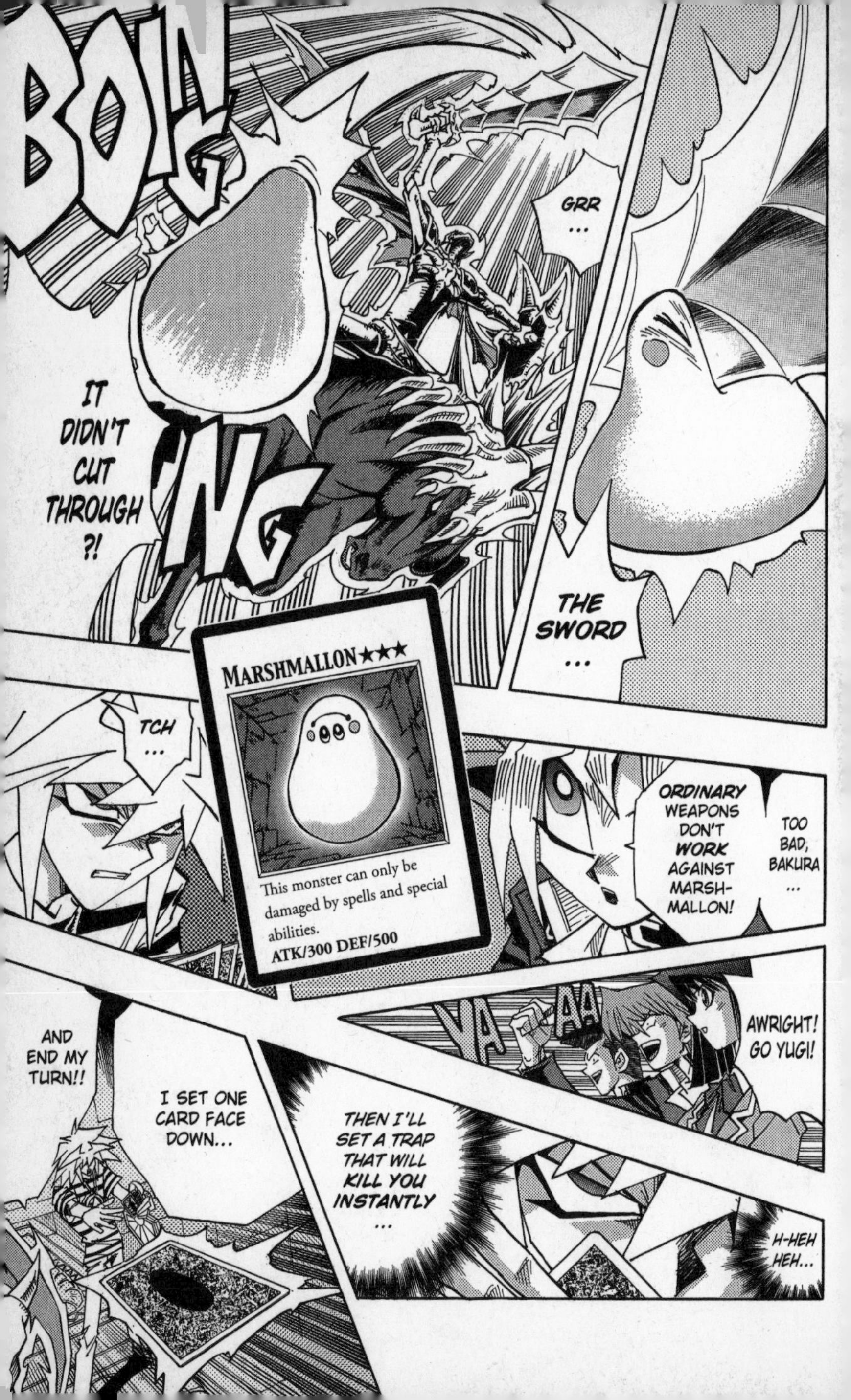
GRR...
THE SWORD...
BOING
IT DIDN'T CUT THROUGH?!
TOO BAD, BAKURA...
ORDINARY WEAPONS DON'T WORK AGAINST MARSHMALLON!
MARSHMALLON★★★
This monster can only be damaged by spells and special abilities.
ATK/300 DEF/500
TCH...
AWRIGHT! GO YUGI!
YAAA
H-HEH HEH...
THEN I'LL SET A TRAP THAT WILL KILL YOU INSTANTLY...
I SET ONE CARD FACE DOWN...
AND END MY TURN!!

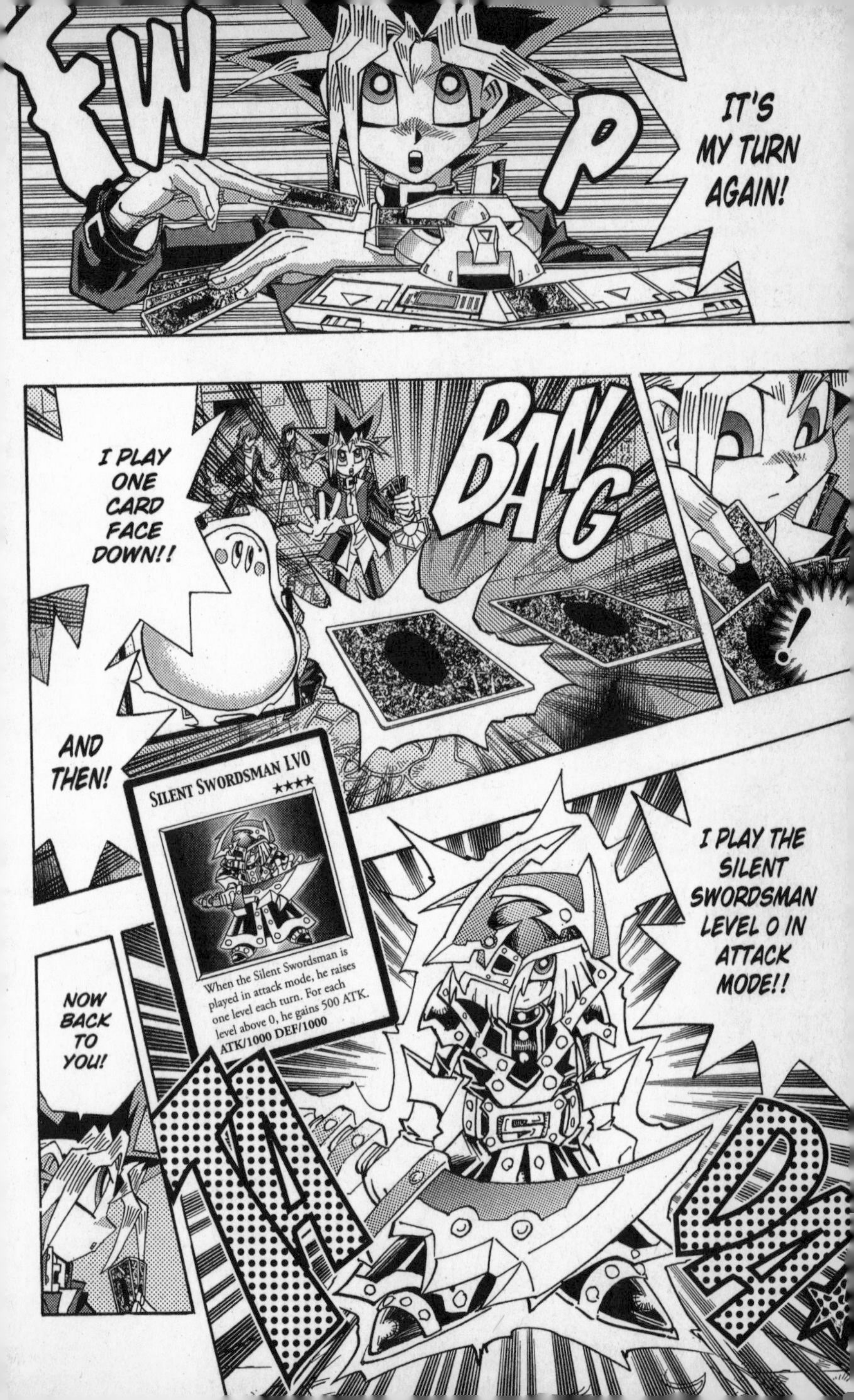
FWP
IT'S MY TURN AGAIN!
!
BANG
I PLAY ONE CARD FACE DOWN!!
AND THEN!
I PLAY THE SILENT SWORDSMAN LEVEL 0 IN ATTACK MODE!!
SILENT SWORDSMAN LV0
★★★★
When the Silent Swordsman is played in attack mode, he raises one level each turn. For each level above 0, he gains 500 ATK.
ATK/1000 DEF/1000
NOW BACK TO YOU!

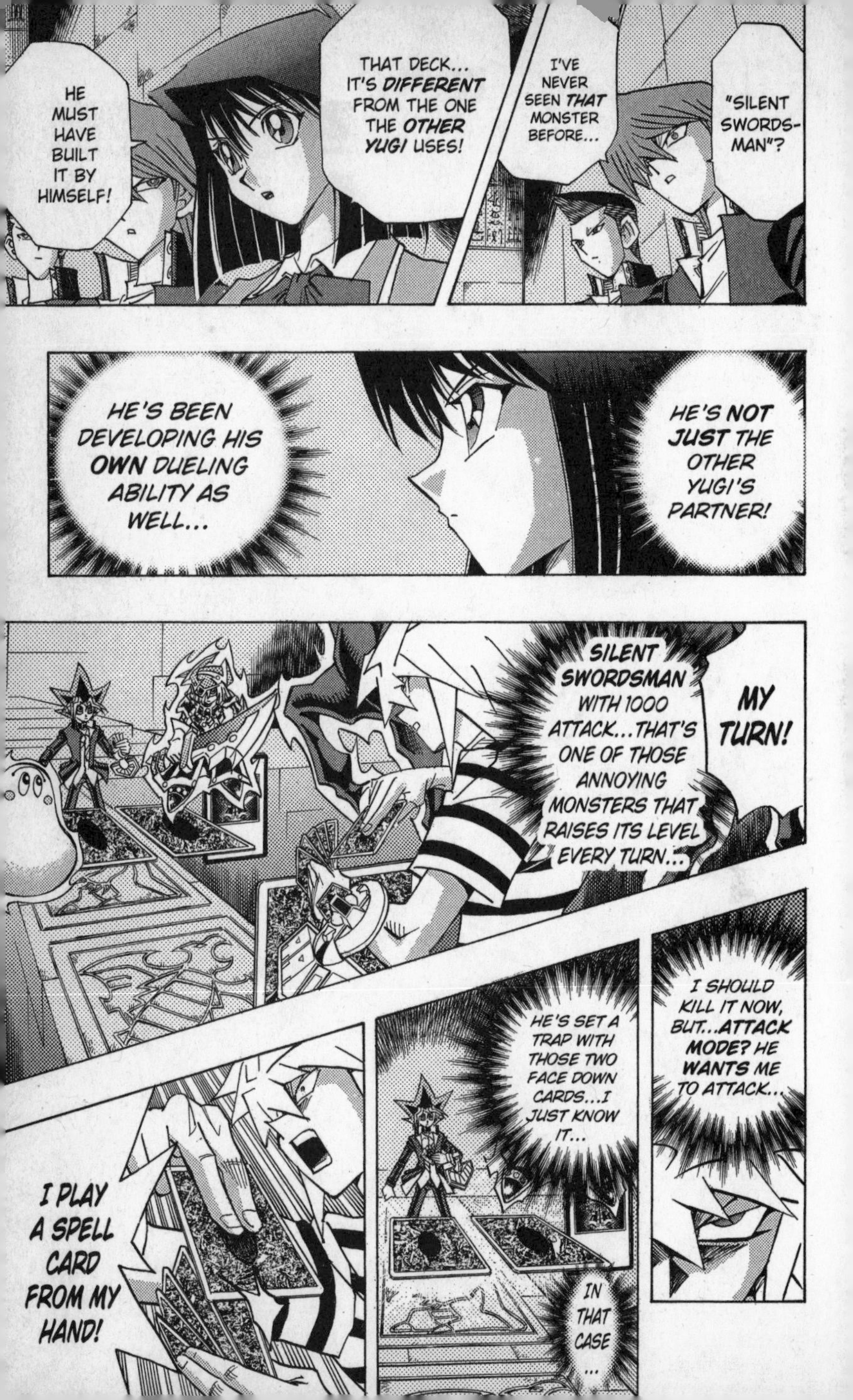
"SILENT SWORDS-MAN"?
I'VE NEVER SEEN THAT MONSTER BEFORE...
THAT DECK... IT'S DIFFERENT FROM THE ONE THE OTHER YUGI USES!
HE MUST HAVE BUILT IT BY HIMSELF!
HE'S NOT JUST THE OTHER YUGI'S PARTNER!
HE'S BEEN DEVELOPING HIS OWN DUELING ABILITY AS WELL...
MY TURN!
SILENT SWORDSMAN WITH 1000 ATTACK...THAT'S ONE OF THOSE ANNOYING MONSTERS THAT RAISES ITS LEVEL EVERY TURN...
I SHOULD KILL IT NOW, BUT...ATTACK MODE? HE WANTS ME TO ATTACK...
HE'S SET A TRAP WITH THOSE TWO FACE DOWN CARDS...I JUST KNOW IT...
IN THAT CASE...
I PLAY A SPELL CARD FROM MY HAND!

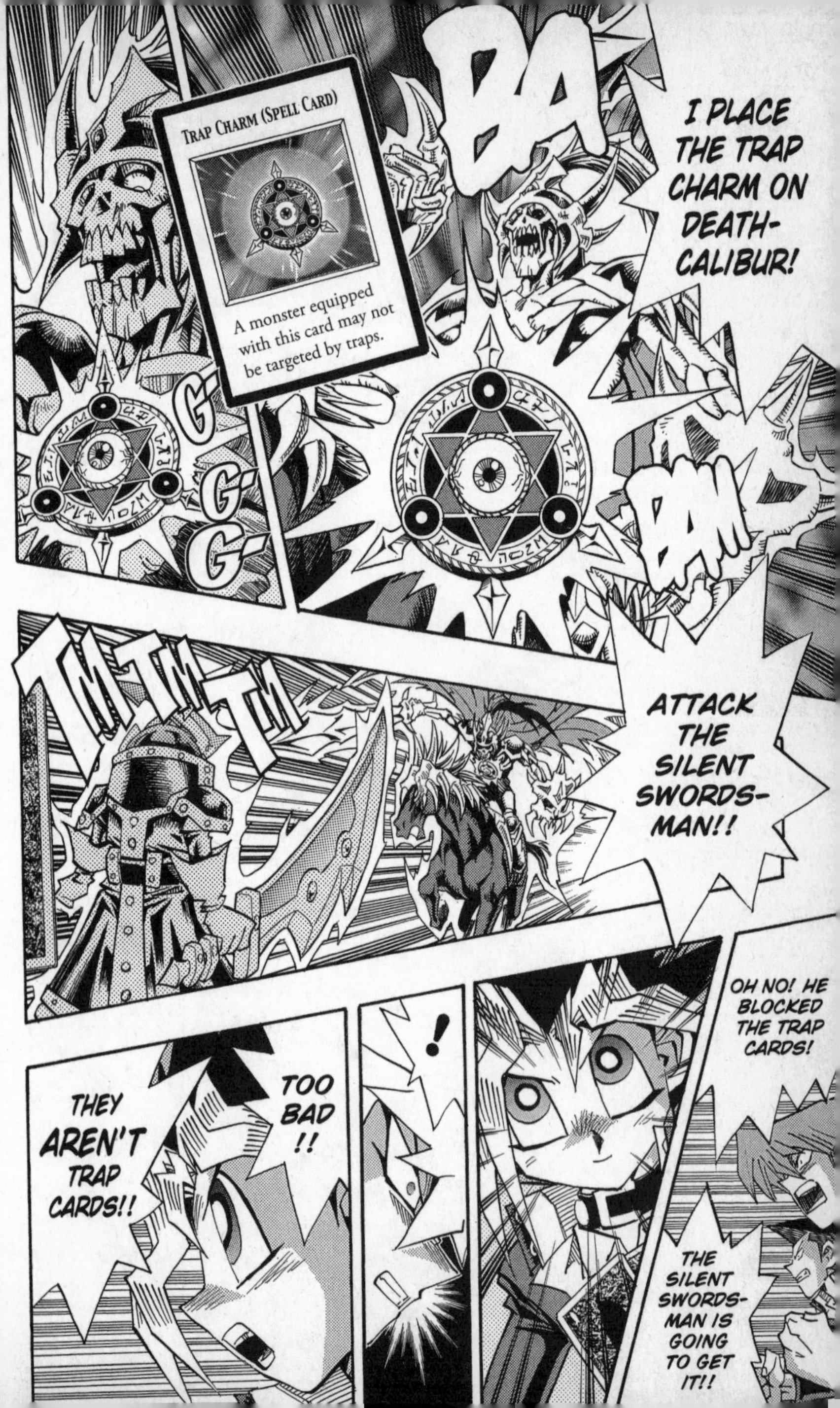
BA
I PLACE THE TRAP CHARM ON DEATH-CALIBUR!
BAM
TRAP CHARM (SPELL CARD)
A monster equipped with this card may not be targeted by traps.
G-G-G-
ATTACK THE SILENT SWORDS-MAN!!
TMTMTM
OH NO! HE BLOCKED THE TRAP CARDS!
THE SILENT SWORDS-MAN IS GOING TO GET IT!!
!
TOO BAD!!
THEY AREN'T TRAP CARDS!!

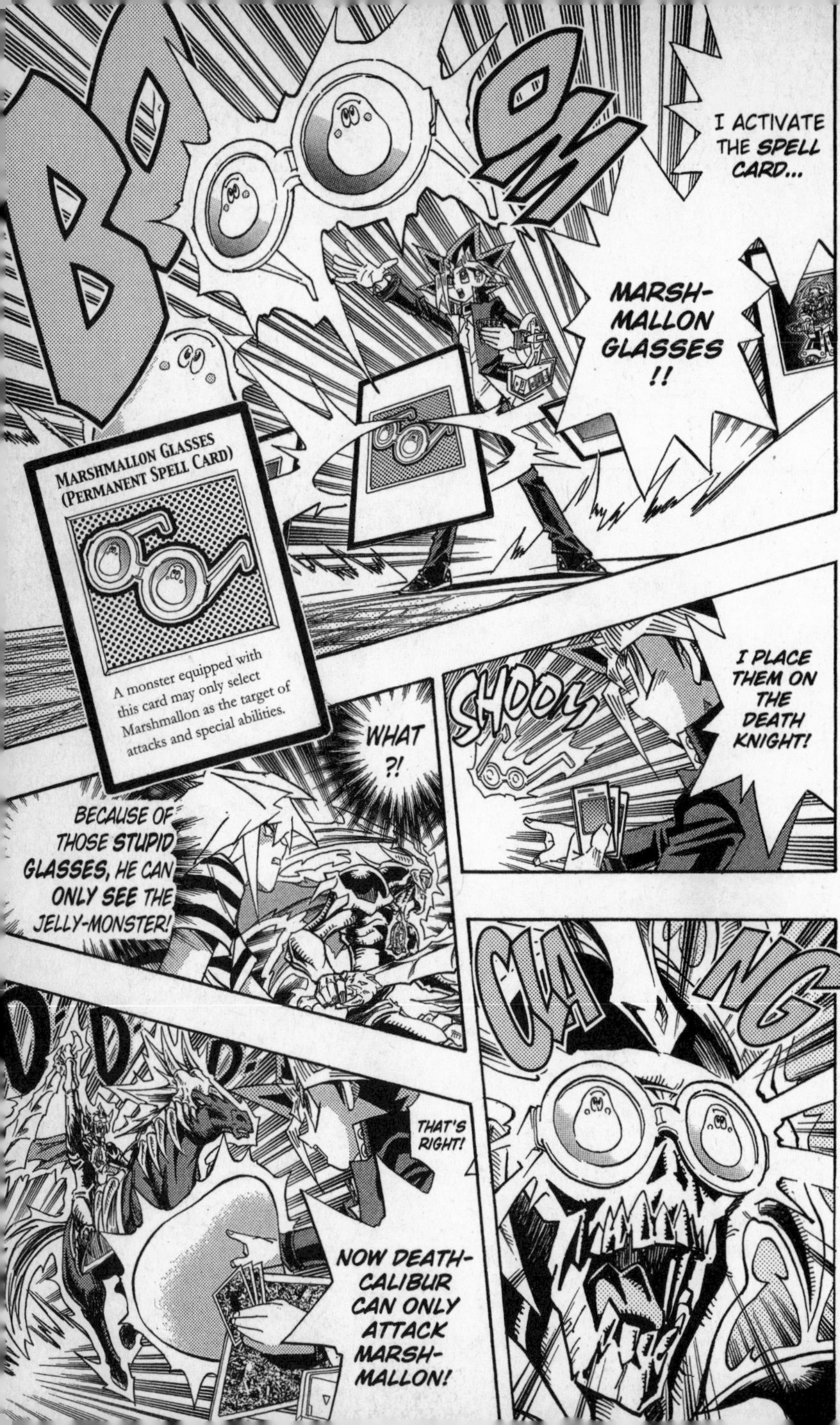
BOOM
I ACTIVATE THE SPELL CARD...
MARSH-MALLON GLASSES!!
MARSHMALLON GLASSES (PERMANENT SPELL CARD)
A monster equipped with this card may only select Marshmallon as the target of attacks and special abilities.
SHOOM
I PLACE THEM ON THE DEATH KNIGHT!
WHAT?!
BECAUSE OF THOSE STUPID GLASSES, HE CAN ONLY SEE THE JELLY-MONSTER!
CLANG
D D D
THAT'S RIGHT!
NOW DEATH-CALIBUR CAN ONLY ATTACK MARSH-MALLON!

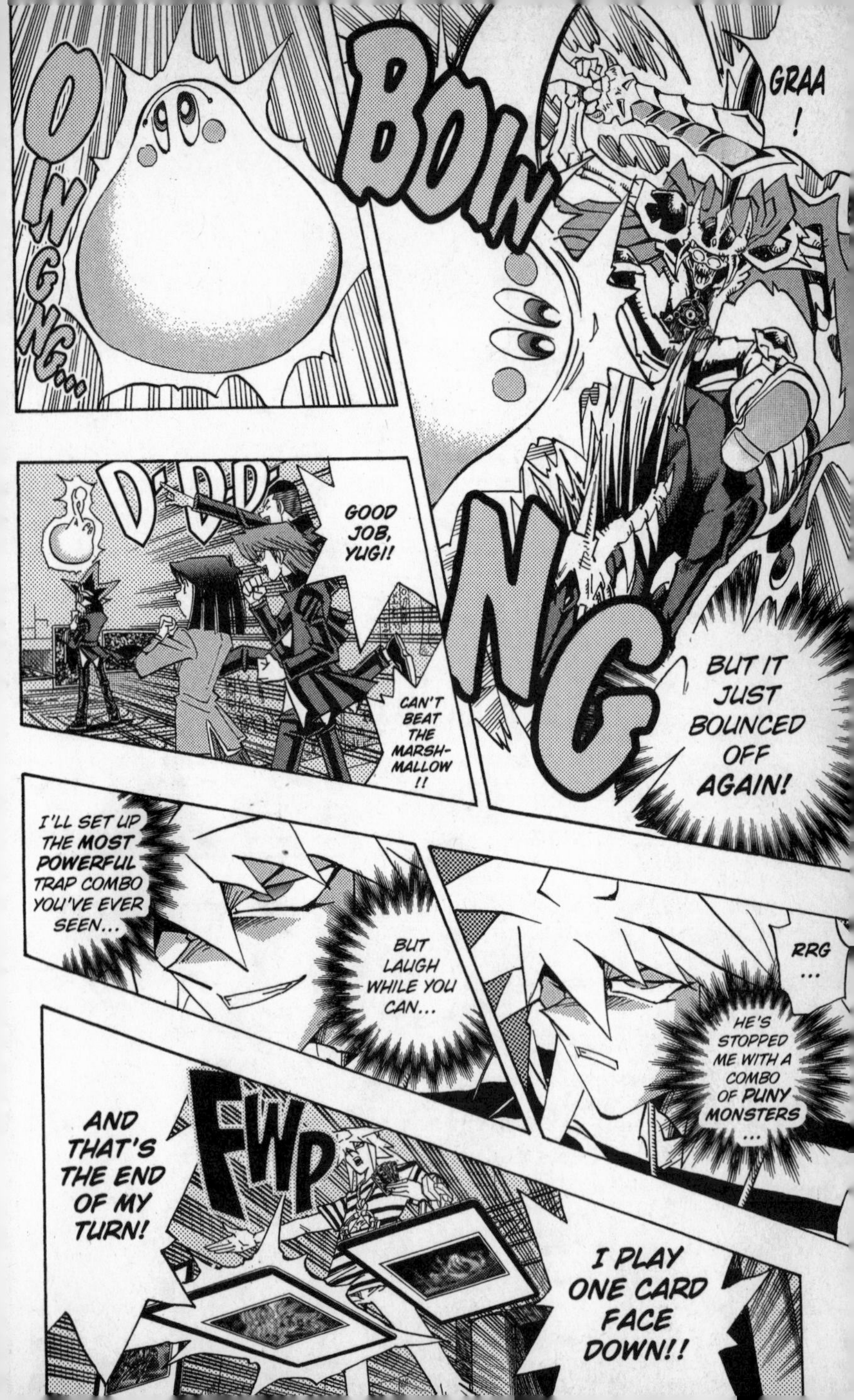
GRAA!
BOIN
NG
BUT IT JUST BOUNCED OFF AGAIN!
OINGNG...
D-D-D
GOOD JOB, YUGI!
CAN'T BEAT THE MARSHMALLOW!!
RRG...
HE'S STOPPED ME WITH A COMBO OF PUNY MONSTERS...
I'LL SET UP THE MOST POWERFUL TRAP COMBO YOU'VE EVER SEEN...
BUT LAUGH WHILE YOU CAN...
I PLAY ONE CARD FACE DOWN!!
FWP
AND THAT'S THE END OF MY TURN!

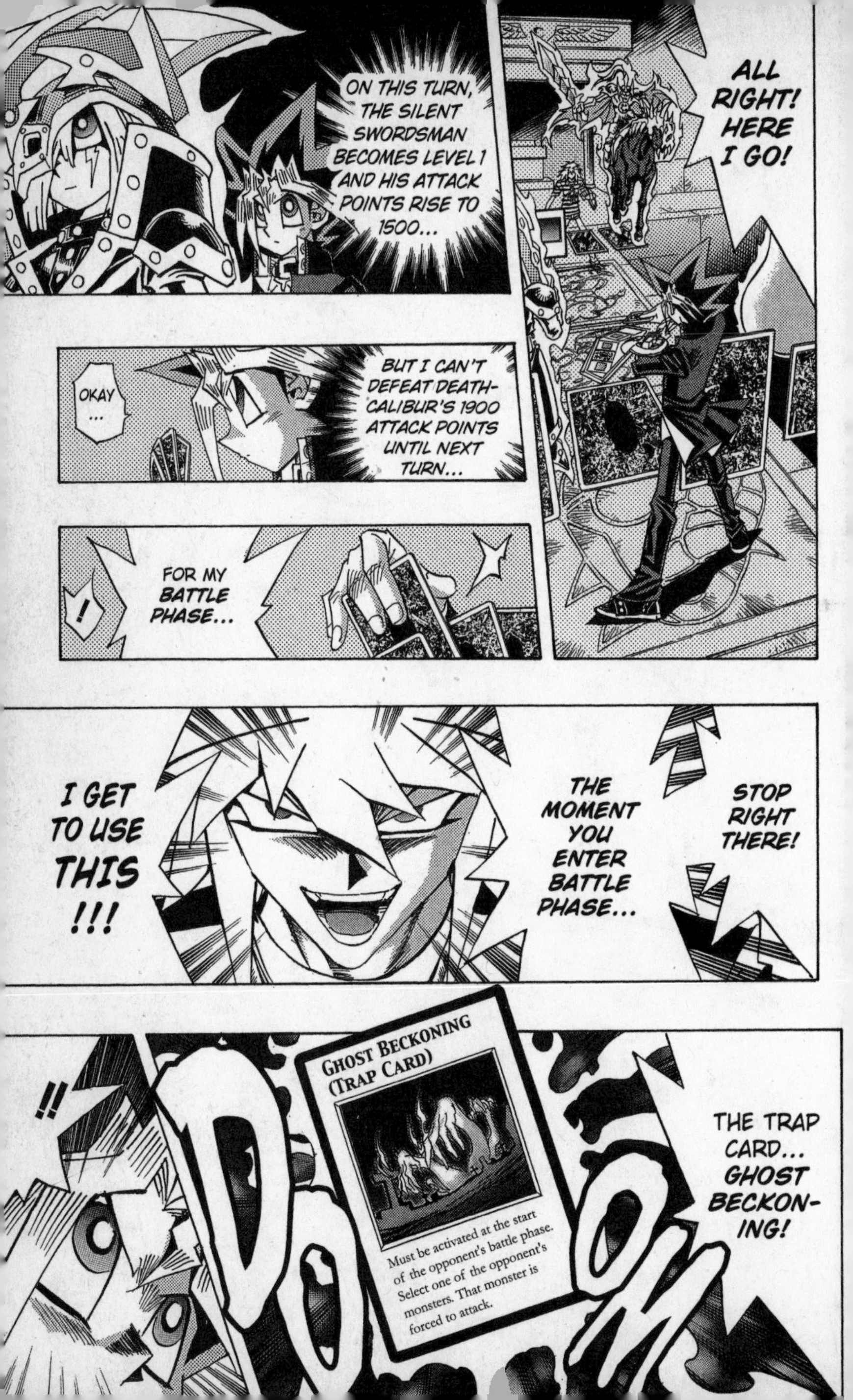
ALL RIGHT! HERE I GO!
ON THIS TURN, THE SILENT SWORDSMAN BECOMES LEVEL 1 AND HIS ATTACK POINTS RISE TO 1500...
BUT I CAN'T DEFEAT DEATH-CALIBUR'S 1900 ATTACK POINTS UNTIL NEXT TURN...
OKAY...
FOR MY BATTLE PHASE...
!
STOP RIGHT THERE!
THE MOMENT YOU ENTER BATTLE PHASE...
I GET TO USE THIS!!!
THE TRAP CARD... GHOST BECKONING!
GHOST BECKONING (TRAP CARD)
Must be activated at the start of the opponent's battle phase. Select one of the opponent's monsters. That monster is forced to attack.
DOOM
!!

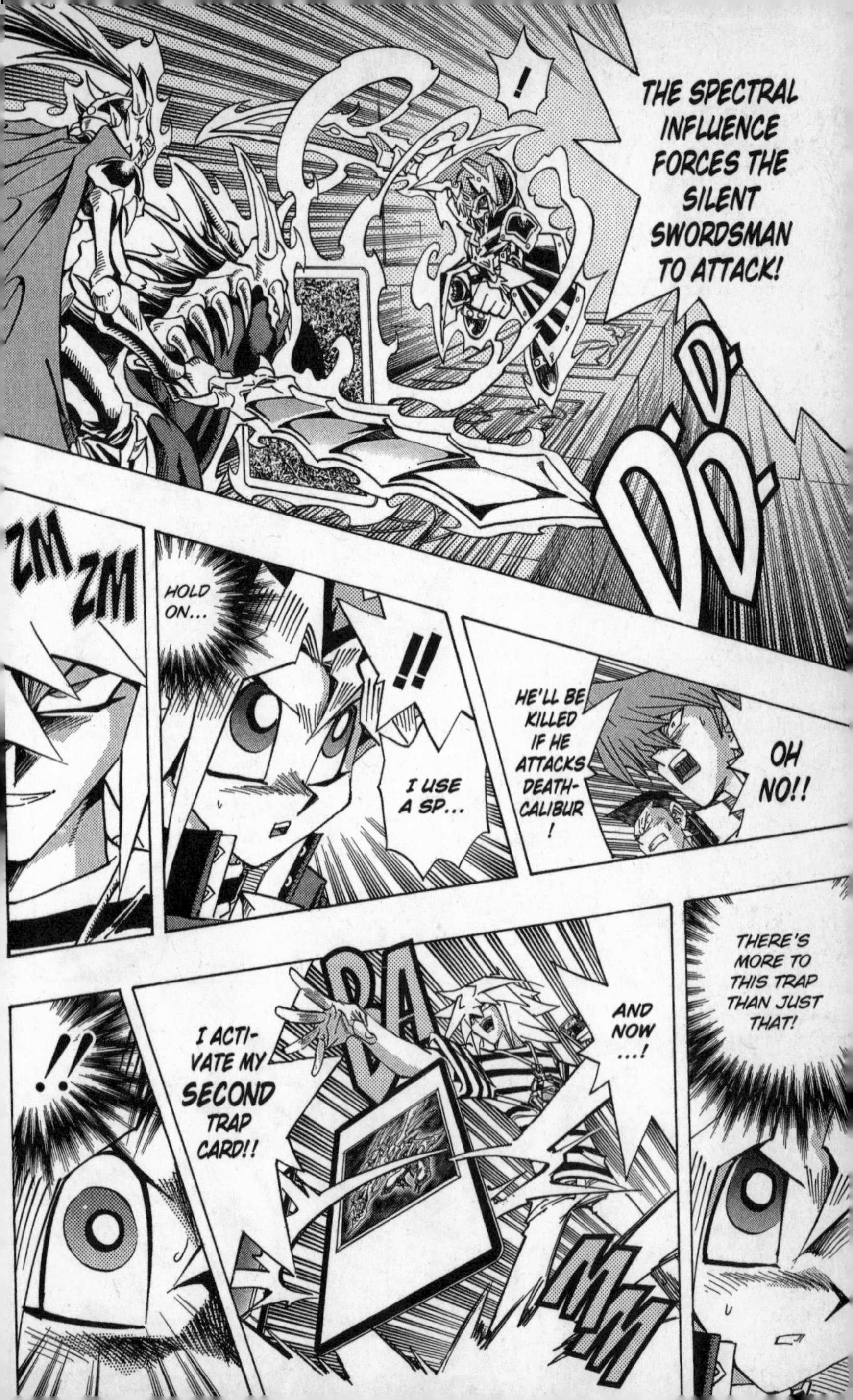
!
THE SPECTRAL INFLUENCE FORCES THE SILENT SWORDSMAN TO ATTACK!
OH NO!!
HE'LL BE KILLED IF HE ATTACKS DEATH-CALIBUR!
HOLD ON...
!!
I USE A SP...
ZM ZM
THERE'S MORE TO THIS TRAP THAN JUST THAT!
AND NOW ...!
I ACTI-VATE MY SECOND TRAP CARD!!
BA
!!

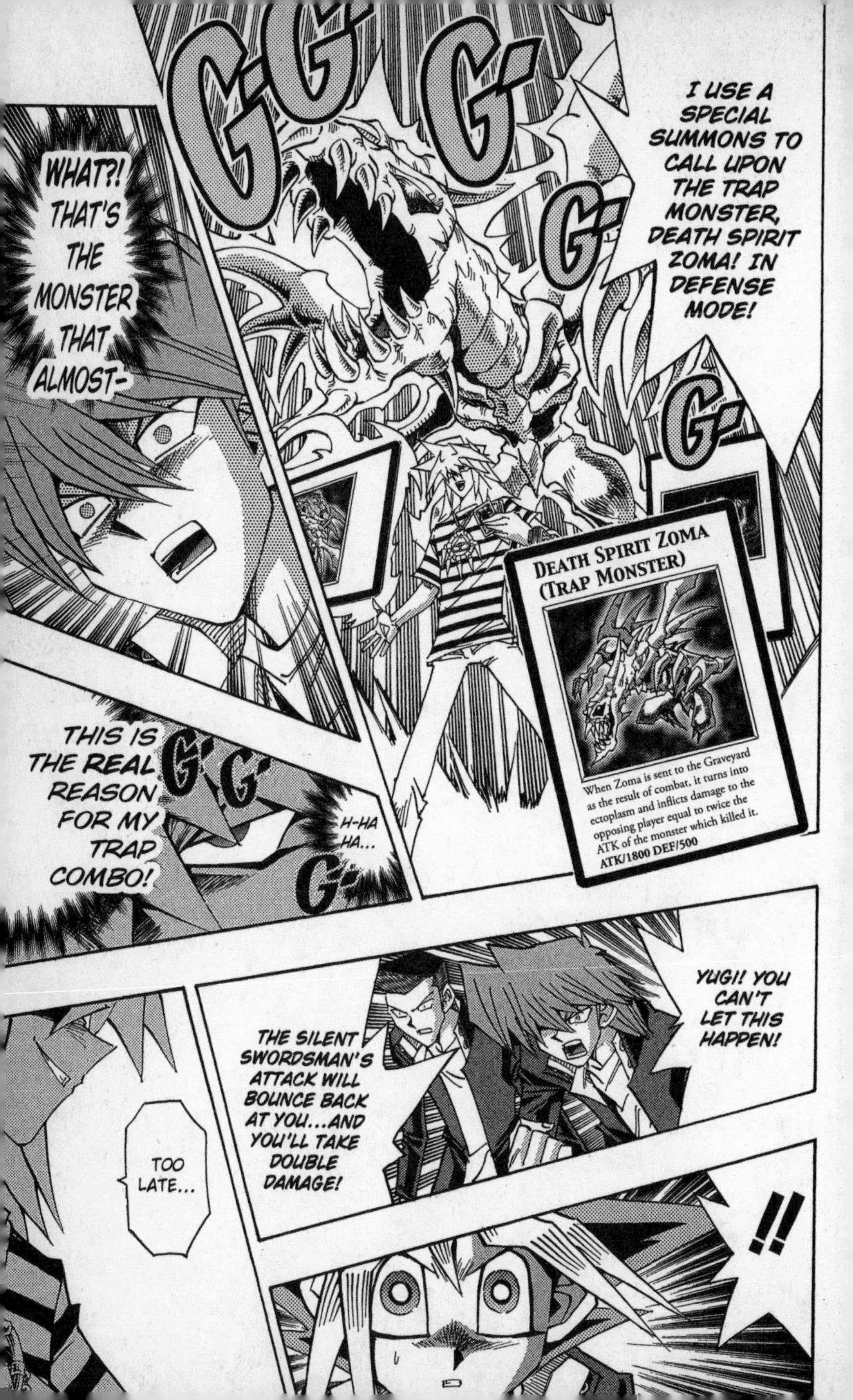
G-G-G-G-G-
I USE A SPECIAL SUMMONS TO CALL UPON THE TRAP MONSTER, DEATH SPIRIT ZOMA! IN DEFENSE MODE!
DEATH SPIRIT ZOMA (TRAP MONSTER)
When Zoma is sent to the Graveyard as the result of combat, it turns into ectoplasm and inflicts damage to the opposing player equal to twice the ATK of the monster which killed it.
ATK/1800 DEF/500
WHAT?! THAT'S THE MONSTER THAT ALMOST-
THIS IS THE REAL REASON FOR MY TRAP COMBO!
G-G-
H-HA HA...
G-
YUGI! YOU CAN'T LET THIS HAPPEN!
THE SILENT SWORDSMAN'S ATTACK WILL BOUNCE BACK AT YOU...AND YOU'LL TAKE DOUBLE DAMAGE!
TOO LATE...
!!

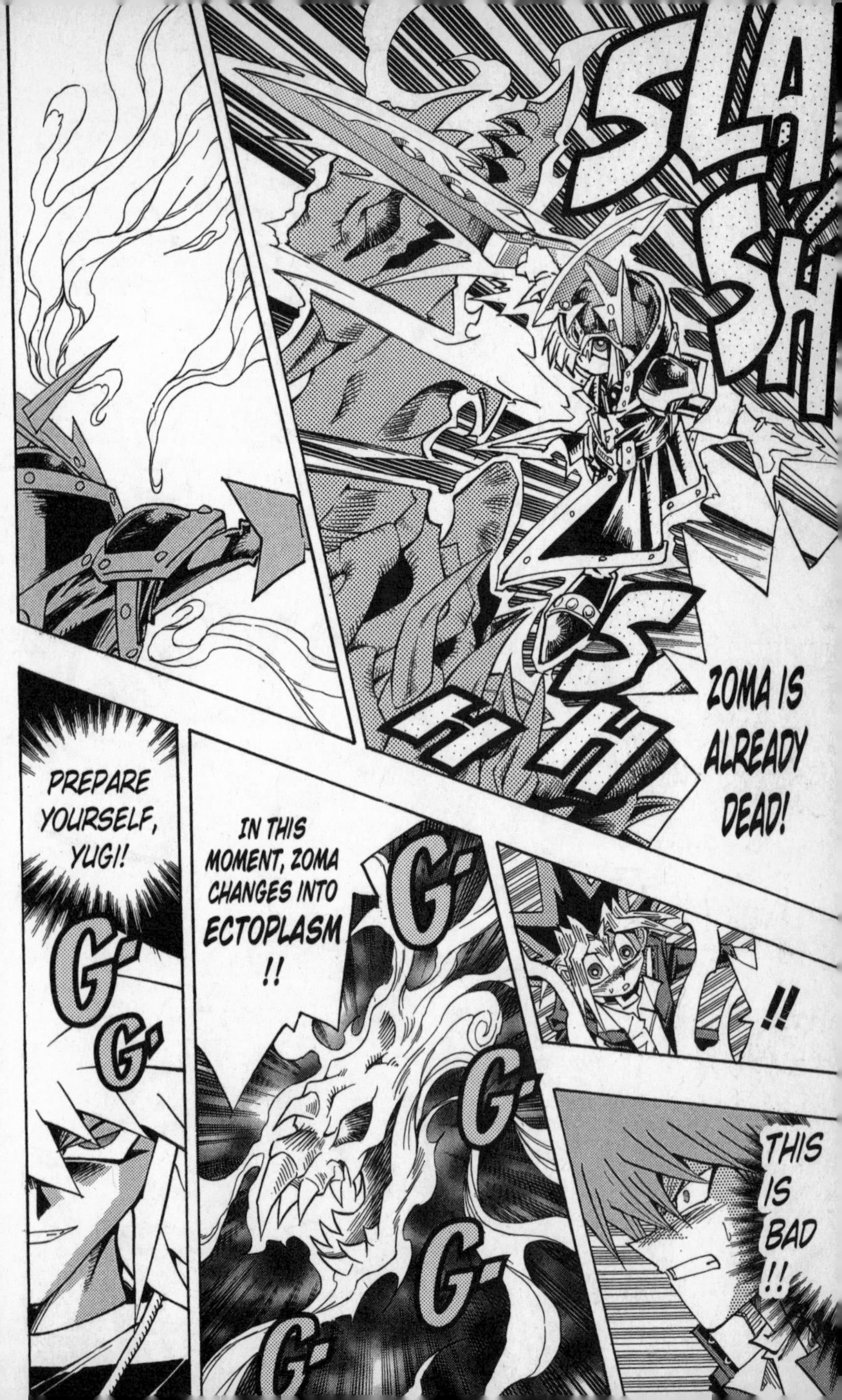
SLA
SH
SHH
ZOMA IS ALREADY DEAD!
!!
THIS IS BAD!!
IN THIS MOMENT, ZOMA CHANGES INTO ECTOPLASM!!
G- G- G- G-
PREPARE YOURSELF, YUGI!
G- G-

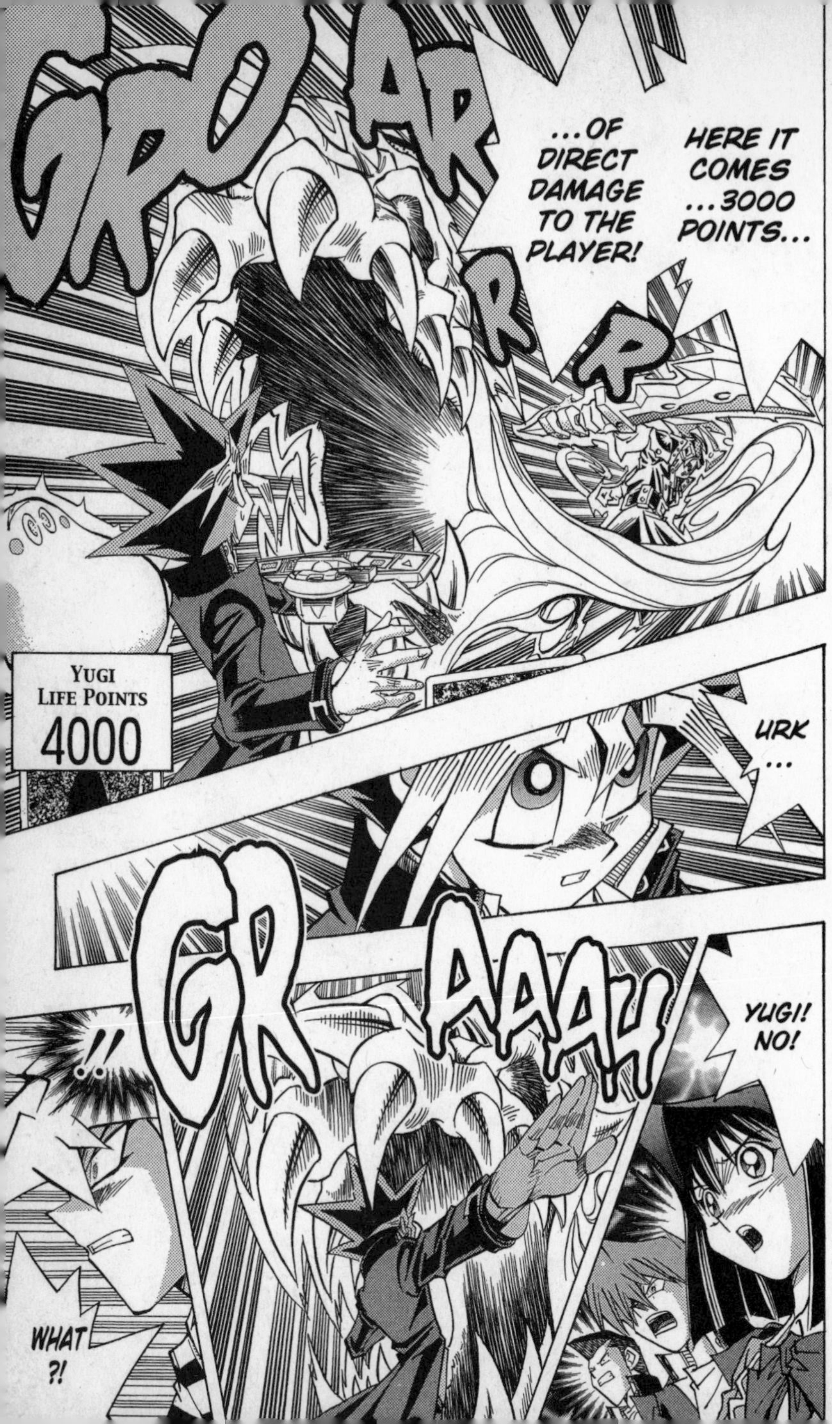
GROOAR
R
R
HERE IT COMES ...3000 POINTS...
...OF DIRECT DAMAGE TO THE PLAYER!
YUGI LIFE POINTS
4000
URK ...
GRAAAH
YUGI! NO!
!!
WHAT ?!

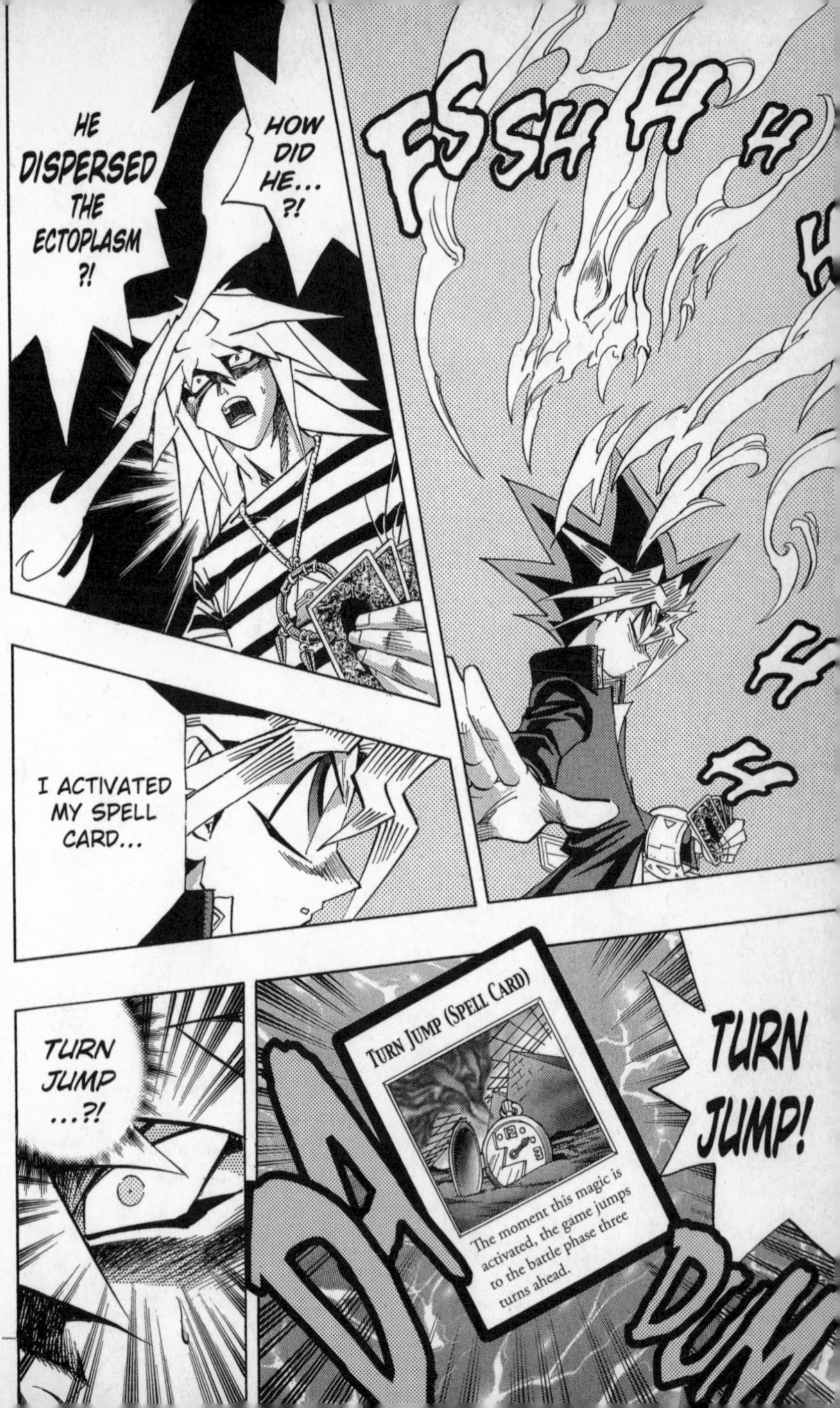
FSSHHHHHHH
HOW DID HE...?!
HE DISPERSED THE ECTOPLASM ?!
I ACTIVATED MY SPELL CARD...
TURN JUMP!
TURN JUMP (SPELL CARD)
The moment this magic is activated, the game jumps to the battle phase three turns ahead.
TURN JUMP ...?!

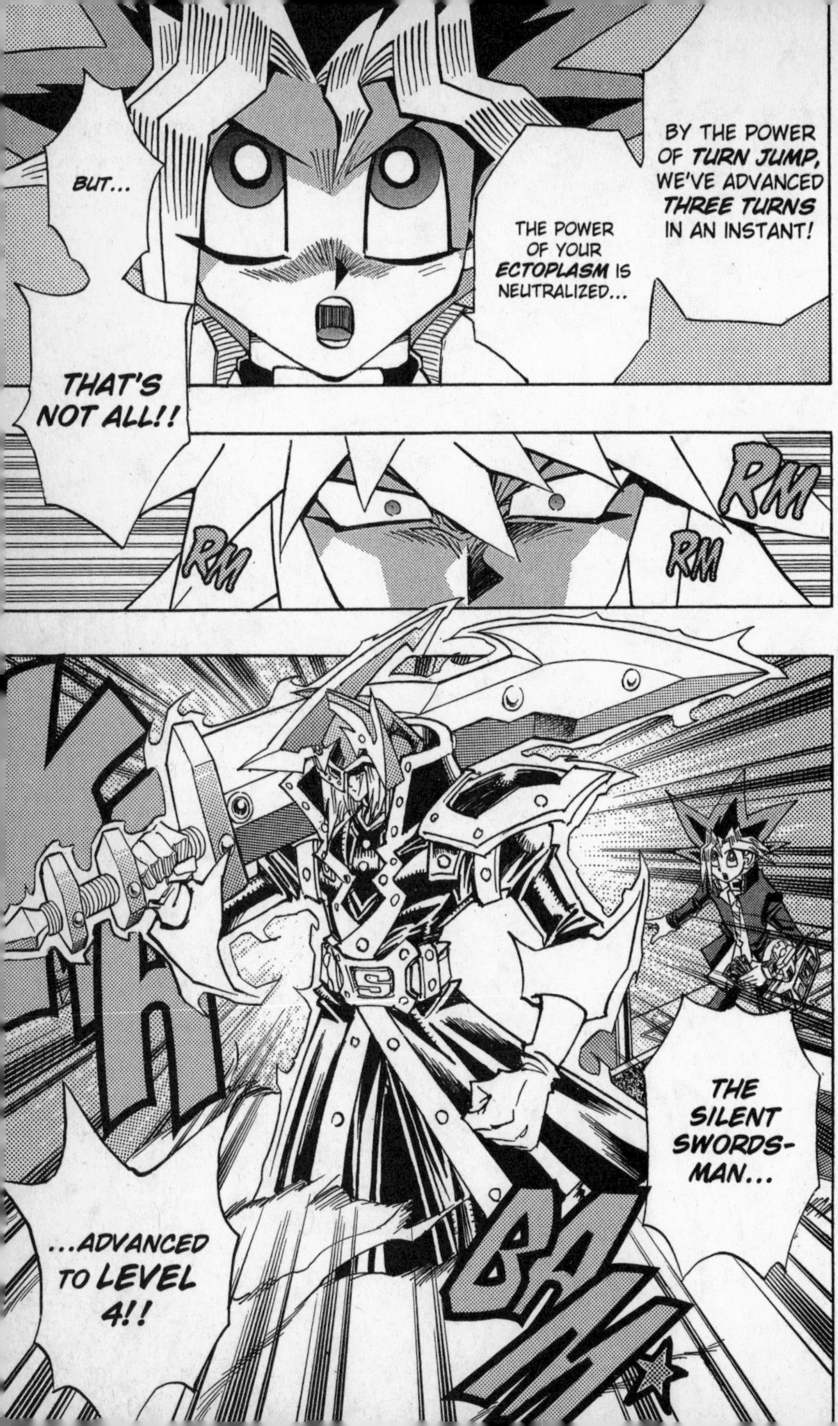
BY THE POWER OF TURN JUMP, WE'VE ADVANCED THREE TURNS IN AN INSTANT!
THE POWER OF YOUR ECTOPLASM IS NEUTRALIZED...
BUT...
THAT'S NOT ALL!!
RM
RM
RM
THE SILENT SWORDS-MAN...
...ADVANCED TO LEVEL 4!!

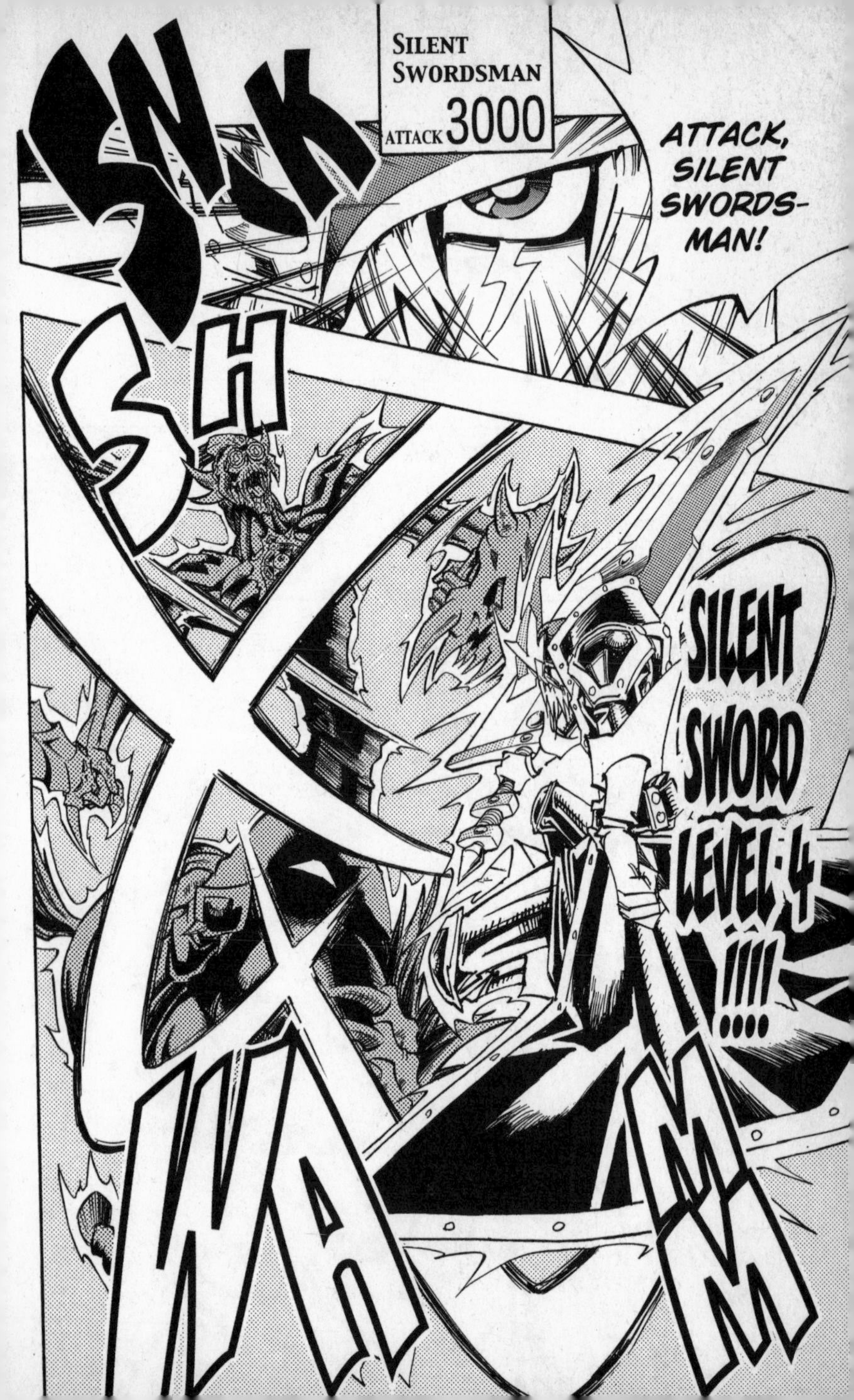
SILENT SWORDSMAN
ATTACK 3000
ATTACK, SILENT SWORDS-MAN!
SNK
SH
SILENT SWORD LEVEL 4 !!!!
WHAM

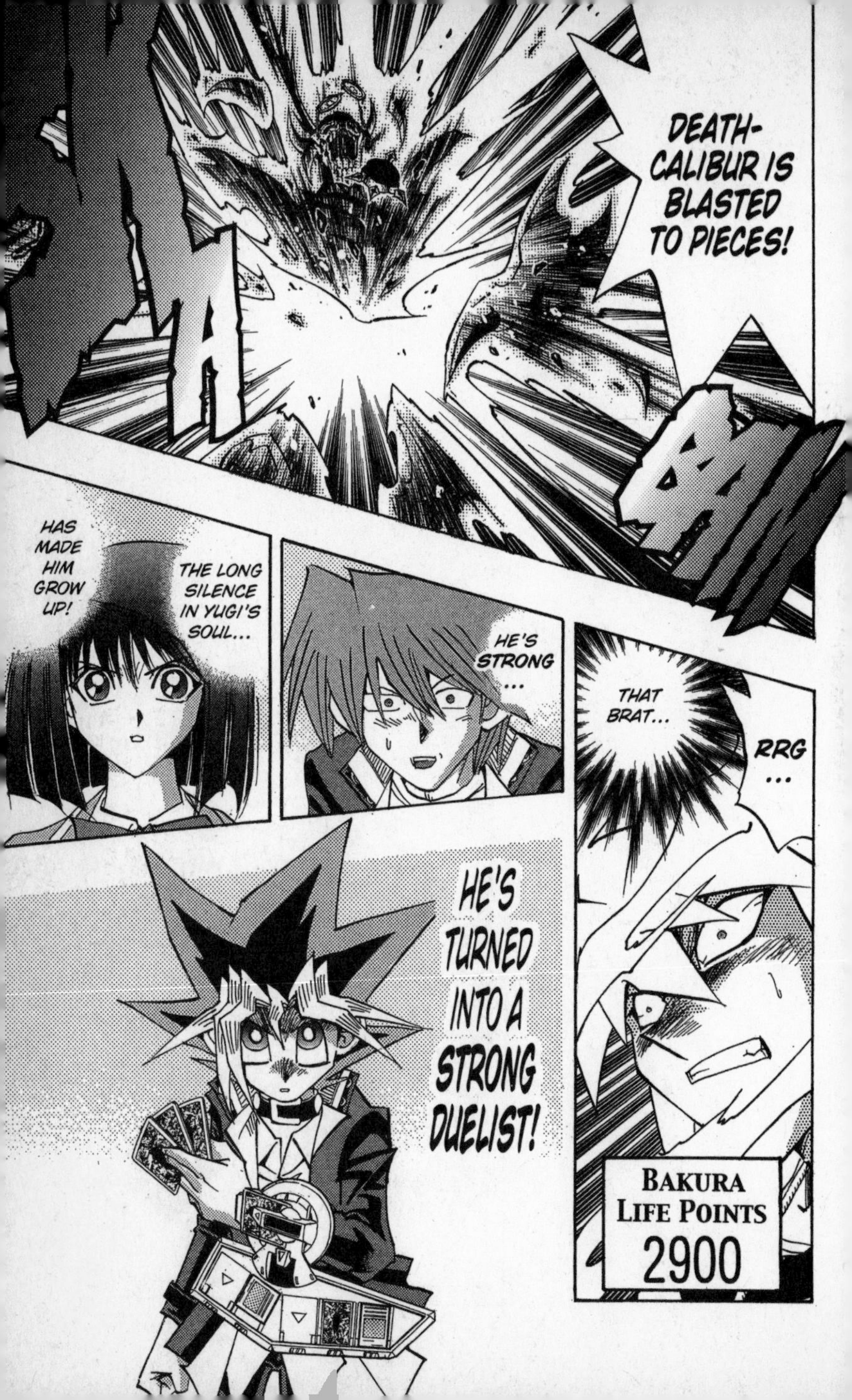
DEATH-CALIBUR IS BLASTED TO PIECES!
THAT BRAT...
RRG...
BAKURA LIFE POINTS 2900
HE'S STRONG...
THE LONG SILENCE IN YUGI'S SOUL...
HAS MADE HIM GROW UP!
HE'S TURNED INTO A STRONG DUELIST!

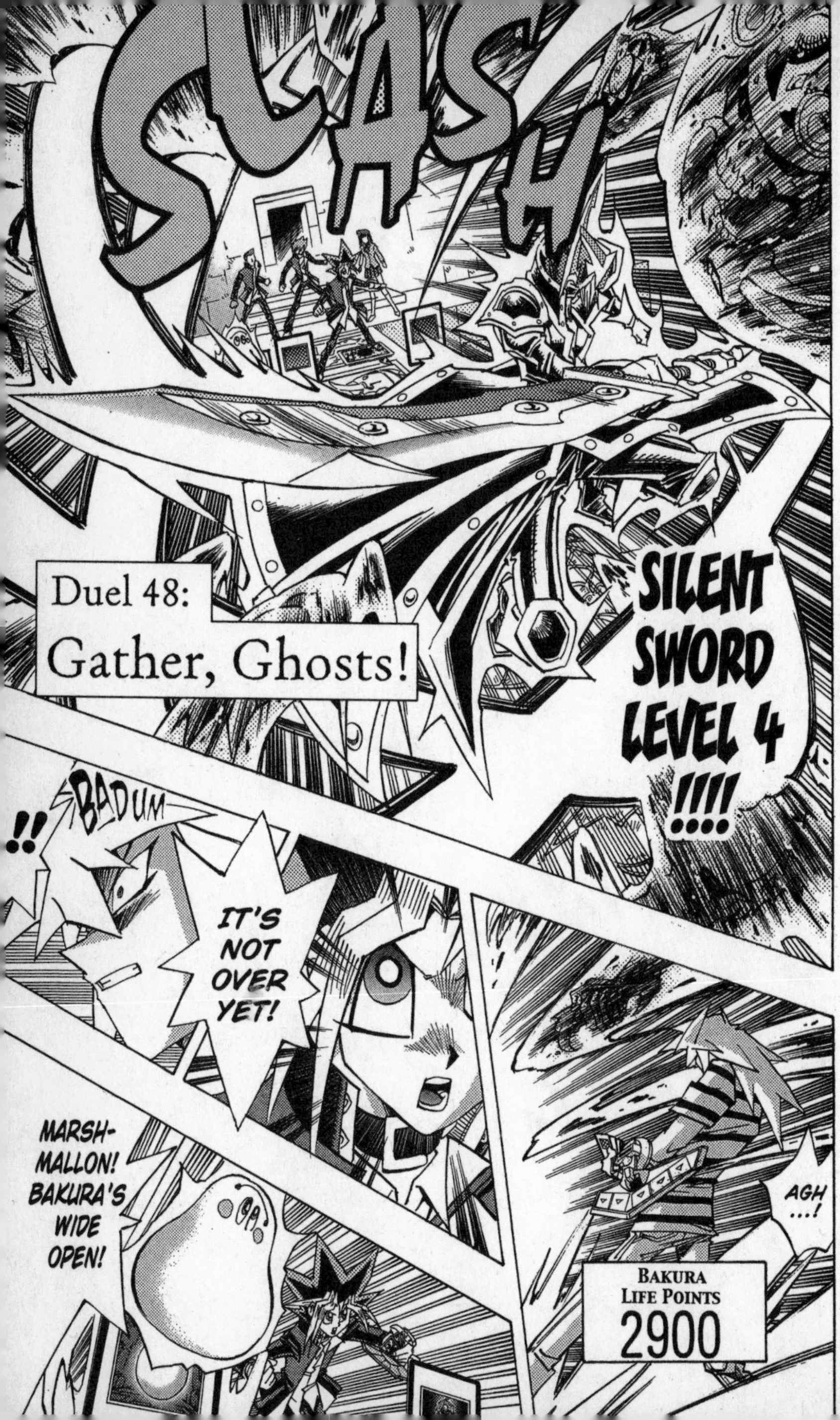
SLASH
SILENT SWORD LEVEL 4 !!!!
Duel 48:
Gather, Ghosts!
AGH ...!
BAKURA LIFE POINTS 2900
BADUM
!!
IT'S NOT OVER YET!
MARSH-MALLON! BAKURA'S WIDE OPEN!

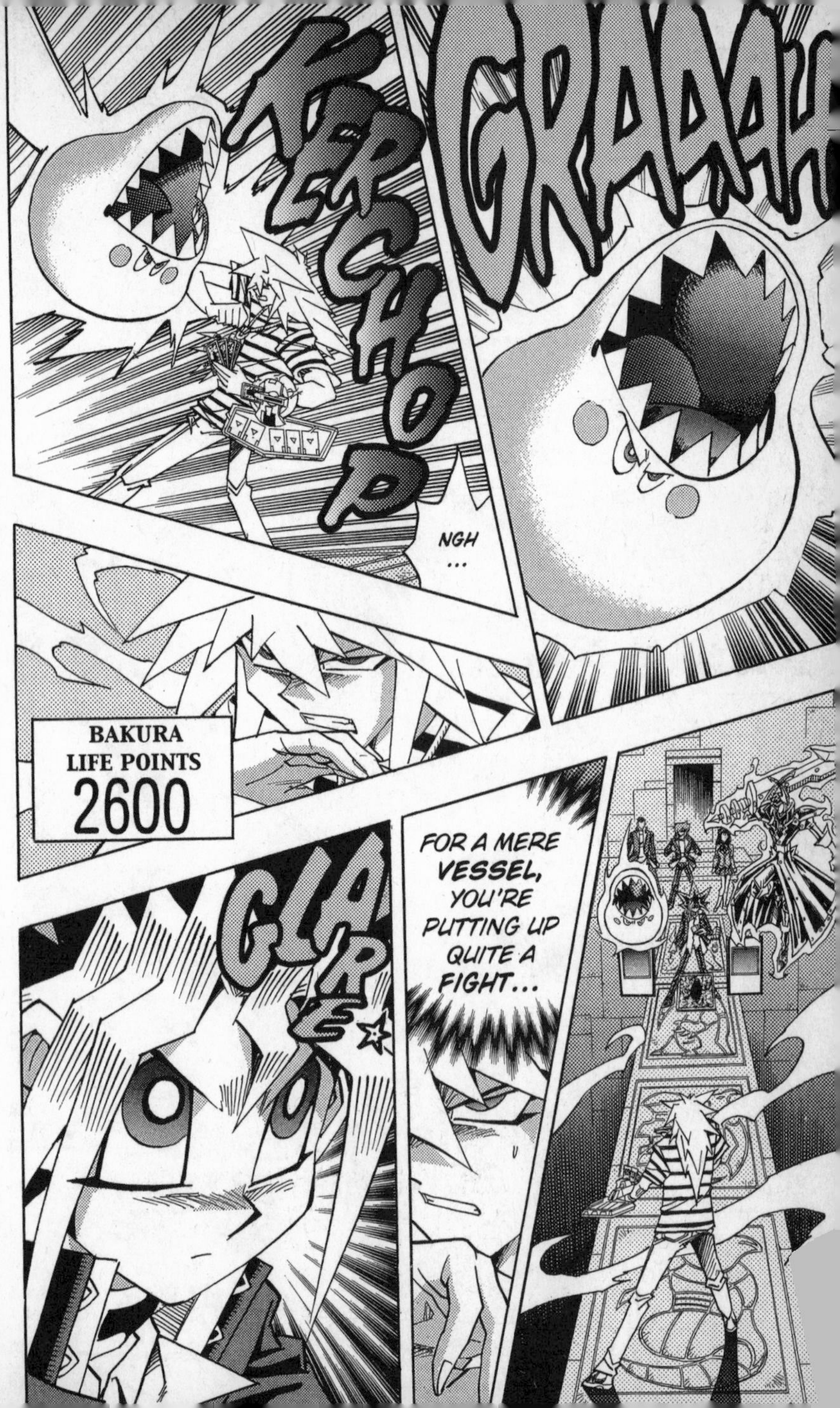

GRAAAH
KERCHOP
NGH ...
BAKURA LIFE POINTS 2600
FOR A MERE VESSEL, YOU'RE PUTTING UP QUITE A FIGHT...
GLARE

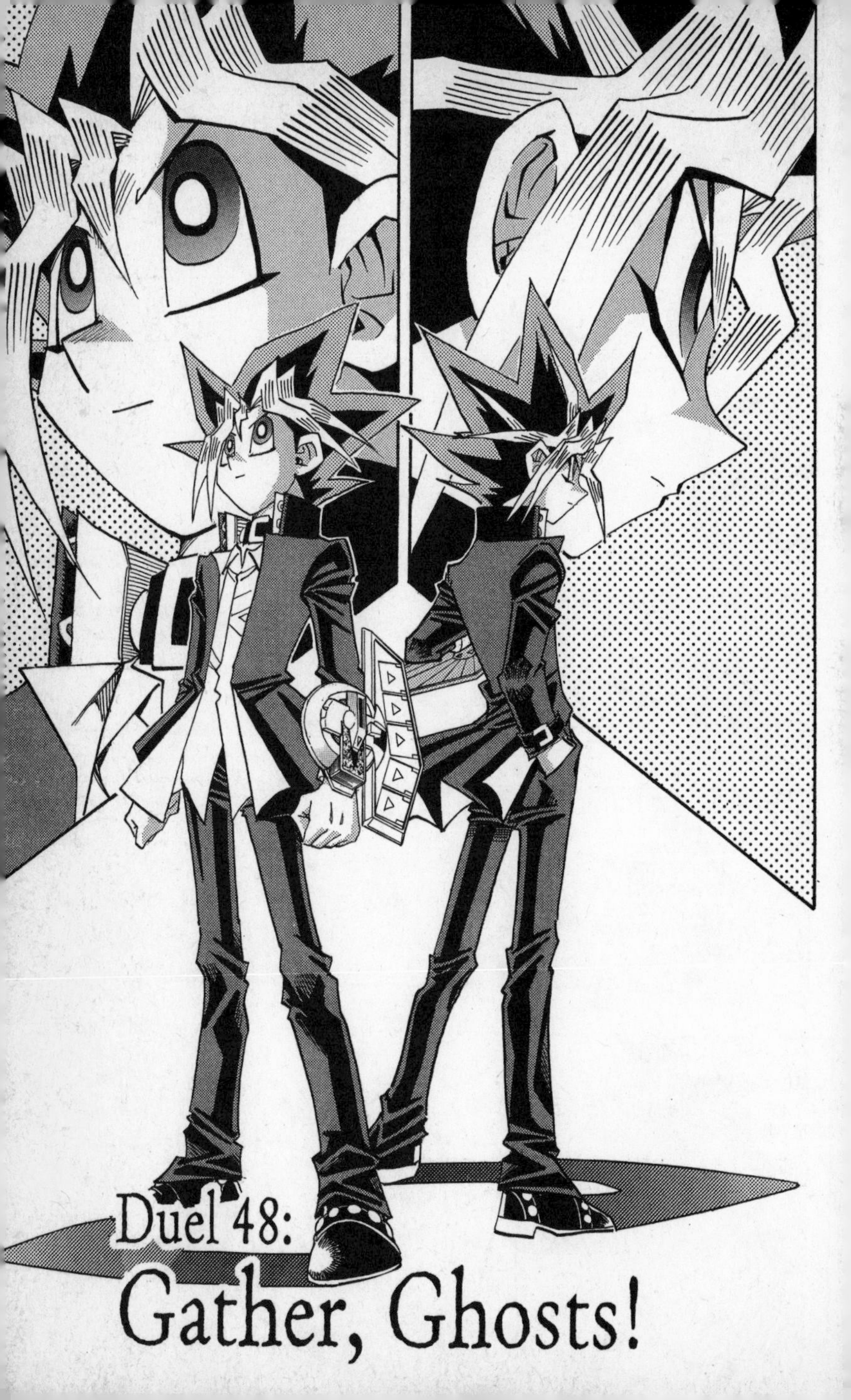
Duel 48:
Gather, Ghosts!

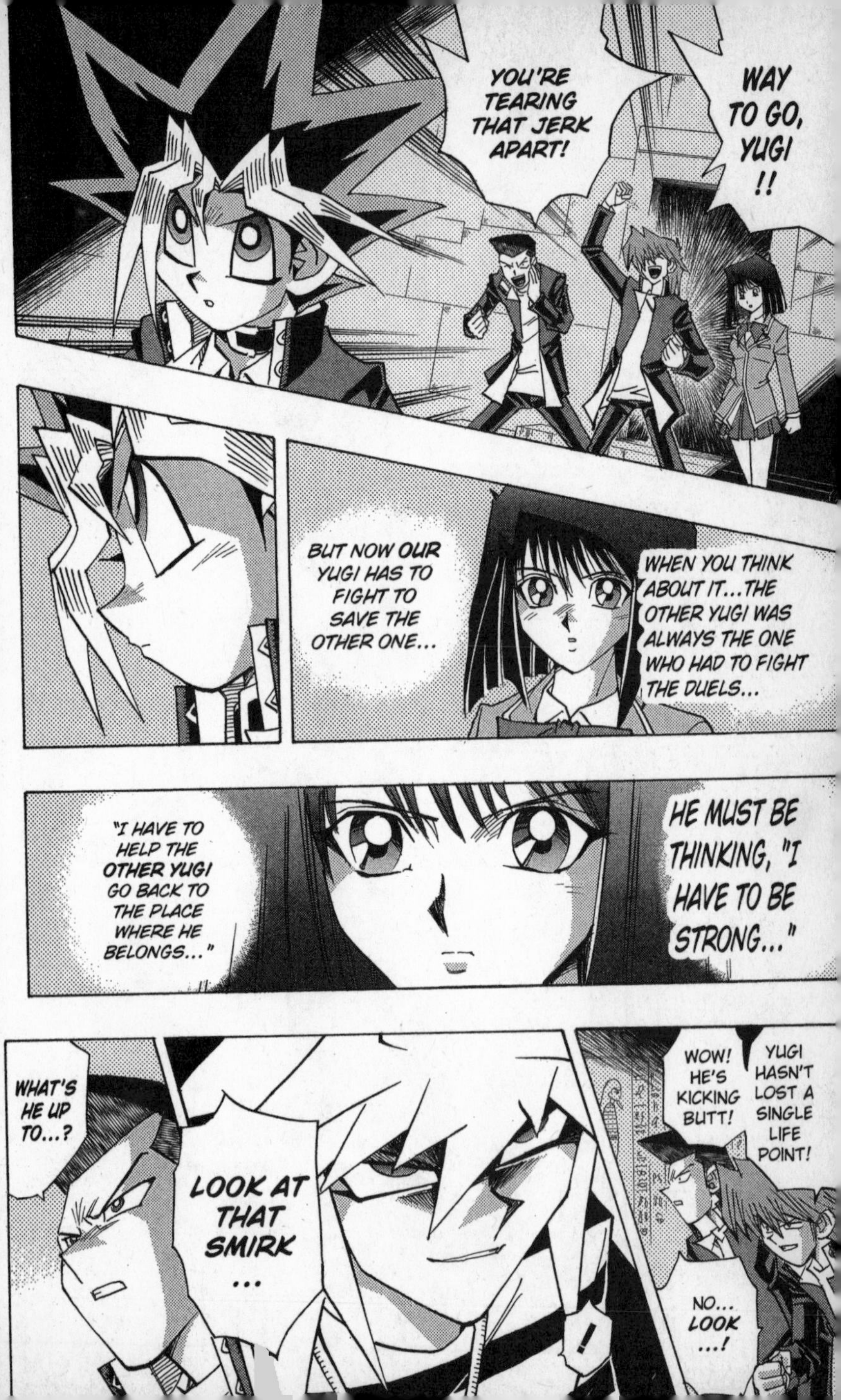

WAY TO GO, YUGI !!
YOU'RE TEARING THAT JERK APART!
WHEN YOU THINK ABOUT IT...THE OTHER YUGI WAS ALWAYS THE ONE WHO HAD TO FIGHT THE DUELS...
BUT NOW OUR YUGI HAS TO FIGHT TO SAVE THE OTHER ONE...
HE MUST BE THINKING, "I HAVE TO BE STRONG..."
"I HAVE TO HELP THE OTHER YUGI GO BACK TO THE PLACE WHERE HE BELONGS..."
YUGI HASN'T LOST A SINGLE LIFE POINT!
WOW! HE'S KICKING BUTT!
NO... LOOK ...!
LOOK AT THAT SMIRK ...
WHAT'S HE UP TO...?
!

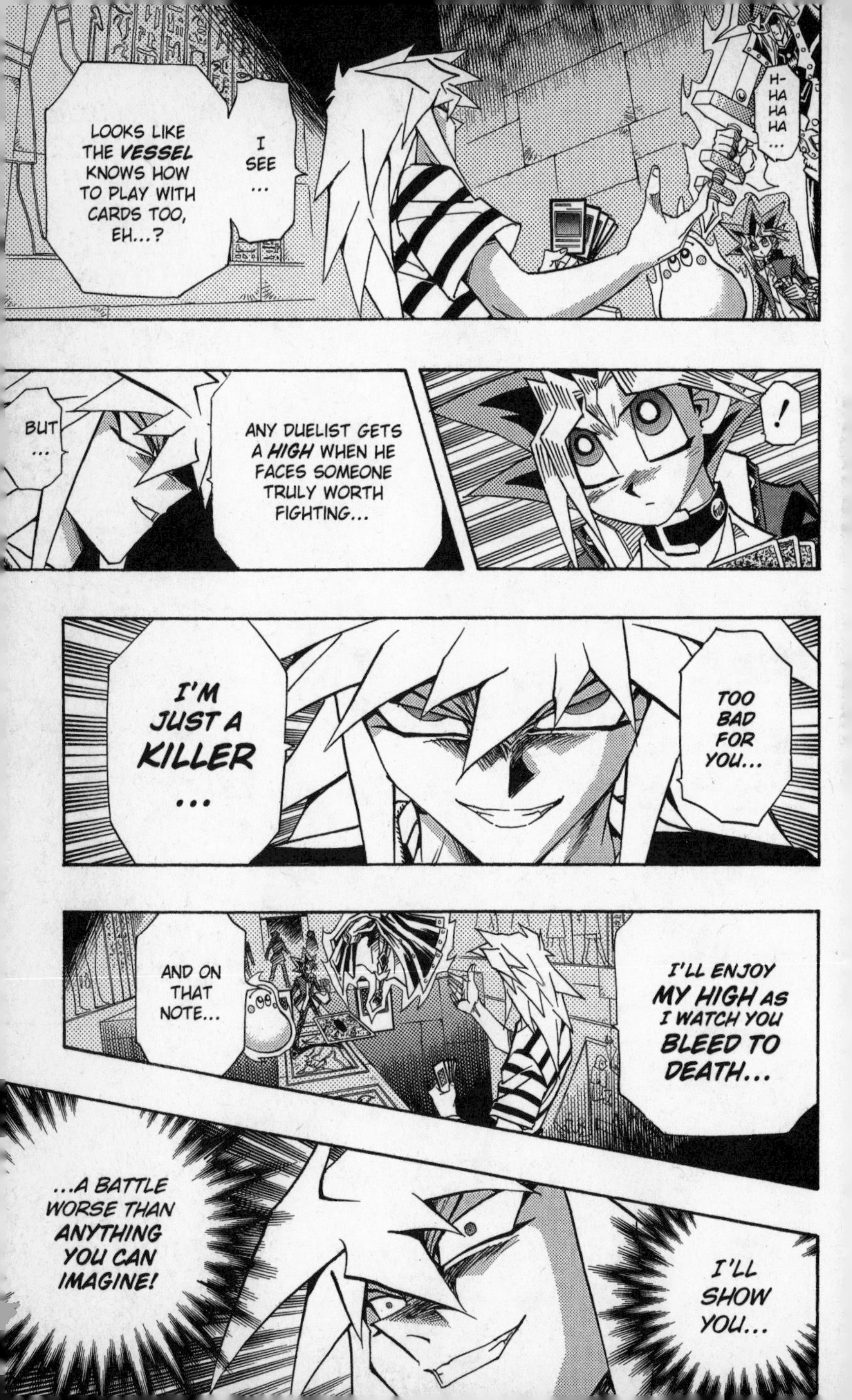
H-HA HA HA...
I SEE...
LOOKS LIKE THE VESSEL KNOWS HOW TO PLAY WITH CARDS TOO, EH...?
!
ANY DUELIST GETS A HIGH WHEN HE FACES SOMEONE TRULY WORTH FIGHTING...
BUT...
TOO BAD FOR YOU...
I'M JUST A KILLER...
I'LL ENJOY MY HIGH AS I WATCH YOU BLEED TO DEATH...
AND ON THAT NOTE...
I'LL SHOW YOU...
...A BATTLE WORSE THAN ANYTHING YOU CAN IMAGINE!

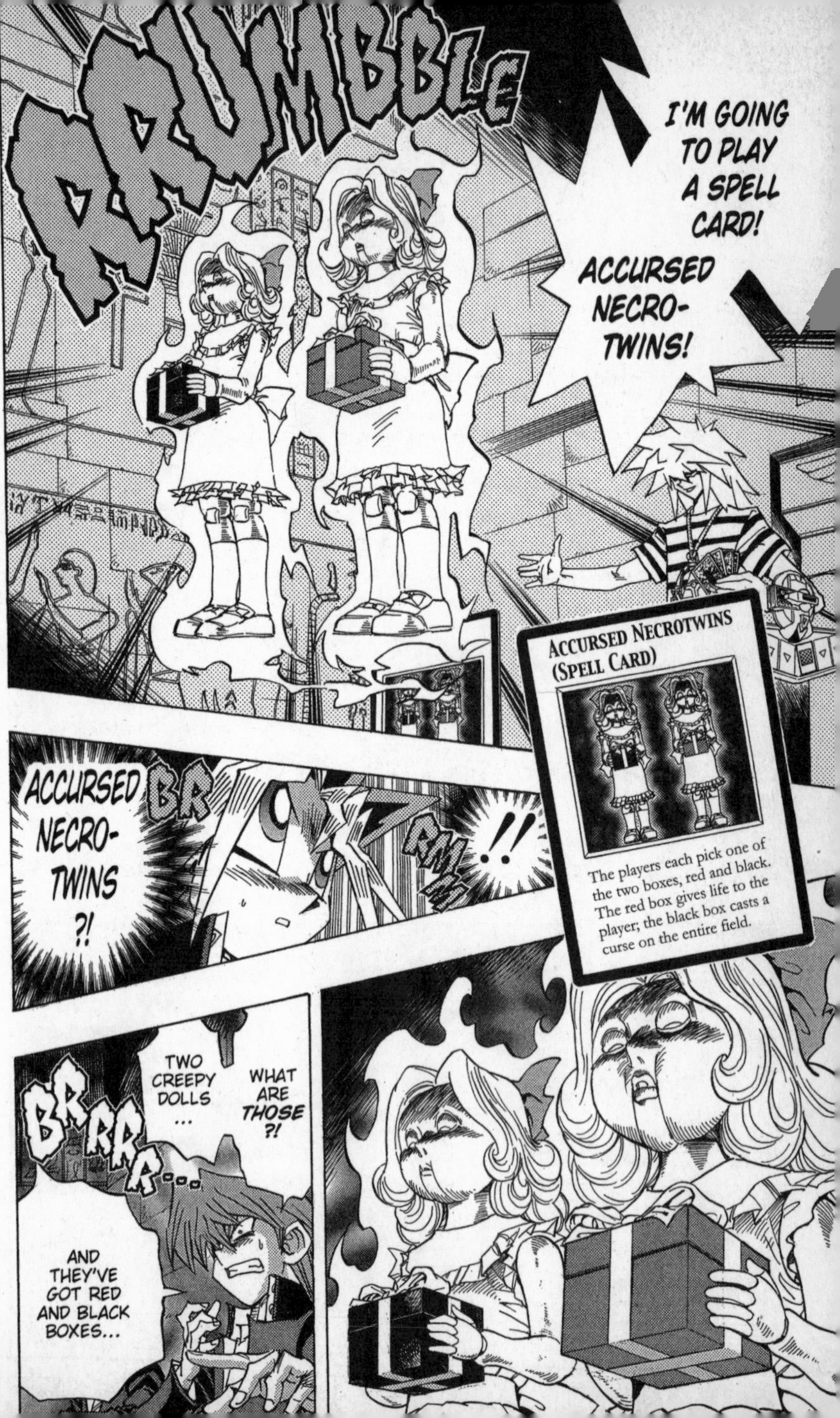
RRUMBBLE
I'M GOING TO PLAY A SPELL CARD!
ACCURSED NECRO-TWINS!
ACCURSED NECROTWINS (SPELL CARD)
The players each pick one of the two boxes, red and black. The red box gives life to the player; the black box casts a curse on the entire field.
!!
BRRMM
ACCURSED NECRO-TWINS ?!
WHAT ARE THOSE ?!
TWO CREEPY DOLLS ...
BRRRR...
AND THEY'VE GOT RED AND BLACK BOXES...

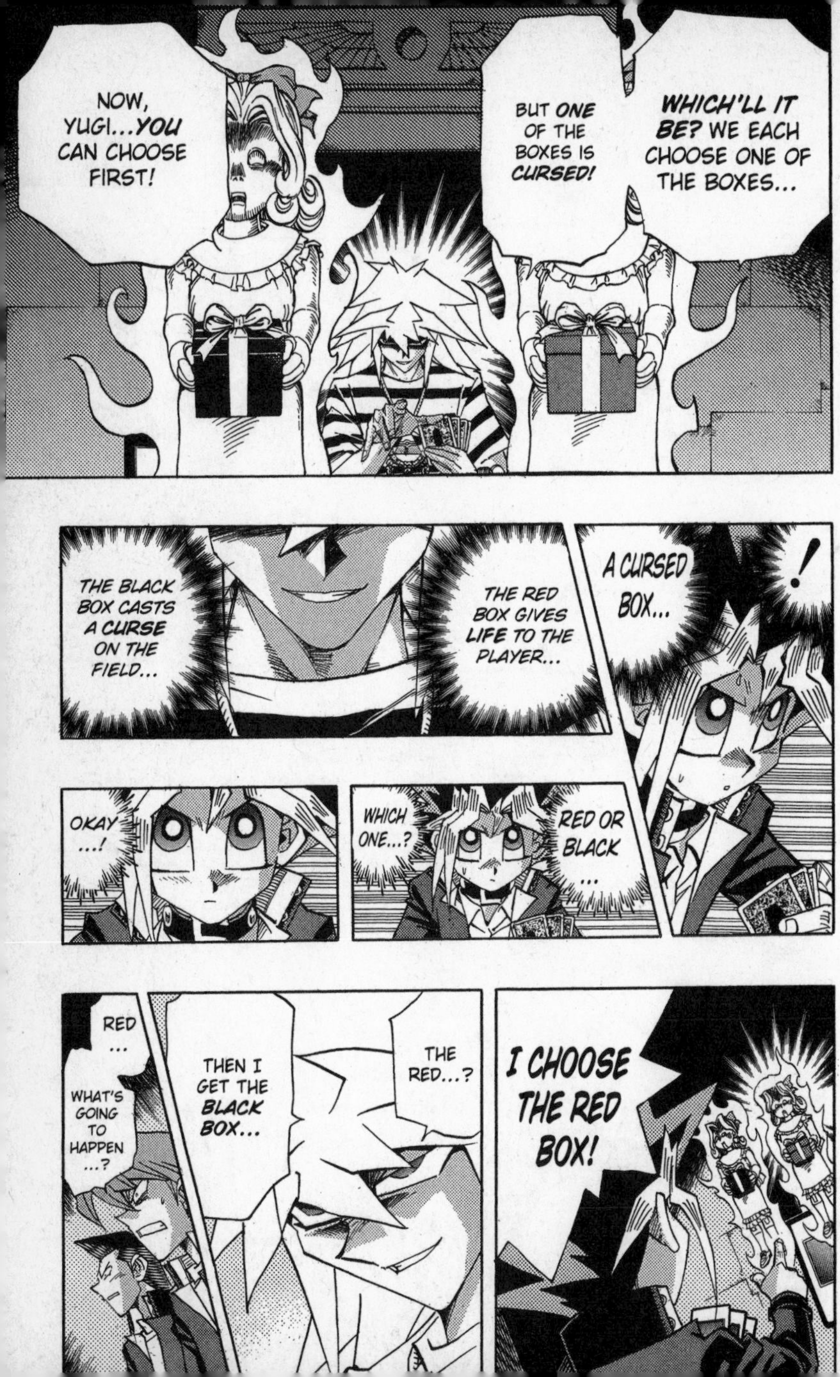
WHICH'LL IT BE? WE EACH CHOOSE ONE OF THE BOXES...
BUT ONE OF THE BOXES IS CURSED!
NOW, YUGI...YOU CAN CHOOSE FIRST!
!
A CURSED BOX...
THE RED BOX GIVES LIFE TO THE PLAYER...
THE BLACK BOX CASTS A CURSE ON THE FIELD...
RED OR BLACK...
WHICH ONE...?
OKAY...!
I CHOOSE THE RED BOX!
THE RED...?
THEN I GET THE BLACK BOX...
RED...
WHAT'S GOING TO HAPPEN...?

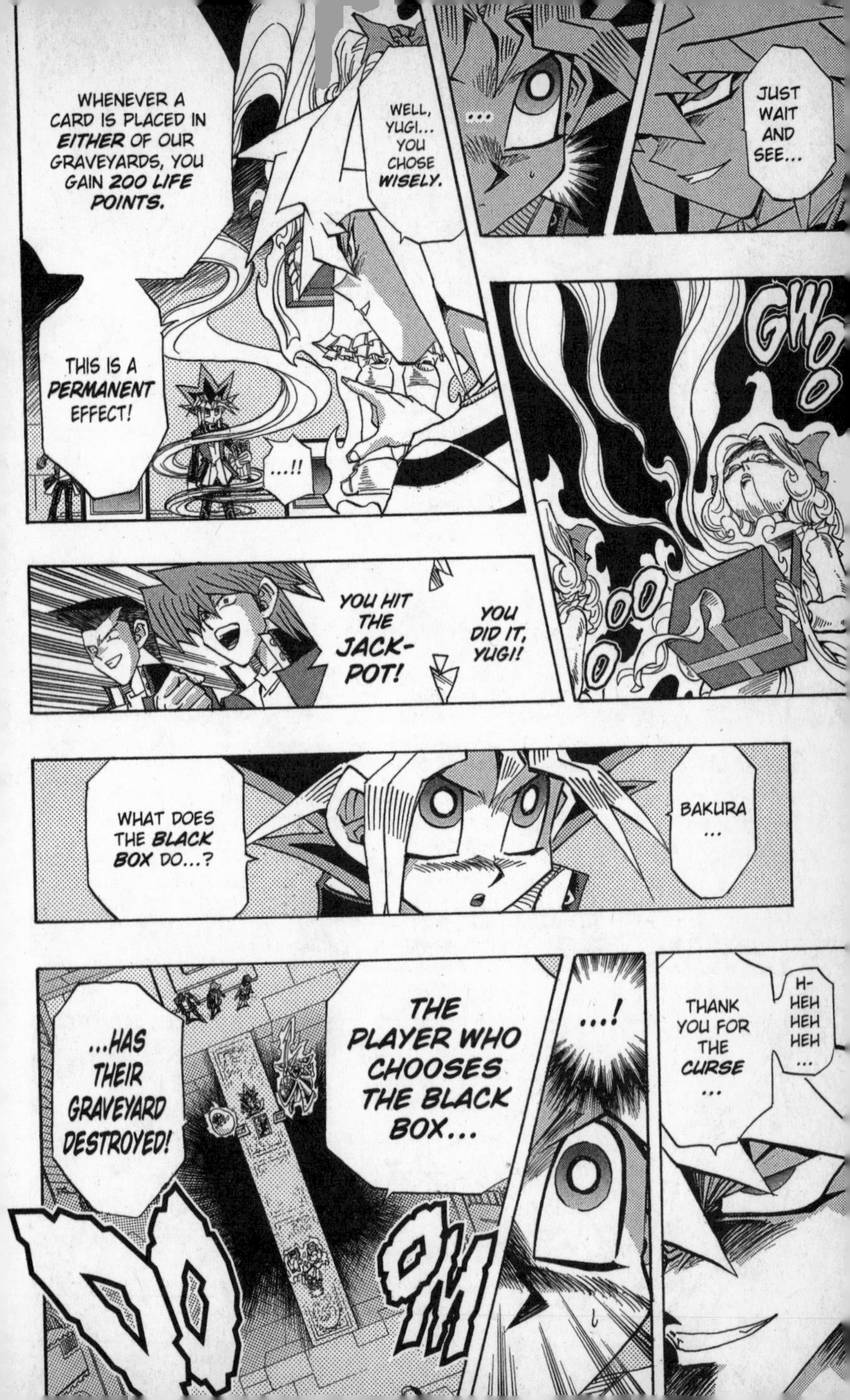
JUST WAIT AND SEE...
...
WELL, YUGI... YOU CHOSE WISELY.
WHENEVER A CARD IS PLACED IN EITHER OF OUR GRAVEYARDS, YOU GAIN 200 LIFE POINTS.
THIS IS A PERMANENT EFFECT!
...!!
GWOOO
YOU DID IT, YUGI!
YOU HIT THE JACK-POT!
BAKURA...
WHAT DOES THE BLACK BOX DO...?
H-HEH HEH HEH...
THANK YOU FOR THE CURSE...
...!
THE PLAYER WHO CHOOSES THE BLACK BOX...
...HAS THEIR GRAVEYARD DESTROYED!
DOOM

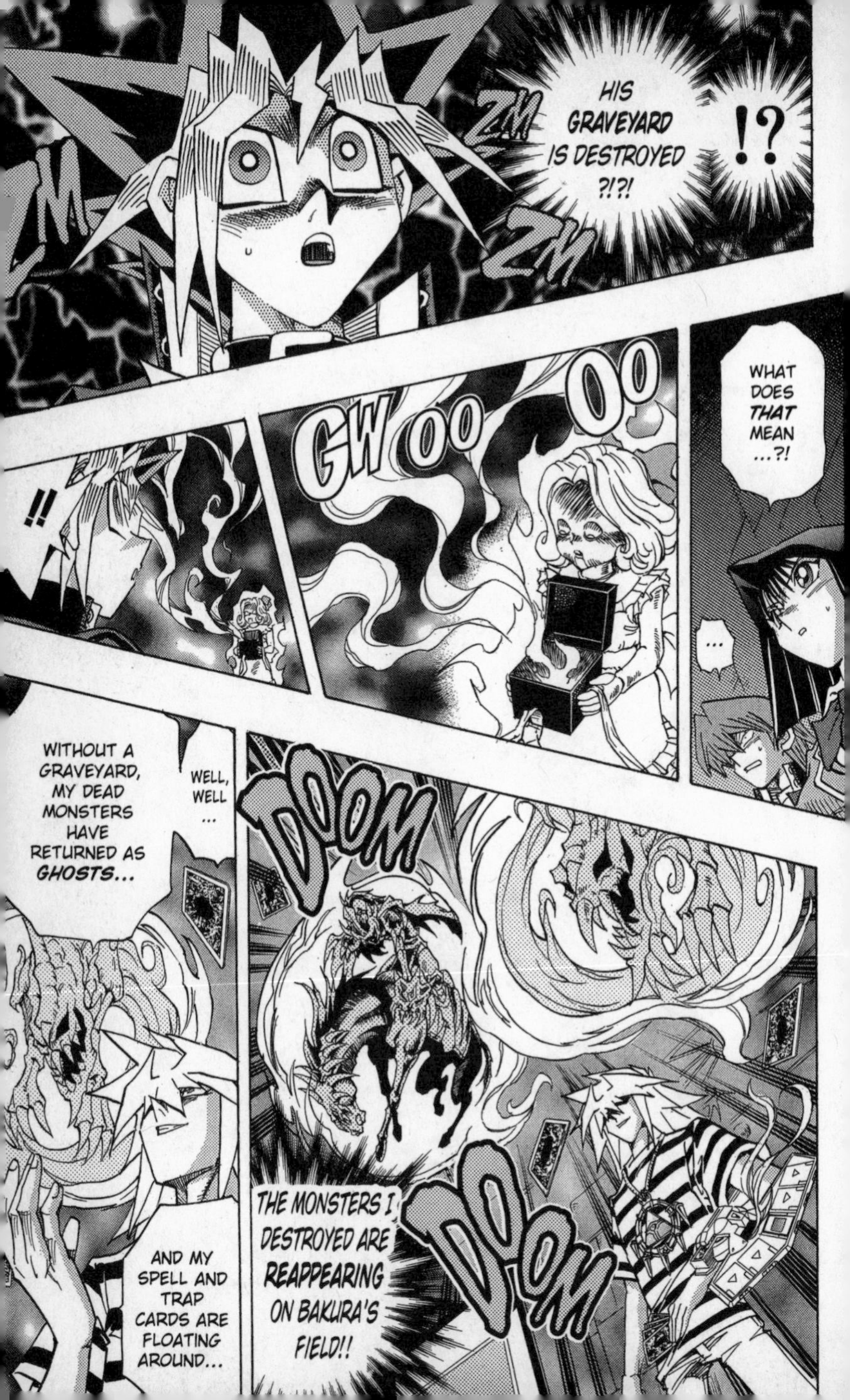
!?
HIS GRAVEYARD IS DESTROYED ?!?!
ZM
ZM
ZM
WHAT DOES THAT MEAN ...?!
...
GW OO OO
!!
DOOM
WELL, WELL ...
WITHOUT A GRAVEYARD, MY DEAD MONSTERS HAVE RETURNED AS GHOSTS...
DOOM
THE MONSTERS I DESTROYED ARE REAPPEARING ON BAKURA'S FIELD!!
AND MY SPELL AND TRAP CARDS ARE FLOATING AROUND...

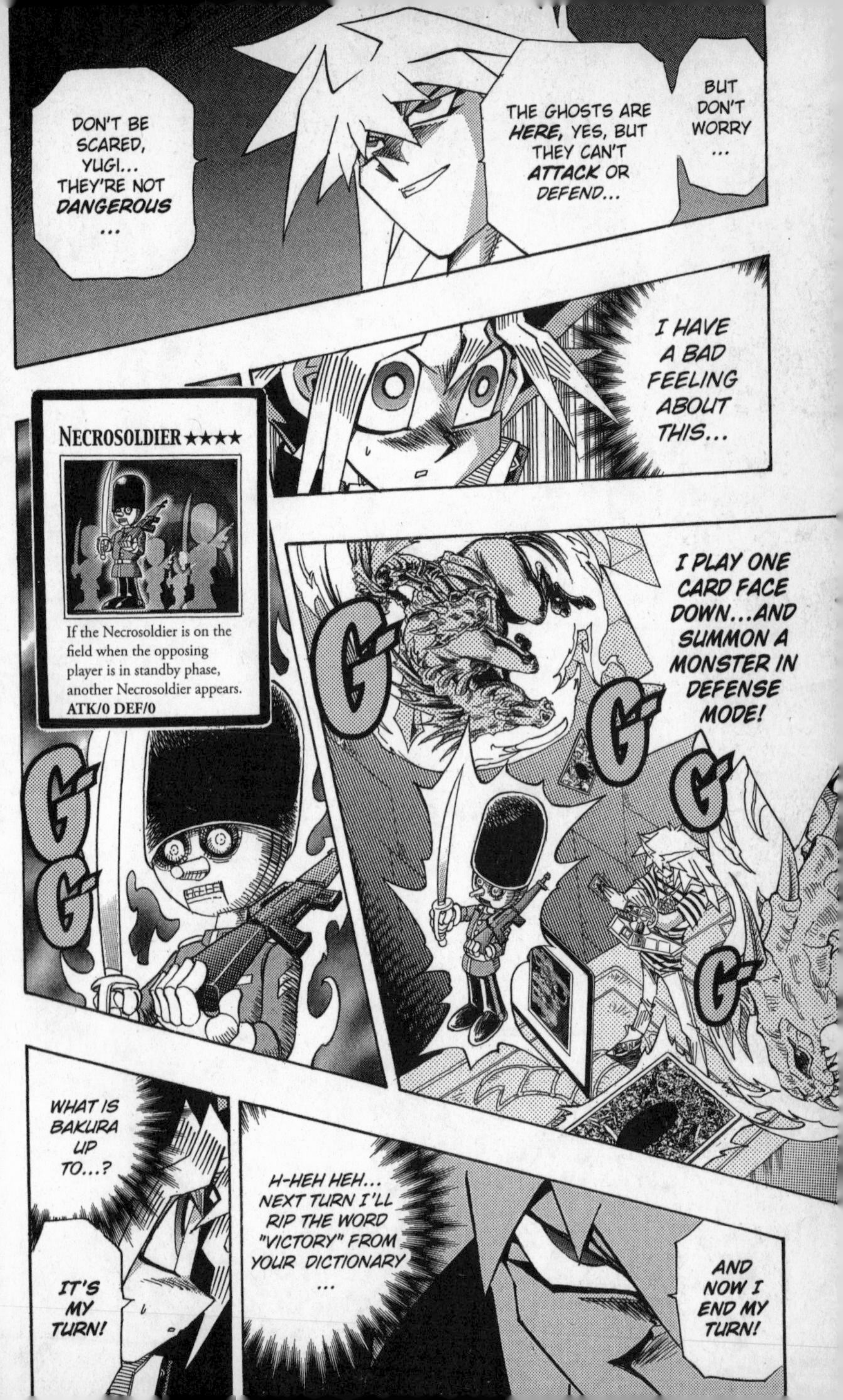
BUT DON'T WORRY ...
THE GHOSTS ARE HERE, YES, BUT THEY CAN'T ATTACK OR DEFEND...
DON'T BE SCARED, YUGI... THEY'RE NOT DANGEROUS ...
I HAVE A BAD FEELING ABOUT THIS...
I PLAY ONE CARD FACE DOWN...AND SUMMON A MONSTER IN DEFENSE MODE!
G
G
G
G
NECROSOLDIER ★★★★
If the Necrosoldier is on the field when the opposing player is in standby phase, another Necrosoldier appears.
ATK/0 DEF/0
G
G
AND NOW I END MY TURN!
H-HEH HEH... NEXT TURN I'LL RIP THE WORD "VICTORY" FROM YOUR DICTIONARY ...
WHAT IS BAKURA UP TO...?
IT'S MY TURN!

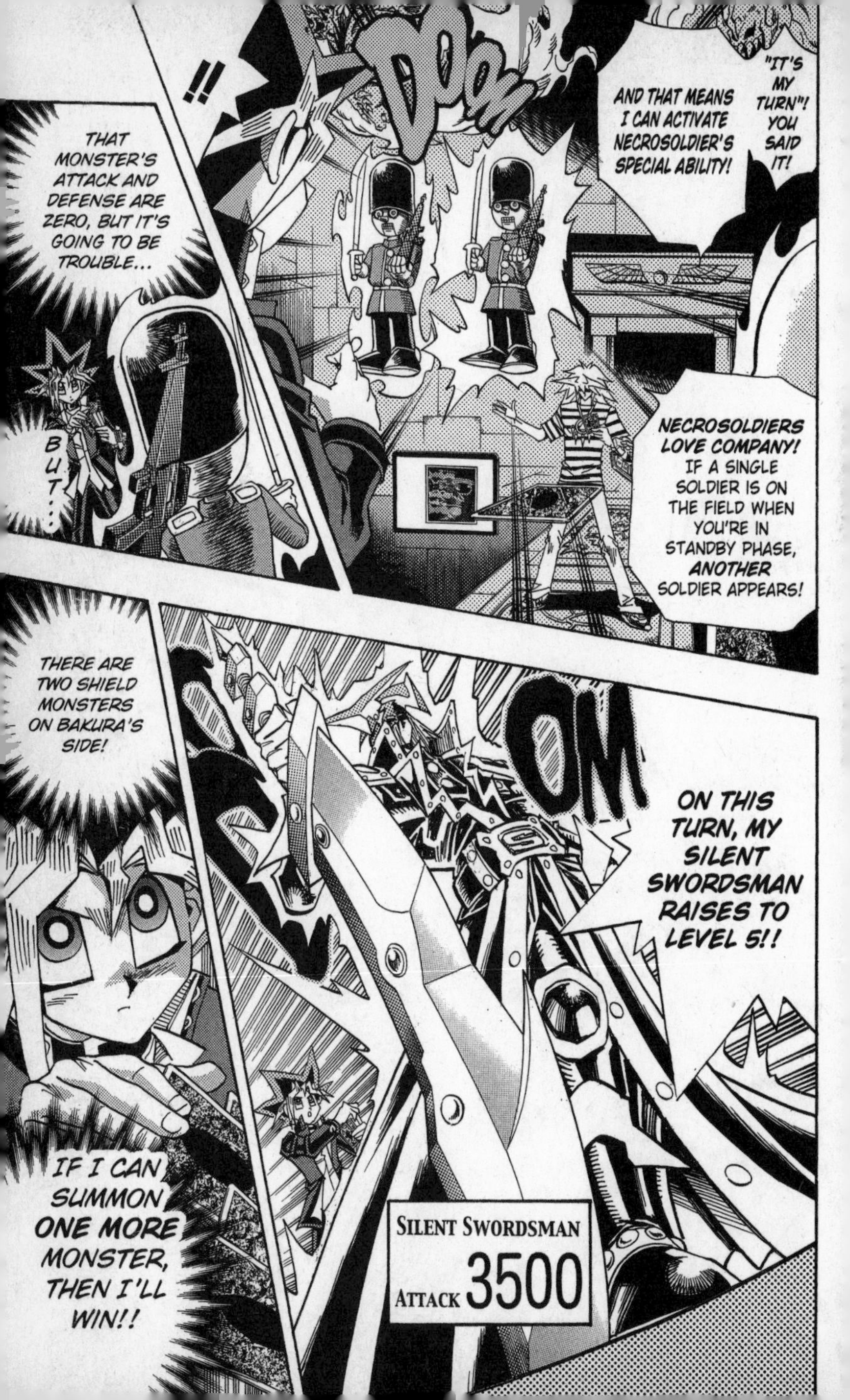
DOOM
"IT'S MY TURN"! YOU SAID IT!
AND THAT MEANS I CAN ACTIVATE NECROSOLDIER'S SPECIAL ABILITY!
NECROSOLDIERS LOVE COMPANY! IF A SINGLE SOLDIER IS ON THE FIELD WHEN YOU'RE IN STANDBY PHASE, ANOTHER SOLDIER APPEARS!
!!
THAT MONSTER'S ATTACK AND DEFENSE ARE ZERO, BUT IT'S GOING TO BE TROUBLE...
BUT...
OM
ON THIS TURN, MY SILENT SWORDSMAN RAISES TO LEVEL 5!!
SILENT SWORDSMAN
ATTACK 3500
THERE ARE TWO SHIELD MONSTERS ON BAKURA'S SIDE!
IF I CAN SUMMON ONE MORE MONSTER, THEN I'LL WIN!!

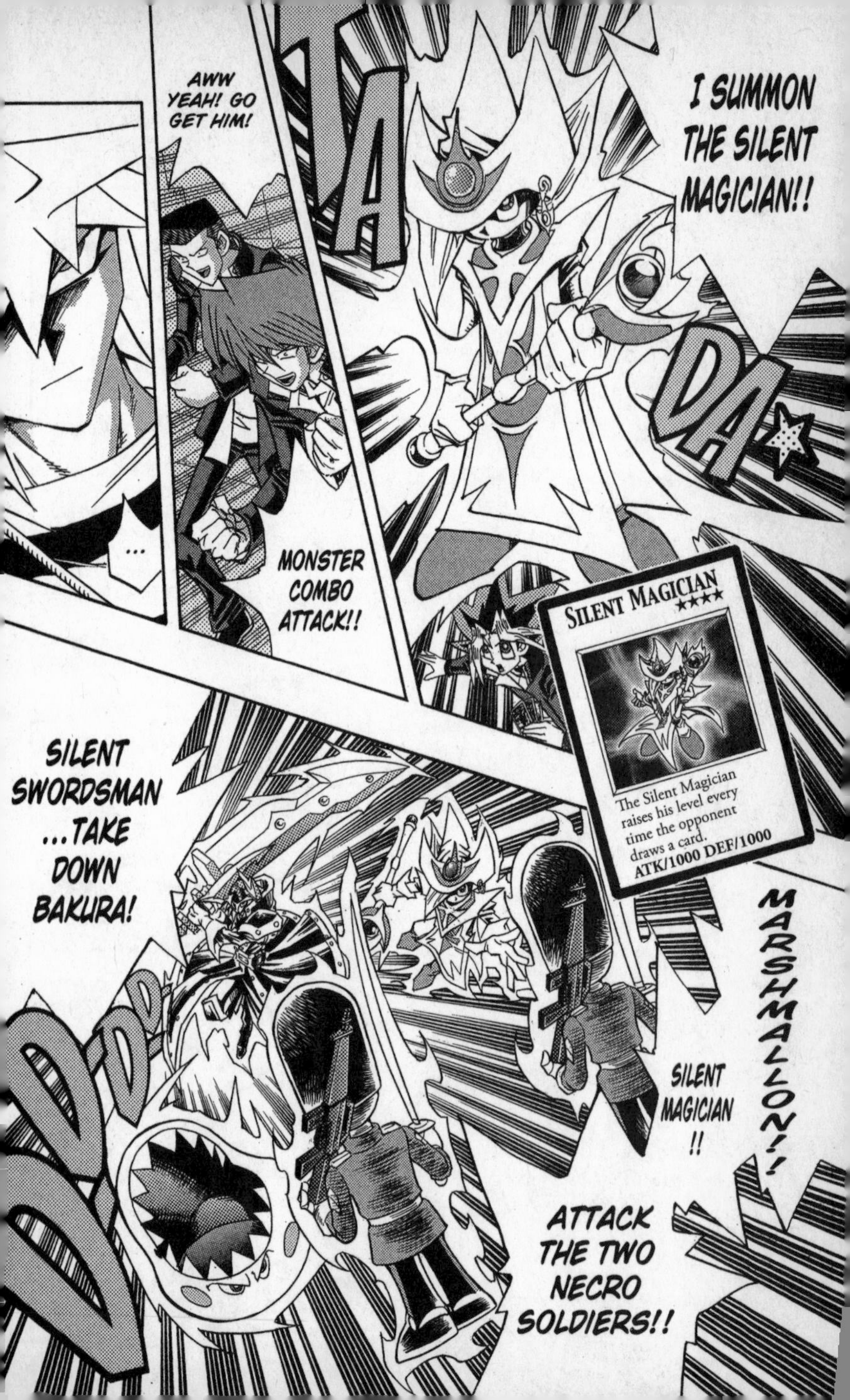
TA
DA
I SUMMON THE SILENT MAGICIAN!!
SILENT MAGICIAN ★★★★
The Silent Magician raises his level every time the opponent draws a card.
ATK/1000 DEF/1000
AWW YEAH! GO GET HIM!
MONSTER COMBO ATTACK!!
...
MARSHMALLON!!
SILENT MAGICIAN !!
ATTACK THE TWO NECRO SOLDIERS!!
SILENT SWORDSMAN ...TAKE DOWN BAKURA!

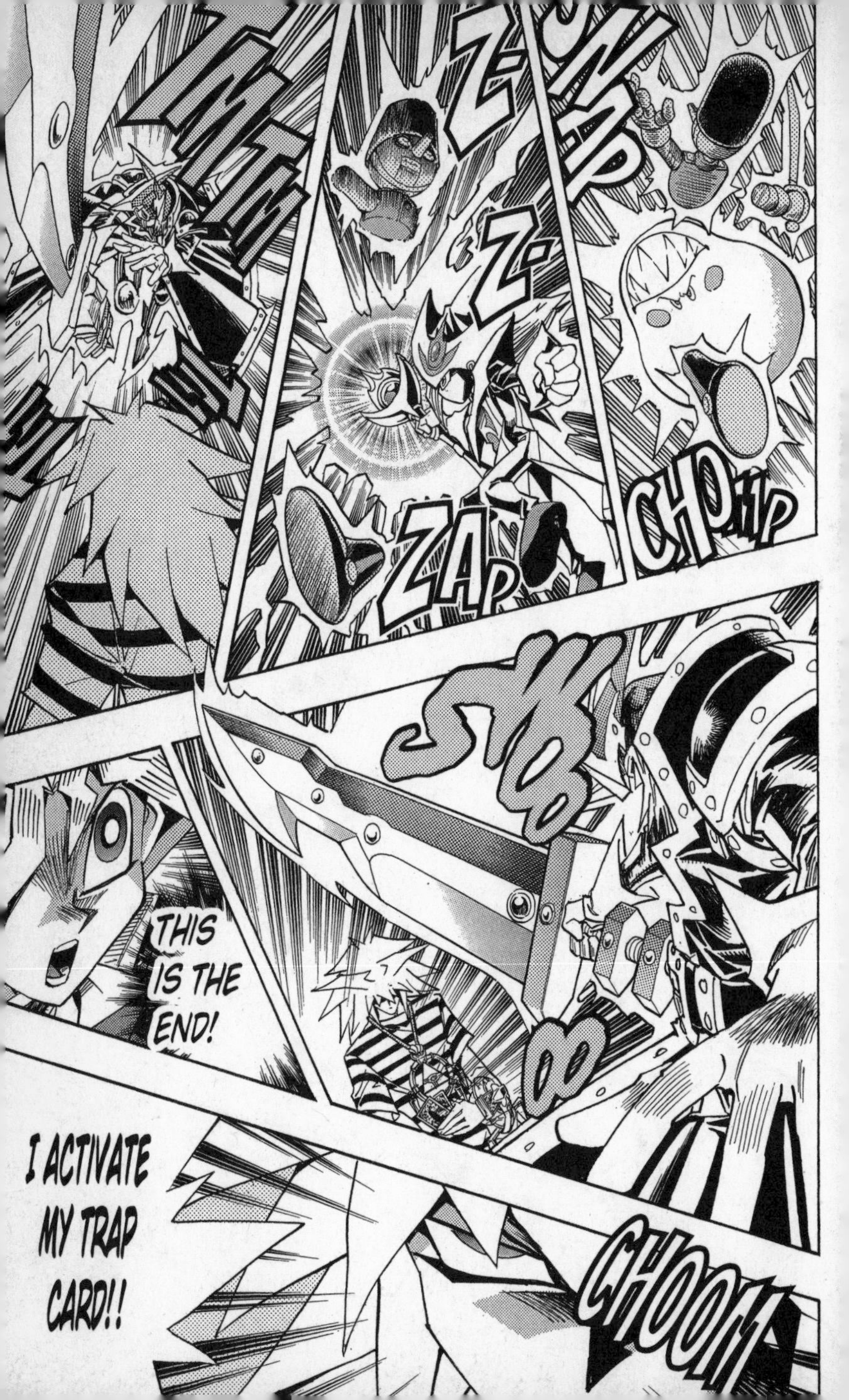
ZAP
THIS IS THE END!
I ACTIVATE MY TRAP CARD!!

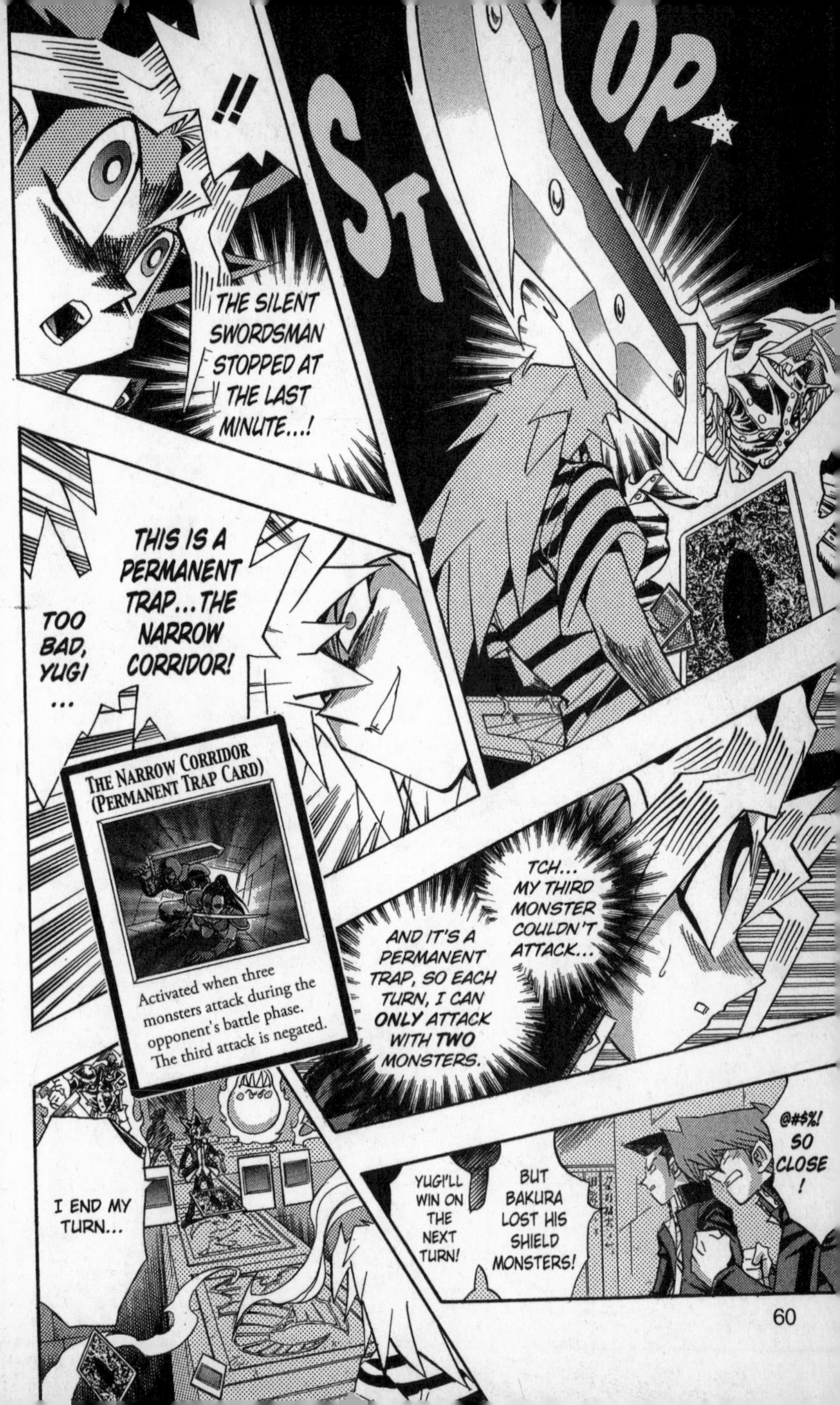
STOP☆
!!
THE SILENT SWORDSMAN STOPPED AT THE LAST MINUTE...!
THIS IS A PERMANENT TRAP...THE NARROW CORRIDOR!
TOO BAD, YUGI...
THE NARROW CORRIDOR (PERMANENT TRAP CARD)
Activated when three monsters attack during the opponent's battle phase. The third attack is negated.
TCH... MY THIRD MONSTER COULDN'T ATTACK...
AND IT'S A PERMANENT TRAP, SO EACH TURN, I CAN ONLY ATTACK WITH TWO MONSTERS.
@#$%! SO CLOSE!
BUT BAKURA LOST HIS SHIELD MONSTERS!
YUGI'LL WIN ON THE NEXT TURN!
I END MY TURN...

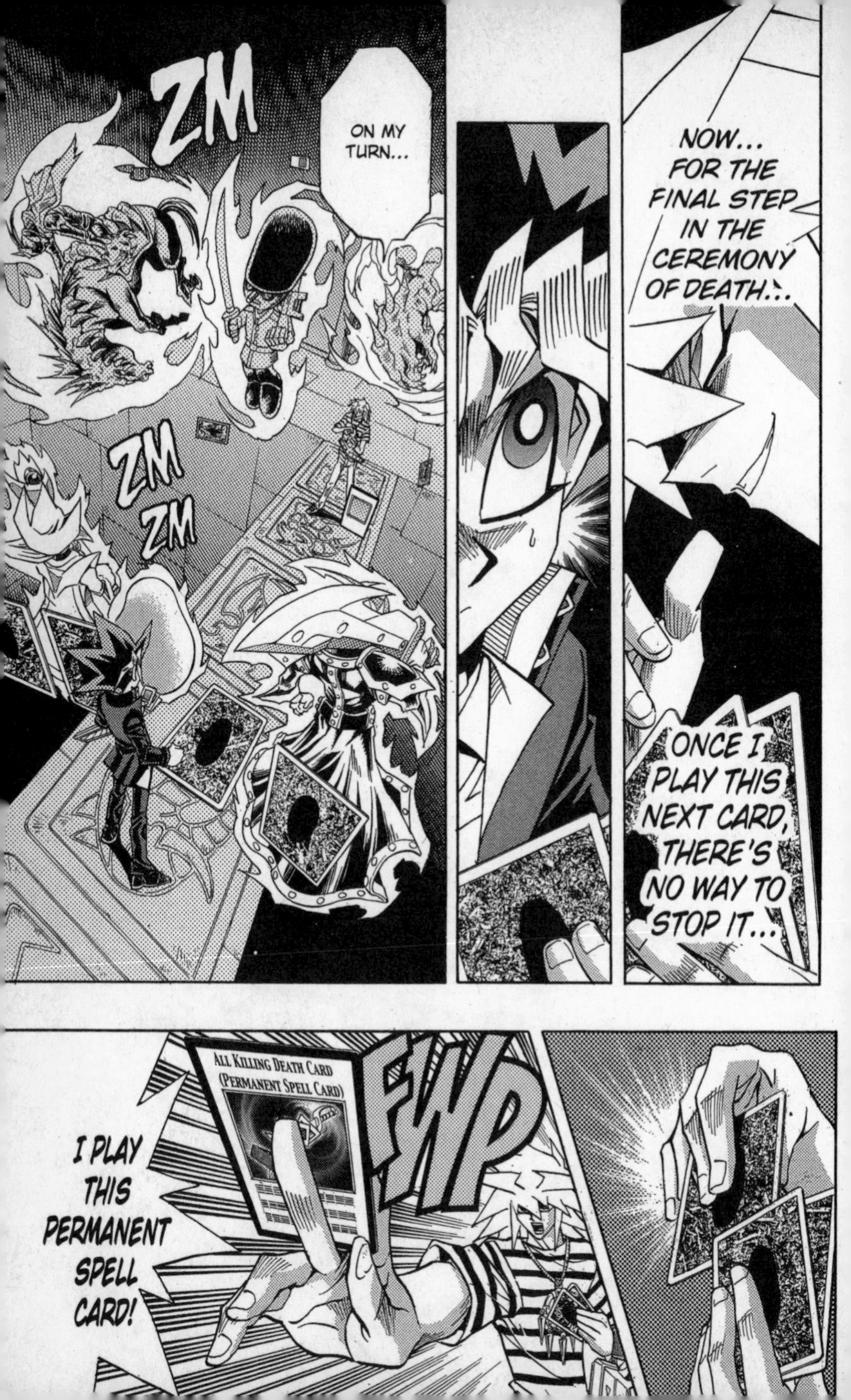
NOW... FOR THE FINAL STEP IN THE CEREMONY OF DEATH...
ONCE I PLAY THIS NEXT CARD, THERE'S NO WAY TO STOP IT...
ON MY TURN...
ZM
ZM ZM
FWP
ALL KILLING DEATH CARD (PERMANENT SPELL CARD)
I PLAY THIS PERMANENT SPELL CARD!

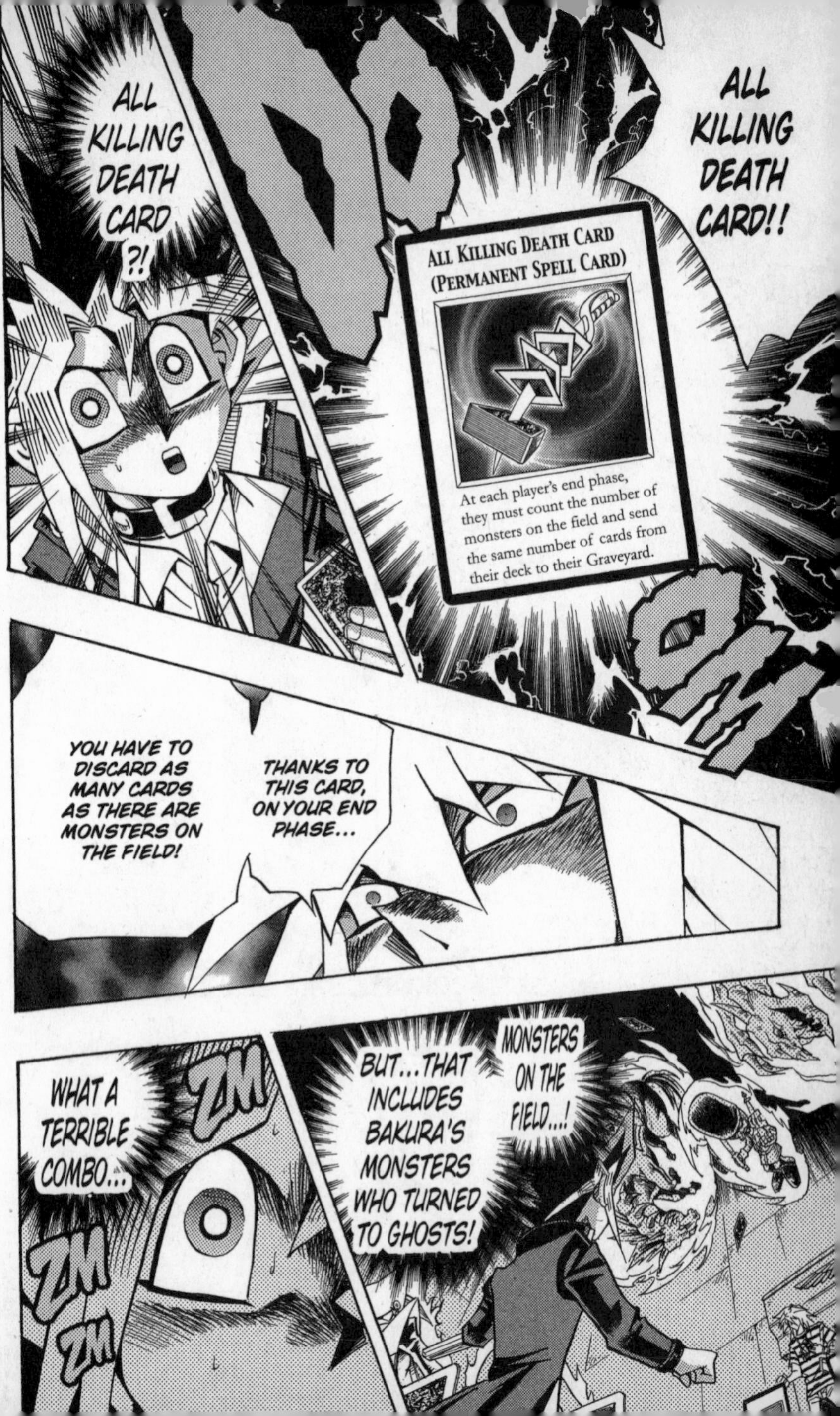
ALL KILLING DEATH CARD!!
ALL KILLING DEATH CARD
(PERMANENT SPELL CARD)
At each player's end phase, they must count the number of monsters on the field and send the same number of cards from their deck to their Graveyard.
DOOM
ALL KILLING DEATH CARD ?!
THANKS TO THIS CARD, ON YOUR END PHASE...
YOU HAVE TO DISCARD AS MANY CARDS AS THERE ARE MONSTERS ON THE FIELD!
MONSTERS ON THE FIELD...!
BUT...THAT INCLUDES BAKURA'S MONSTERS WHO TURNED TO GHOSTS!
ZM
WHAT A TERRIBLE COMBO...
ZM
ZM

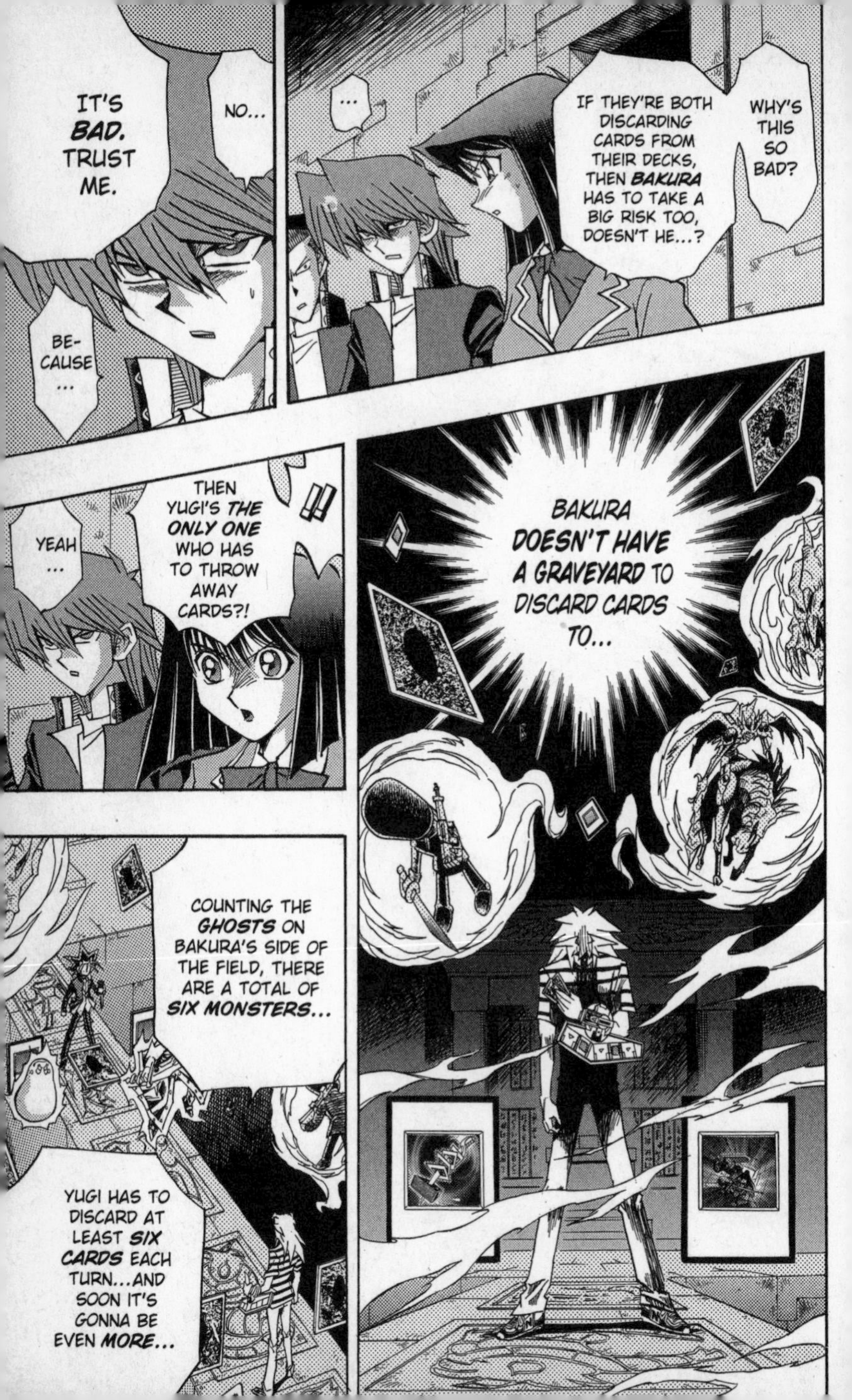
WHY'S THIS SO BAD?
IF THEY'RE BOTH DISCARDING CARDS FROM THEIR DECKS, THEN BAKURA HAS TO TAKE A BIG RISK TOO, DOESN'T HE...?
...
NO...
IT'S BAD. TRUST ME.
BE- CAUSE ...
BAKURA DOESN'T HAVE A GRAVEYARD TO DISCARD CARDS TO...
!!
THEN YUGI'S THE ONLY ONE WHO HAS TO THROW AWAY CARDS?!
YEAH ...
COUNTING THE GHOSTS ON BAKURA'S SIDE OF THE FIELD, THERE ARE A TOTAL OF SIX MONSTERS...
YUGI HAS TO DISCARD AT LEAST SIX CARDS EACH TURN...AND SOON IT'S GONNA BE EVEN MORE...

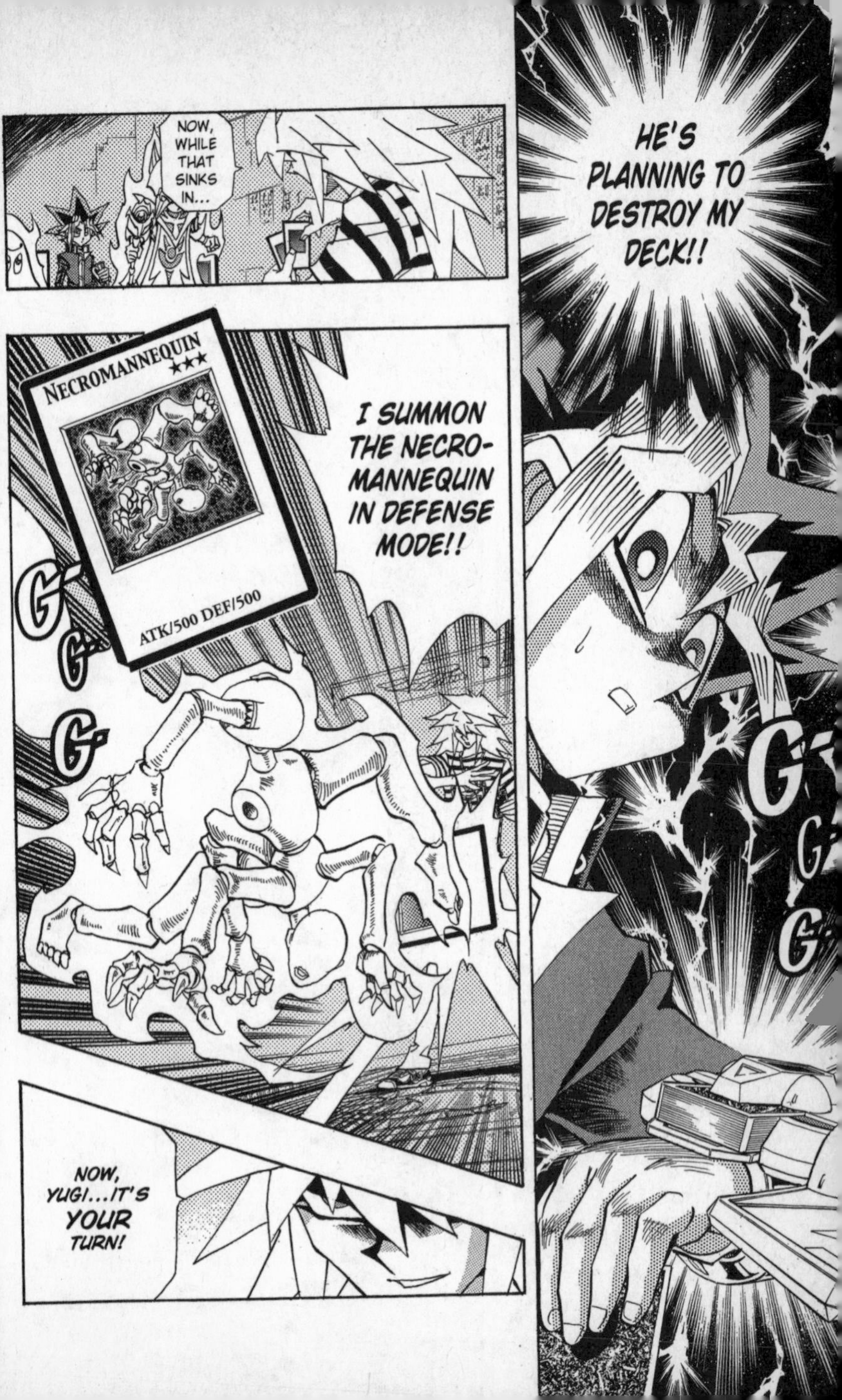
HE'S PLANNING TO DESTROY MY DECK!!
G- G- G-
NOW, WHILE THAT SINKS IN...
NECROMANNEQUIN
ATK/500 DEF/500
I SUMMON THE NECRO-MANNEQUIN IN DEFENSE MODE!!
G- G- G-
NOW, YUGI...IT'S YOUR TURN!

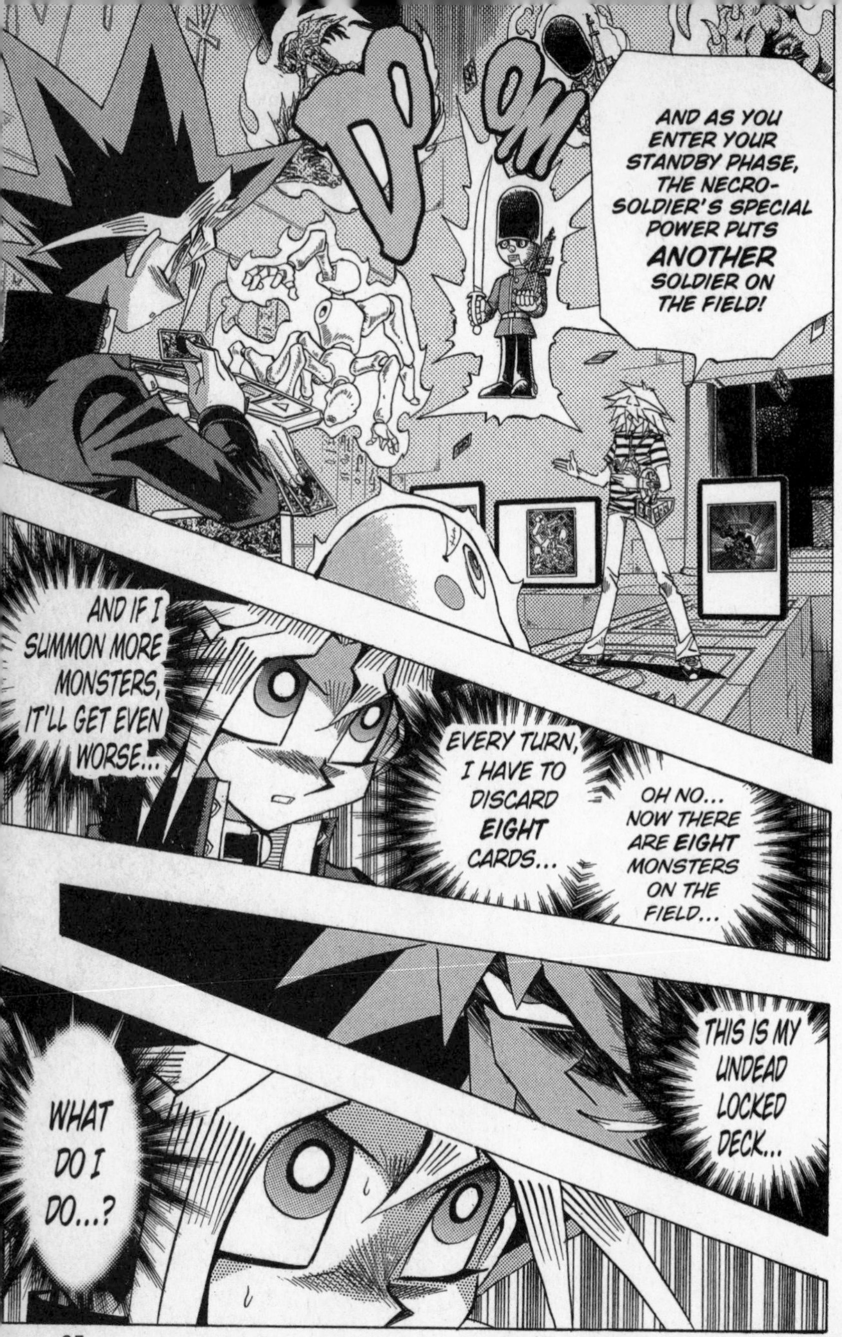
AND AS YOU ENTER YOUR STANDBY PHASE, THE NECRO-SOLDIER'S SPECIAL POWER PUTS ANOTHER SOLDIER ON THE FIELD!
OH NO... NOW THERE ARE EIGHT MONSTERS ON THE FIELD...
EVERY TURN, I HAVE TO DISCARD EIGHT CARDS...
AND IF I SUMMON MORE MONSTERS, IT'LL GET EVEN WORSE...
THIS IS MY UNDEAD LOCKED DECK...
WHAT DO I DO...?

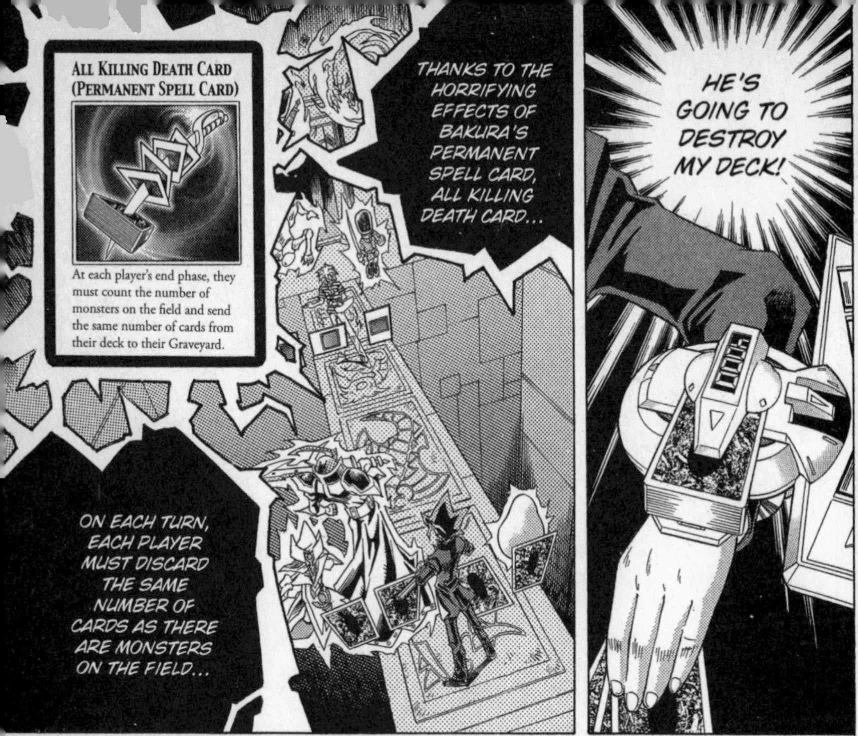
HE'S GOING TO DESTROY MY DECK!
THANKS TO THE HORRIFYING EFFECTS OF BAKURA'S PERMANENT SPELL CARD, ALL KILLING DEATH CARD...
All Killing Death Card (Permanent Spell Card)
At each player's end phase, they must count the number of monsters on the field and send the same number of cards from their deck to their Graveyard.
ON EACH TURN, EACH PLAYER MUST DISCARD THE SAME NUMBER OF CARDS AS THERE ARE MONSTERS ON THE FIELD...

Duel 49: I Won't Give Up!!

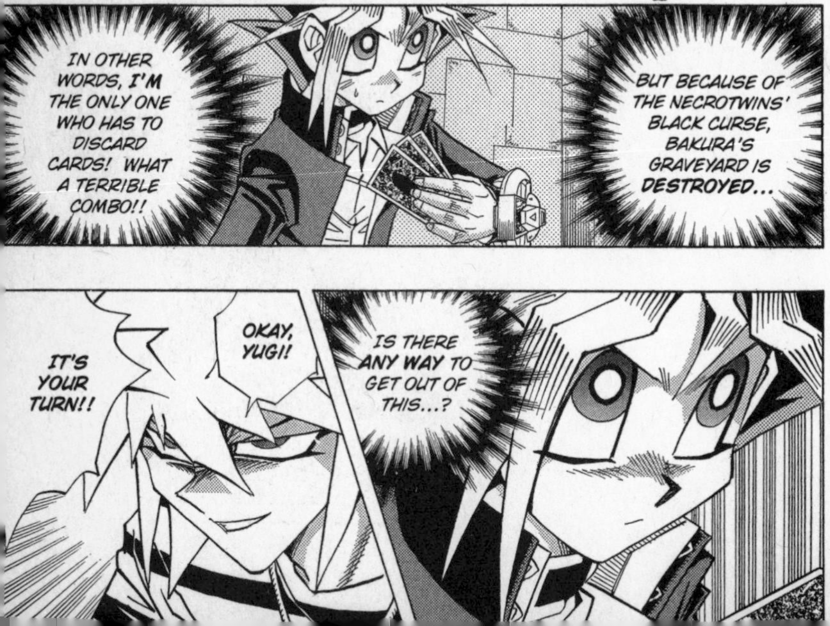
BUT BECAUSE OF THE NECROTWINS' BLACK CURSE, BAKURA'S GRAVEYARD IS DESTROYED...
IN OTHER WORDS, I'M THE ONLY ONE WHO HAS TO DISCARD CARDS! WHAT A TERRIBLE COMBO!!
IS THERE ANY WAY TO GET OUT OF THIS...?
OKAY, YUGI!
IT'S YOUR TURN!!

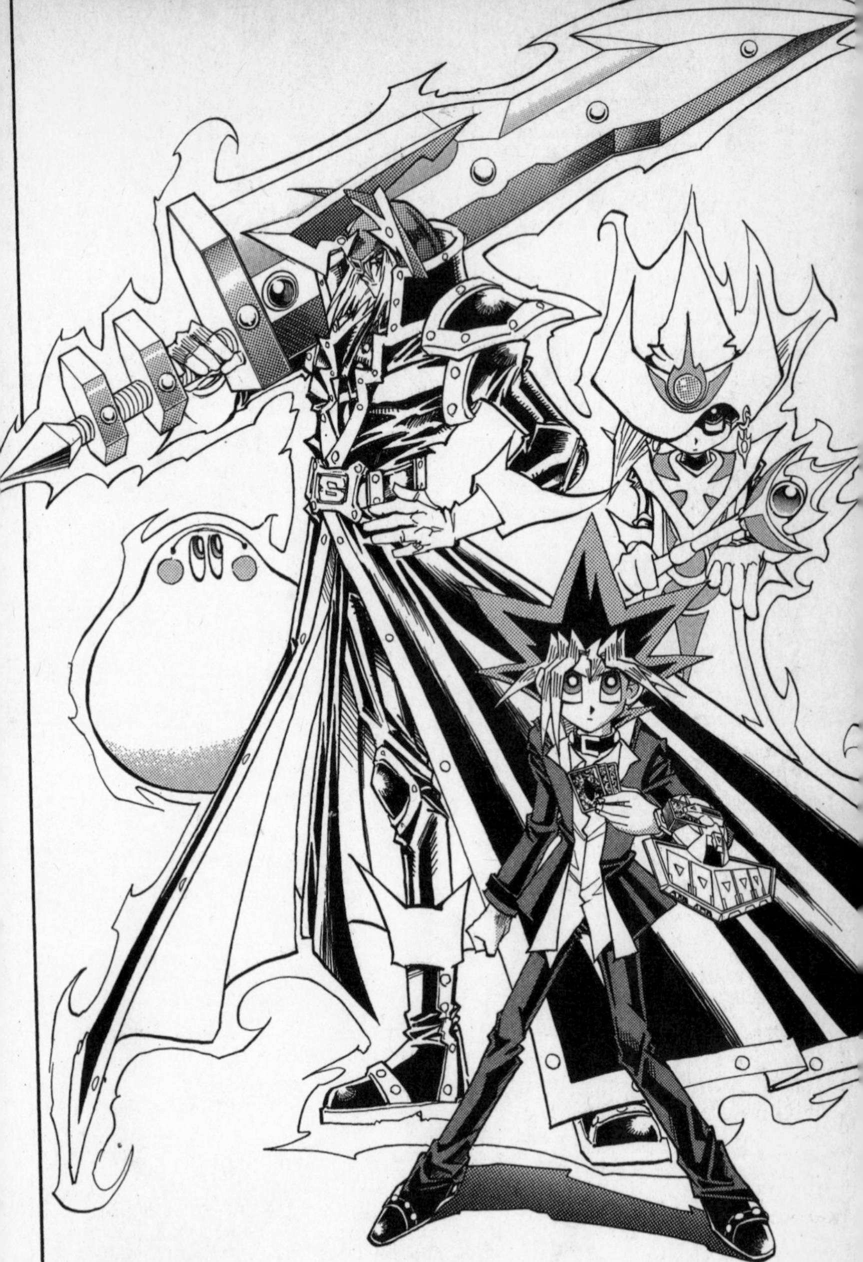

Duel 49: I Won't Give Up!!

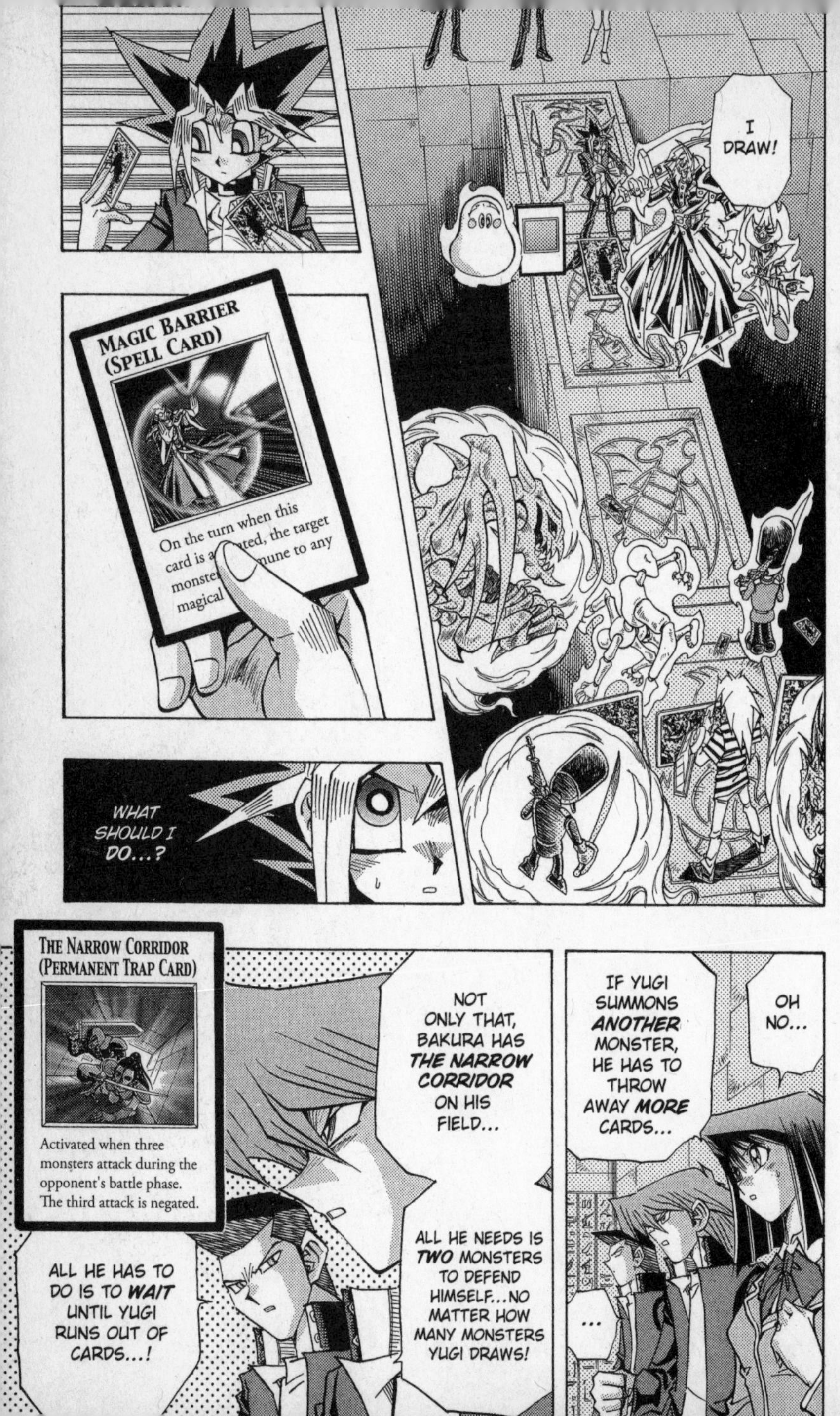
I DRAW!
Magic Barrier (Spell Card)
On the turn when this
card is a ted, the target
card is a mune to any
monster
magical
WHAT SHOULD I DO...?
OH NO...
IF YUGI SUMMONS ANOTHER MONSTER, HE HAS TO THROW AWAY MORE CARDS...
...
NOT ONLY THAT, BAKURA HAS THE NARROW CORRIDOR ON HIS FIELD...
The Narrow Corridor (Permanent Trap Card)
Activated when three monsters attack during the opponent's battle phase. The third attack is negated.
ALL HE NEEDS IS TWO MONSTERS TO DEFEND HIMSELF...NO MATTER HOW MANY MONSTERS YUGI DRAWS!
ALL HE HAS TO DO IS TO WAIT UNTIL YUGI RUNS OUT OF CARDS...!

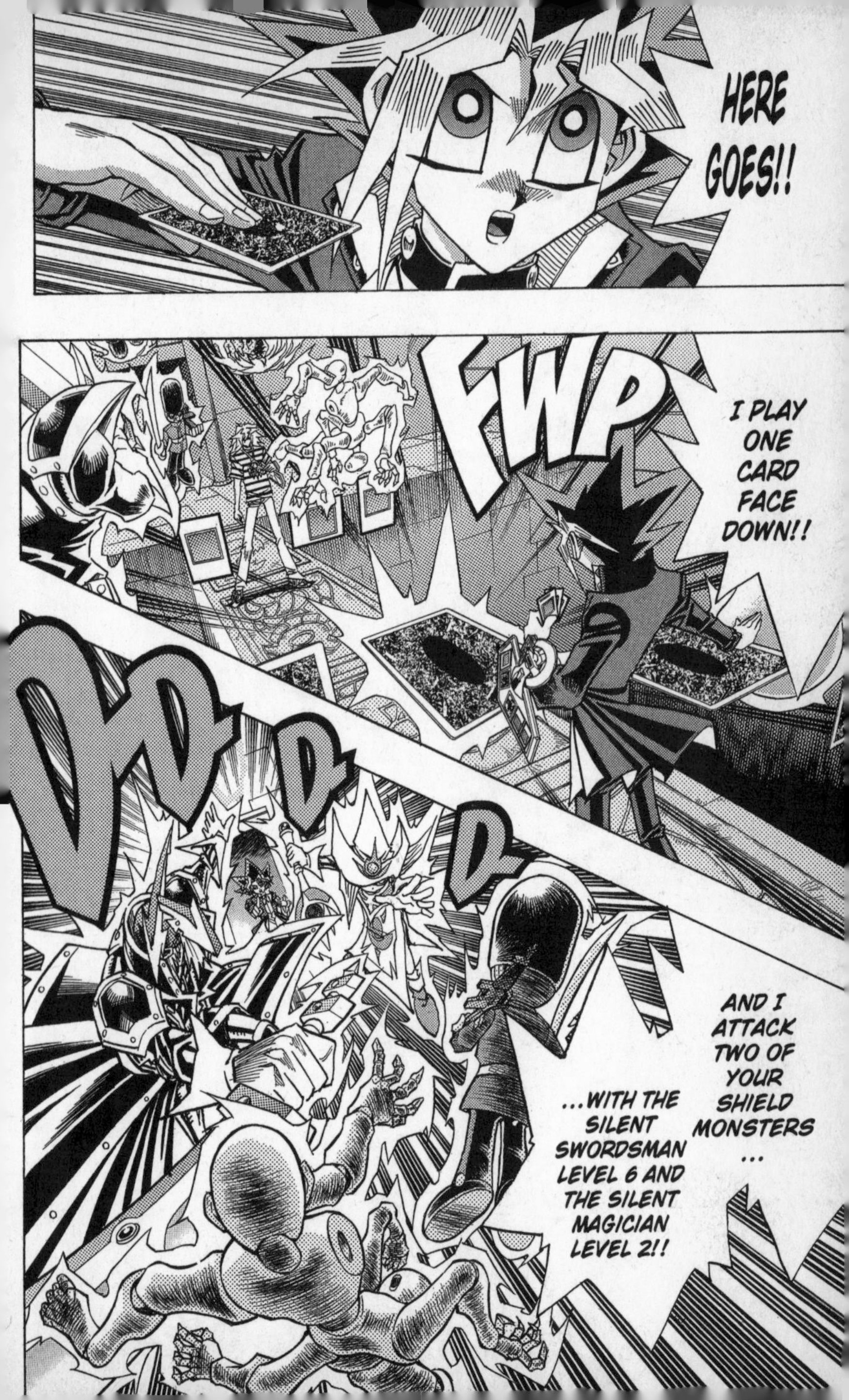
HERE GOES!!
FWP
I PLAY ONE CARD FACE DOWN!!
DDD
AND I ATTACK TWO OF YOUR SHIELD MONSTERS...
...WITH THE SILENT SWORDSMAN LEVEL 6 AND THE SILENT MAGICIAN LEVEL 2!!

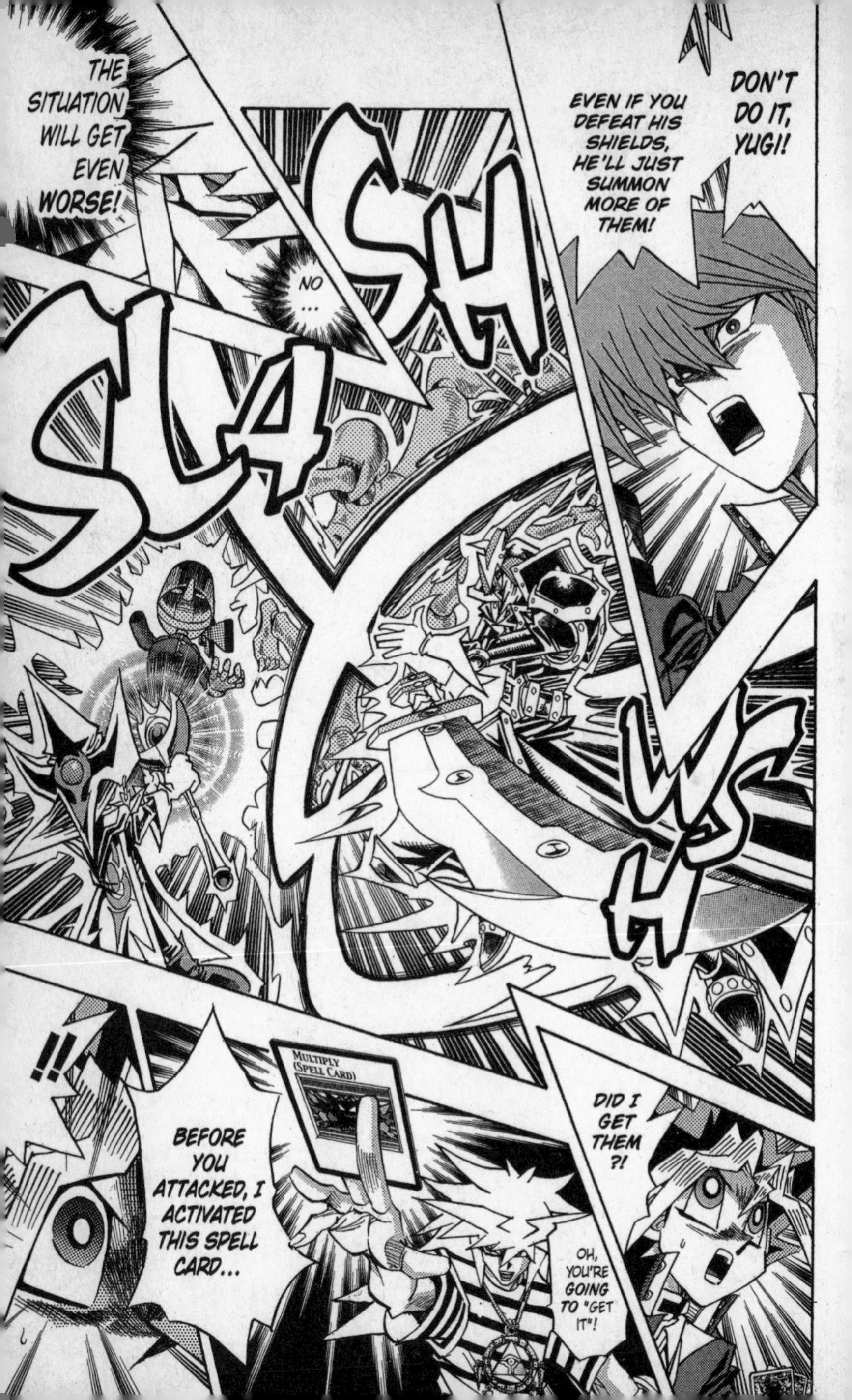
DON'T DO IT, YUGI!
EVEN IF YOU DEFEAT HIS SHIELDS, HE'LL JUST SUMMON MORE OF THEM!
SLASH
NO ...
THE SITUATION WILL GET EVEN WORSE!
DID I GET THEM?!
OH, YOU'RE GOING TO "GET IT"!
MULTIPLY (SPELL CARD)
BEFORE YOU ATTACKED, I ACTIVATED THIS SPELL CARD...
!!

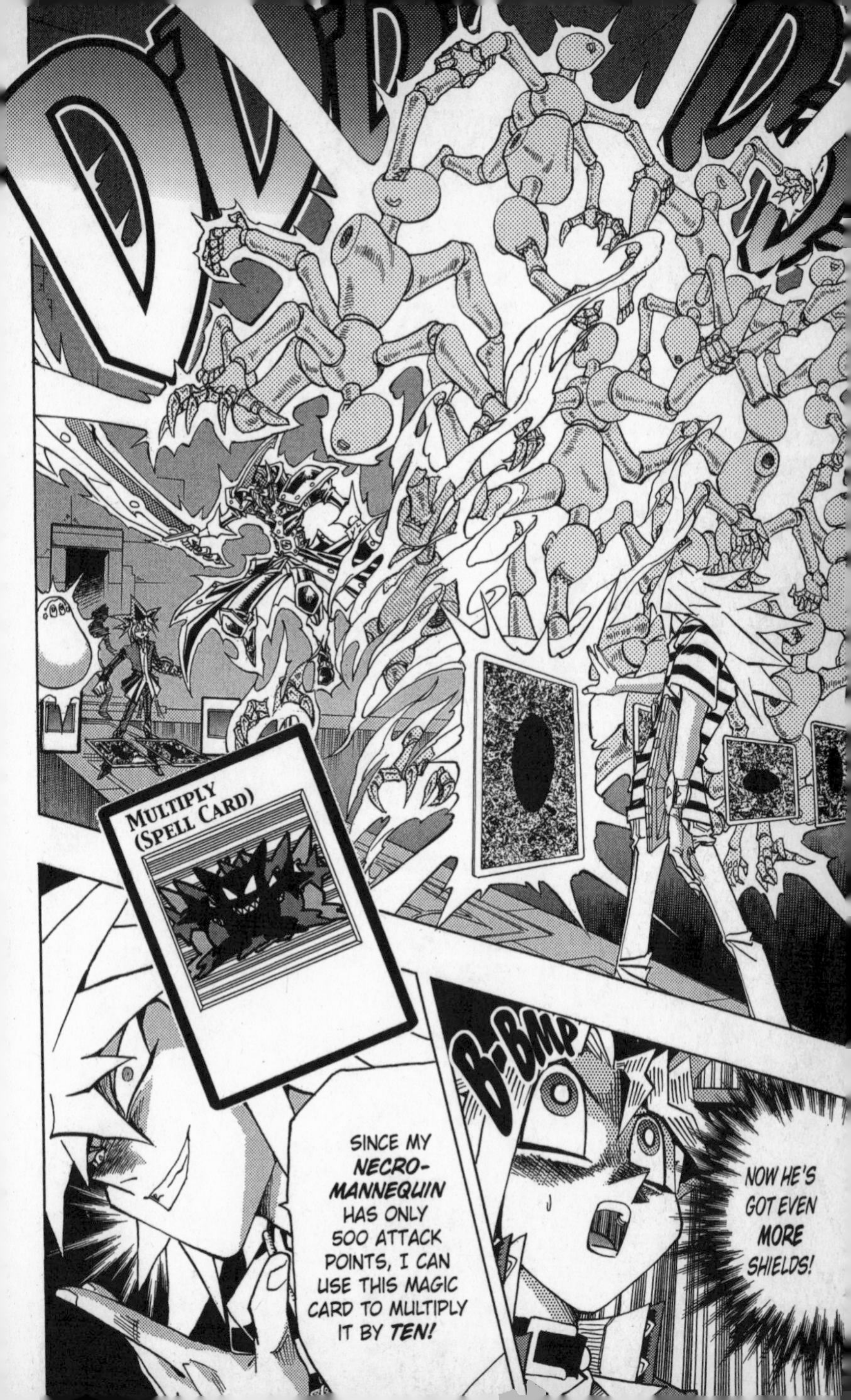
B-BMP
NOW HE'S GOT EVEN MORE SHIELDS!
MULTIPLY (SPELL CARD)
SINCE MY NECRO-MANNEQUIN HAS ONLY 500 ATTACK POINTS, I CAN USE THIS MAGIC CARD TO MULTIPLY IT BY TEN!

READ THIS WAY

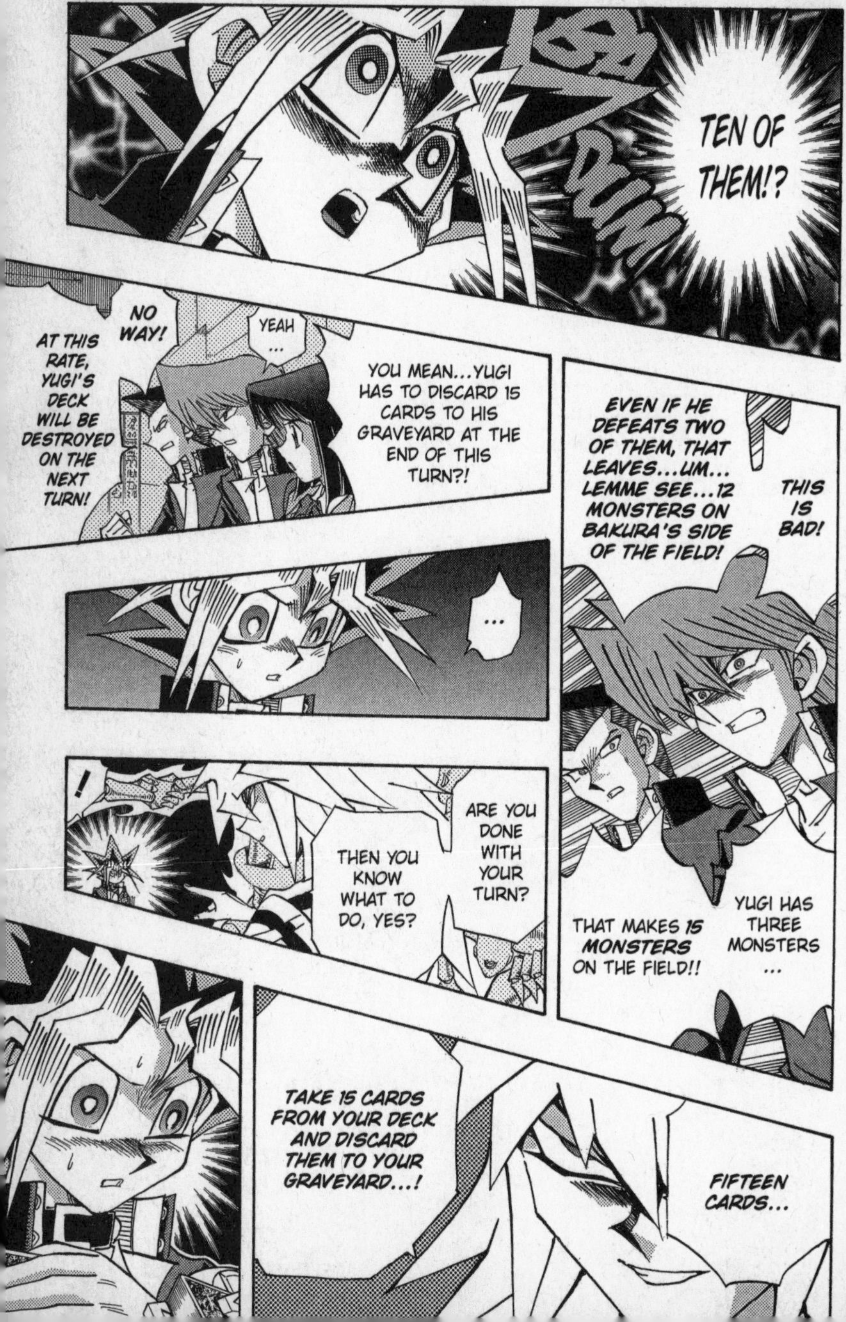
BA
DUM
TEN OF THEM!?
EVEN IF HE DEFEATS TWO OF THEM, THAT LEAVES...UM... LEMME SEE...12 MONSTERS ON BAKURA'S SIDE OF THE FIELD!
THIS IS BAD!
YUGI HAS THREE MONSTERS ...
THAT MAKES 15 MONSTERS ON THE FIELD!!
YOU MEAN...YUGI HAS TO DISCARD 15 CARDS TO HIS GRAVEYARD AT THE END OF THIS TURN?!
YEAH ...
NO WAY!
AT THIS RATE, YUGI'S DECK WILL BE DESTROYED ON THE NEXT TURN!
...
ARE YOU DONE WITH YOUR TURN?
THEN YOU KNOW WHAT TO DO, YES?
!
FIFTEEN CARDS...
TAKE 15 CARDS FROM YOUR DECK AND DISCARD THEM TO YOUR GRAVEYARD...!

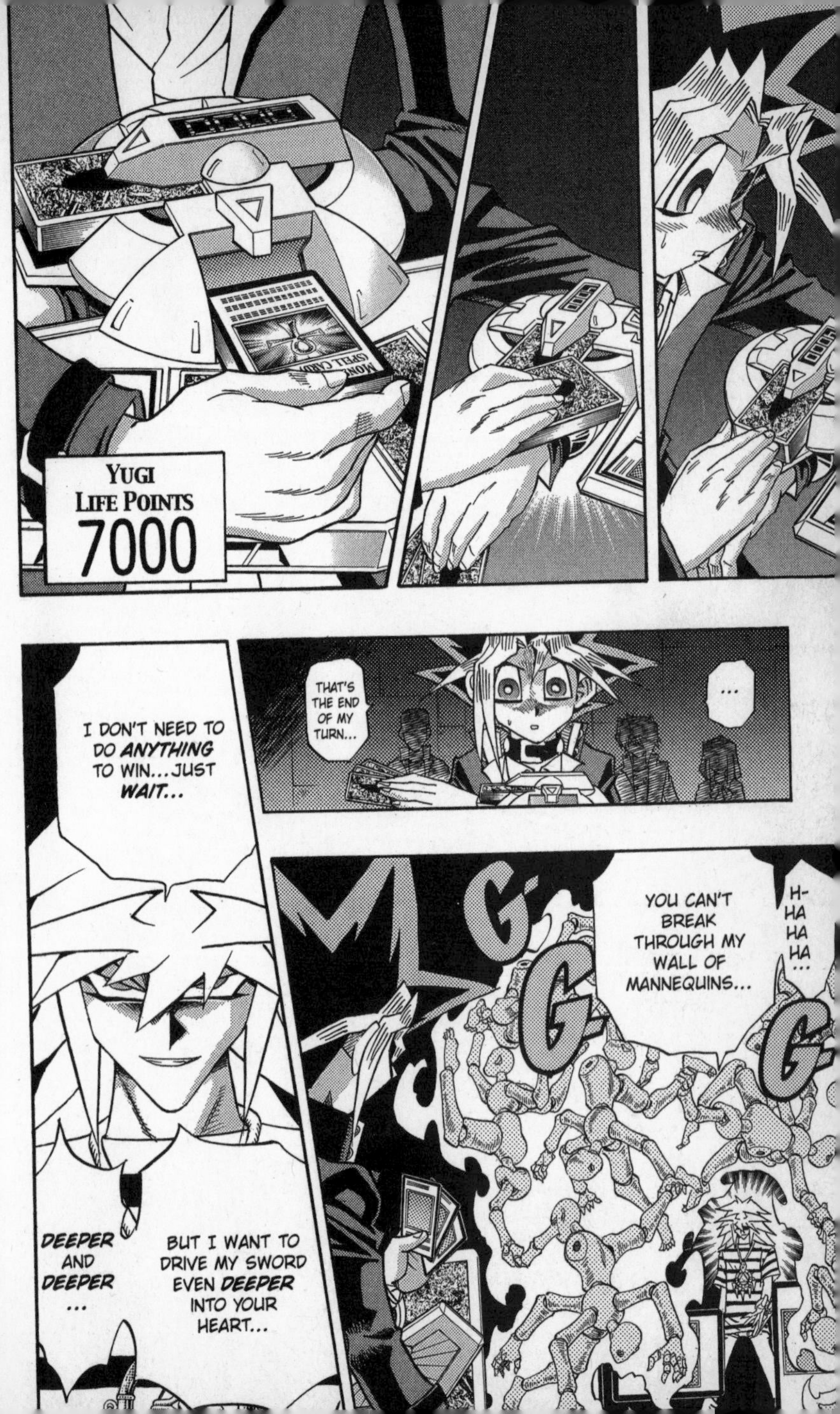

YUGI LIFE POINTS 7000
...
THAT'S THE END OF MY TURN...
H-HA HA HA...
YOU CAN'T BREAK THROUGH MY WALL OF MANNEQUINS...
G G G
M
I DON'T NEED TO DO ANYTHING TO WIN... JUST WAIT...
BUT I WANT TO DRIVE MY SWORD EVEN DEEPER INTO YOUR HEART...
DEEPER AND DEEPER ...

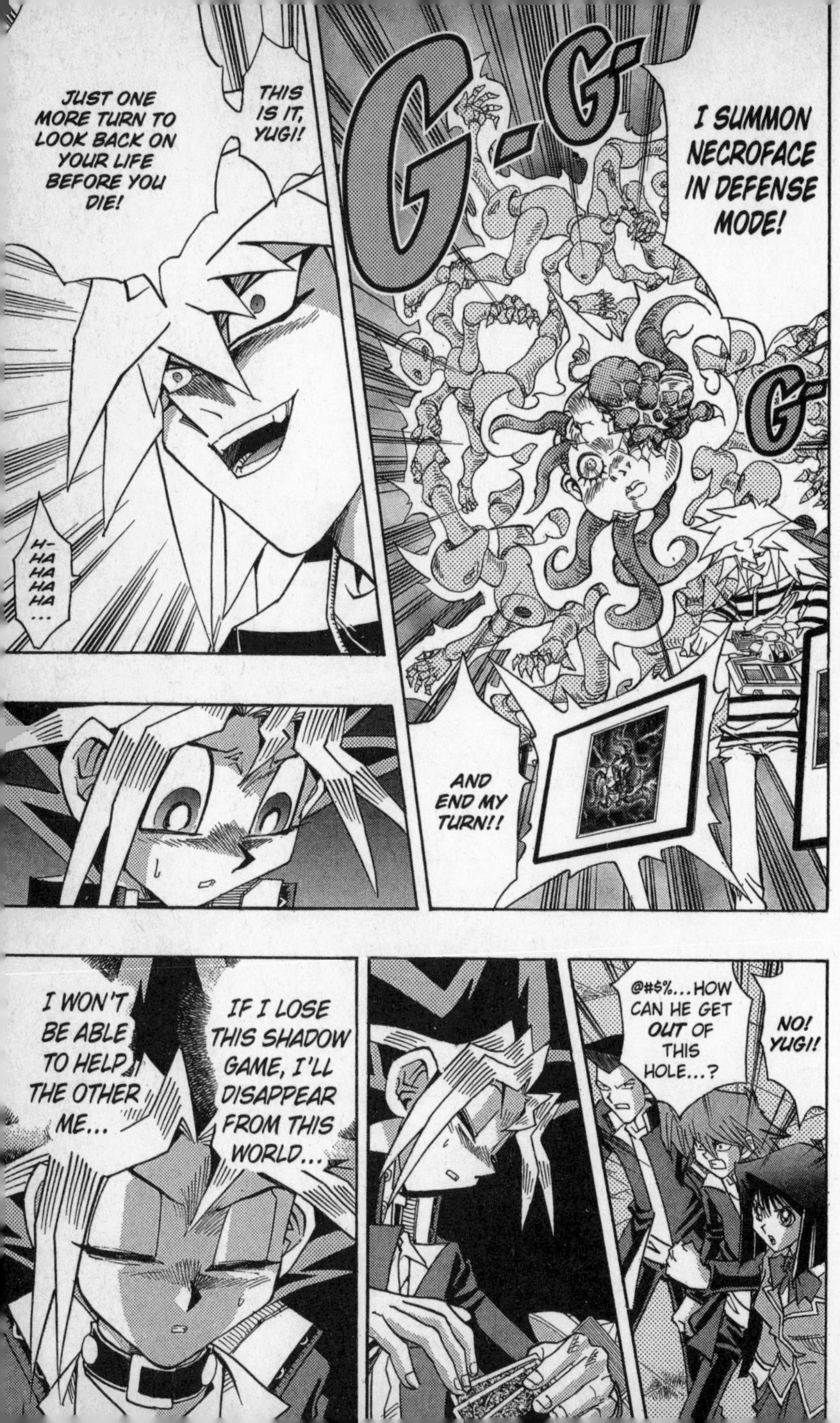

I SUMMON NECROFACE IN DEFENSE MODE!
G-G-
G-
AND END MY TURN!!
THIS IS IT, YUGI!
JUST ONE MORE TURN TO LOOK BACK ON YOUR LIFE BEFORE YOU DIE!
H-HA HA HA HA...
NO! YUGI!
@#$%... HOW CAN HE GET OUT OF THIS HOLE...?
IF I LOSE THIS SHADOW GAME, I'LL DISAPPEAR FROM THIS WORLD...
I WON'T BE ABLE TO HELP THE OTHER ME...

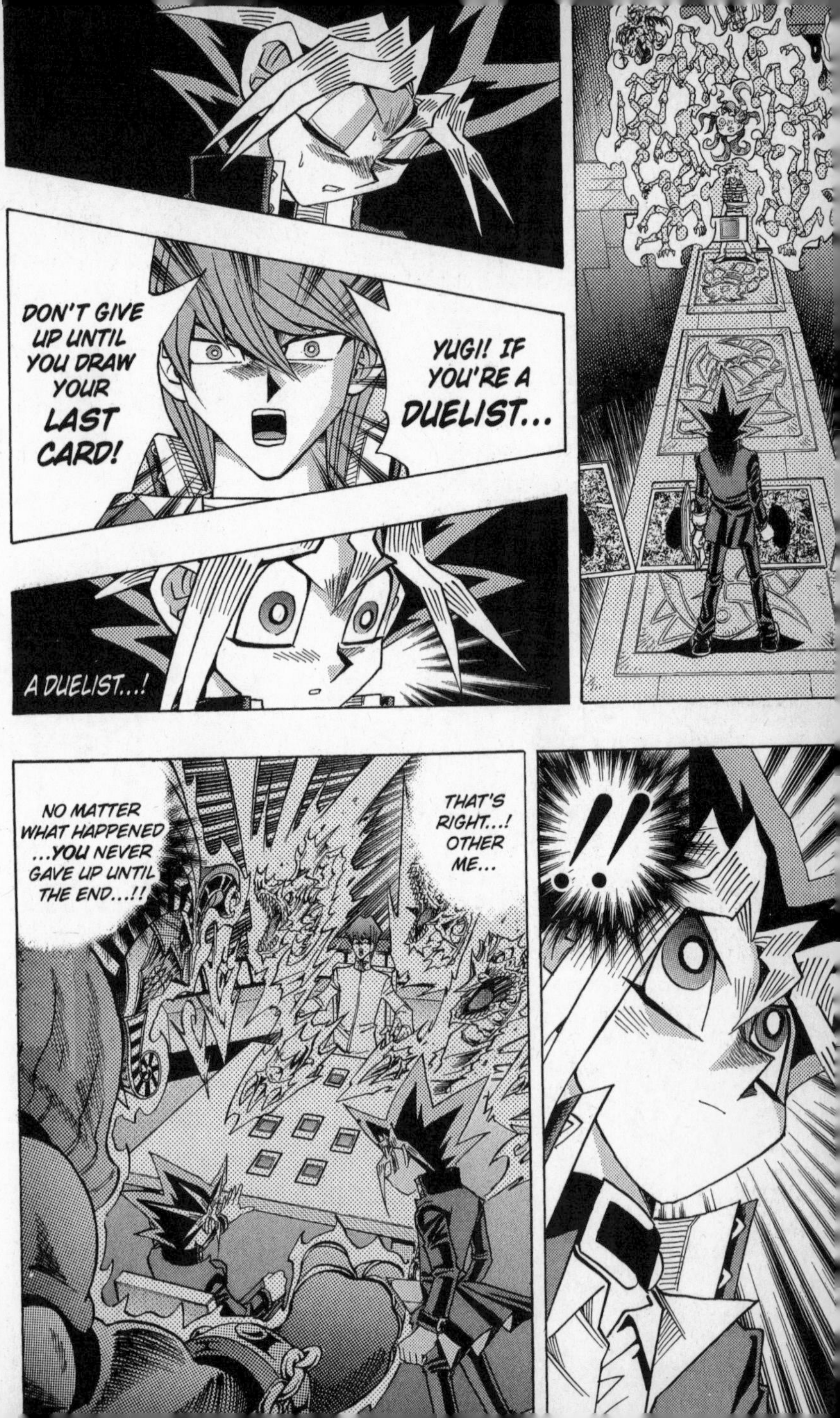
YUGI! IF YOU'RE A DUELIST...
DON'T GIVE UP UNTIL YOU DRAW YOUR LAST CARD!
A DUELIST...!
!!
THAT'S RIGHT...! OTHER ME...
NO MATTER WHAT HAPPENED ...YOU NEVER GAVE UP UNTIL THE END...!!

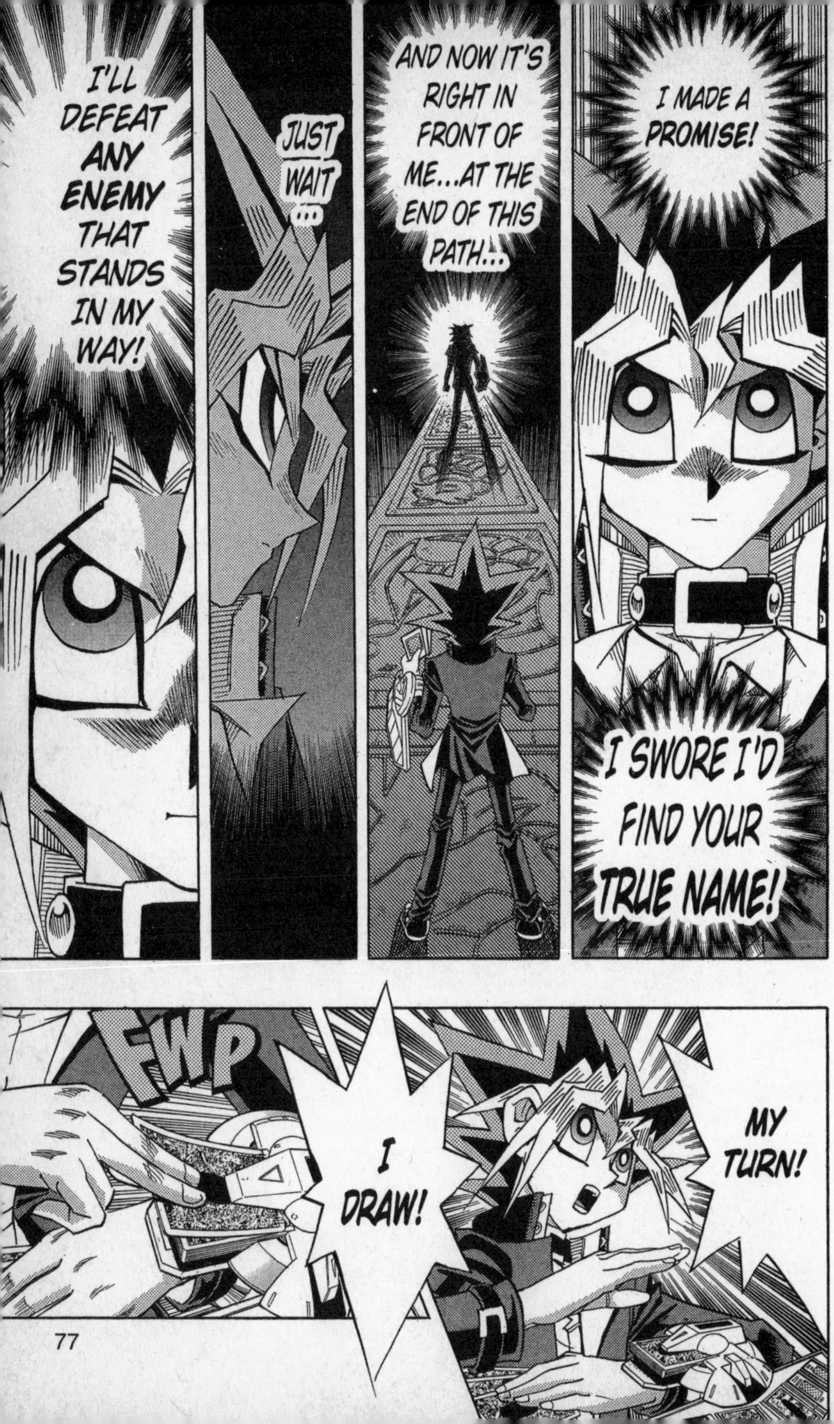
I MADE A PROMISE!
I SWORE I'D FIND YOUR TRUE NAME!
AND NOW IT'S RIGHT IN FRONT OF ME...AT THE END OF THIS PATH...
JUST WAIT...
I'LL DEFEAT ANY ENEMY THAT STANDS IN MY WAY!
MY TURN!
I DRAW!
FWP

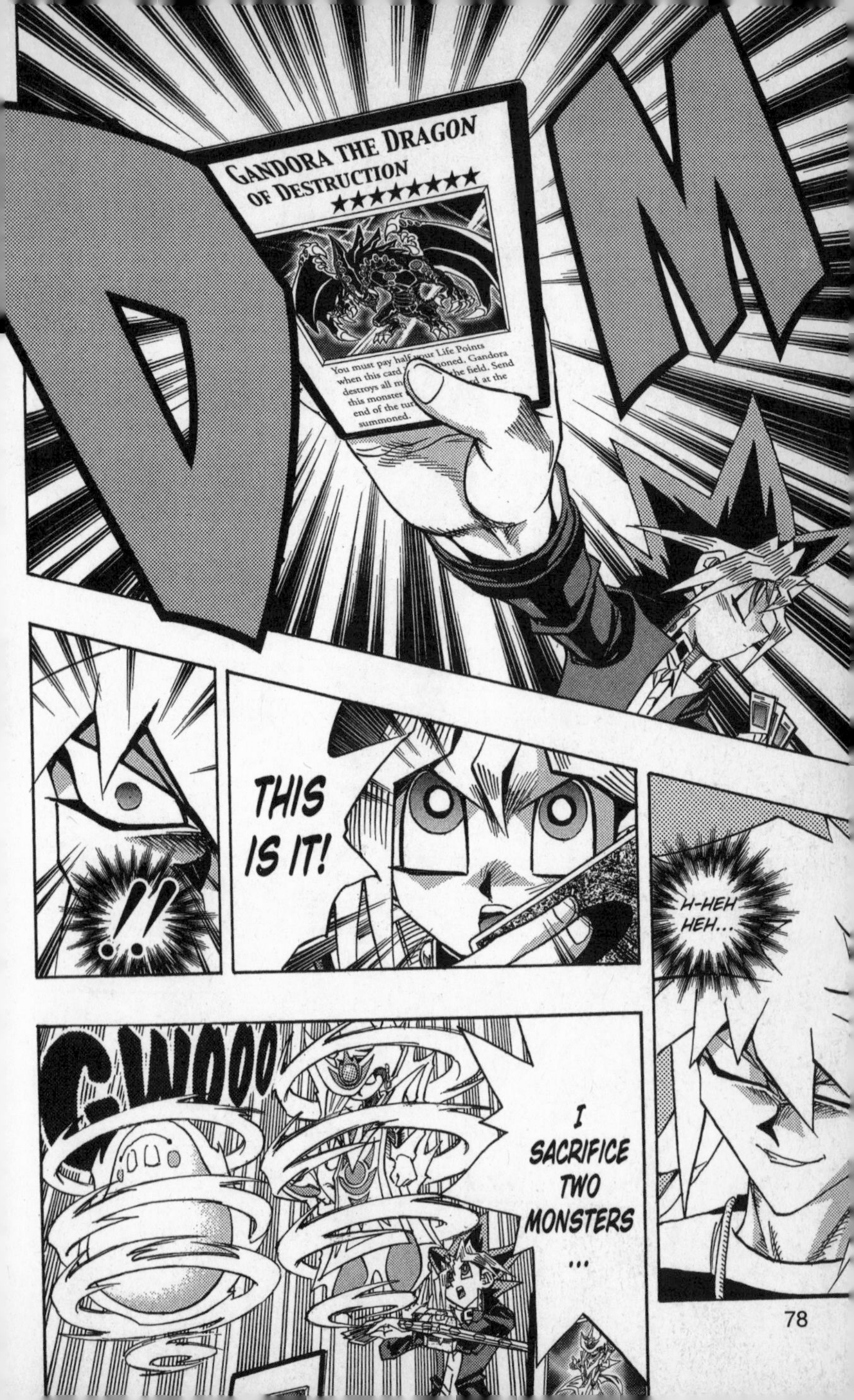
DOM
GANDORA THE DRAGON OF DESTRUCTION
You must pay half your Life Points when this card moned. Gandora destroys all m the field. Send this monster d at the end of the tur summoned.
H-HEH HEH...
THIS IS IT!
!!
I SACRIFICE TWO MONSTERS ...
GWOOO

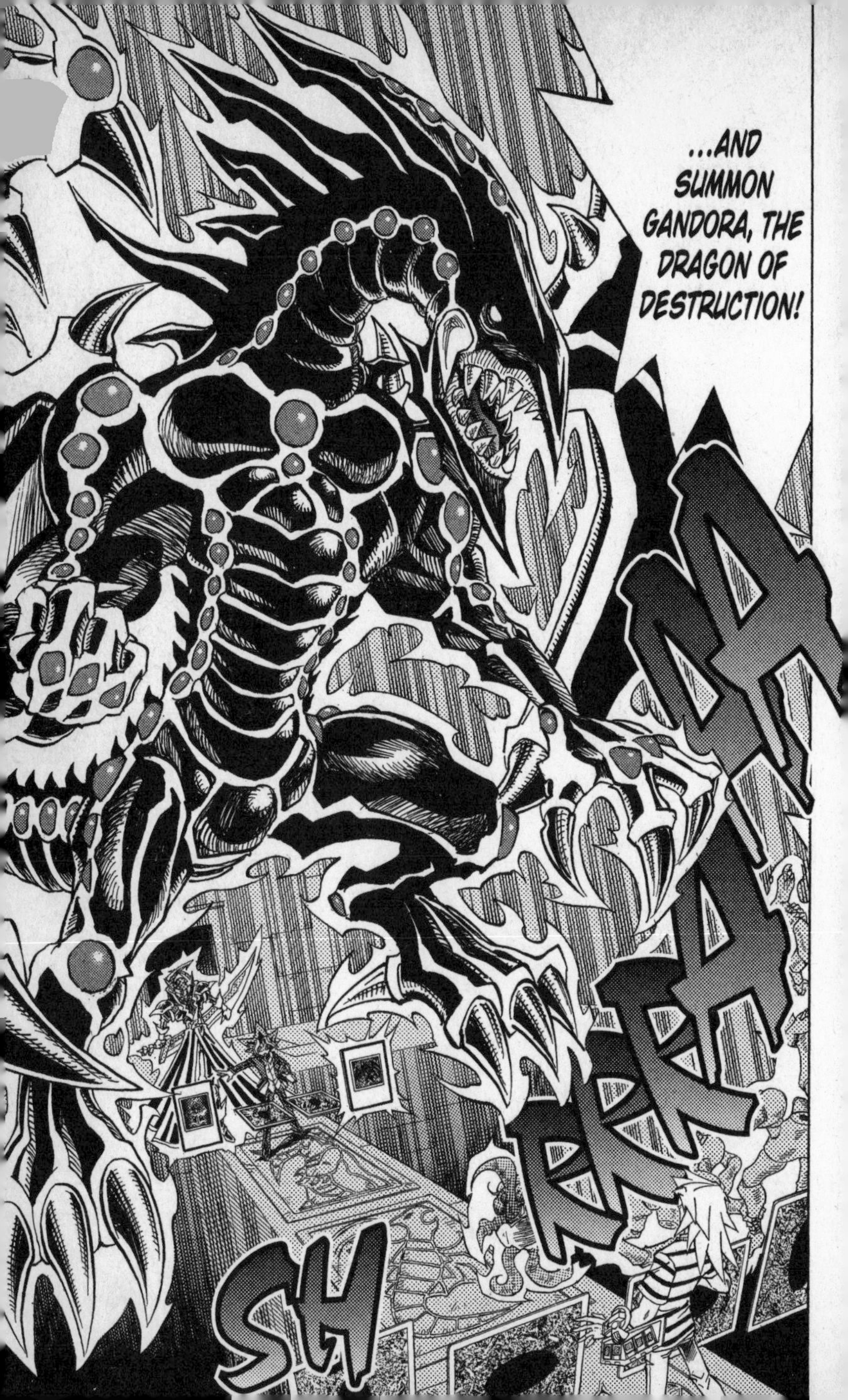
...AND SUMMON GANDORA, THE DRAGON OF DESTRUCTION!
SH

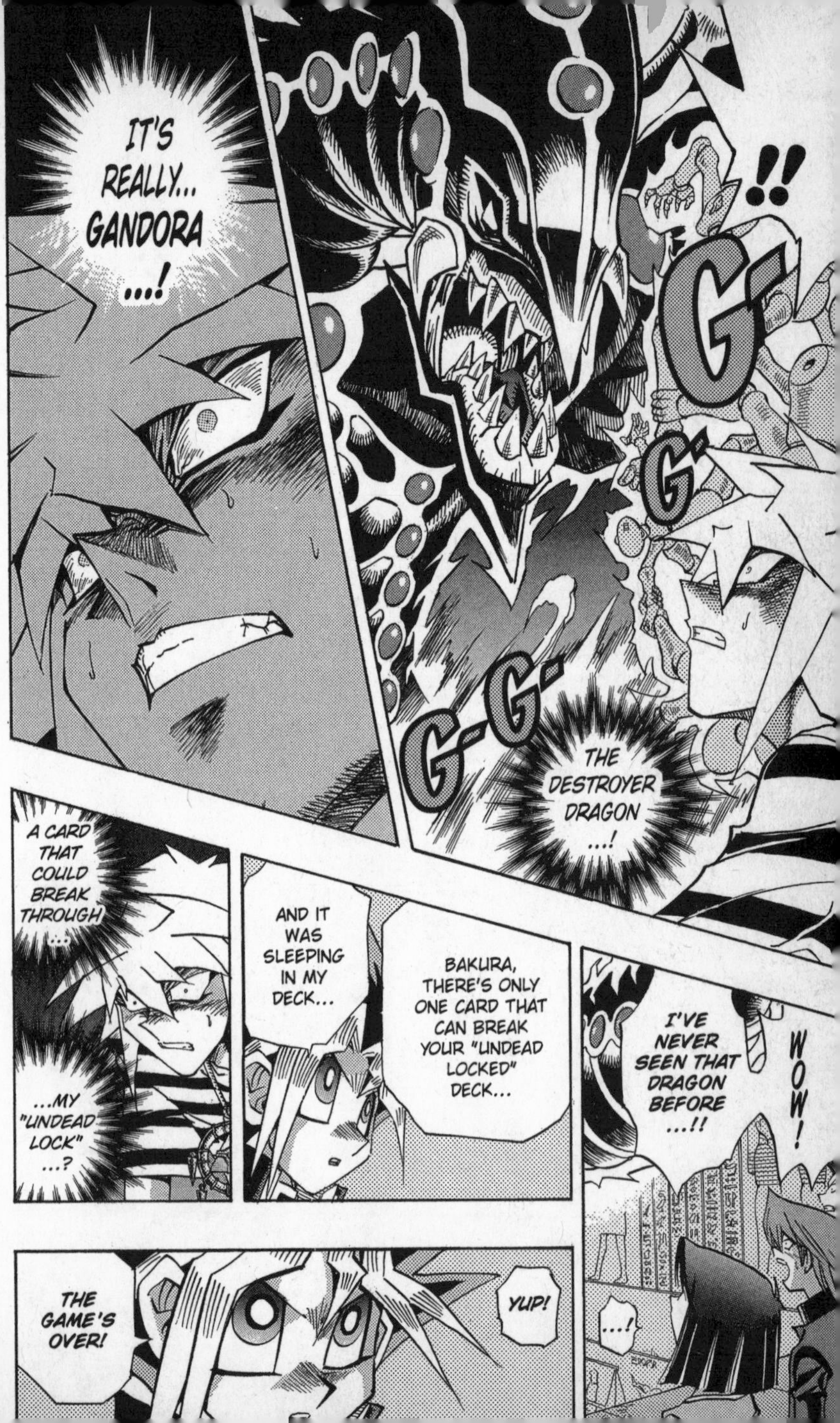
!!
G-
G-
G-G-
THE DESTROYER DRAGON ...!
IT'S REALLY... GANDORA ...!
I'VE NEVER SEEN THAT DRAGON BEFORE ...!!
WOW!
BAKURA, THERE'S ONLY ONE CARD THAT CAN BREAK YOUR "UNDEAD LOCKED" DECK...
AND IT WAS SLEEPING IN MY DECK...
A CARD THAT COULD BREAK THROUGH ...
...MY "UNDEAD LOCK" ...?
...!
YUP!
THE GAME'S OVER!

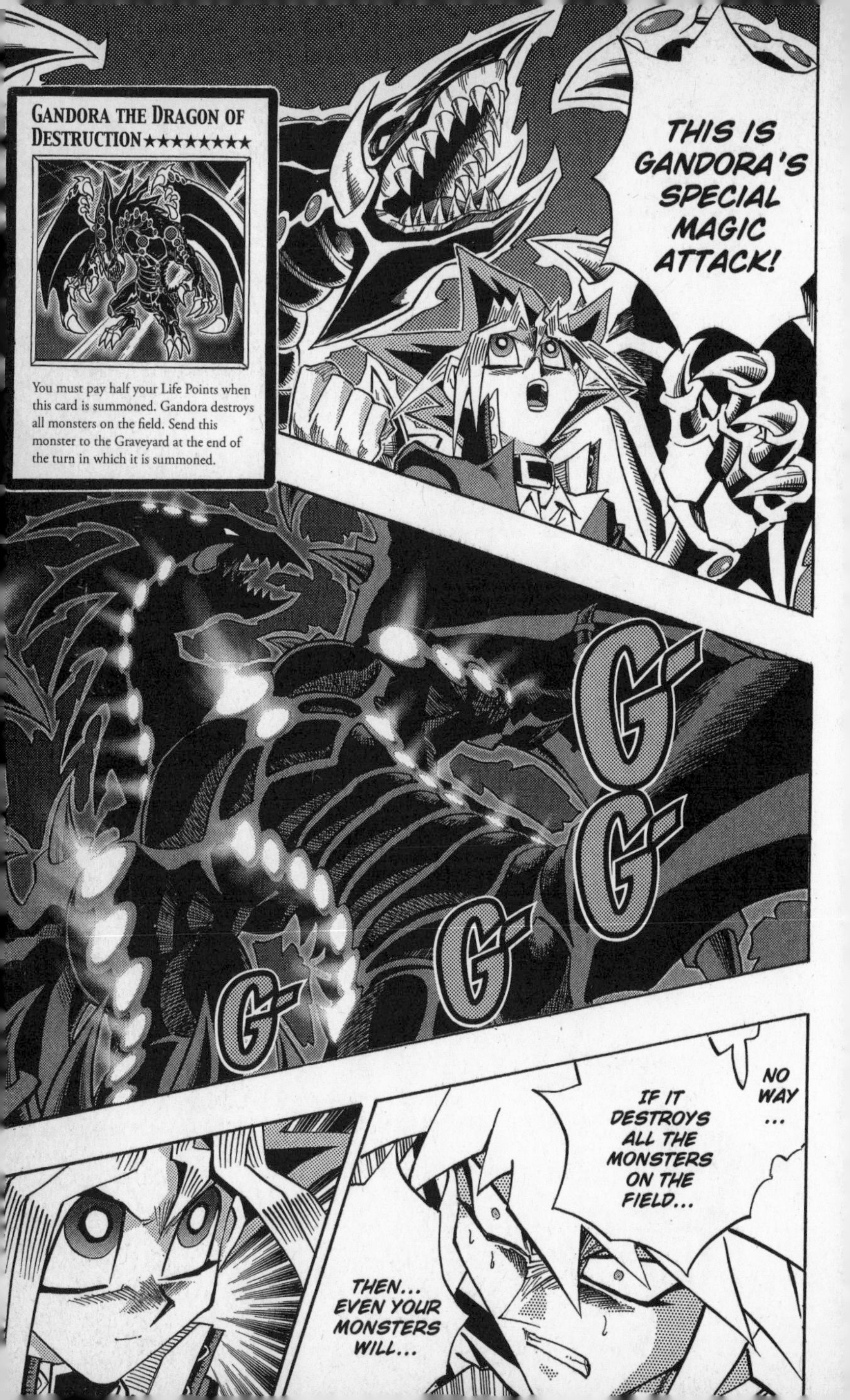
THIS IS GANDORA'S SPECIAL MAGIC ATTACK!
GANDORA THE DRAGON OF DESTRUCTION★★★★★★★★
You must pay half your Life Points when this card is summoned. Gandora destroys all monsters on the field. Send this monster to the Graveyard at the end of the turn in which it is summoned.
G G G G
NO WAY...
IF IT DESTROYS ALL THE MONSTERS ON THE FIELD...
THEN... EVEN YOUR MONSTERS WILL...

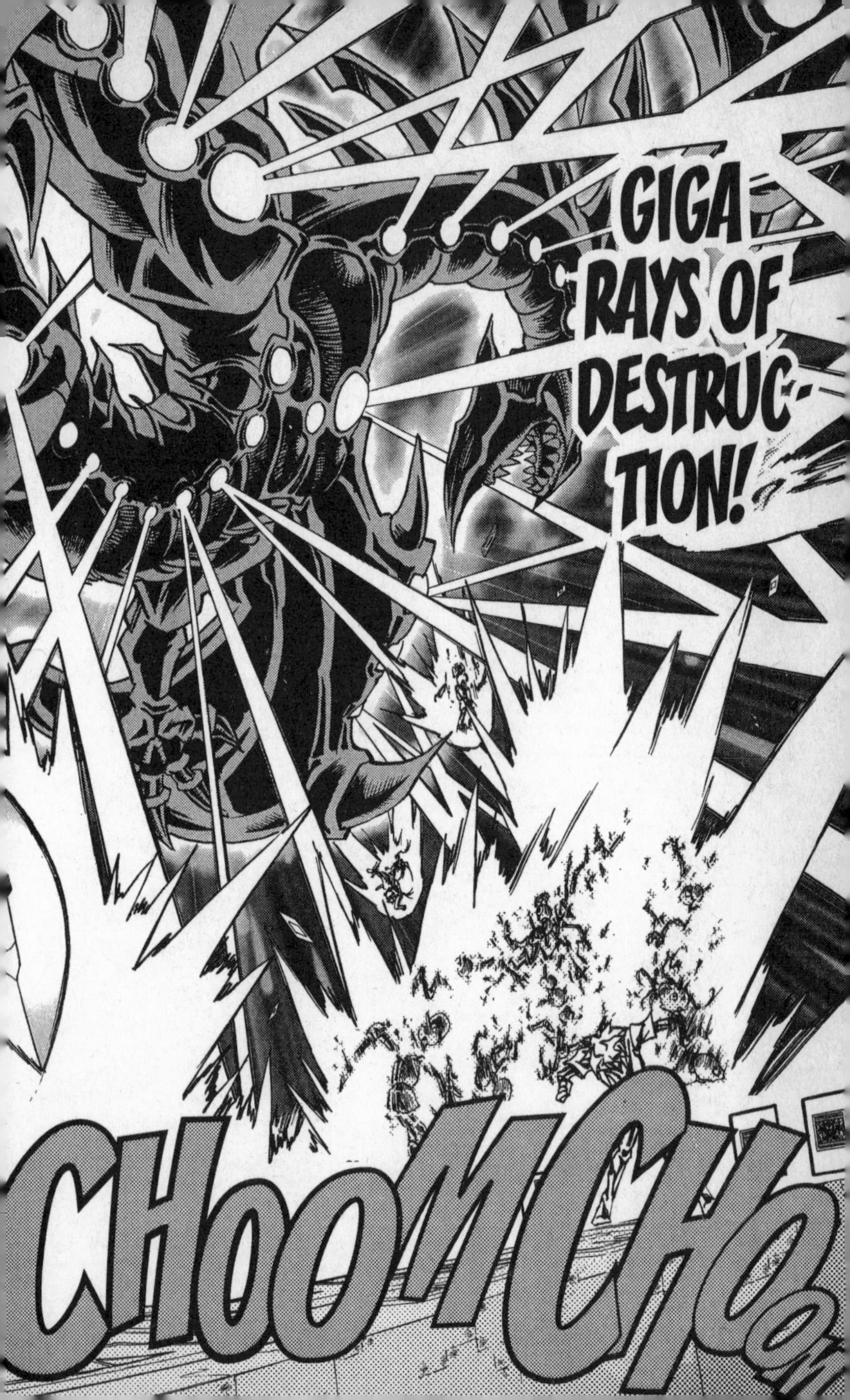
GIGA RAYS OF DESTRUC-TION!
CHOOMCHOOM

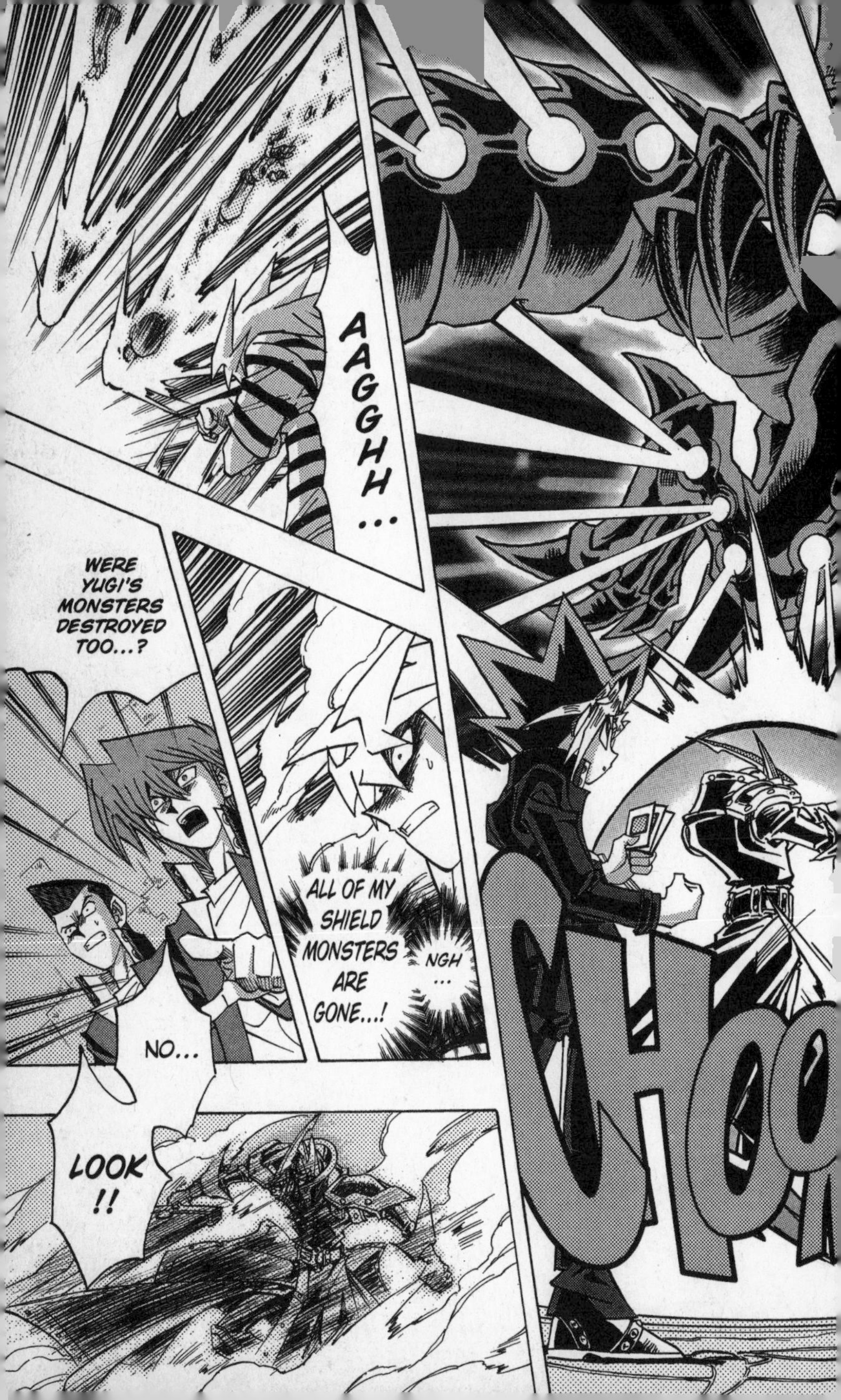
AAGGHH...
CHOO
ALL OF MY SHIELD MONSTERS ARE GONE...!
NGH...
WERE YUGI'S MONSTERS DESTROYED TOO...?
NO...
LOOK!!

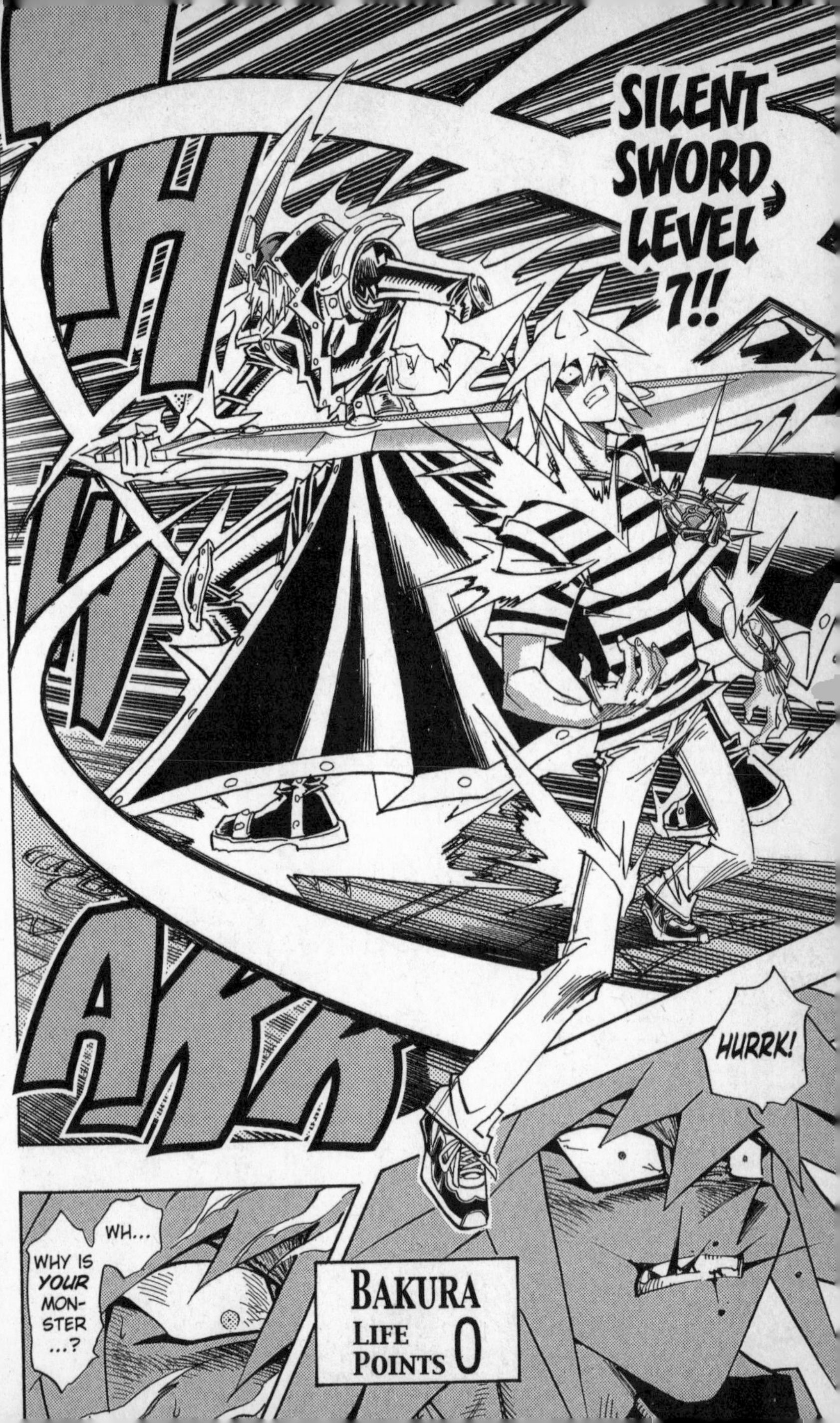
SILENT SWORD, LEVEL 7!!
HURRK!
BAKURA LIFE POINTS 0
WH...
WHY IS *YOUR* MONSTER ...?

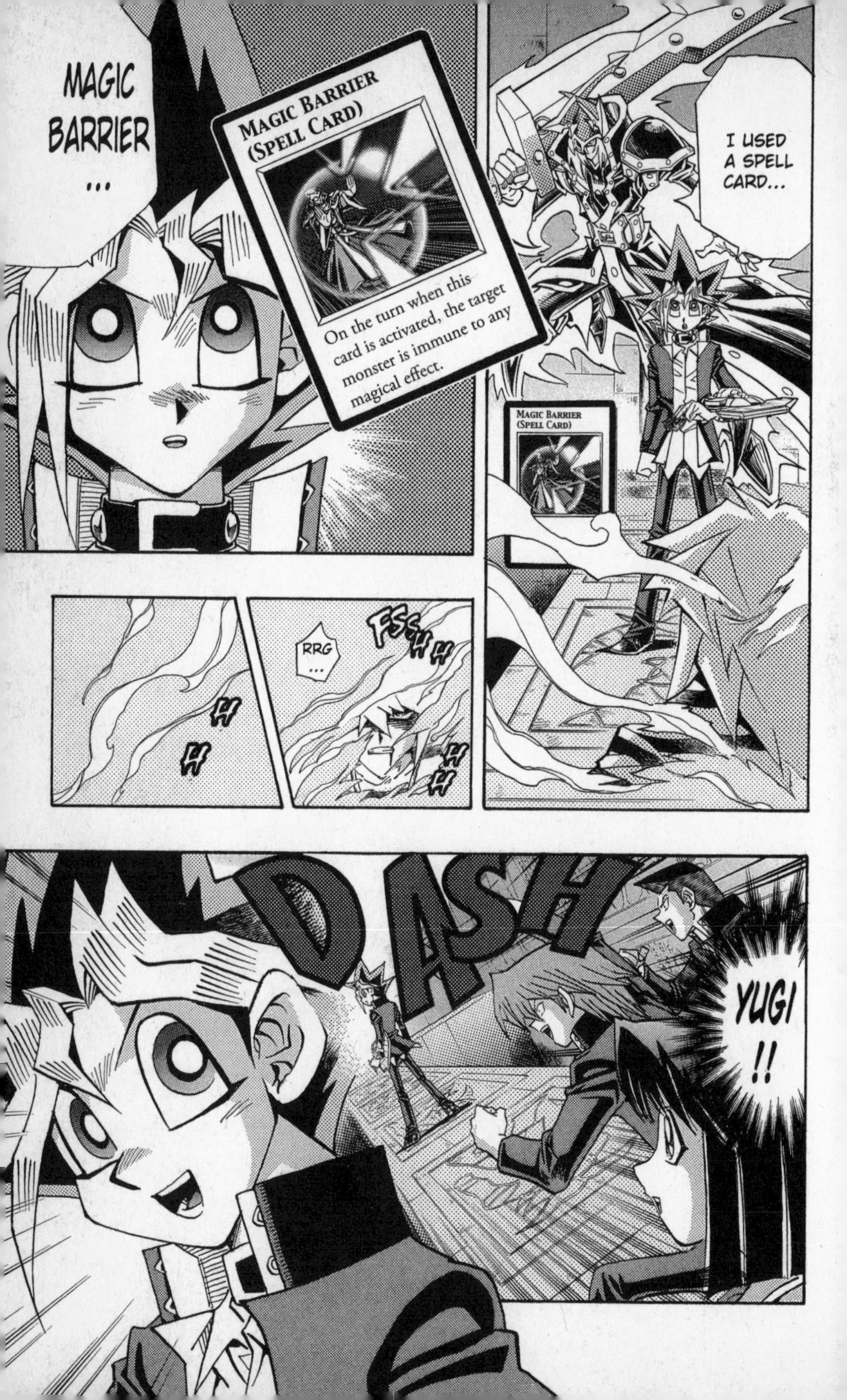
I USED A SPELL CARD...
MAGIC BARRIER (SPELL CARD)
MAGIC BARRIER ...
MAGIC BARRIER (SPELL CARD)
On the turn when this card is activated, the target monster is immune to any magical effect.
RRG ...
FSSHHHH
HH
DASH
YUGI !!

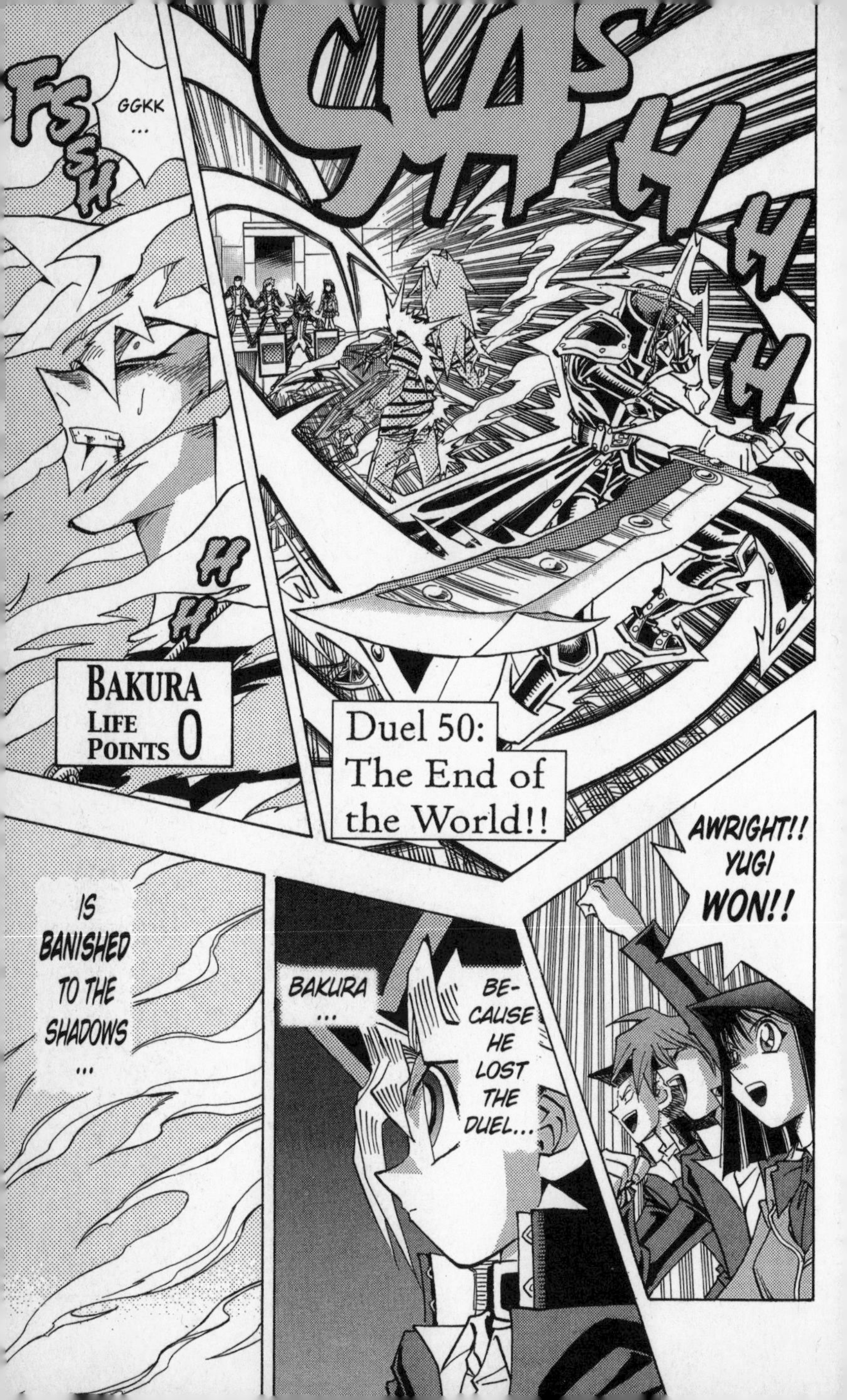

Duel 50: The End of the World!!
FSSH
GGKK...
HH
BAKURA LIFE POINTS 0
AWRIGHT!! YUGI WON!!
BE-CAUSE HE LOST THE DUEL...
BAKURA...
IS BANISHED TO THE SHADOWS...

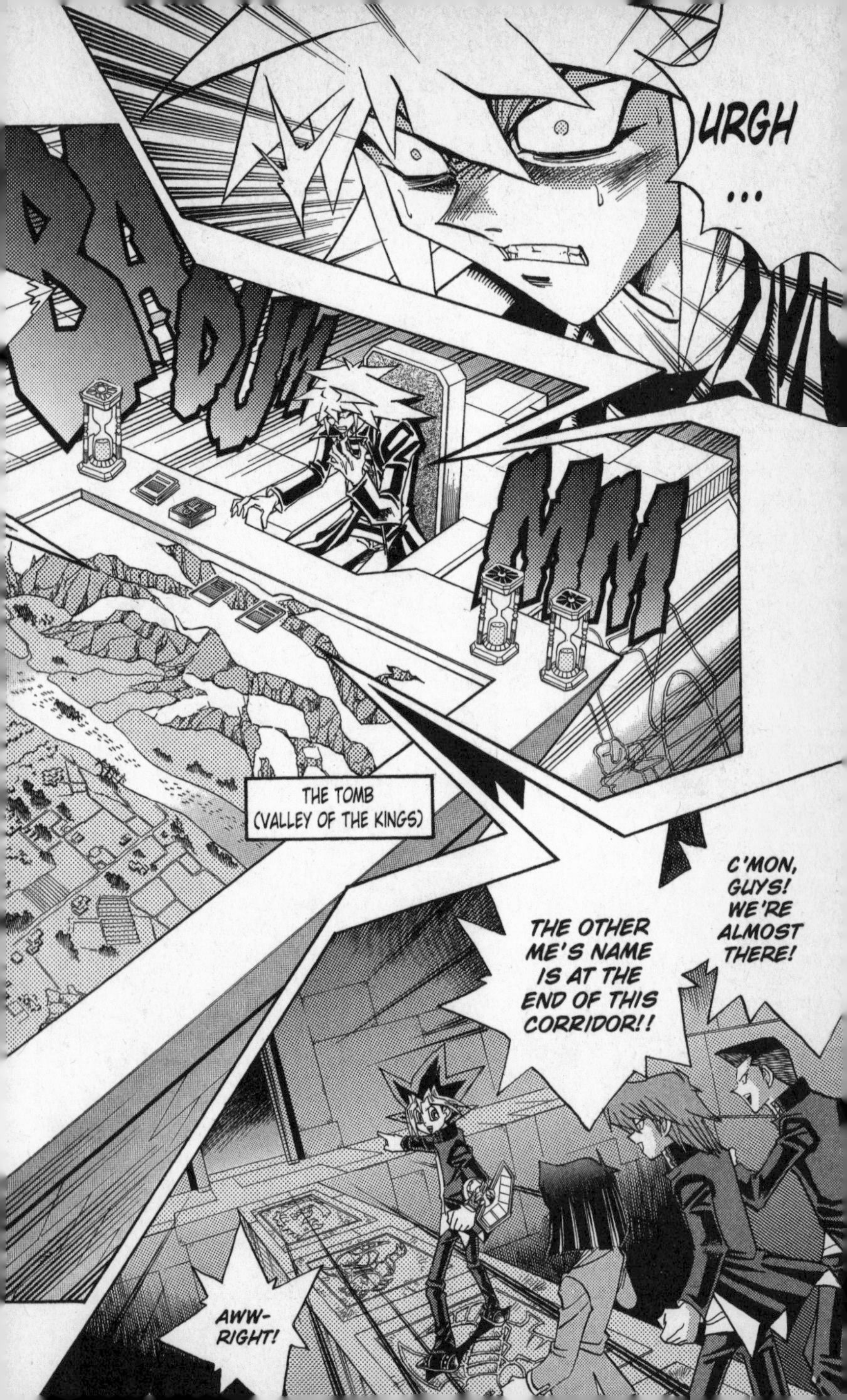
URGH ...
BADUMMM
THE TOMB (VALLEY OF THE KINGS)
C'MON, GUYS! WE'RE ALMOST THERE!
THE OTHER ME'S NAME IS AT THE END OF THIS CORRIDOR!!
AWW-RIGHT!

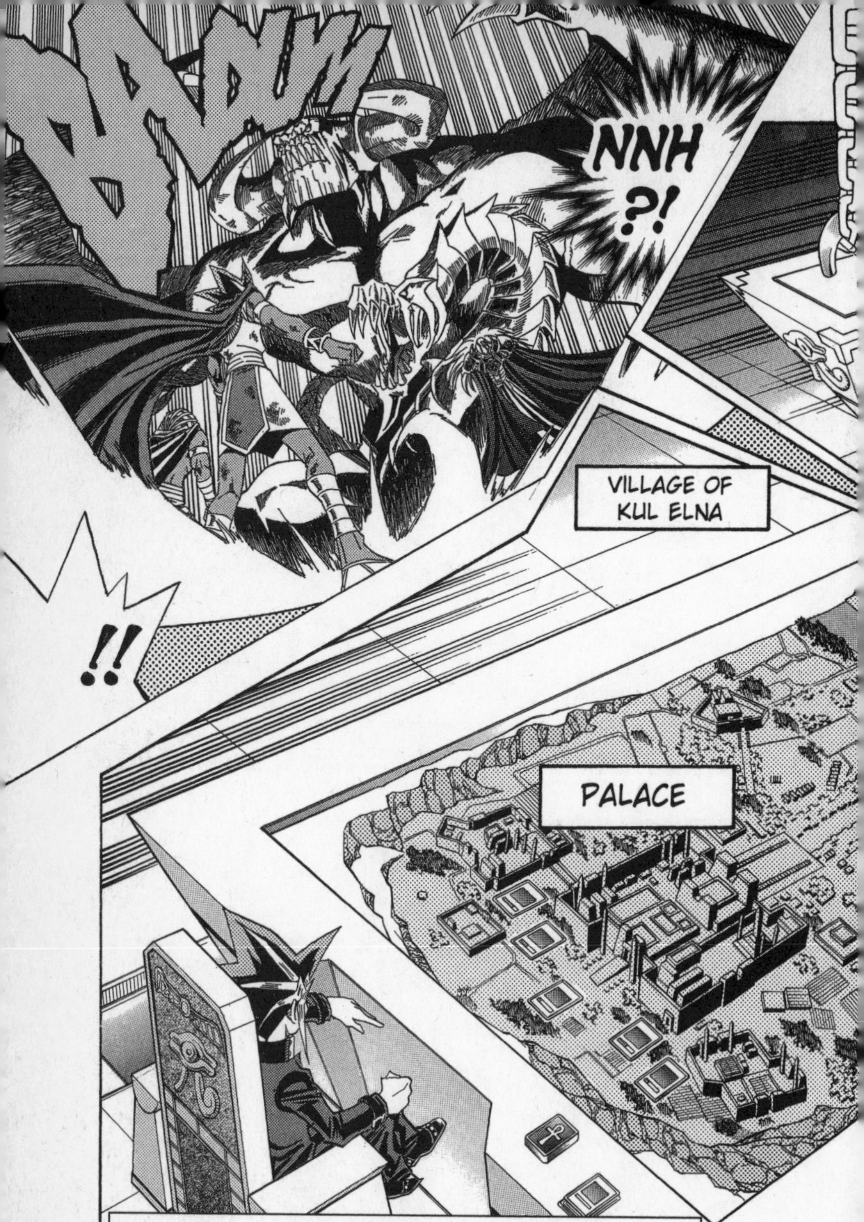
NNH ?!
BADUM
VILLAGE OF KUL ELNA
!!
PALACE

Duel 50: The End of the World!!

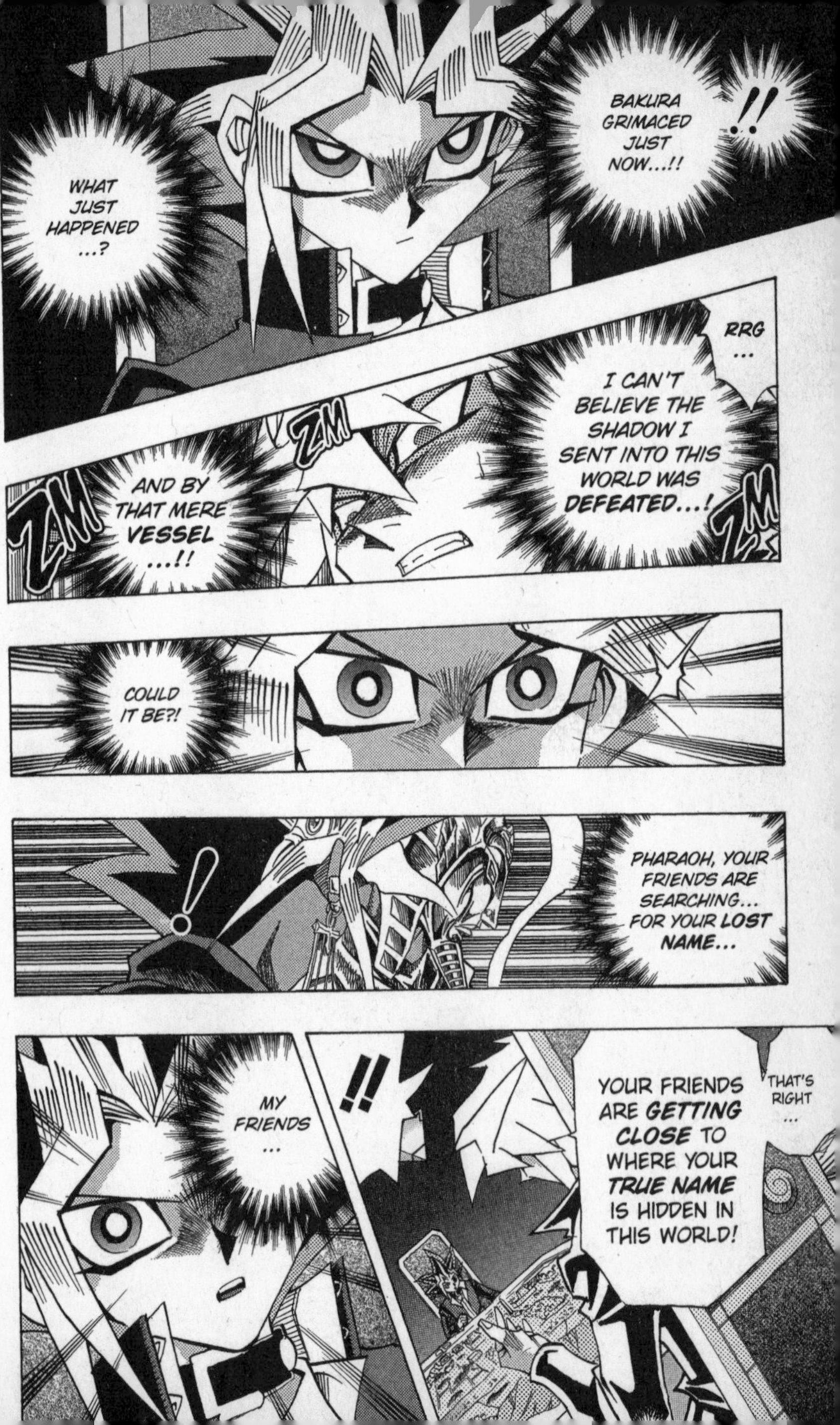

BAKURA GRIMACED JUST NOW...!!
!!
WHAT JUST HAPPENED...?
RRG...
I CAN'T BELIEVE THE SHADOW I SENT INTO THIS WORLD WAS DEFEATED...!
ZM
ZM
AND BY THAT MERE VESSEL...!!
ZM
COULD IT BE?!
PHARAOH, YOUR FRIENDS ARE SEARCHING... FOR YOUR LOST NAME...
!
THAT'S RIGHT...
YOUR FRIENDS ARE GETTING CLOSE TO WHERE YOUR TRUE NAME IS HIDDEN IN THIS WORLD!
!!
MY FRIENDS...

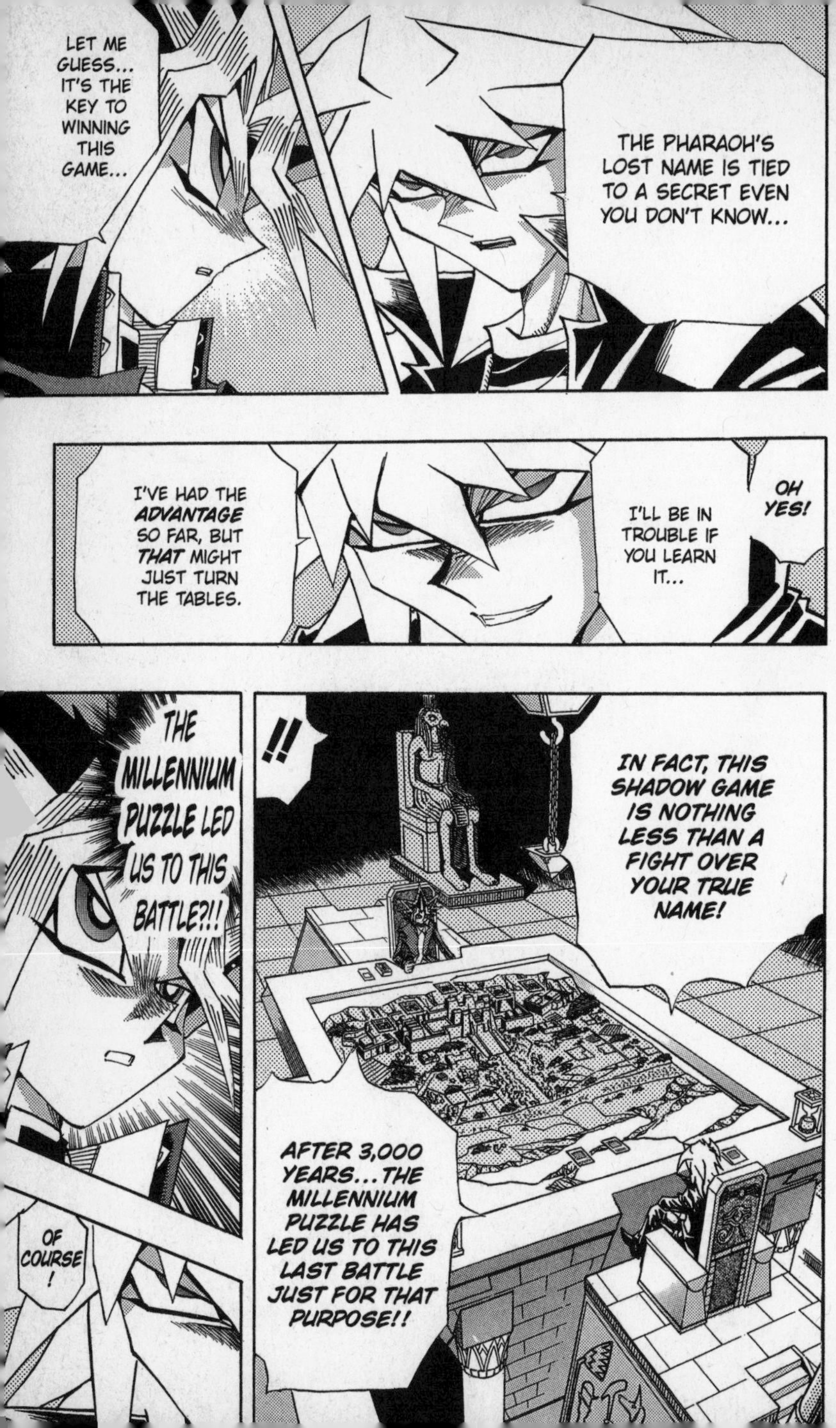
THE PHARAOH'S LOST NAME IS TIED TO A SECRET EVEN YOU DON'T KNOW...
LET ME GUESS... IT'S THE KEY TO WINNING THIS GAME...
OH YES!
I'LL BE IN TROUBLE IF YOU LEARN IT...
I'VE HAD THE **ADVANTAGE** SO FAR, BUT **THAT** MIGHT JUST TURN THE TABLES.
IN FACT, THIS SHADOW GAME IS NOTHING LESS THAN A FIGHT OVER YOUR TRUE NAME!
!!
AFTER 3,000 YEARS...THE MILLENNIUM PUZZLE HAS LED US TO THIS LAST BATTLE JUST FOR THAT PURPOSE!!
THE MILLENNIUM PUZZLE LED US TO THIS BATTLE?!!
OF COURSE!

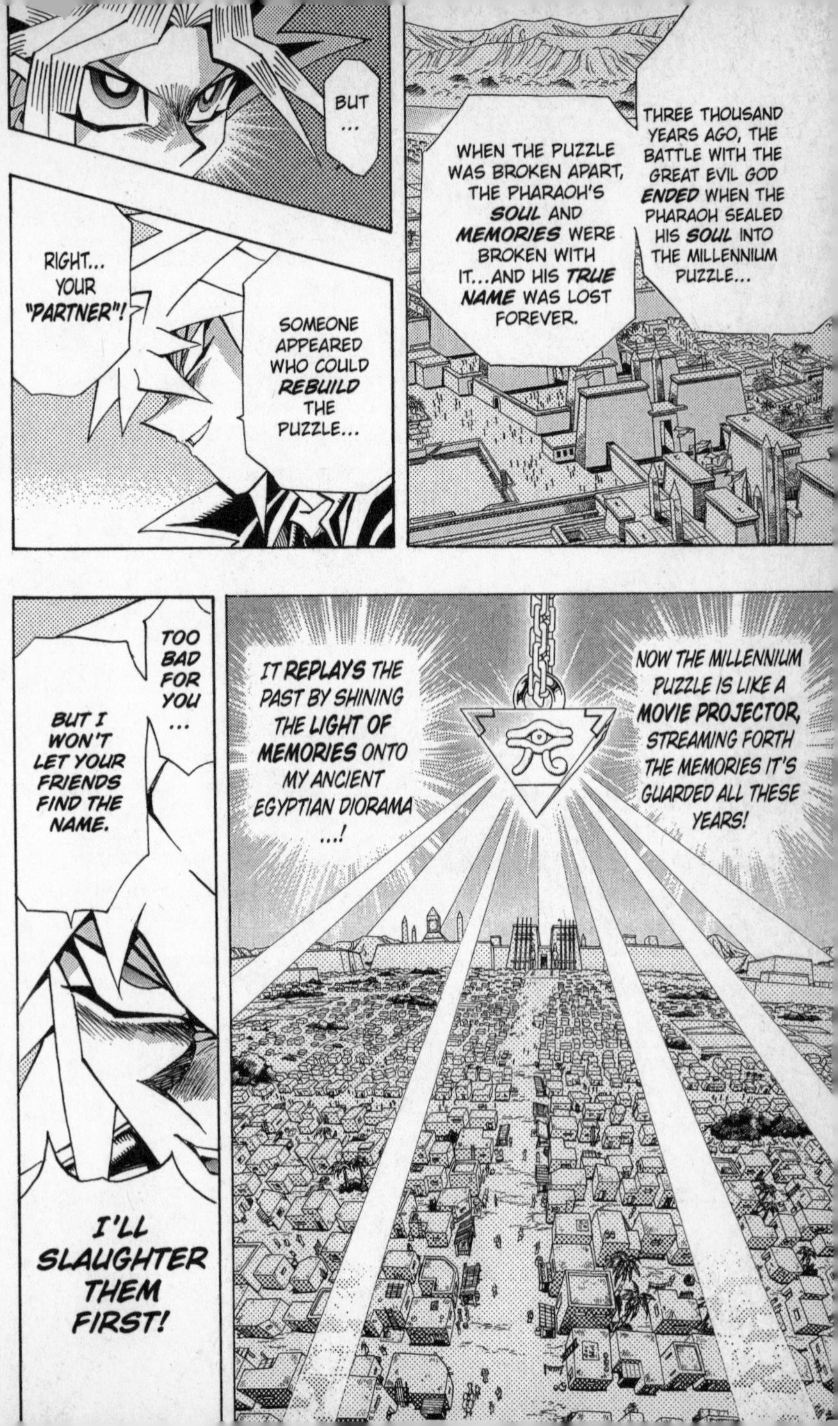
THREE THOUSAND YEARS AGO, THE BATTLE WITH THE GREAT EVIL GOD ENDED WHEN THE PHARAOH SEALED HIS SOUL INTO THE MILLENNIUM PUZZLE...
WHEN THE PUZZLE WAS BROKEN APART, THE PHARAOH'S SOUL AND MEMORIES WERE BROKEN WITH IT...AND HIS TRUE NAME WAS LOST FOREVER.
BUT...
SOMEONE APPEARED WHO COULD REBUILD THE PUZZLE...
RIGHT... YOUR "PARTNER"!
NOW THE MILLENNIUM PUZZLE IS LIKE A MOVIE PROJECTOR, STREAMING FORTH THE MEMORIES IT'S GUARDED ALL THESE YEARS!
IT REPLAYS THE PAST BY SHINING THE LIGHT OF MEMORIES ONTO MY ANCIENT EGYPTIAN DIORAMA...!
TOO BAD FOR YOU...
BUT I WON'T LET YOUR FRIENDS FIND THE NAME.
I'LL SLAUGHTER THEM FIRST!

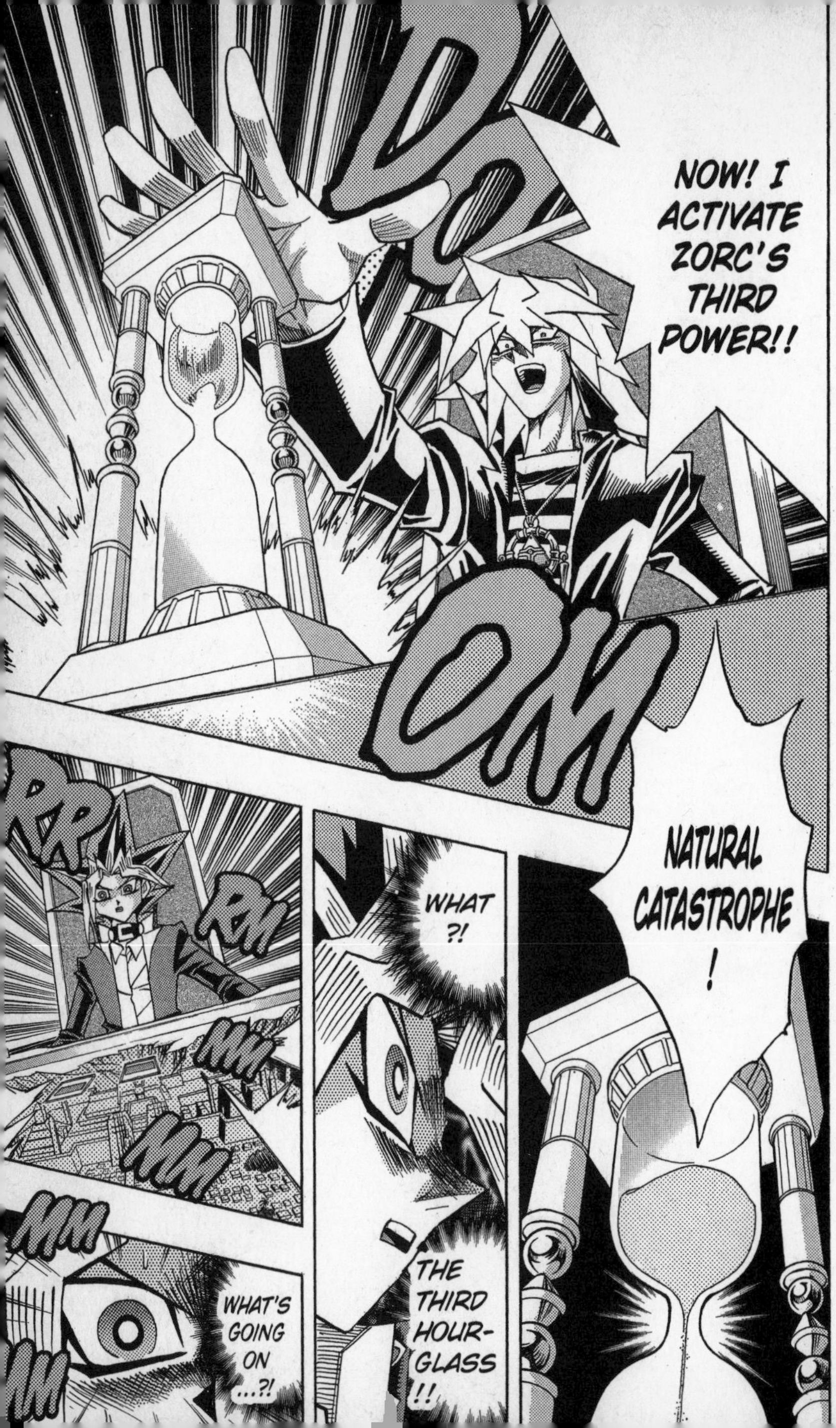
NOW! I ACTIVATE ZORC'S THIRD POWER!!
DOOM
NATURAL CATASTROPHE!
WHAT?!
THE THIRD HOURGLASS!!
WHAT'S GOING ON...?!

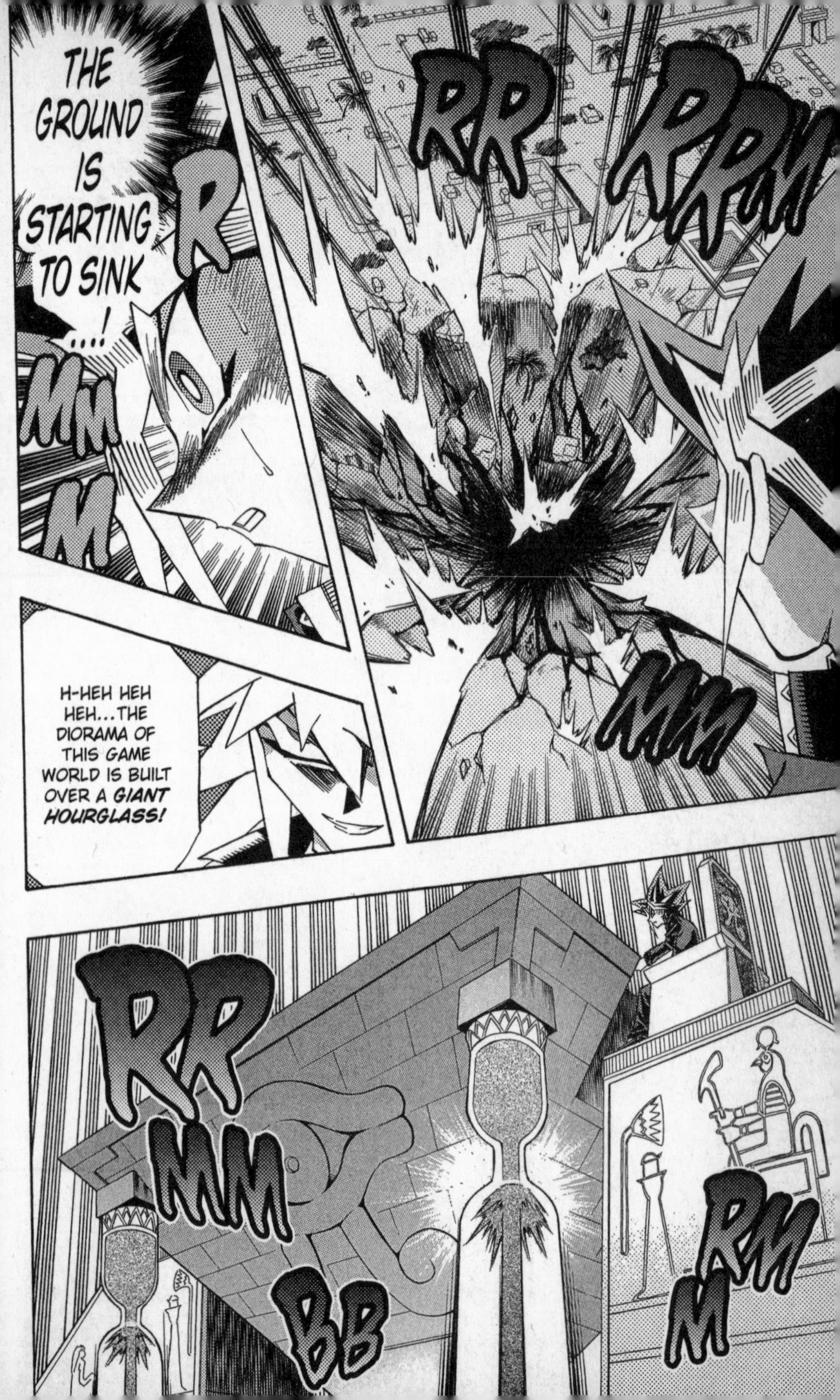
RR
MMM
R
THE GROUND IS STARTING TO SINK ...!
MM
M
H-HEH HEH HEH...THE DIORAMA OF THIS GAME WORLD IS BUILT OVER A *GIANT HOURGLASS!*
RM
M
RR
MM
BB

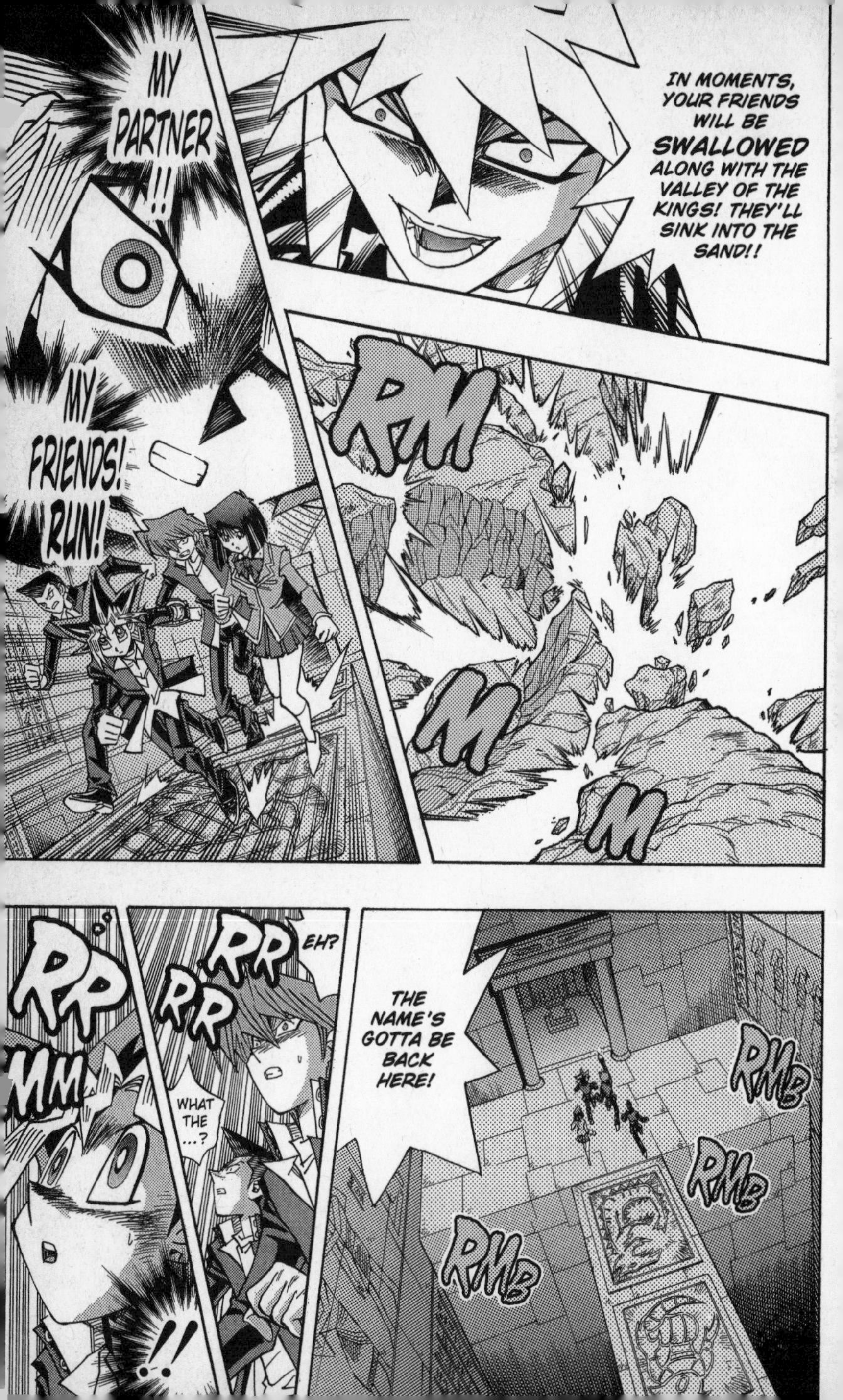
IN MOMENTS, YOUR FRIENDS WILL BE SWALLOWED ALONG WITH THE VALLEY OF THE KINGS! THEY'LL SINK INTO THE SAND!!
RM
M
M
MY PARTNER!!
MY FRIENDS! RUN!
THE NAME'S GOTTA BE BACK HERE!
RMB
RMB
RMB
RR
RR
EH?
WHAT THE ...?
RR
MM
!!

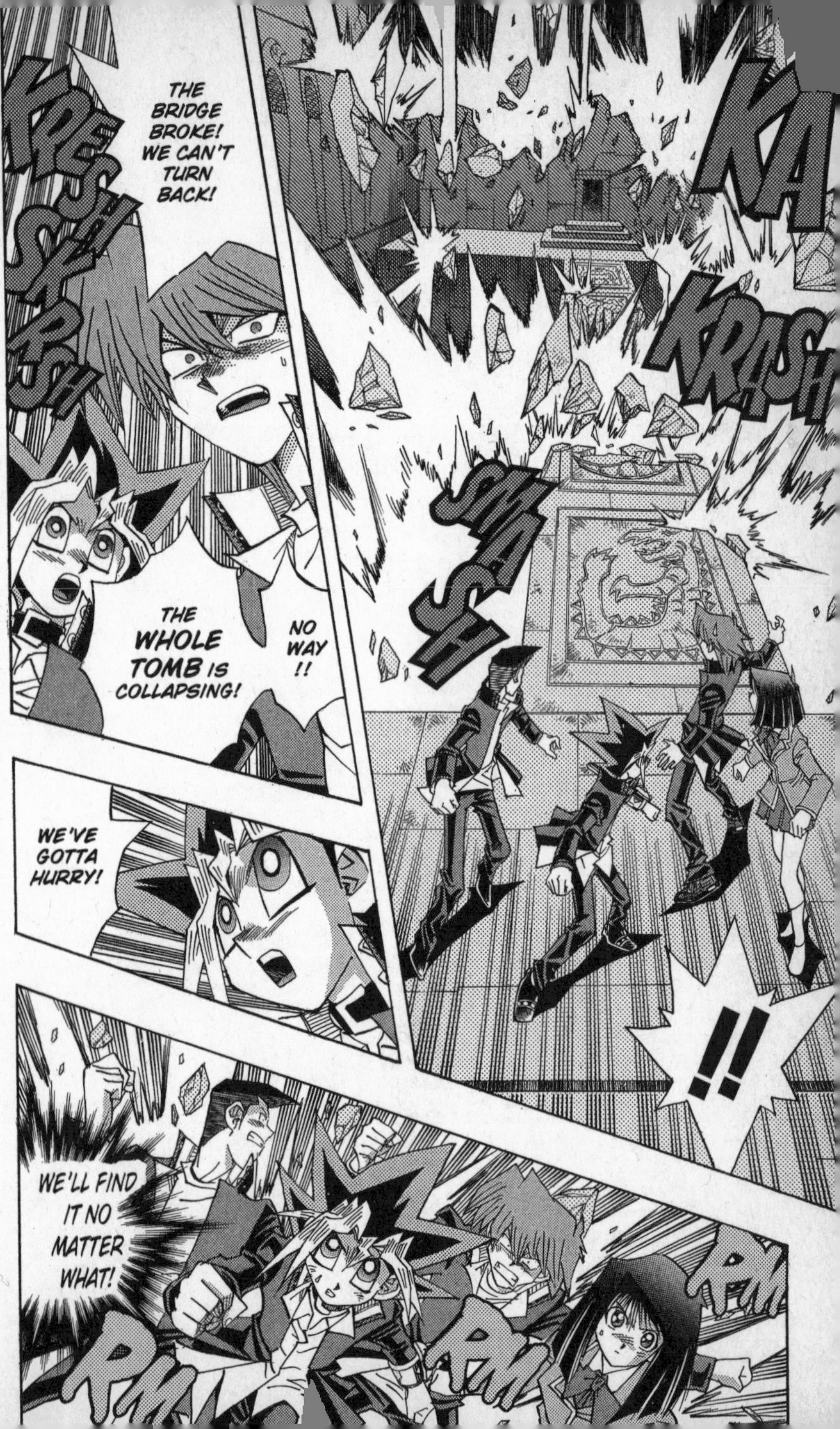
KA
KRASH
SMASH
!!
KRESH
SKRASH
THE BRIDGE BROKE! WE CAN'T TURN BACK!
NO WAY!!
THE WHOLE TOMB IS COLLAPSING!
WE'VE GOTTA HURRY!
RM
WE'LL FIND IT NO MATTER WHAT!
RM
RM

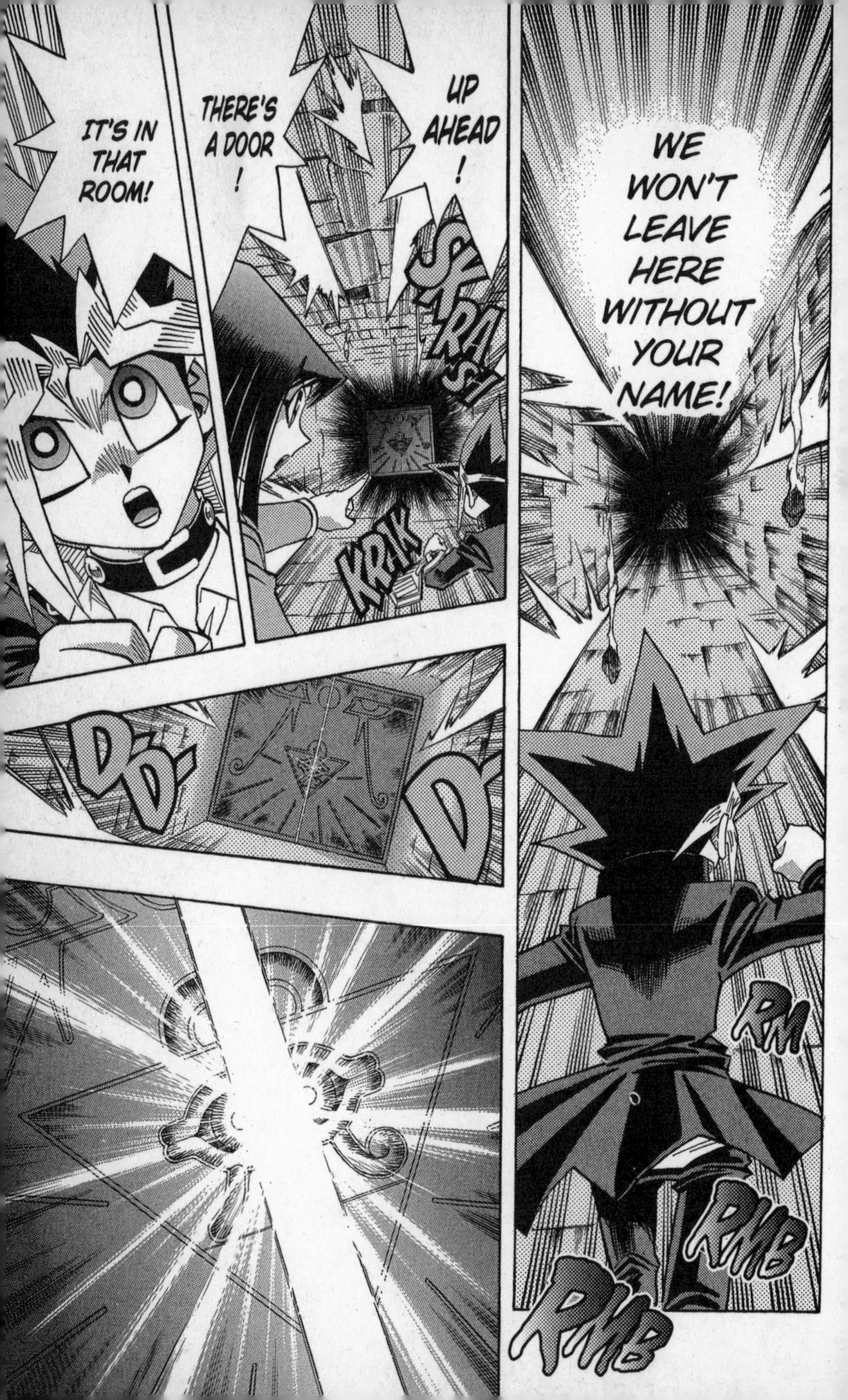
WE WON'T LEAVE HERE WITHOUT YOUR NAME!
RM
RMB
RMB
UP AHEAD!
THERE'S A DOOR!
SKRASH!
KRAK
IT'S IN THAT ROOM!

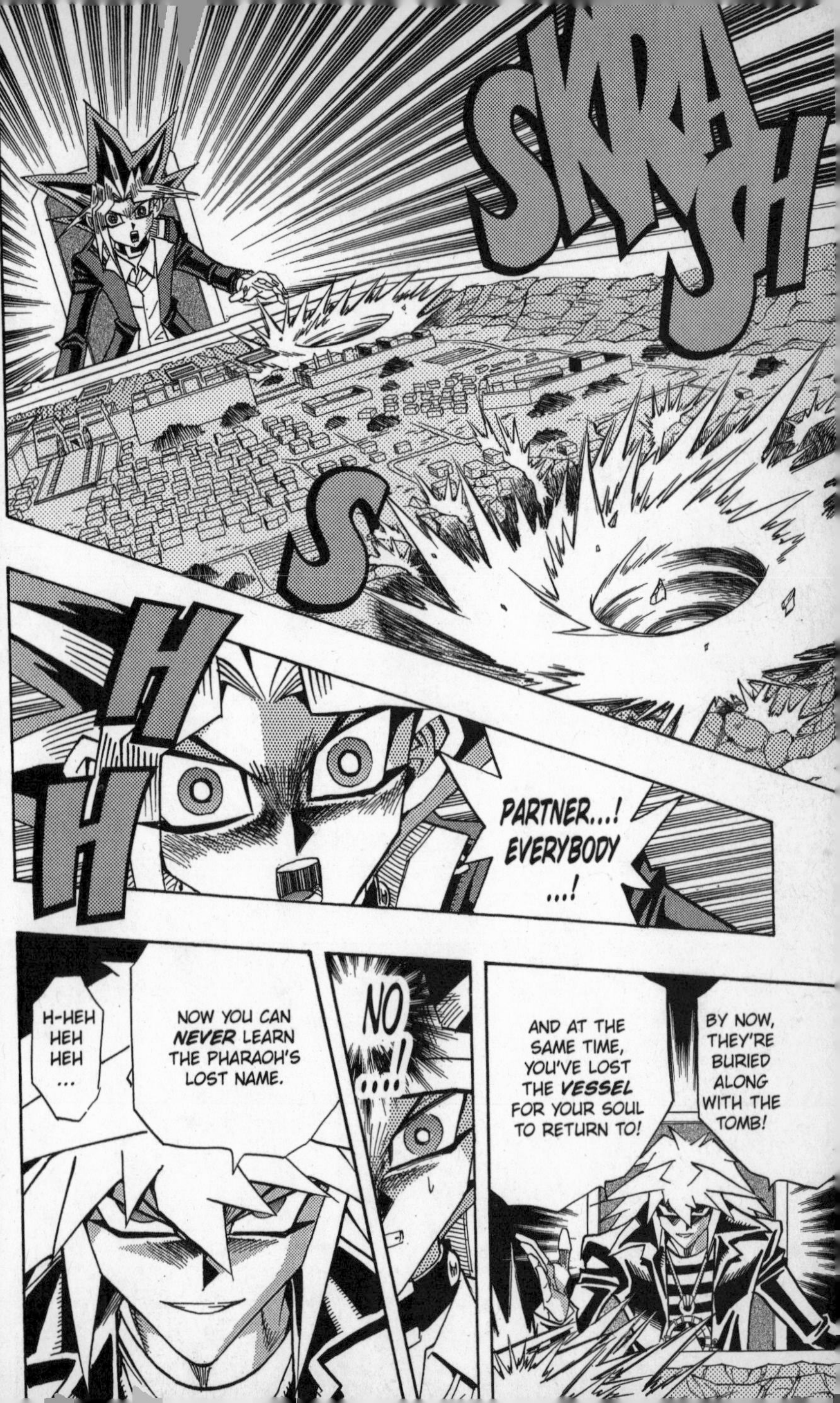
PARTNER...! EVERYBODY ...!
BY NOW, THEY'RE BURIED ALONG WITH THE TOMB!
AND AT THE SAME TIME, YOU'VE LOST THE *VESSEL* FOR YOUR SOUL TO RETURN TO!
NO ...!!
NOW YOU CAN *NEVER* LEARN THE PHARAOH'S LOST NAME.
H-HEH HEH HEH ...

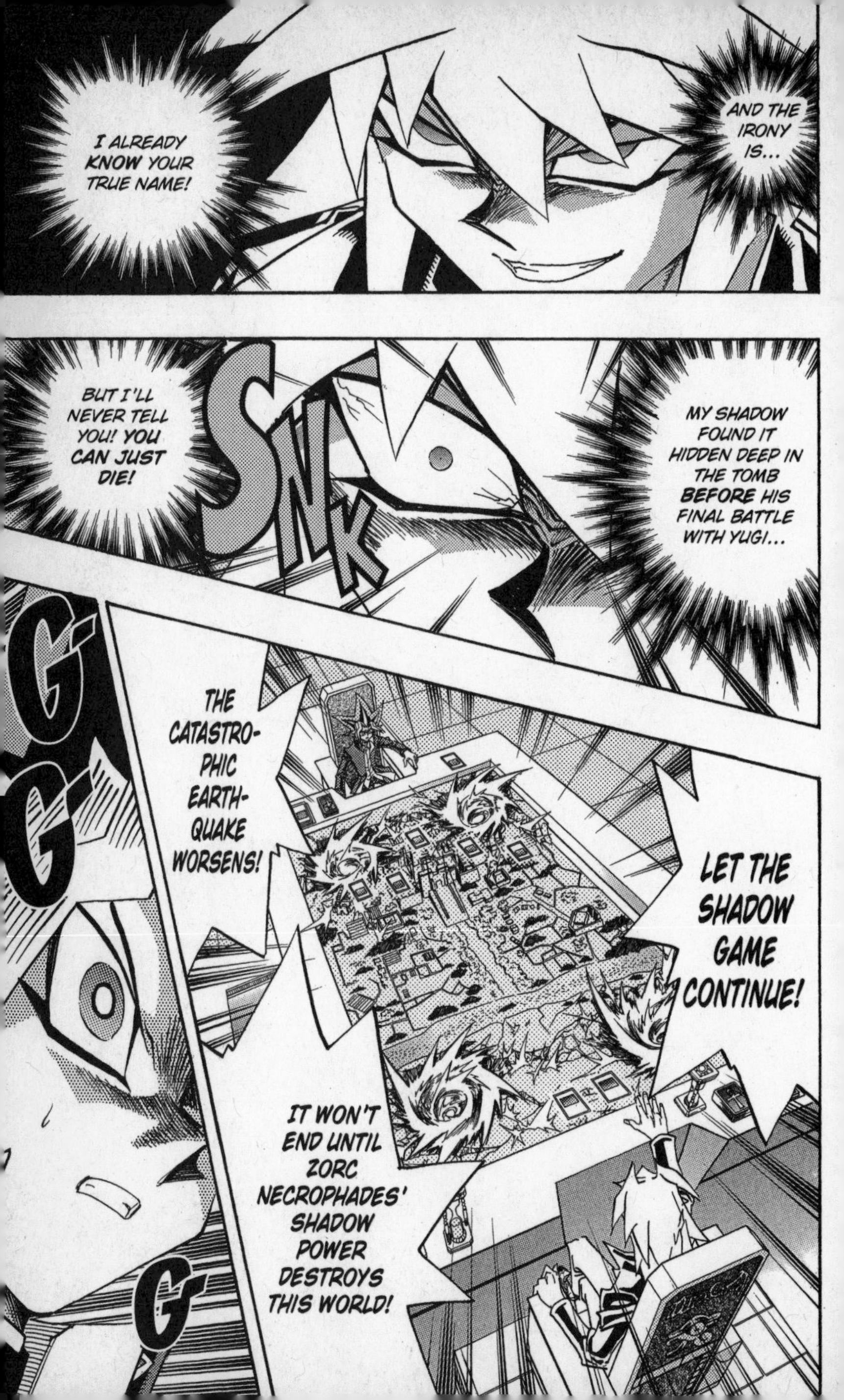
AND THE IRONY IS...
I ALREADY KNOW YOUR TRUE NAME!
MY SHADOW FOUND IT HIDDEN DEEP IN THE TOMB BEFORE HIS FINAL BATTLE WITH YUGI...
SNK
BUT I'LL NEVER TELL YOU! YOU CAN JUST DIE!
THE CATASTROPHIC EARTHQUAKE WORSENS!
LET THE SHADOW GAME CONTINUE!
IT WON'T END UNTIL ZORC NECROPHADES' SHADOW POWER DESTROYS THIS WORLD!
G G G
G

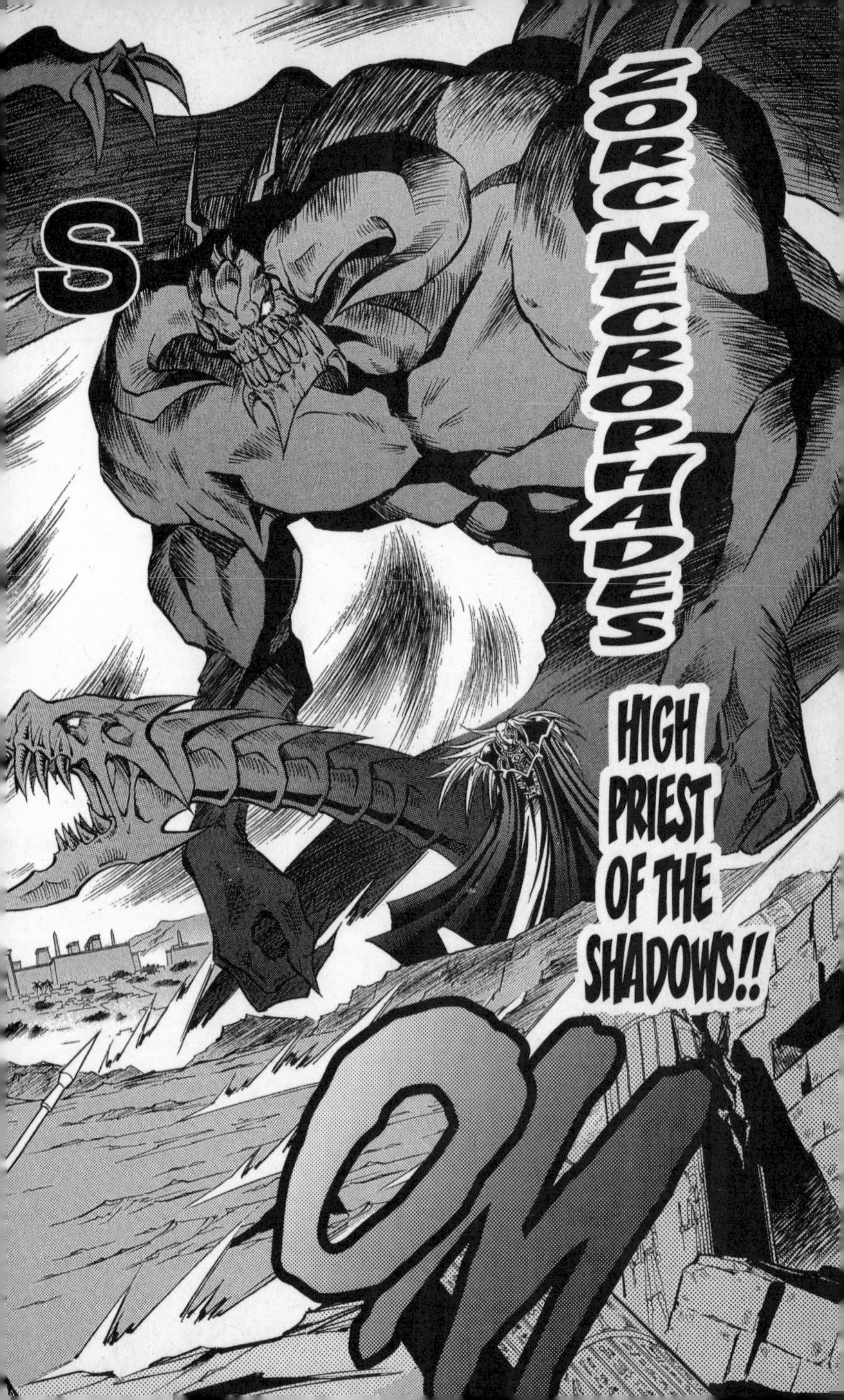
ZORC NECROPHADES
HIGH PRIEST OF THE SHADOWS!!
S

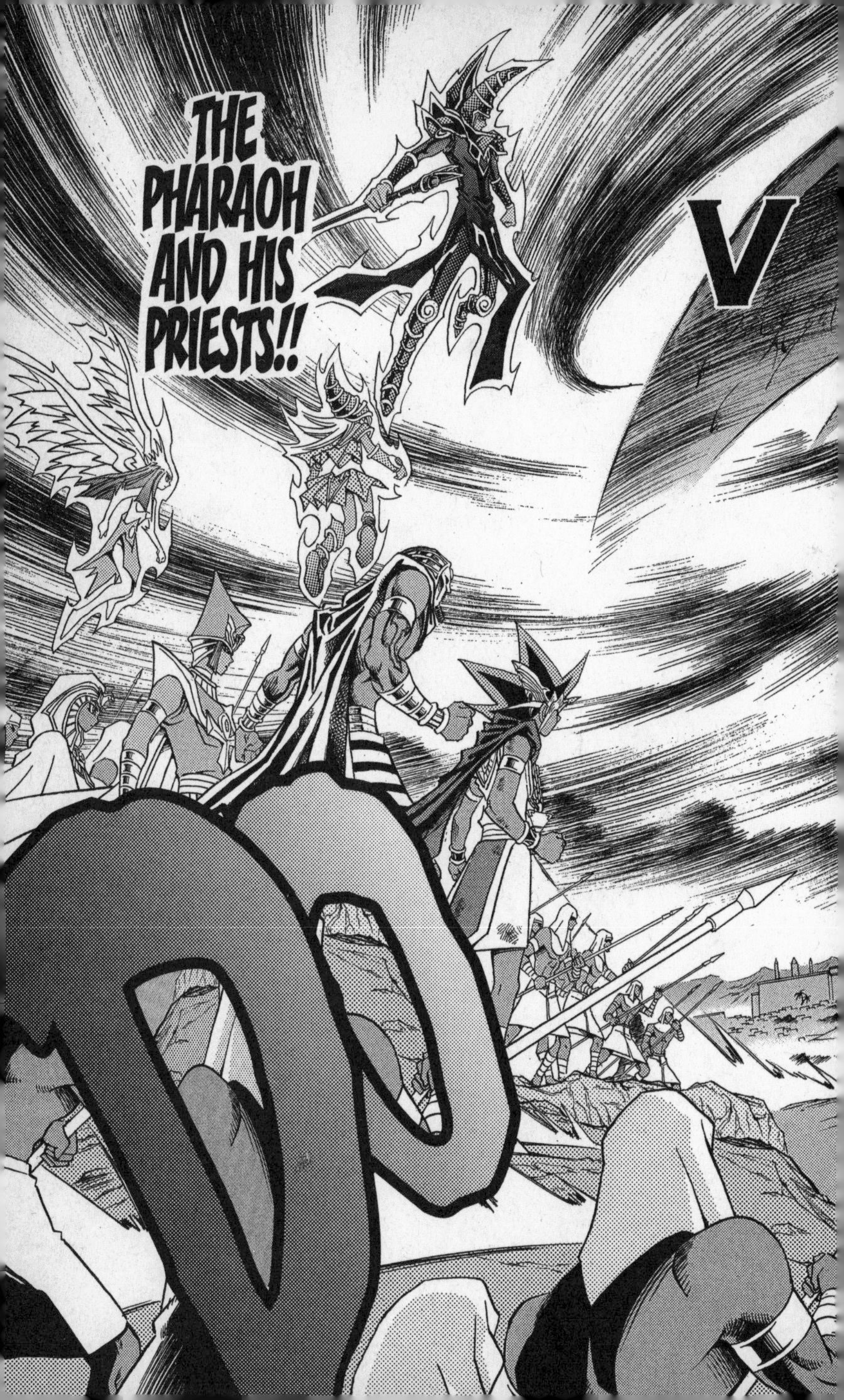
THE PHARAOH AND HIS PRIESTS!!
V

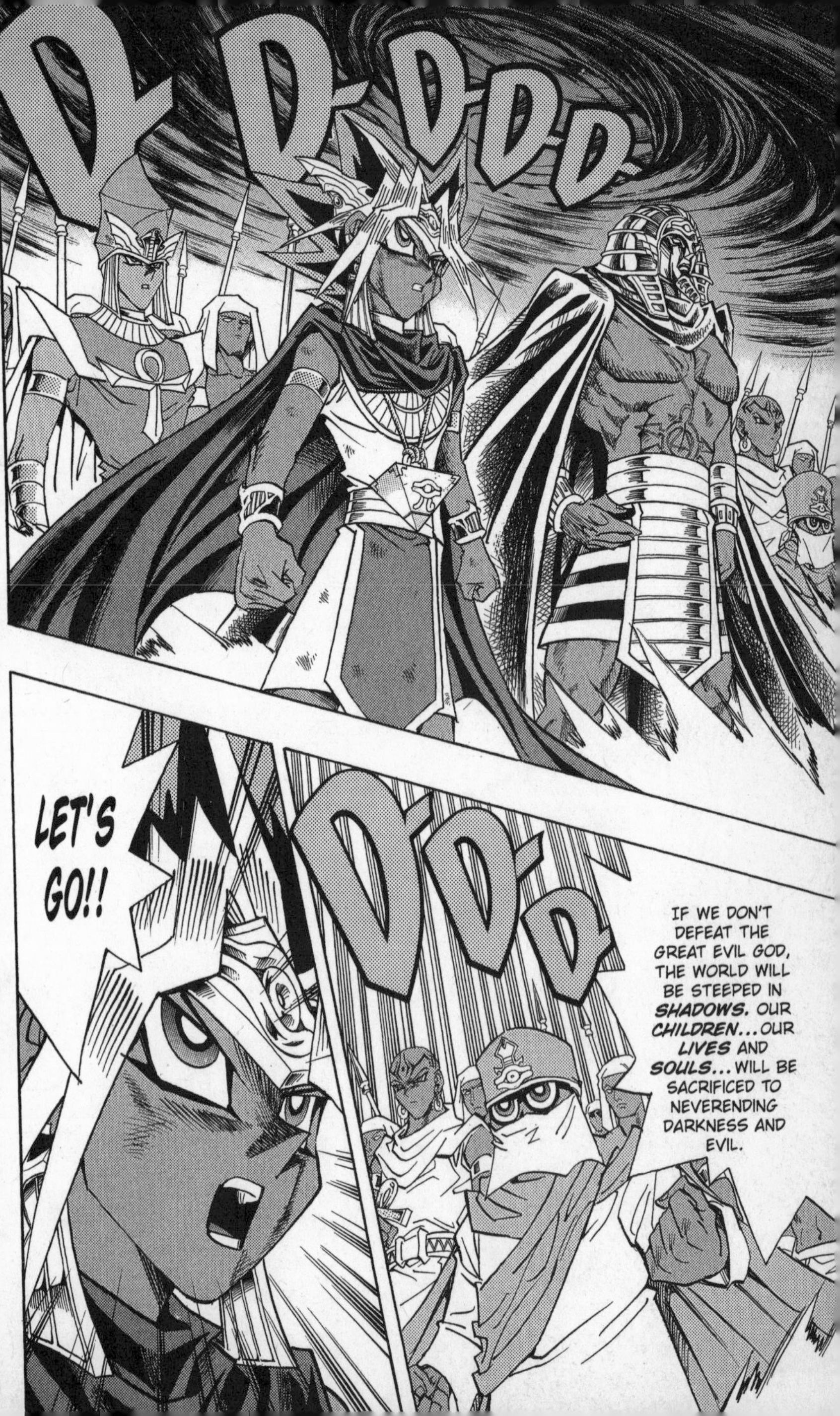
DDDDD
IF WE DON'T DEFEAT THE GREAT EVIL GOD, THE WORLD WILL BE STEEPED IN SHADOWS. OUR CHILDREN...OUR LIVES AND SOULS...WILL BE SACRIFICED TO NEVERENDING DARKNESS AND EVIL.
DDD
LET'S GO!!

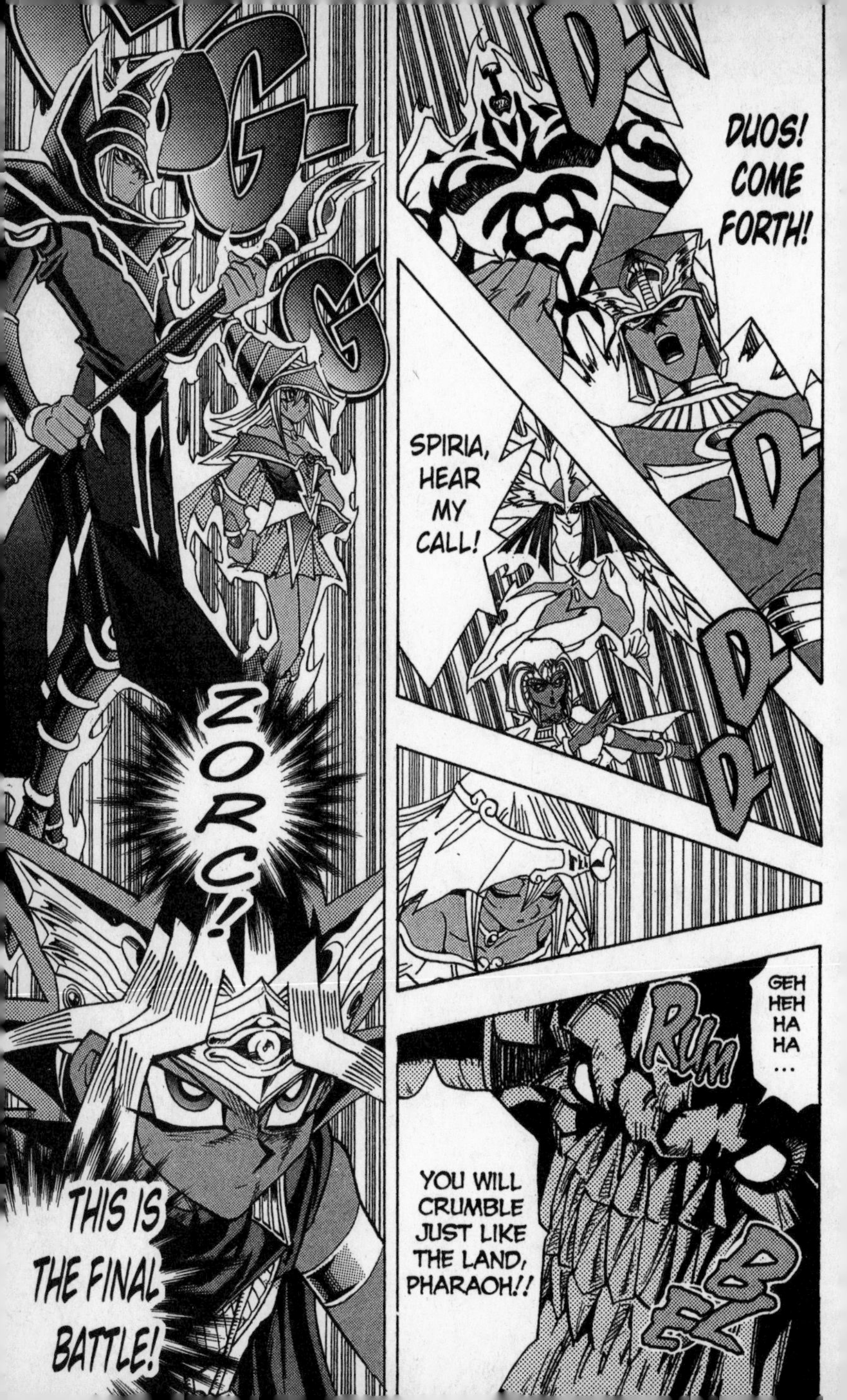
DUOS! COME FORTH!
SPIRIA, HEAR MY CALL!
GEH HEH HA HA...
RUM
YOU WILL CRUMBLE JUST LIKE THE LAND, PHARAOH!!
BLE
ZORC!!
THIS IS THE FINAL BATTLE!

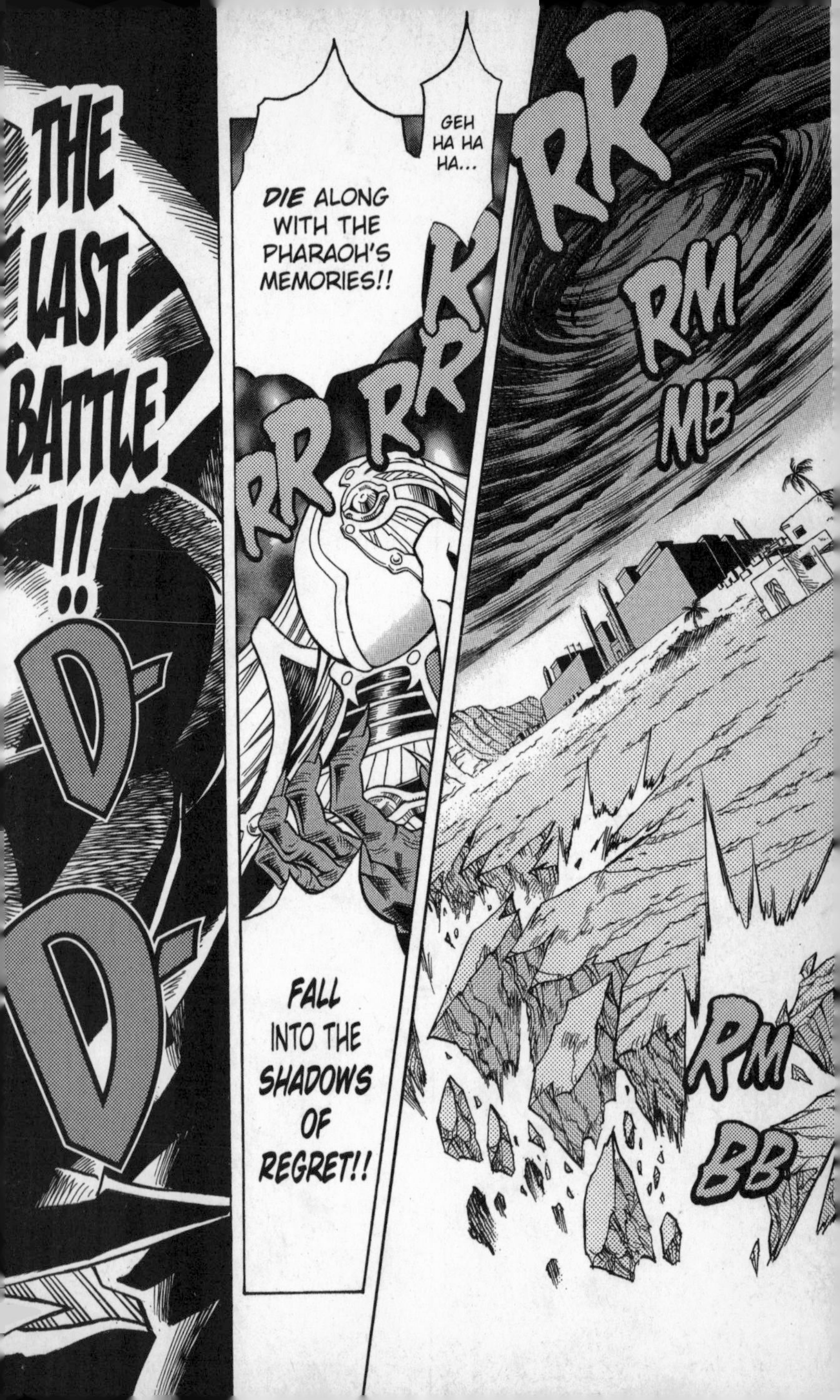

RR
RM
MB
RM
BB
GEH HA HA HA...
DIE ALONG WITH THE PHARAOH'S MEMORIES!!
K
RR
RR
FALL INTO THE SHADOWS OF REGRET!!
THE LAST BATTLE!!
D
D

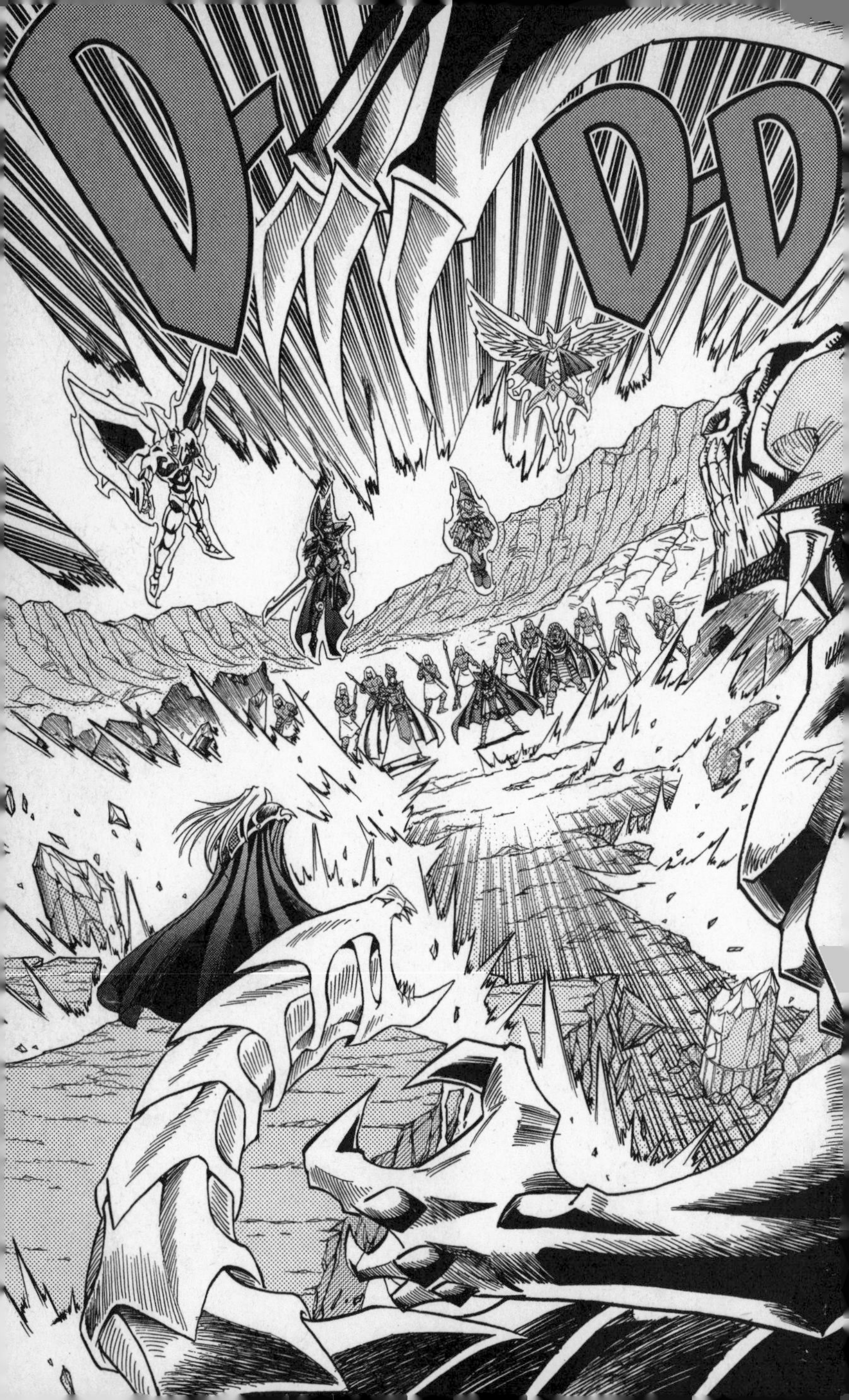

Duel 51: Until our *Ba* Runs Out!

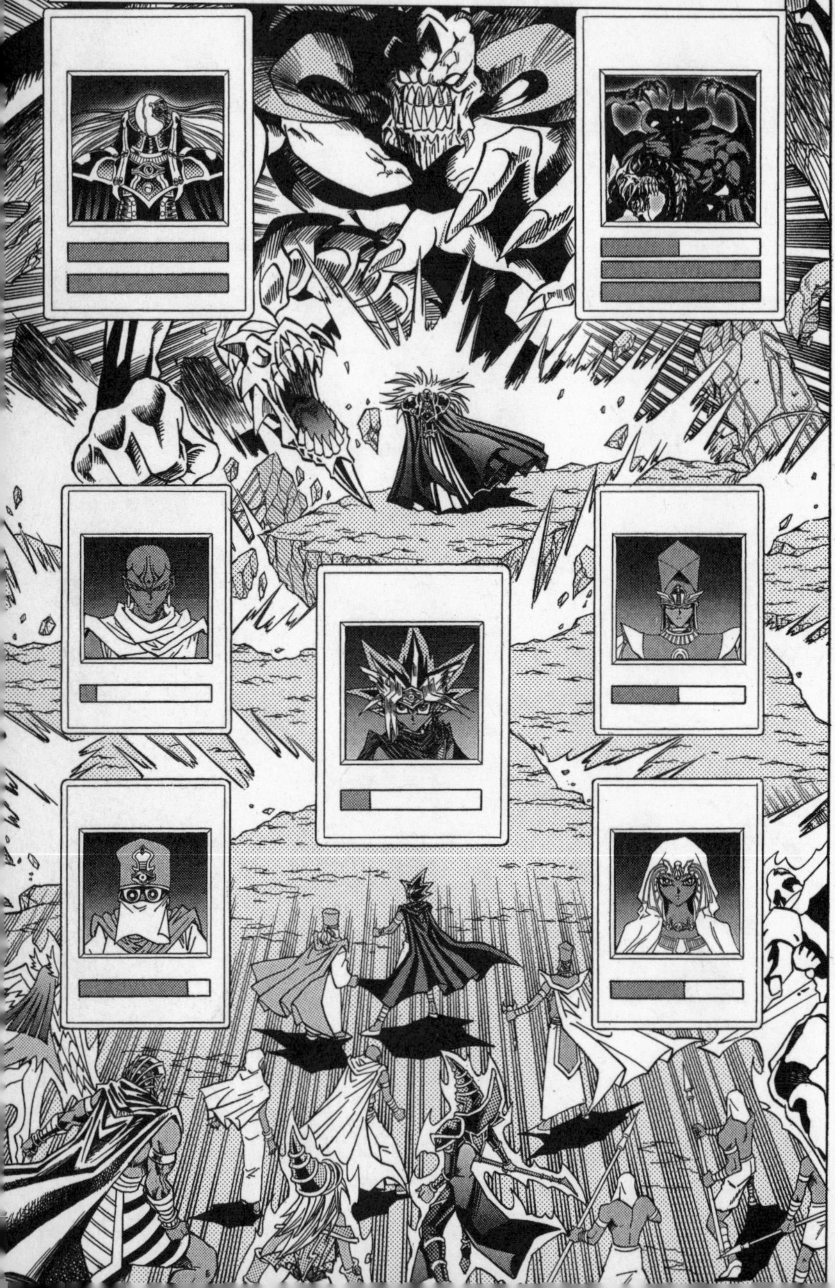

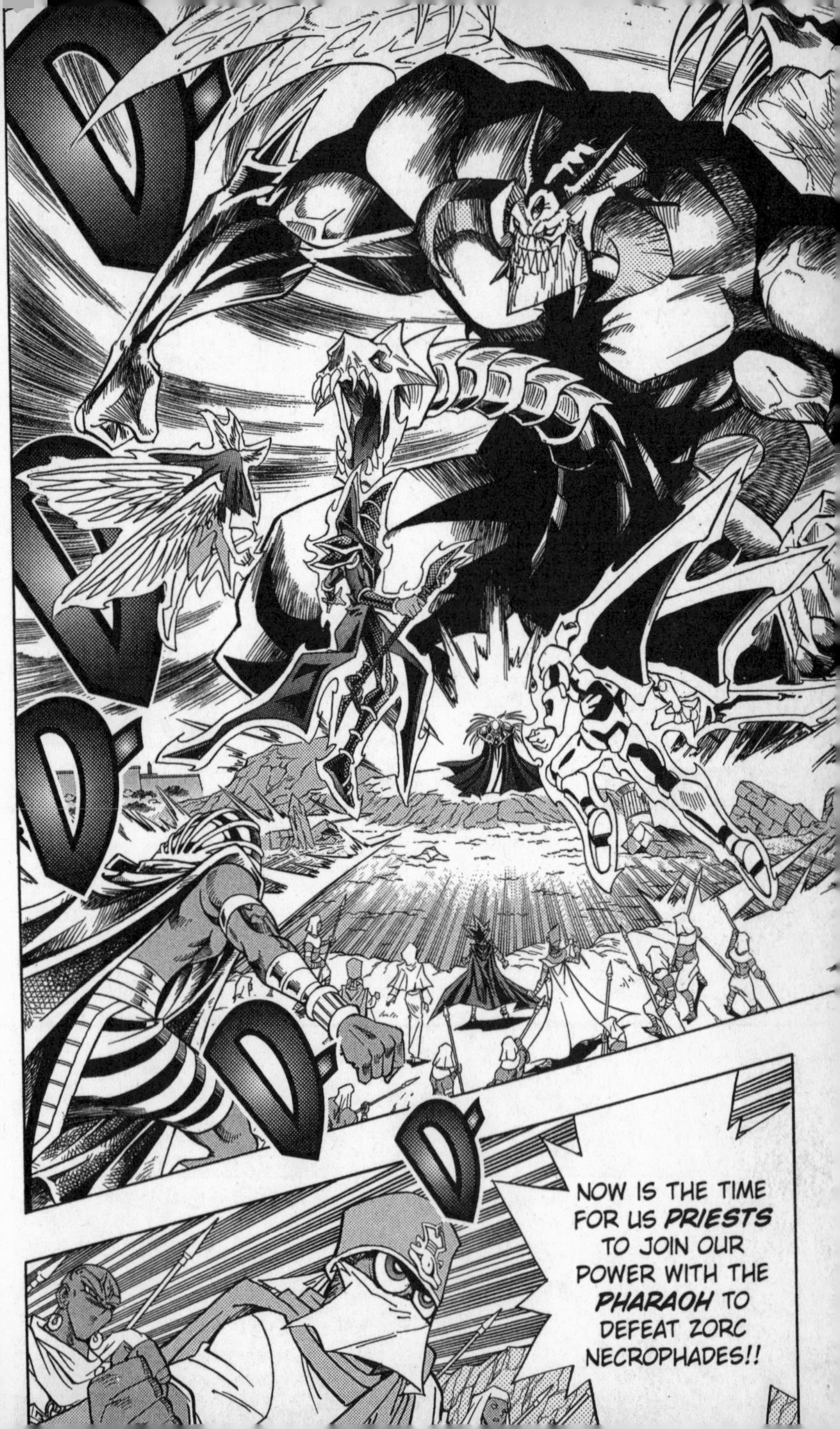
NOW IS THE TIME FOR US PRIESTS TO JOIN OUR POWER WITH THE PHARAOH TO DEFEAT ZORC NECROPHADES!!

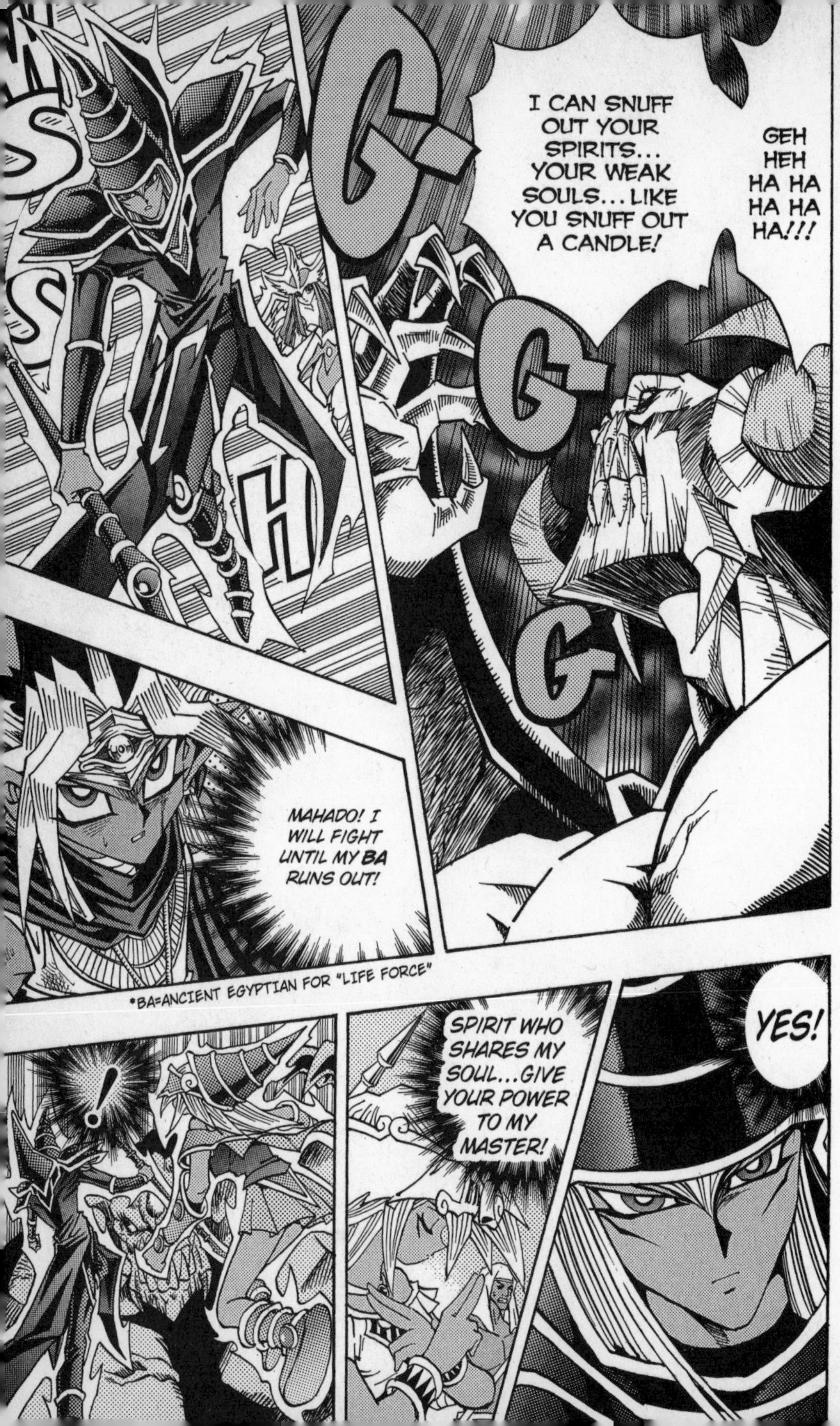
G
G
G
I CAN SNUFF OUT YOUR SPIRITS... YOUR WEAK SOULS... LIKE YOU SNUFF OUT A CANDLE!
GEH HEH HA HA HA HA HA!!!
S
S
H
MAHADO! I WILL FIGHT UNTIL MY BA RUNS OUT!
YES!
SPIRIT WHO SHARES MY SOUL... GIVE YOUR POWER TO MY MASTER!
!
*BA=ANCIENT EGYPTIAN FOR "LIFE FORCE"

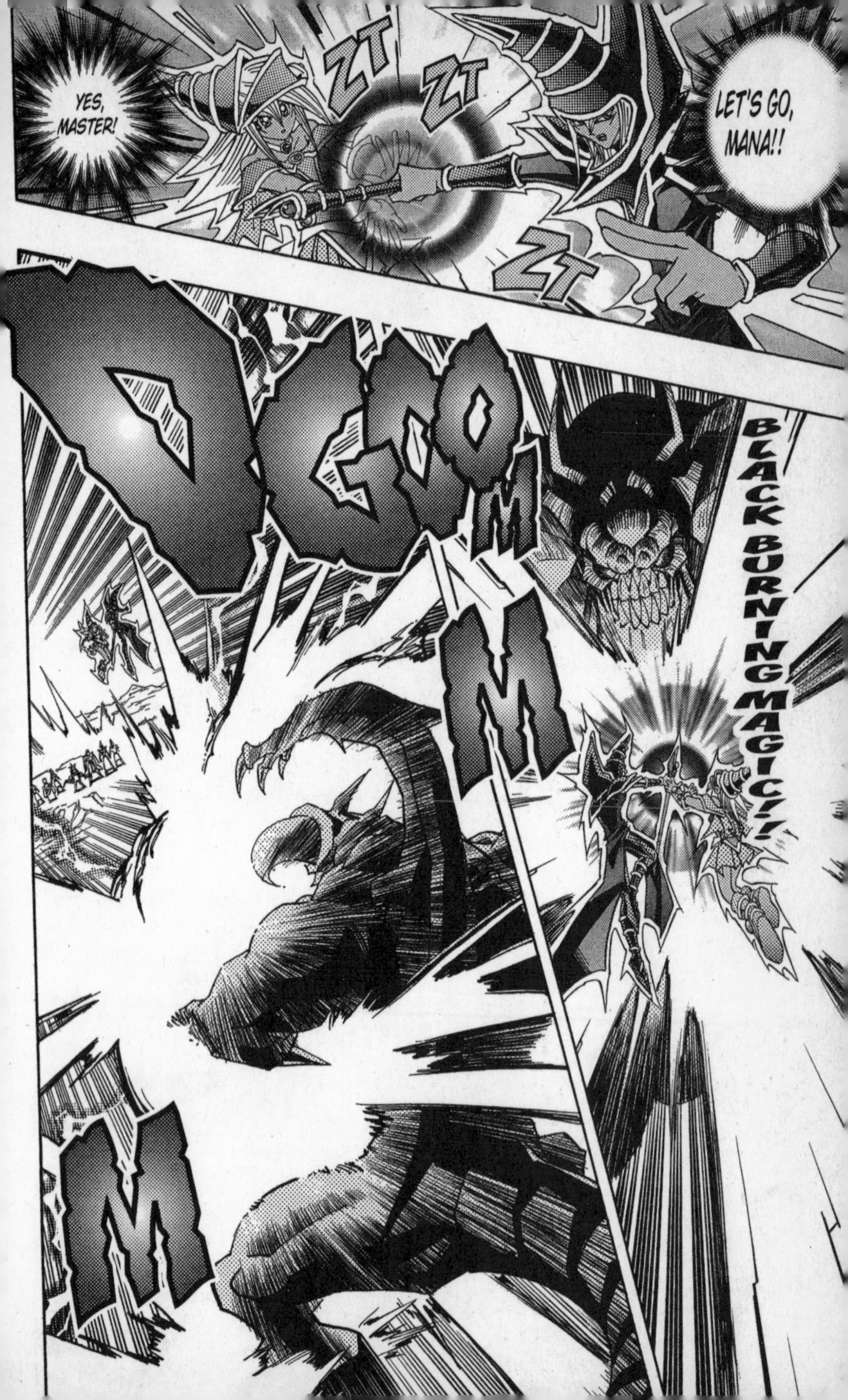
LET'S GO, MANA!!
ZT
ZT
YES, MASTER!
ZT
BLACK BURNING MAGIC!!
DOOOM
M
M

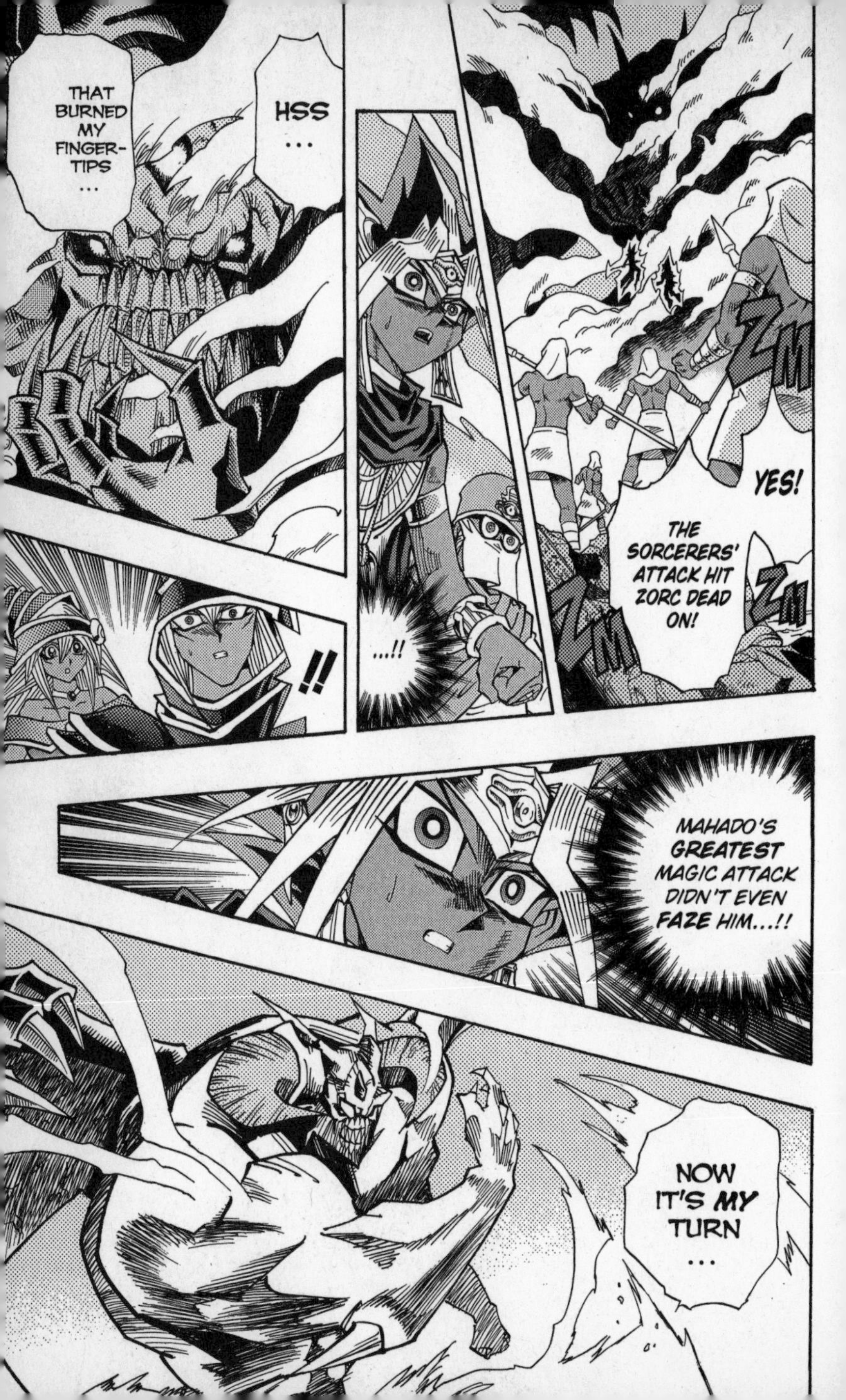
YES!
THE SORCERERS' ATTACK HIT ZORC DEAD ON!
...!!
HSS ...
THAT BURNED MY FINGER-TIPS ...
!!
MAHADO'S GREATEST MAGIC ATTACK DIDN'T EVEN FAZE HIM...!!
NOW IT'S MY TURN ...

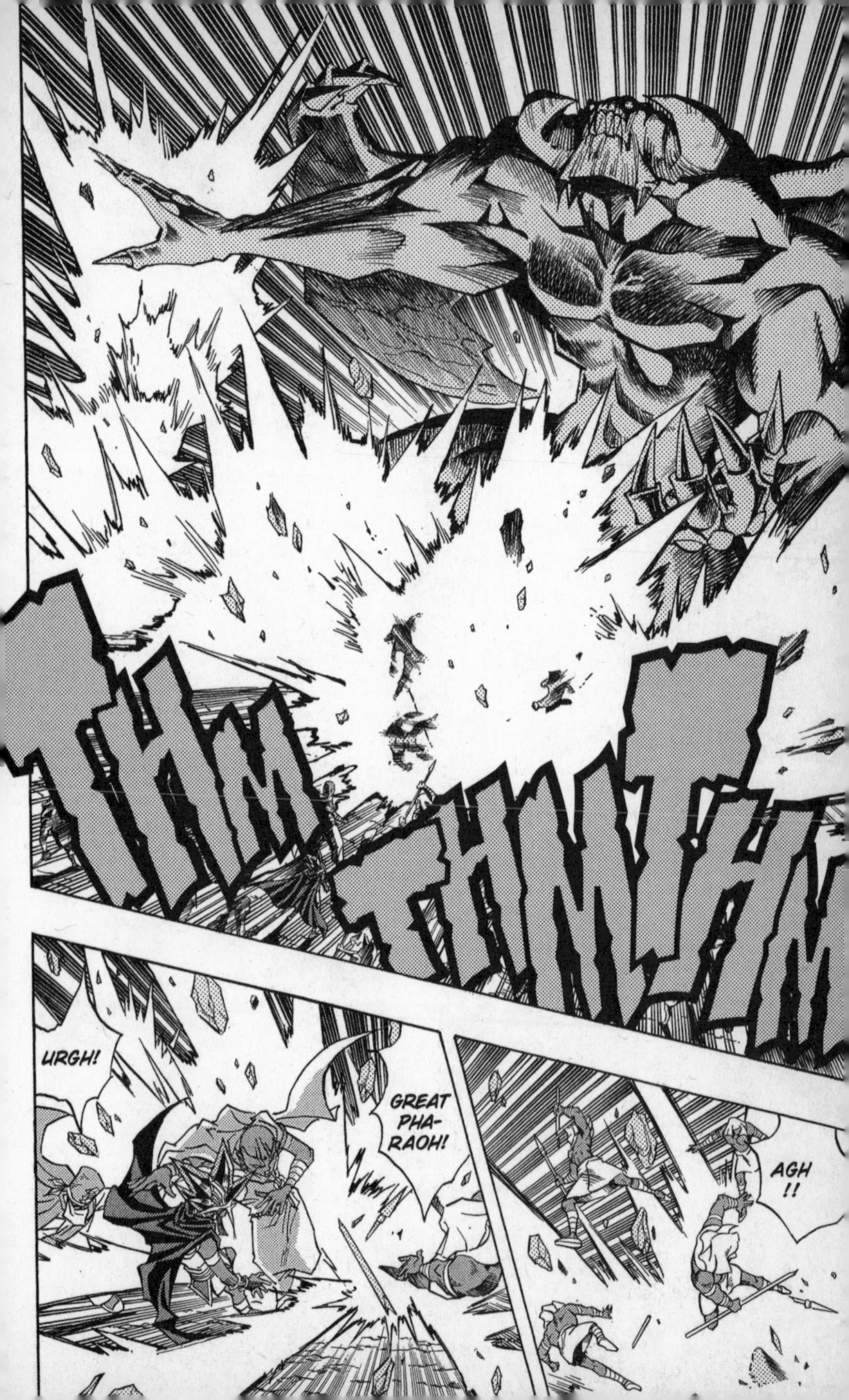
THM THM THM
AGH!!
GREAT PHA-RAOH!
URGH!

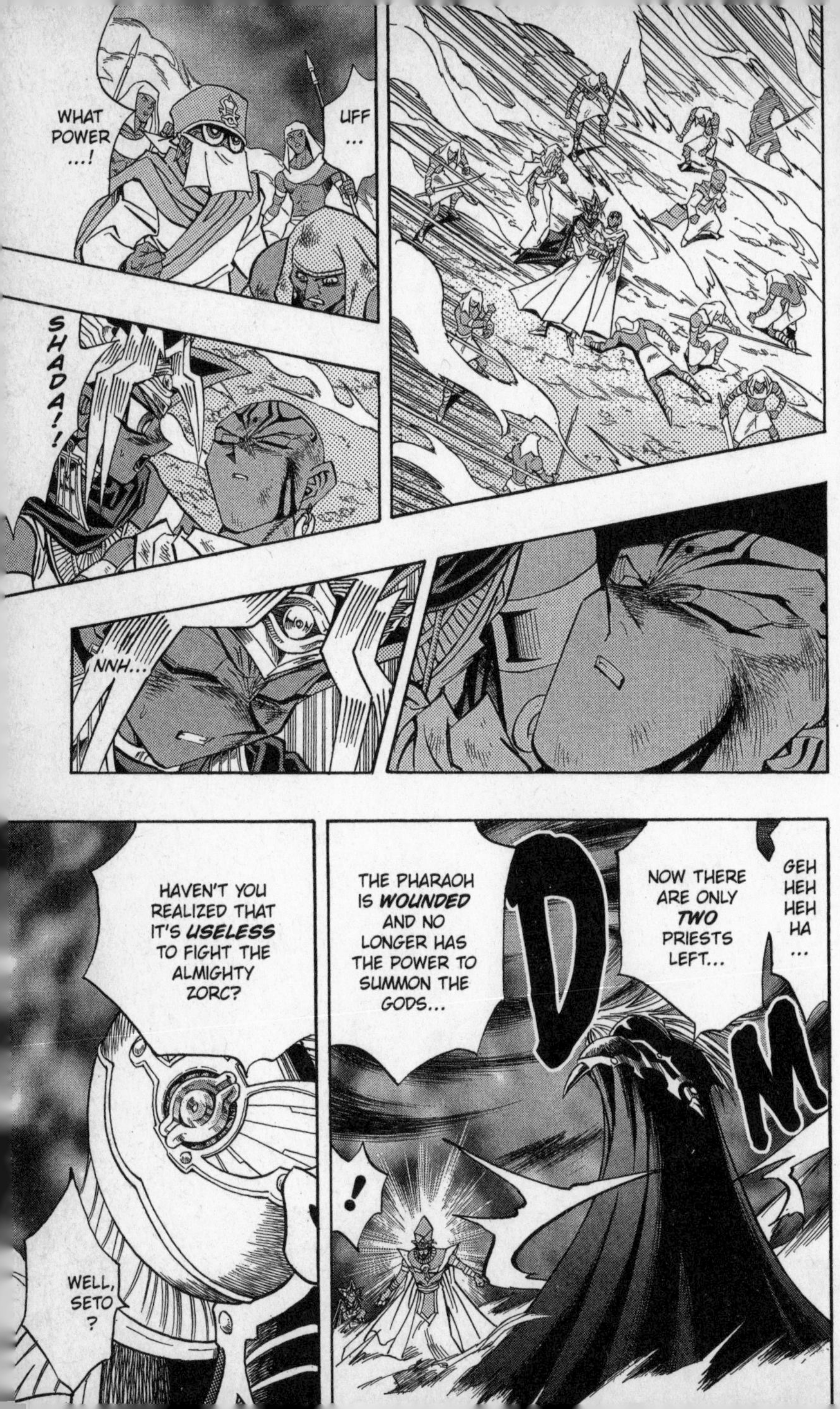
UFF ...
WHAT POWER ...!
SHADA!!
NNH...
GEH HEH HEH HA ...
NOW THERE ARE ONLY TWO PRIESTS LEFT...
THE PHARAOH IS WOUNDED AND NO LONGER HAS THE POWER TO SUMMON THE GODS...
DM
!
HAVEN'T YOU REALIZED THAT IT'S USELESS TO FIGHT THE ALMIGHTY ZORC?
WELL, SETO ?

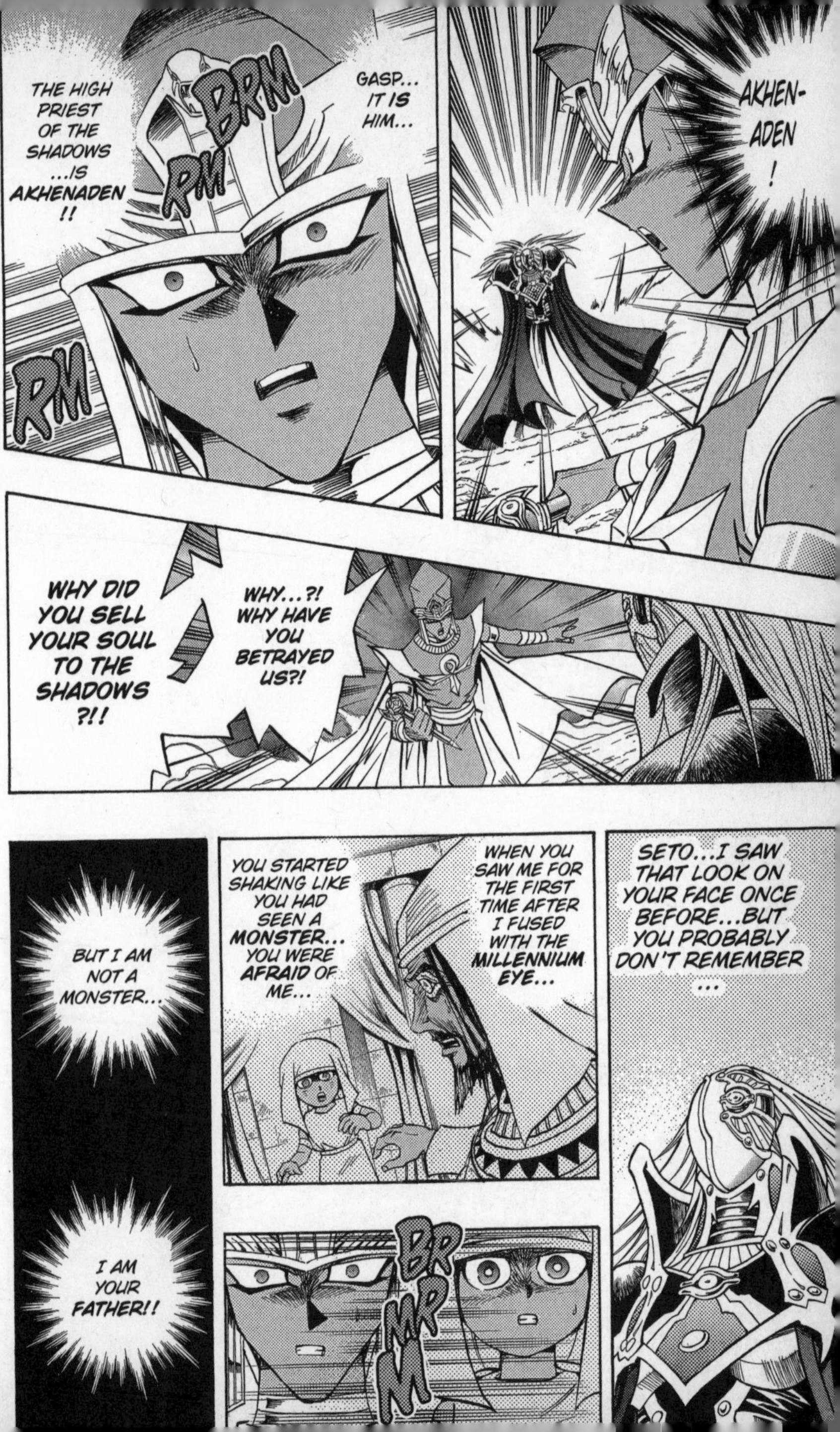
AKHEN-ADEN!
GASP... IT IS HIM...
BRM
RM
THE HIGH PRIEST OF THE SHADOWS ...IS AKHENADEN!!
RM
WHY...?! WHY HAVE YOU BETRAYED US?!
WHY DID YOU SELL YOUR SOUL TO THE SHADOWS?!!
SETO...I SAW THAT LOOK ON YOUR FACE ONCE BEFORE...BUT YOU PROBABLY DON'T REMEMBER...
WHEN YOU SAW ME FOR THE FIRST TIME AFTER I FUSED WITH THE MILLENNIUM EYE...
YOU STARTED SHAKING LIKE YOU HAD SEEN A MONSTER... YOU WERE AFRAID OF ME...
BRMRM
BUT I AM NOT A MONSTER...
I AM YOUR FATHER!!

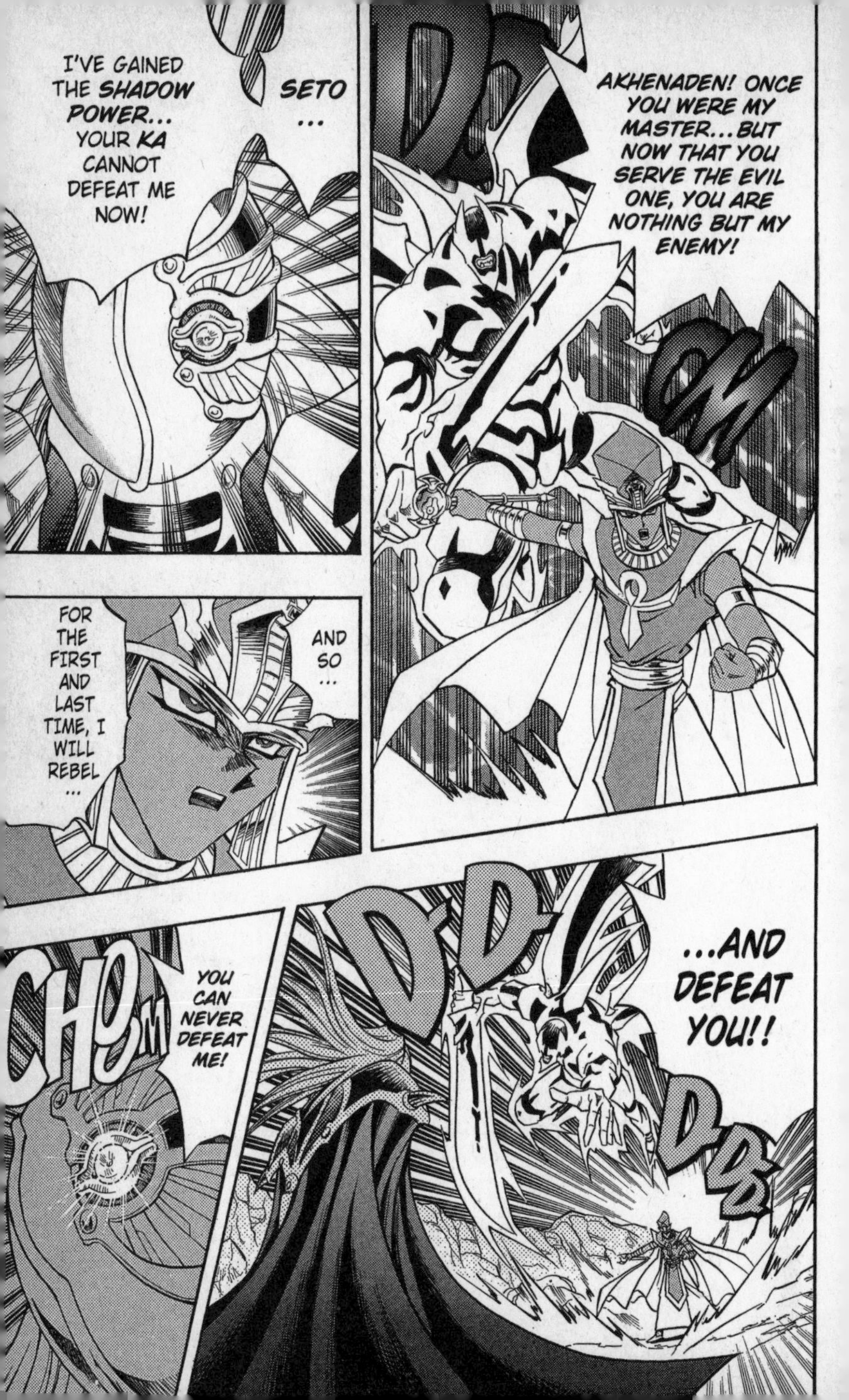
AKHENADEN! ONCE YOU WERE MY MASTER...BUT NOW THAT YOU SERVE THE EVIL ONE, YOU ARE NOTHING BUT MY ENEMY!
OM
SETO...
I'VE GAINED THE SHADOW POWER... YOUR KA CANNOT DEFEAT ME NOW!
AND SO...
FOR THE FIRST AND LAST TIME, I WILL REBEL...
DD
...AND DEFEAT YOU!!
DD
CHOOM
YOU CAN NEVER DEFEAT ME!

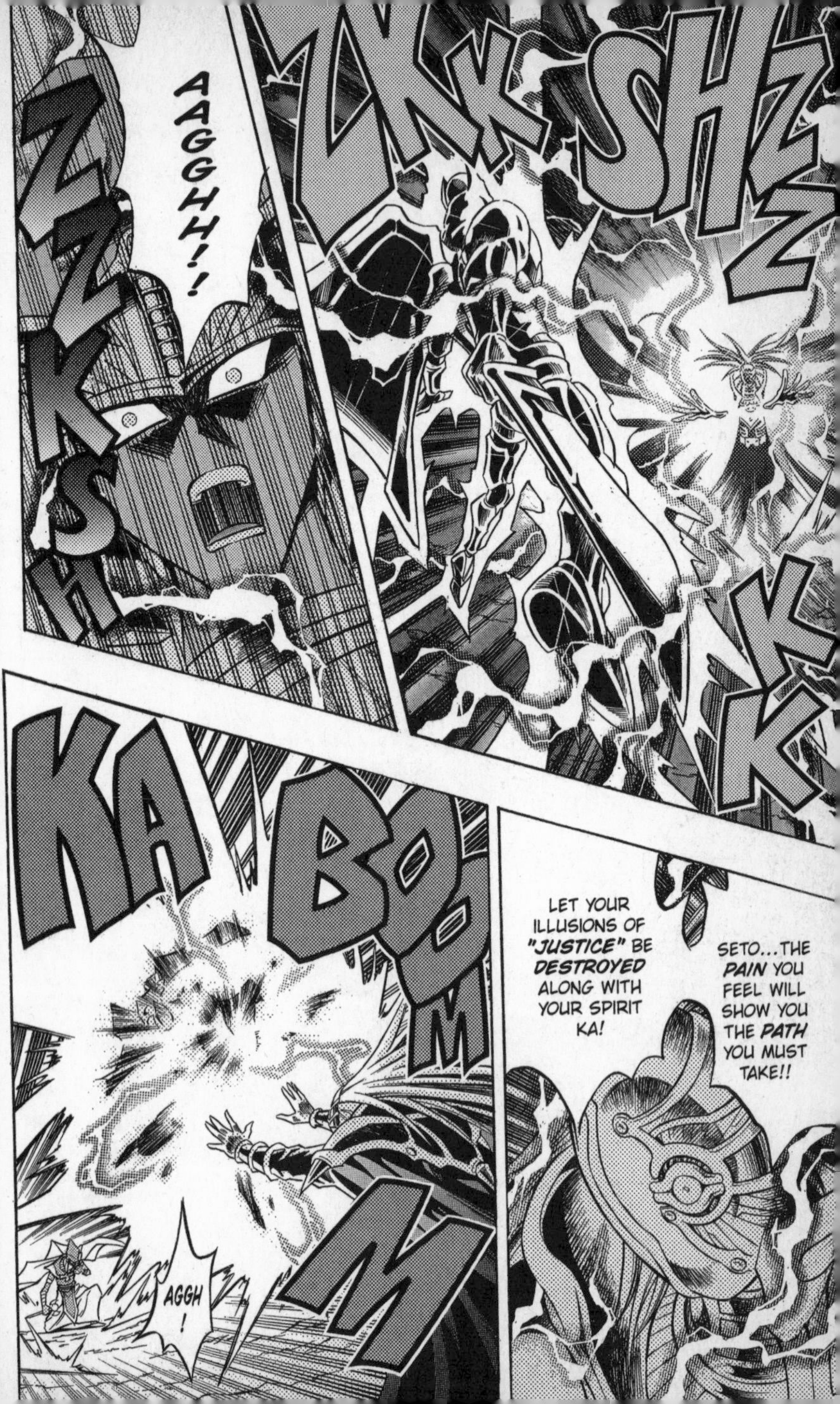

ZKKSHZZ
KKK
ZZZKSH
AAGGHH!!
SETO...THE *PAIN* YOU FEEL WILL SHOW YOU THE *PATH* YOU MUST TAKE!!
LET YOUR ILLUSIONS OF *"JUSTICE"* BE *DESTROYED* ALONG WITH YOUR SPIRIT KA!
KABOOM
AGGH!

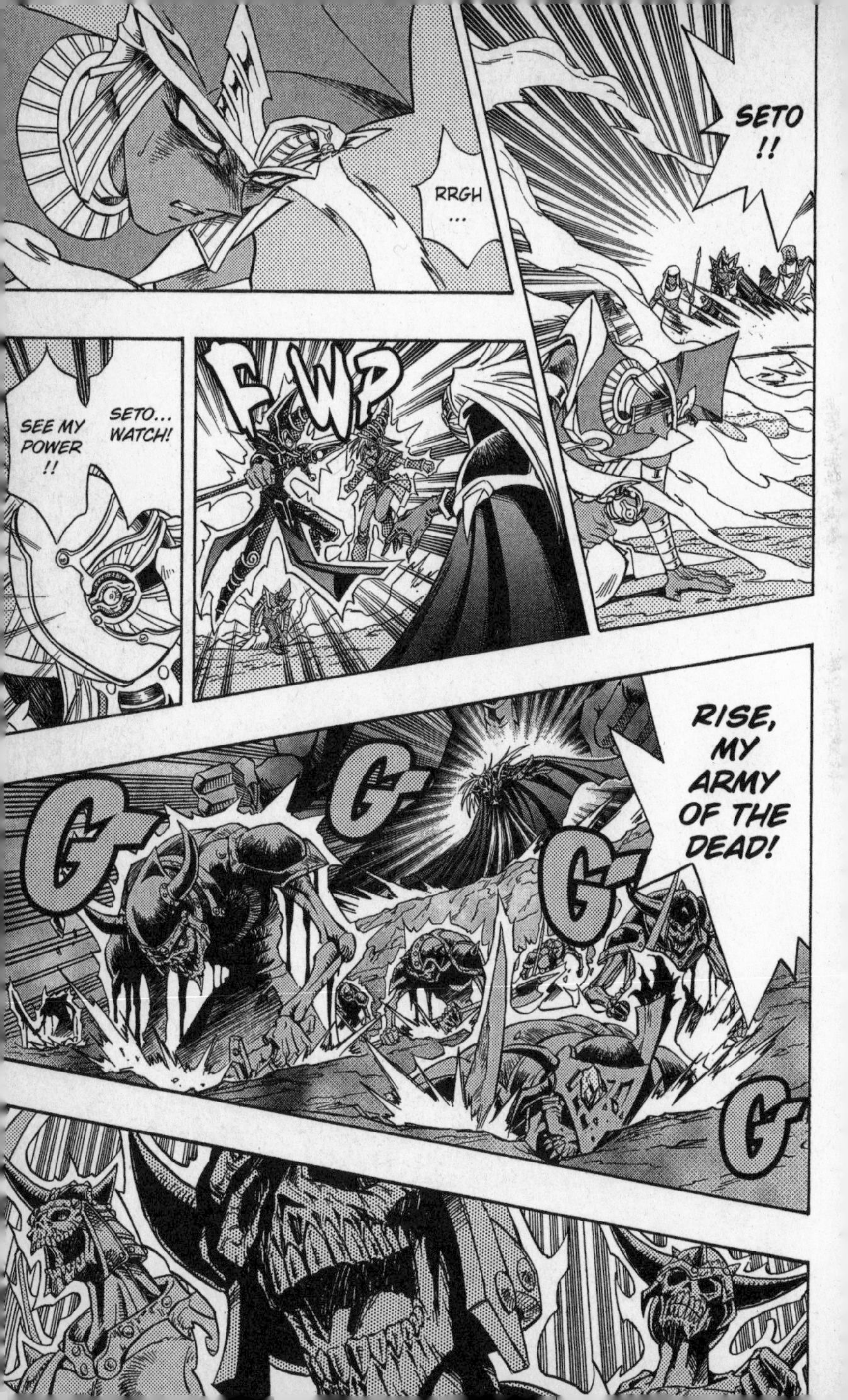
SETO !!
RRGH ...
F W P
SETO... WATCH!
SEE MY POWER !!
RISE, MY ARMY OF THE DEAD!
G
G
G
G

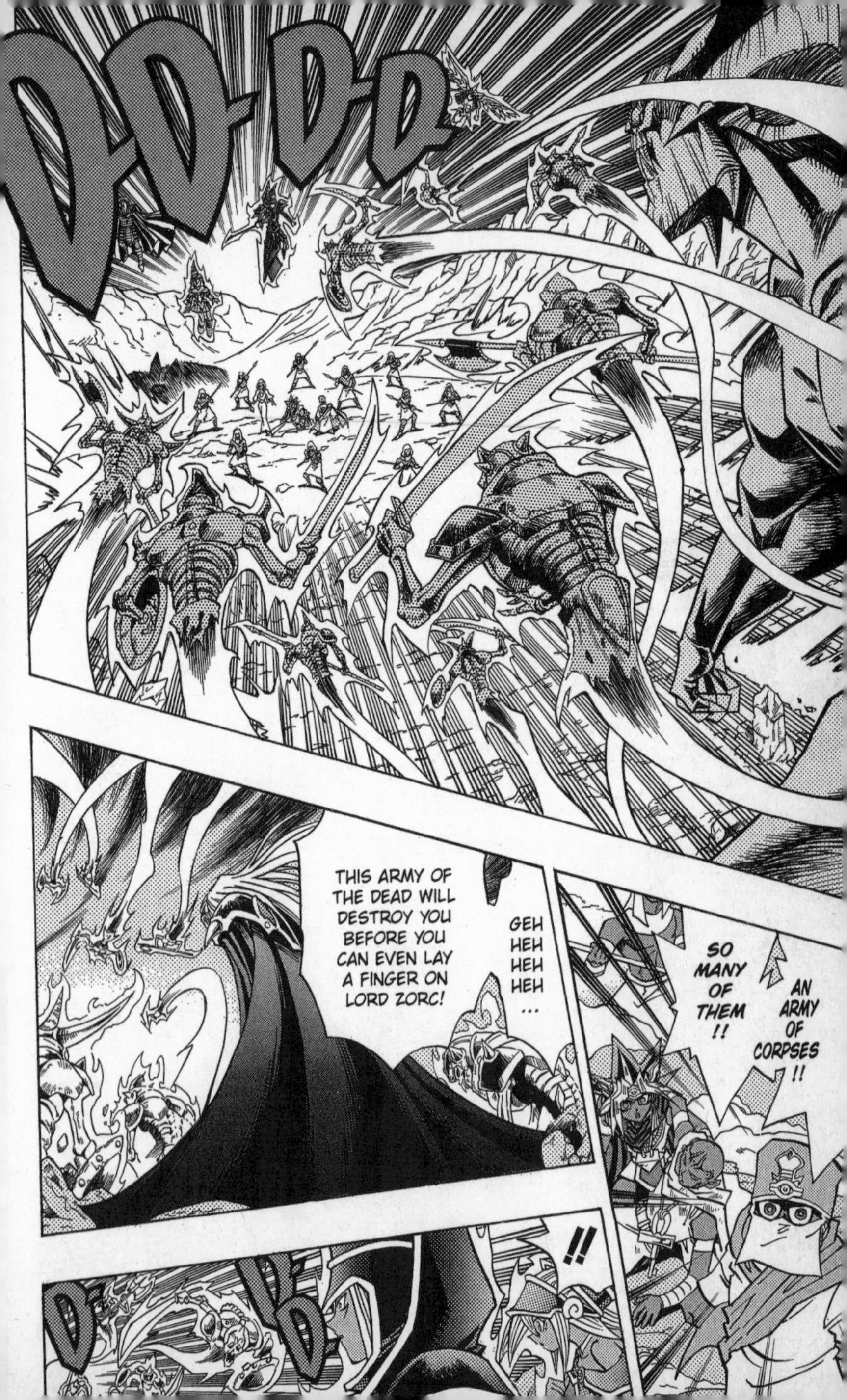
AN ARMY OF CORPSES!!
SO MANY OF THEM!!
GEH HEH HEH HEH...
THIS ARMY OF THE DEAD WILL DESTROY YOU BEFORE YOU CAN EVEN LAY A FINGER ON LORD ZORC!
!!

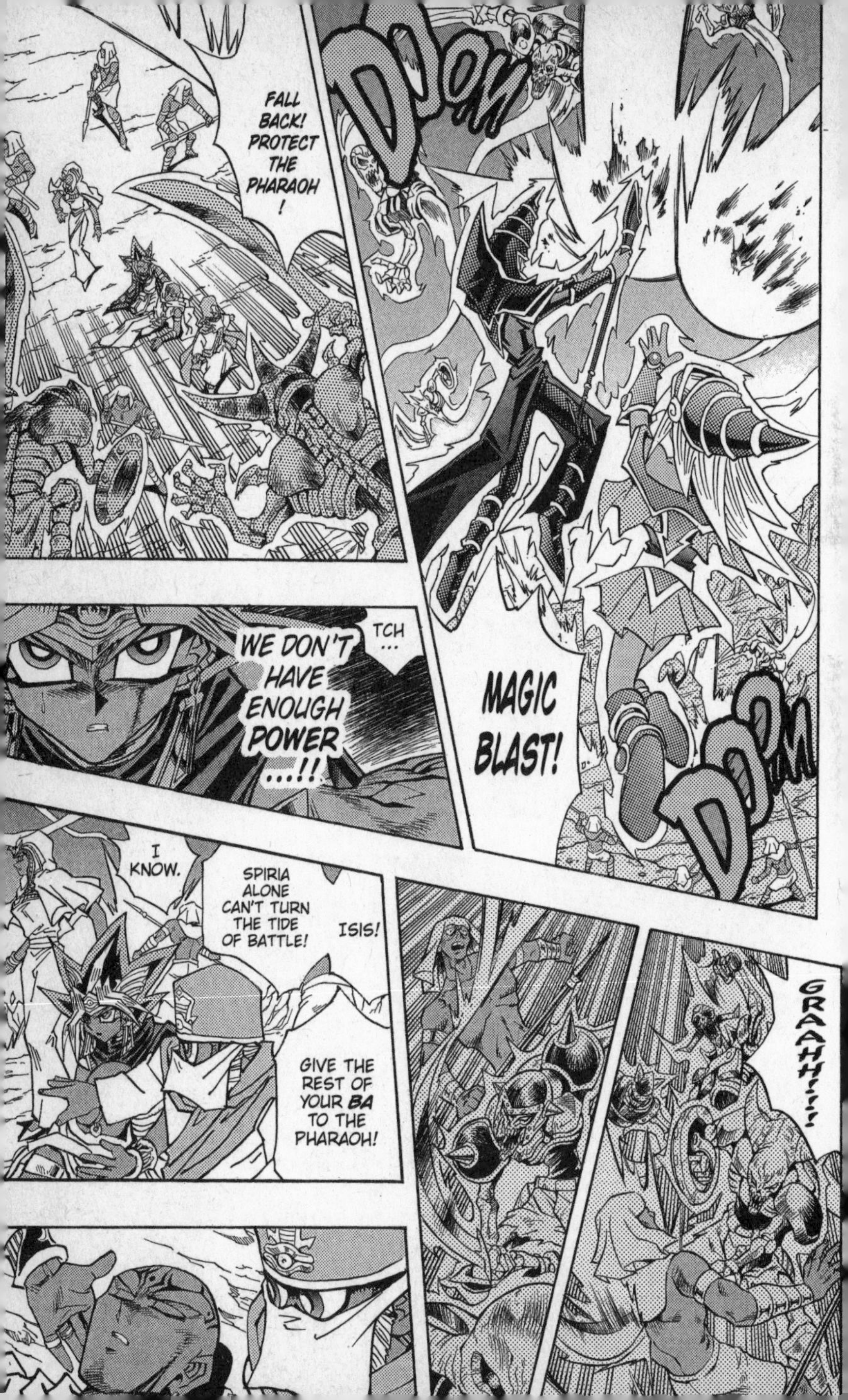
DOOM
MAGIC BLAST!
DOOM
FALL BACK! PROTECT THE PHARAOH!
TCH...
WE DON'T HAVE ENOUGH POWER ...!!
GRAAHH!!!
ISIS!
SPIRIA ALONE CAN'T TURN THE TIDE OF BATTLE!
I KNOW.
GIVE THE REST OF YOUR *BA* TO THE PHARAOH!

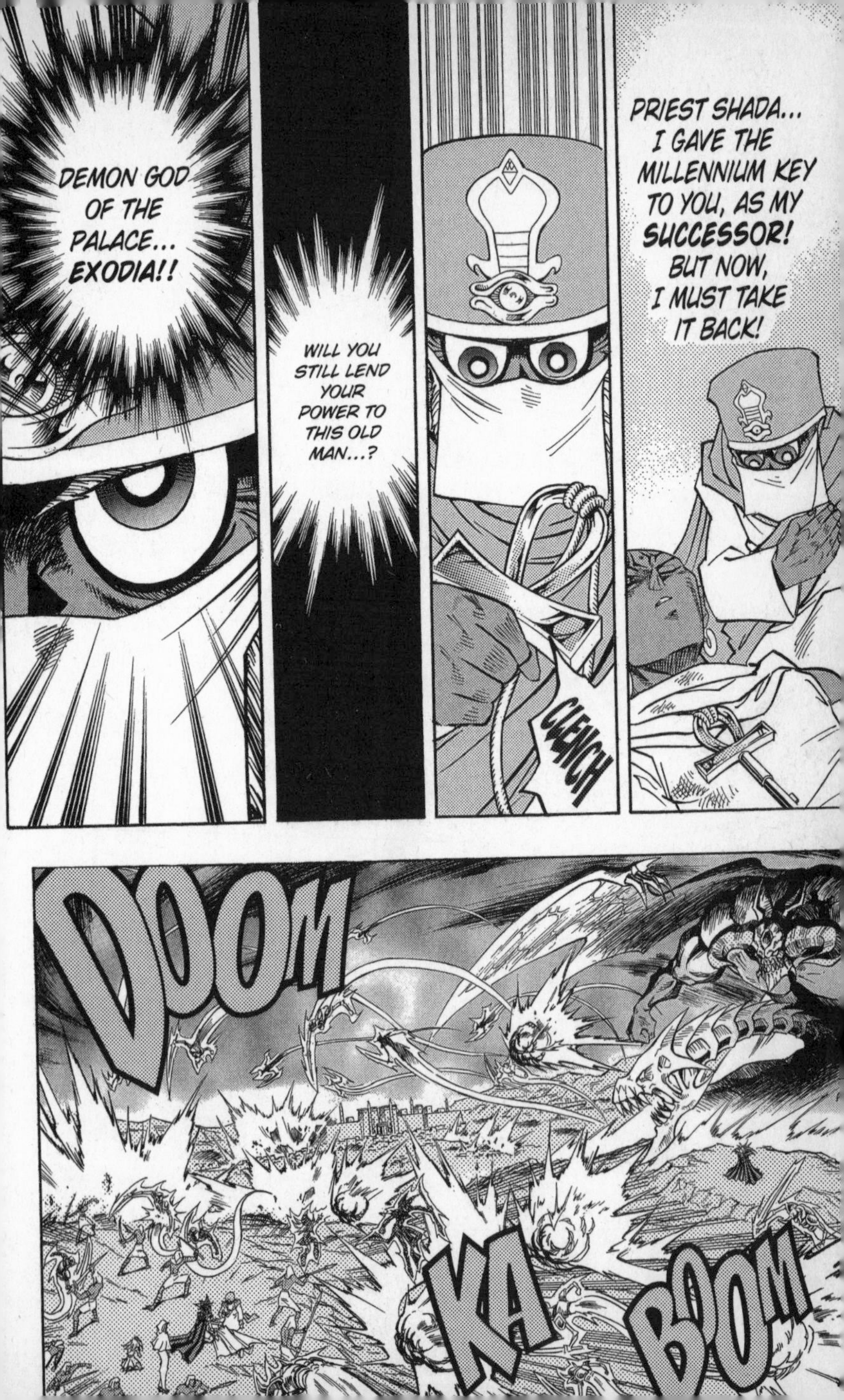
PRIEST SHADA... I GAVE THE MILLENNIUM KEY TO YOU, AS MY SUCCESSOR! BUT NOW, I MUST TAKE IT BACK!
CLENCH
WILL YOU STILL LEND YOUR POWER TO THIS OLD MAN...?
DEMON GOD OF THE PALACE... EXODIA!!
DOOM
KA
BOOM

READ THIS WAY

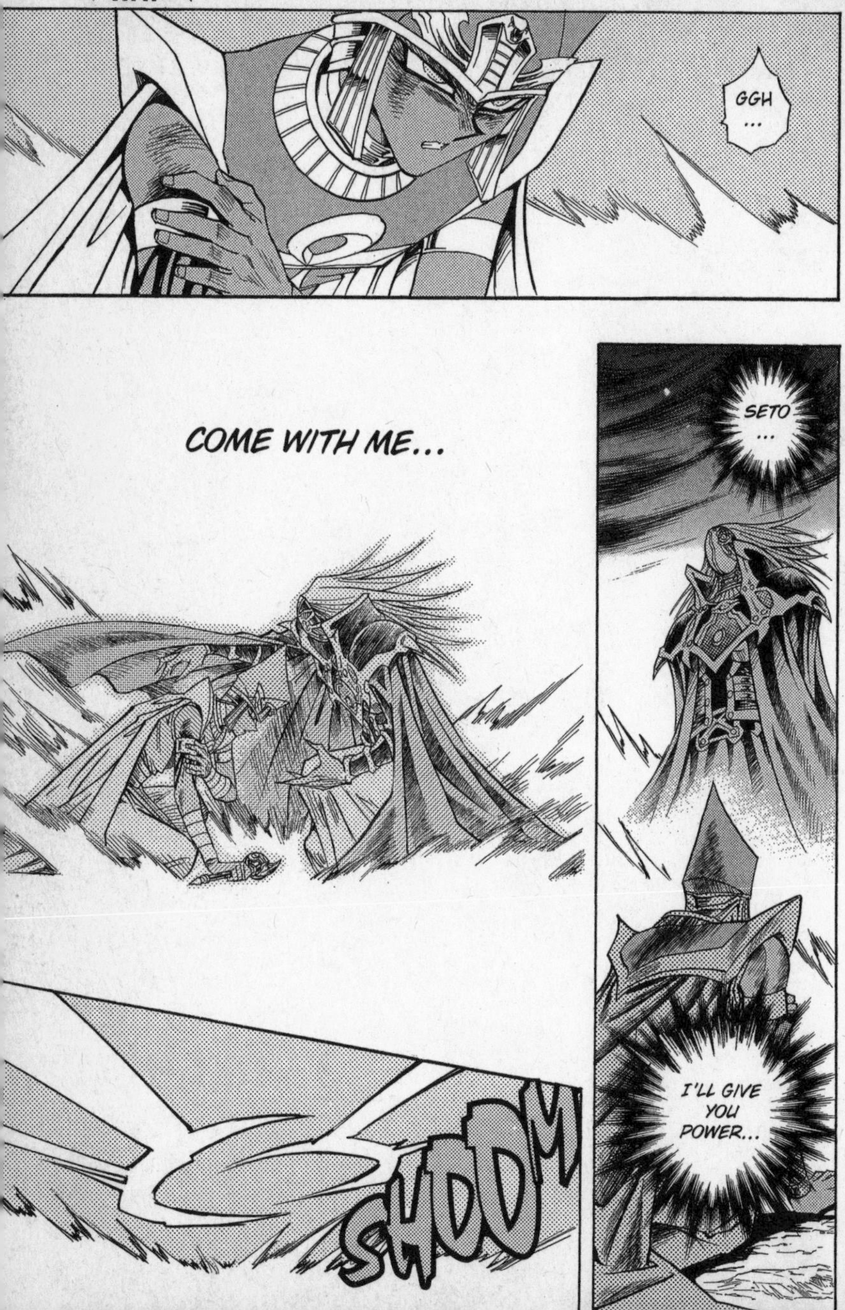
GGH ...
SETO ...
I'LL GIVE YOU POWER...
COME WITH ME...
SHOOM

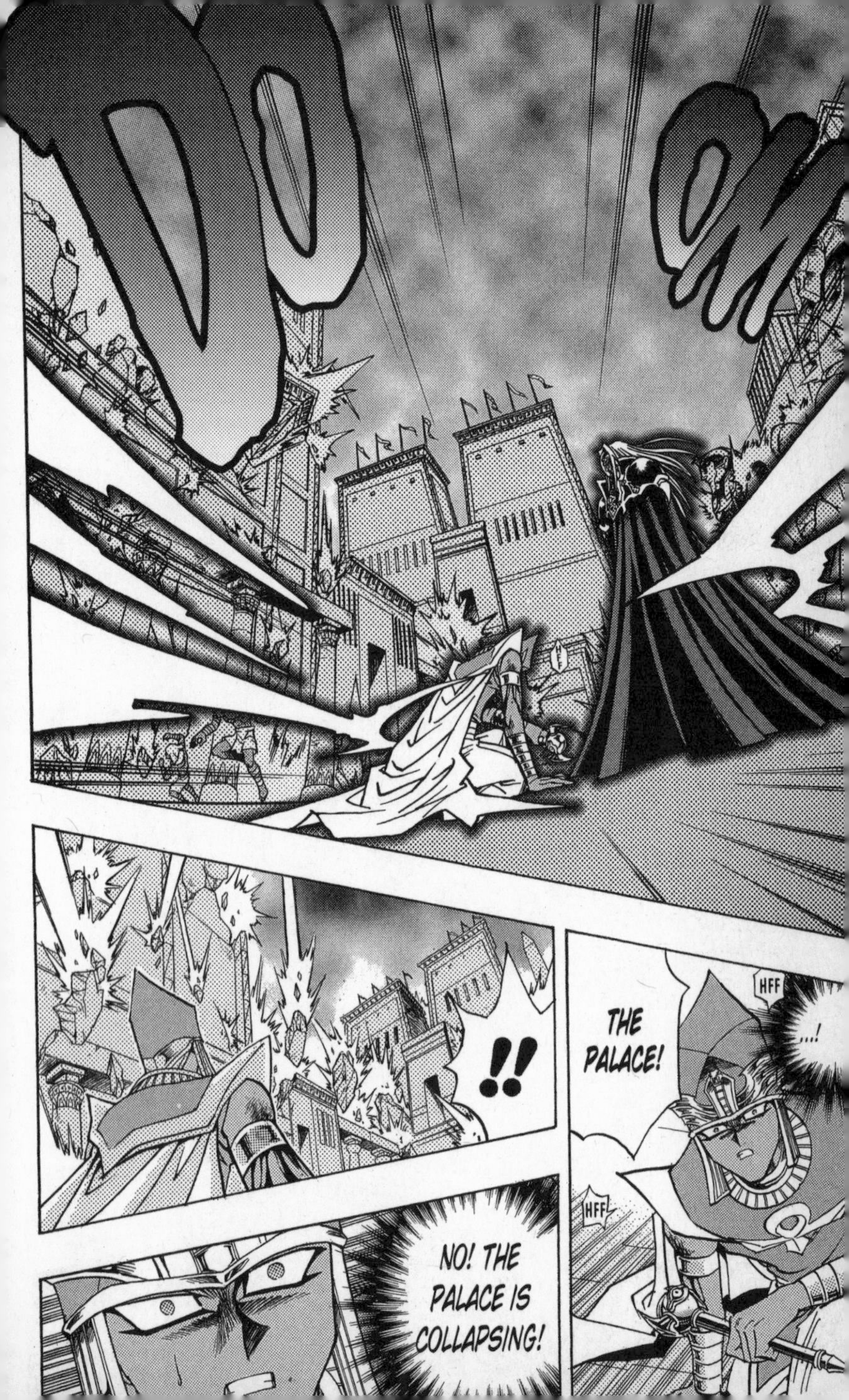
DOOM
HFF
...!
THE PALACE!
HFF
!!
NO! THE PALACE IS COLLAPSING!

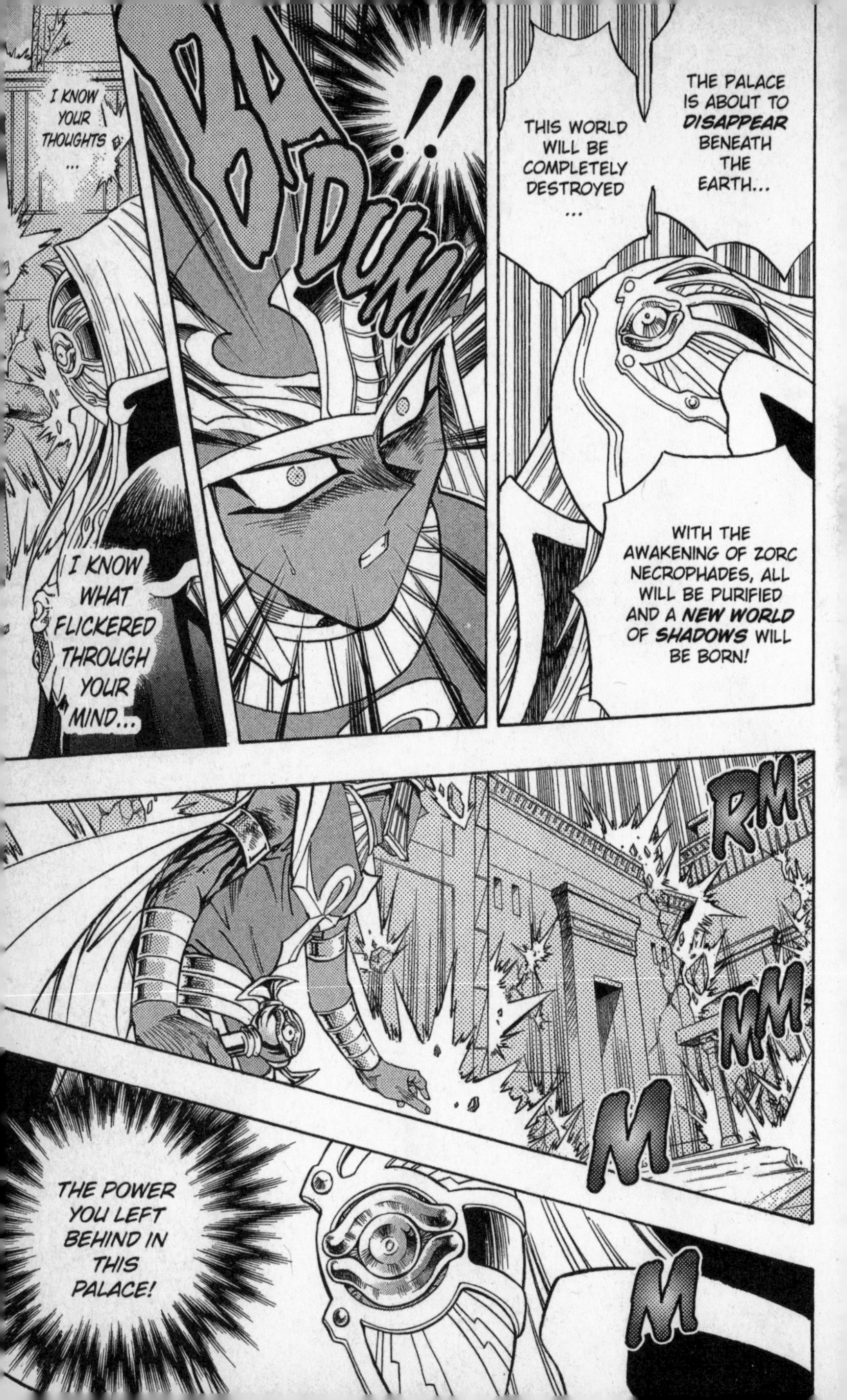
THE PALACE IS ABOUT TO ***DISAPPEAR*** BENEATH THE EARTH...
THIS WORLD WILL BE COMPLETELY DESTROYED ...
WITH THE AWAKENING OF ZORC NECROPHADES, ALL WILL BE PURIFIED AND A ***NEW WORLD*** OF ***SHADOWS*** WILL BE BORN!
BA DUM!!
I KNOW YOUR THOUGHTS ...
I KNOW WHAT FLICKERED THROUGH YOUR MIND...
RM
MM
M
THE POWER YOU LEFT BEHIND IN THIS PALACE!
M

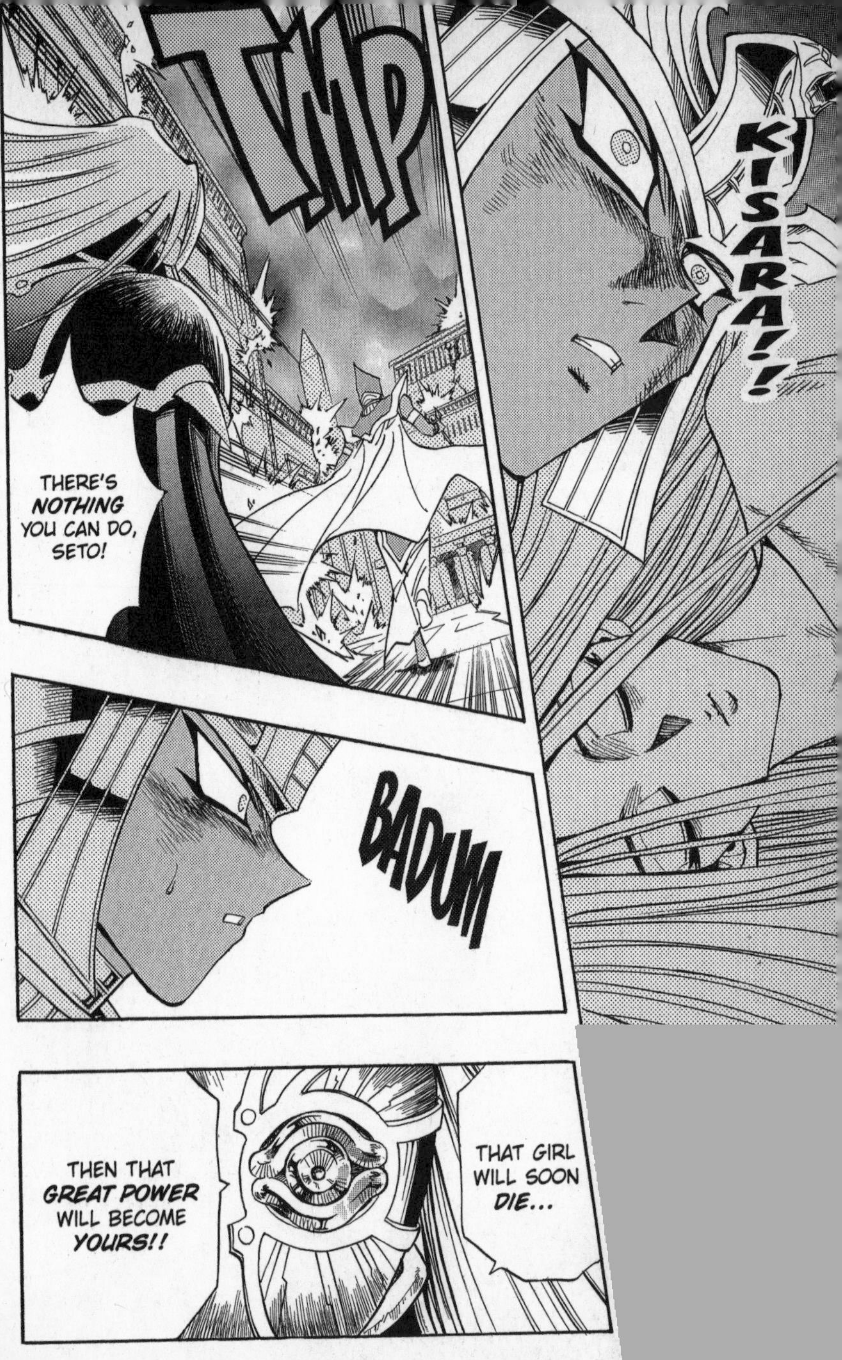
KISARA!!
TMP
THERE'S NOTHING YOU CAN DO, SETO!
BADUM
THAT GIRL WILL SOON DIE...
THEN THAT GREAT POWER WILL BECOME YOURS!!

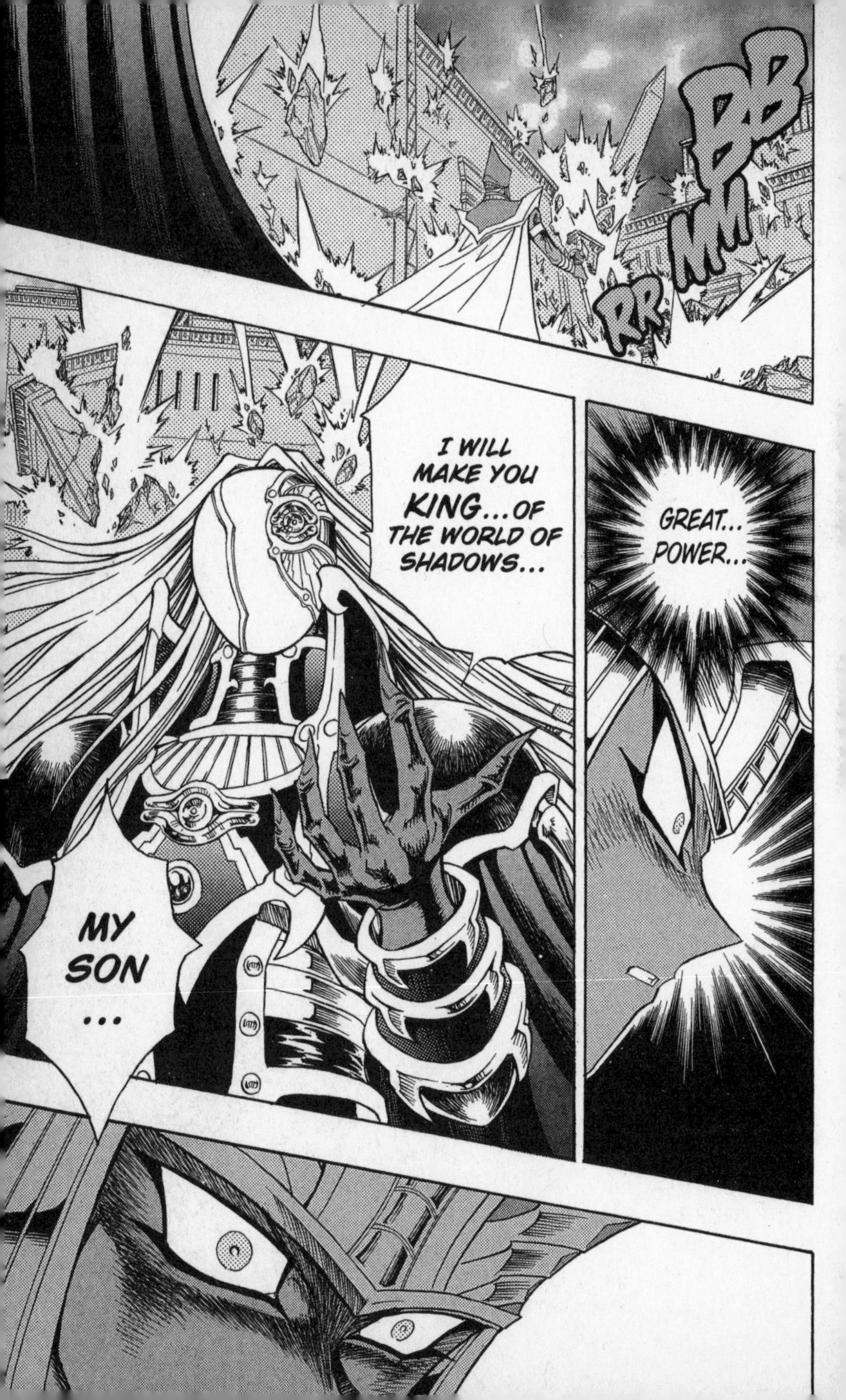
RRMMBB
GREAT... POWER...
I WILL MAKE YOU KING...OF THE WORLD OF SHADOWS...
MY SON ...

Duel 52: The Guardian God!

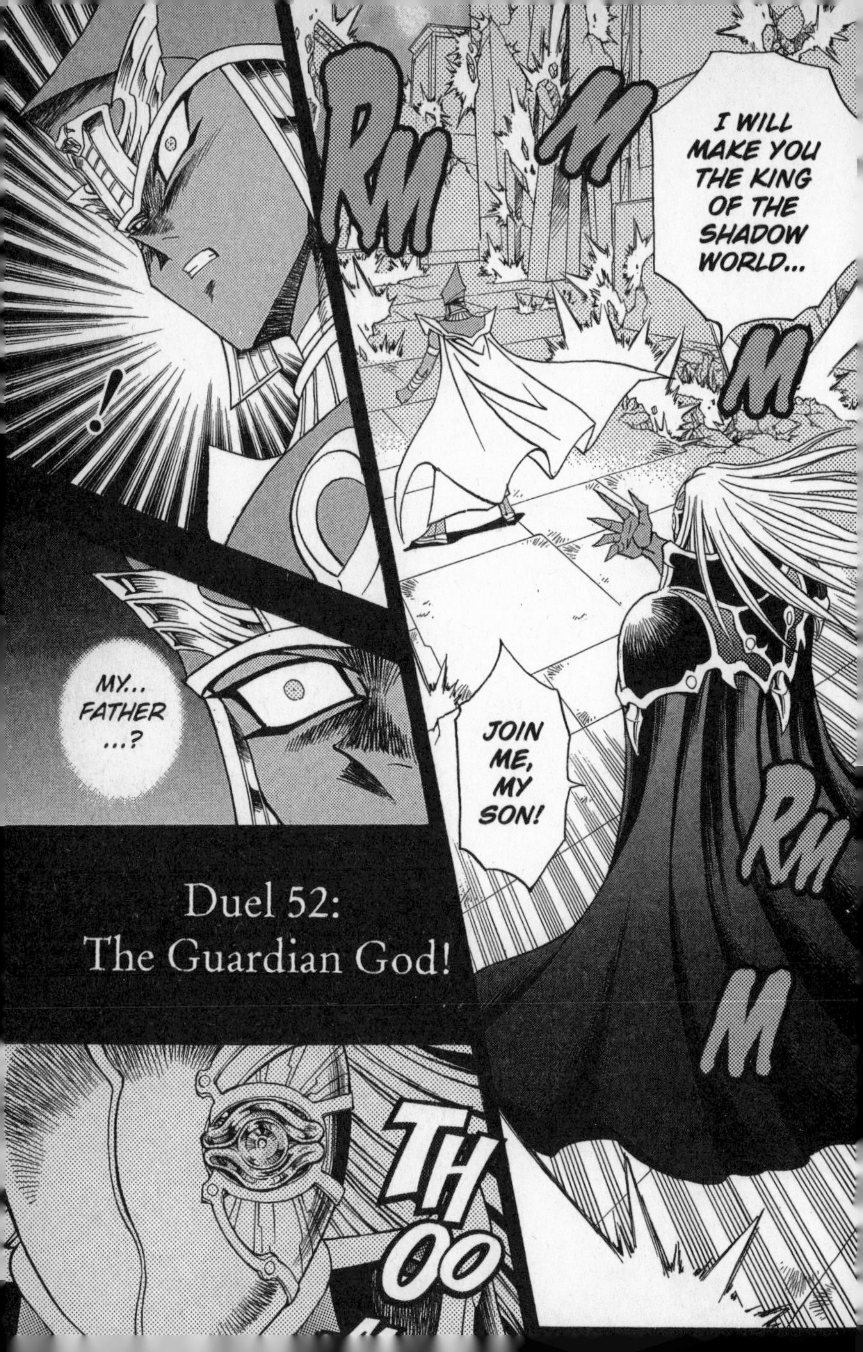
RMMM
I WILL MAKE YOU THE KING OF THE SHADOW WORLD...
JOIN ME, MY SON!
RMM
!
MY... FATHER ...?
THOO

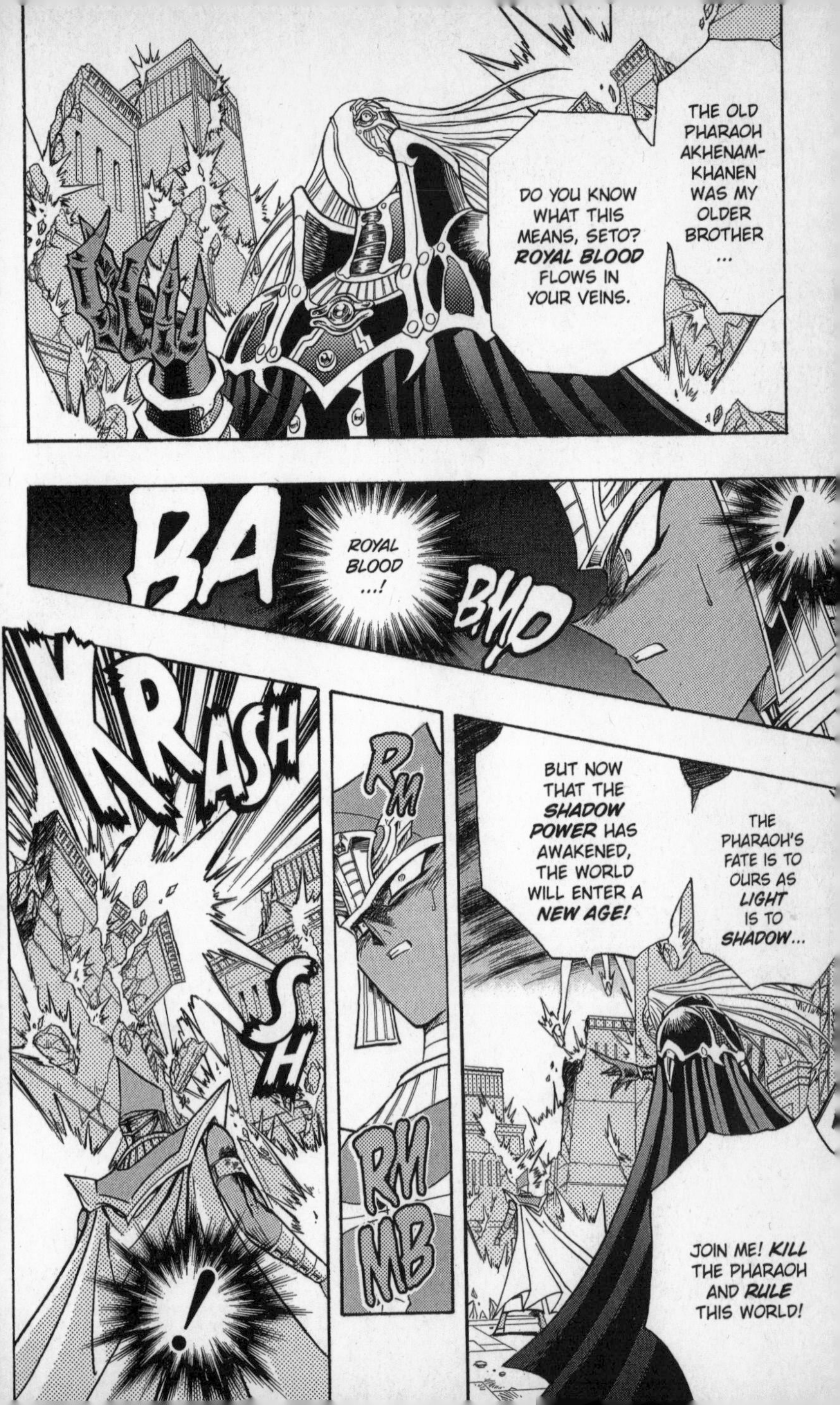
THE OLD PHARAOH AKHENAMKHANEN WAS MY OLDER BROTHER ...
DO YOU KNOW WHAT THIS MEANS, SETO? ROYAL BLOOD FLOWS IN YOUR VEINS.
!
ROYAL BLOOD ...!
BA
THE PHARAOH'S FATE IS TO OURS AS LIGHT IS TO SHADOW...
BUT NOW THAT THE SHADOW POWER HAS AWAKENED, THE WORLD WILL ENTER A NEW AGE!
JOIN ME! KILL THE PHARAOH AND RULE THIS WORLD!
RM
RMMB
KRASH
SH
!

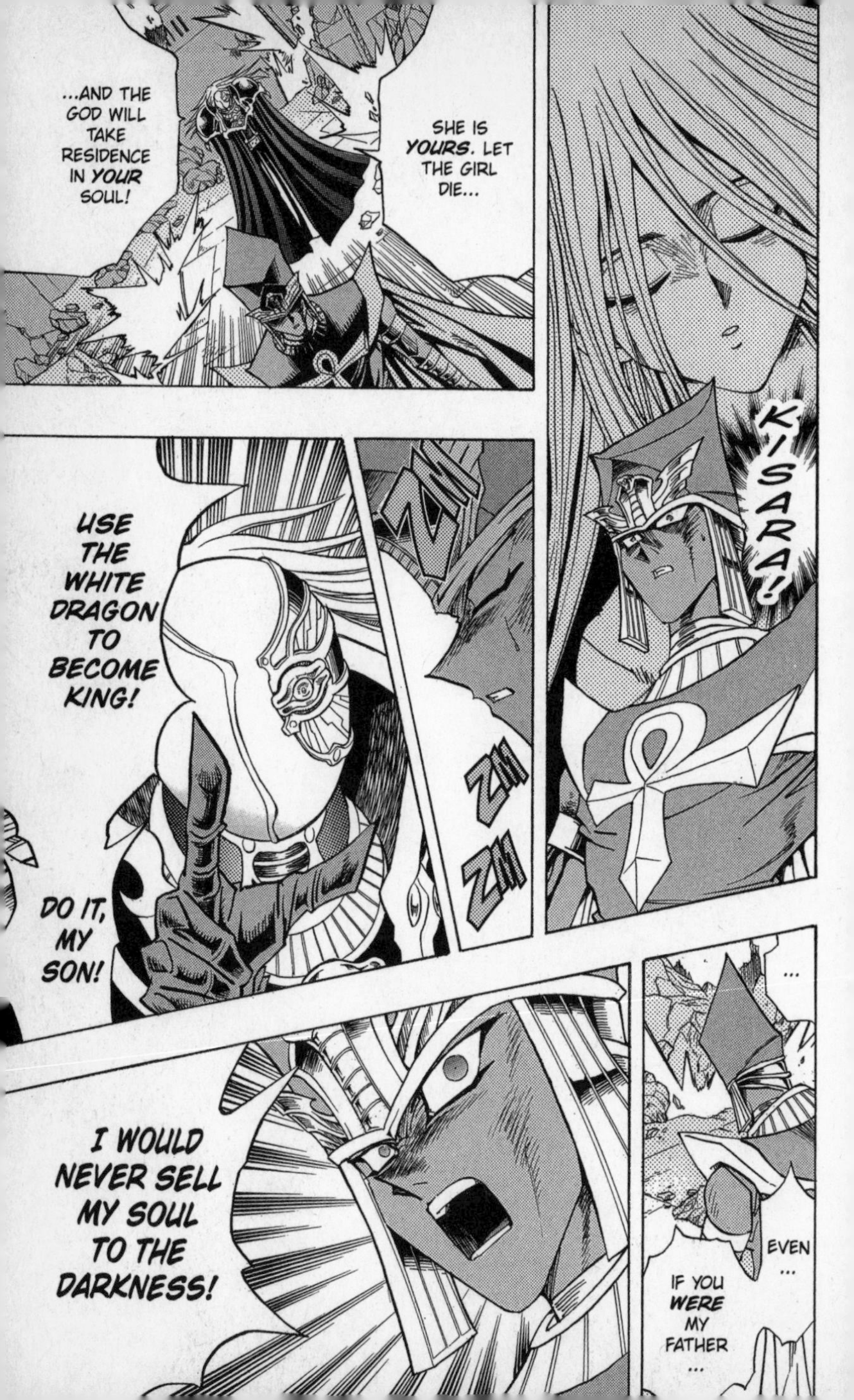
KISARA!
SHE IS YOURS. LET THE GIRL DIE...
...AND THE GOD WILL TAKE RESIDENCE IN YOUR SOUL!
ZM
ZM
ZM
USE THE WHITE DRAGON TO BECOME KING!
DO IT, MY SON!
...
EVEN...
IF YOU WERE MY FATHER...
I WOULD NEVER SELL MY SOUL TO THE DARKNESS!

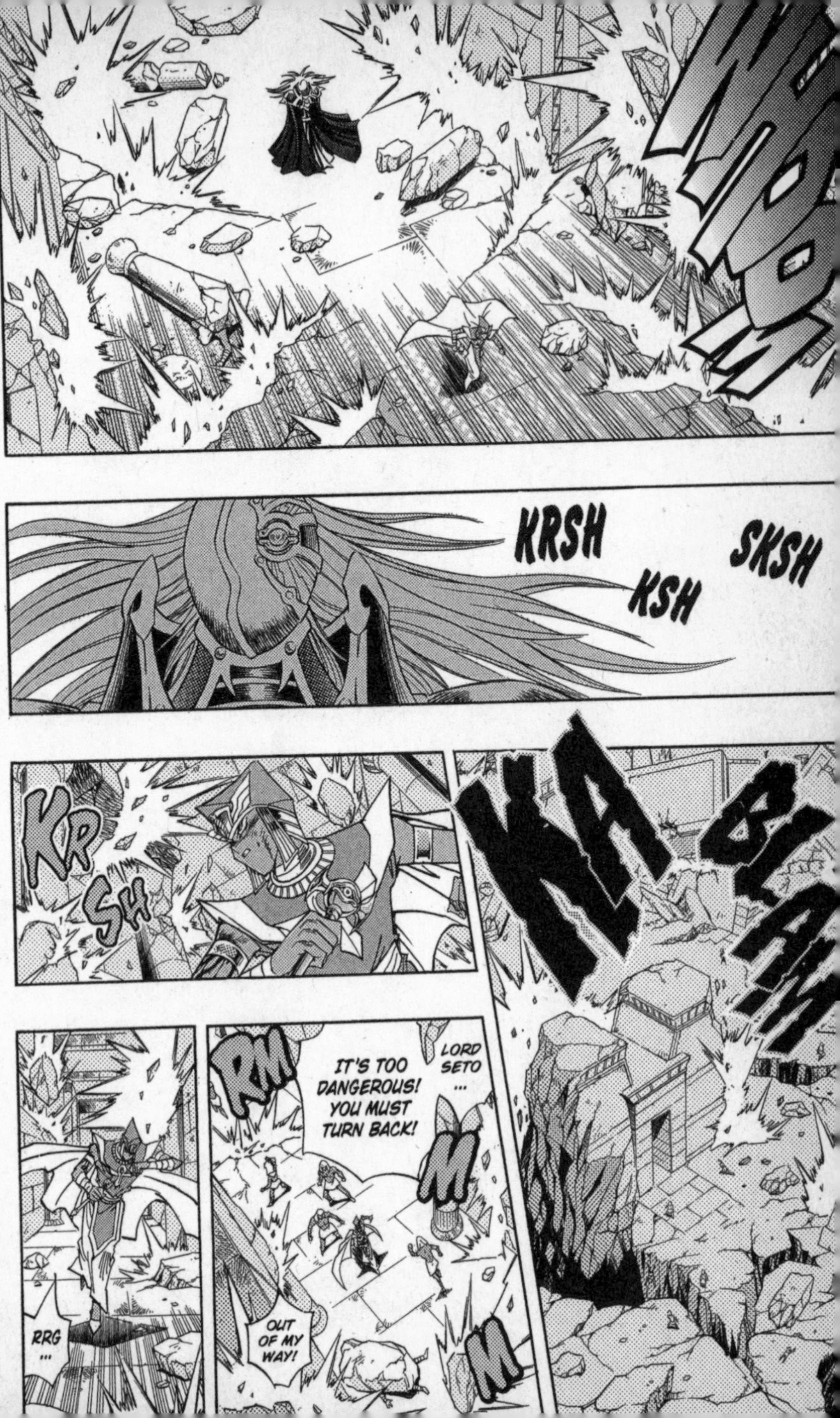
SKSH
KRSH
KSH
KA-BLAM
KRSH
LORD SETO ...
IT'S TOO DANGEROUS! YOU MUST TURN BACK!
RM
M
OUT OF MY WAY!
M
RRG ...

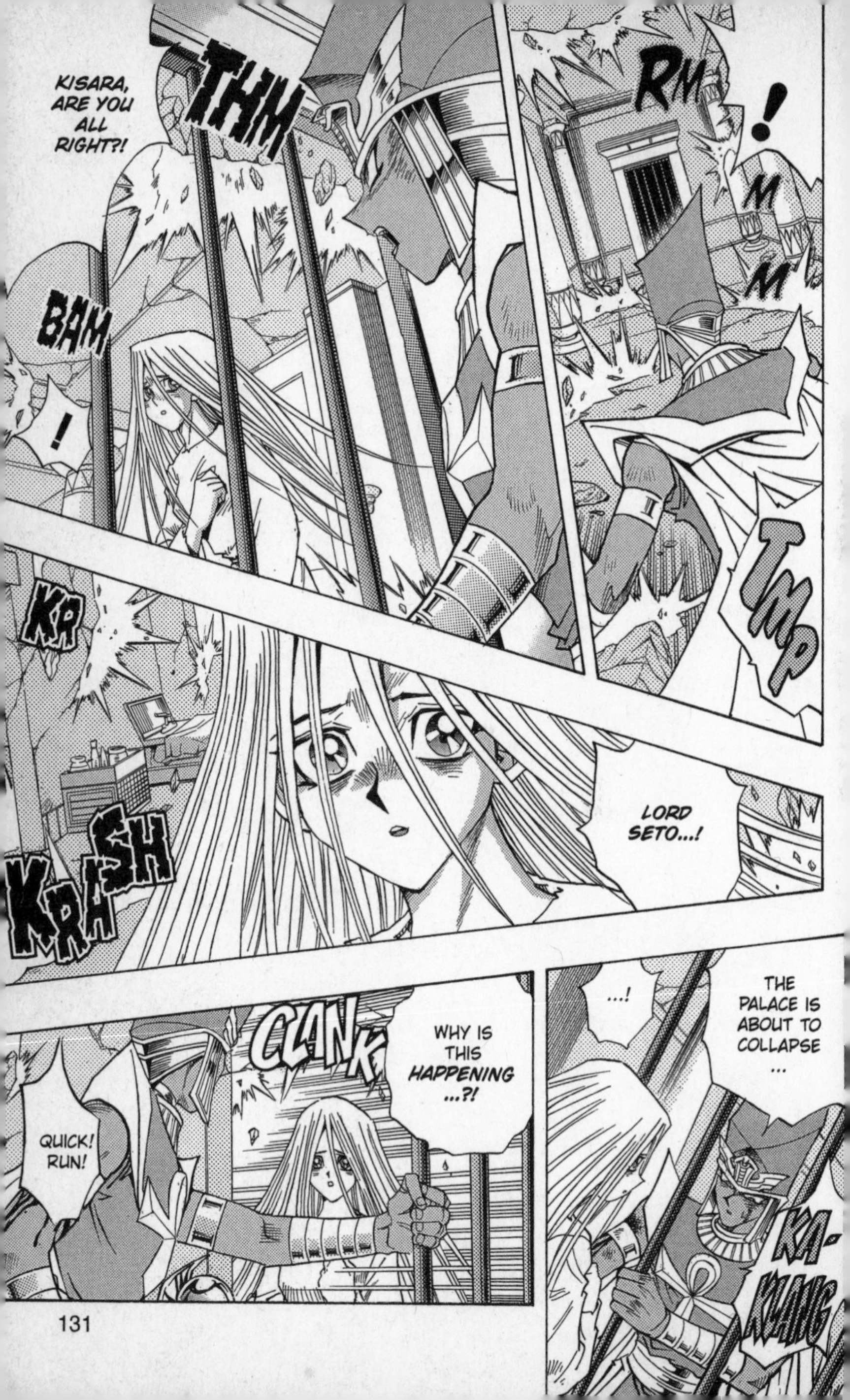
RMMM
!
TMP
THM
KISARA, ARE YOU ALL RIGHT?!
BAM
!
LORD SETO...!
KR
KRASH
THE PALACE IS ABOUT TO COLLAPSE ...
...!
KA-KLANG
WHY IS THIS HAPPENING ...?!
CLANK
QUICK! RUN!

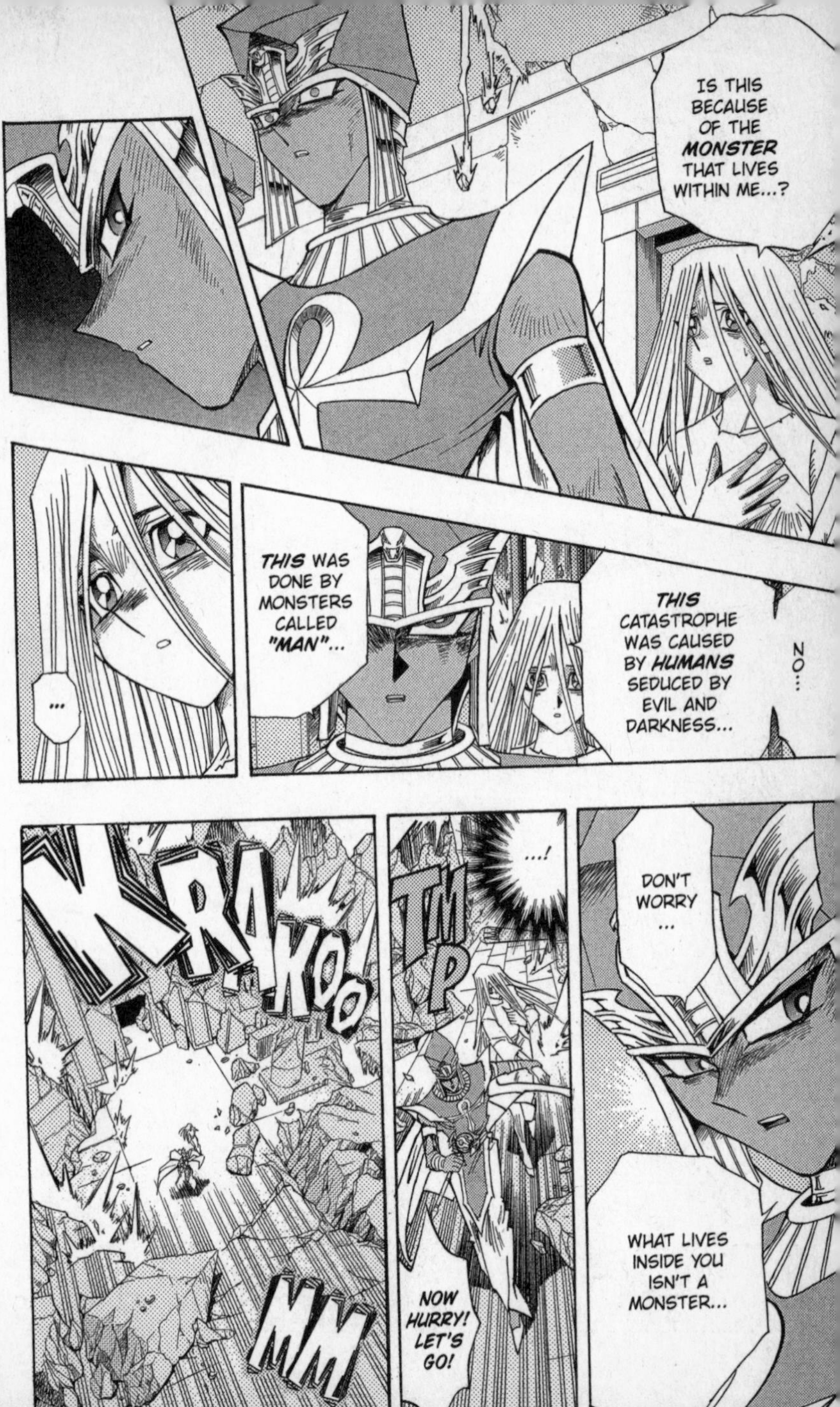
IS THIS BECAUSE OF THE MONSTER THAT LIVES WITHIN ME...?
NO...
THIS CATASTROPHE WAS CAUSED BY HUMANS SEDUCED BY EVIL AND DARKNESS...
THIS WAS DONE BY MONSTERS CALLED "MAN"...
...
DON'T WORRY...
WHAT LIVES INSIDE YOU ISN'T A MONSTER...
...!
TMP
NOW HURRY! LET'S GO!
KRAKOOMM

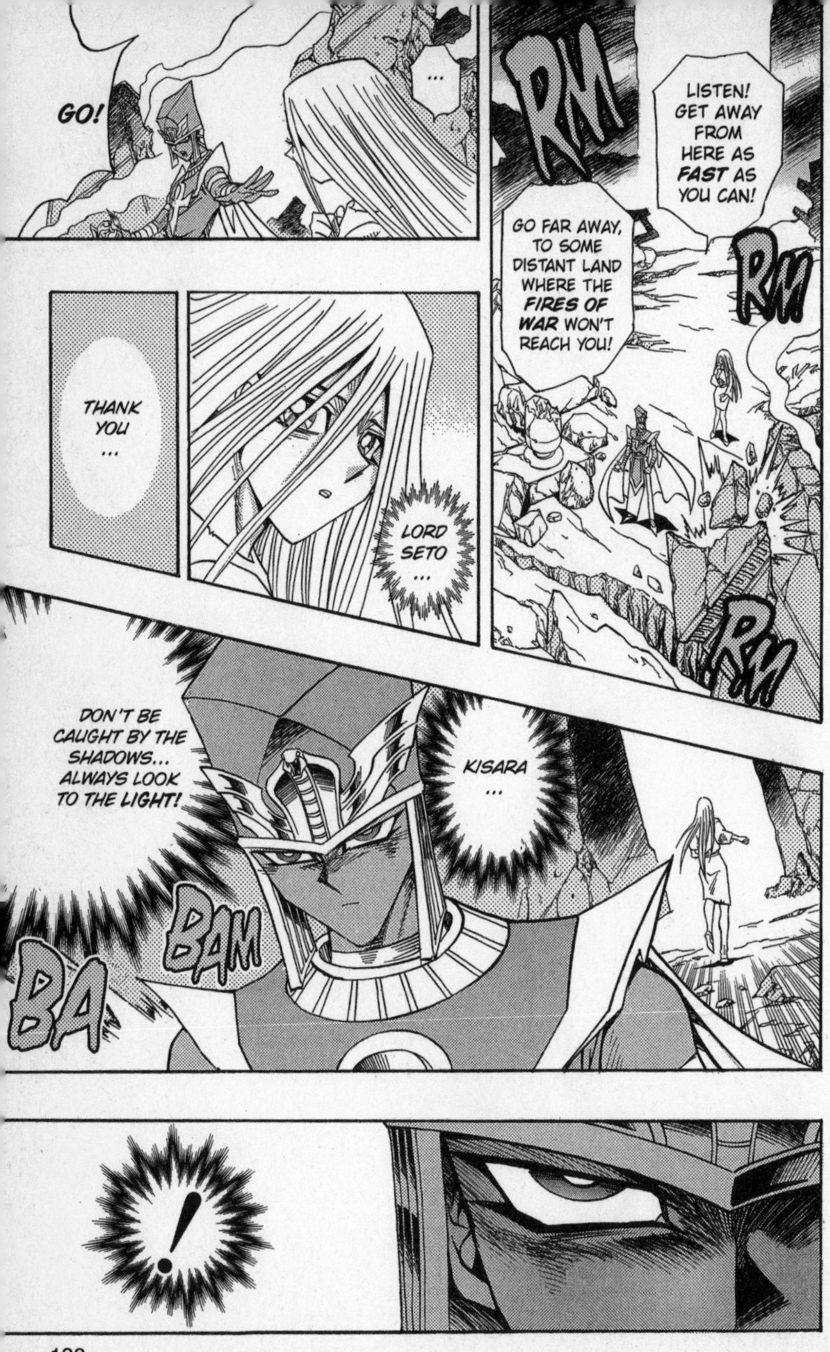
RM
LISTEN! GET AWAY FROM HERE AS FAST AS YOU CAN!
GO FAR AWAY, TO SOME DISTANT LAND WHERE THE FIRES OF WAR WON'T REACH YOU!
RM
RM
...
GO!
LORD SETO ...
THANK YOU ...
KISARA ...
DON'T BE CAUGHT BY THE SHADOWS... ALWAYS LOOK TO THE LIGHT!
BAM
BA
!

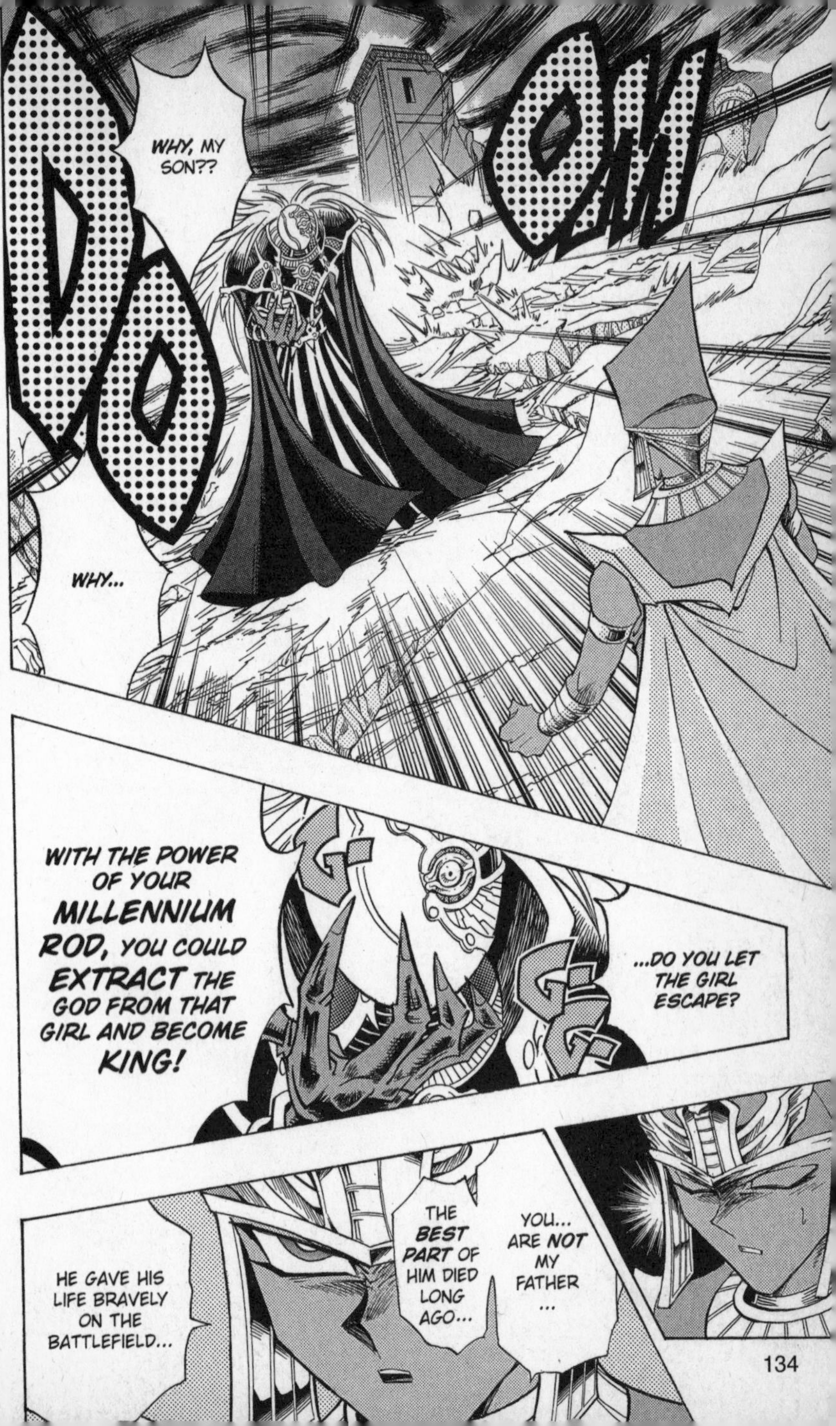
DOOM
WHY, MY SON??
WHY...
...DO YOU LET THE GIRL ESCAPE?
WITH THE POWER OF YOUR **MILLENNIUM ROD,** YOU COULD **EXTRACT** THE GOD FROM THAT GIRL AND BECOME **KING!**
YOU... ARE ***NOT*** MY FATHER ...
THE ***BEST PART*** OF HIM DIED LONG AGO...
HE GAVE HIS LIFE BRAVELY ON THE BATTLEFIELD...

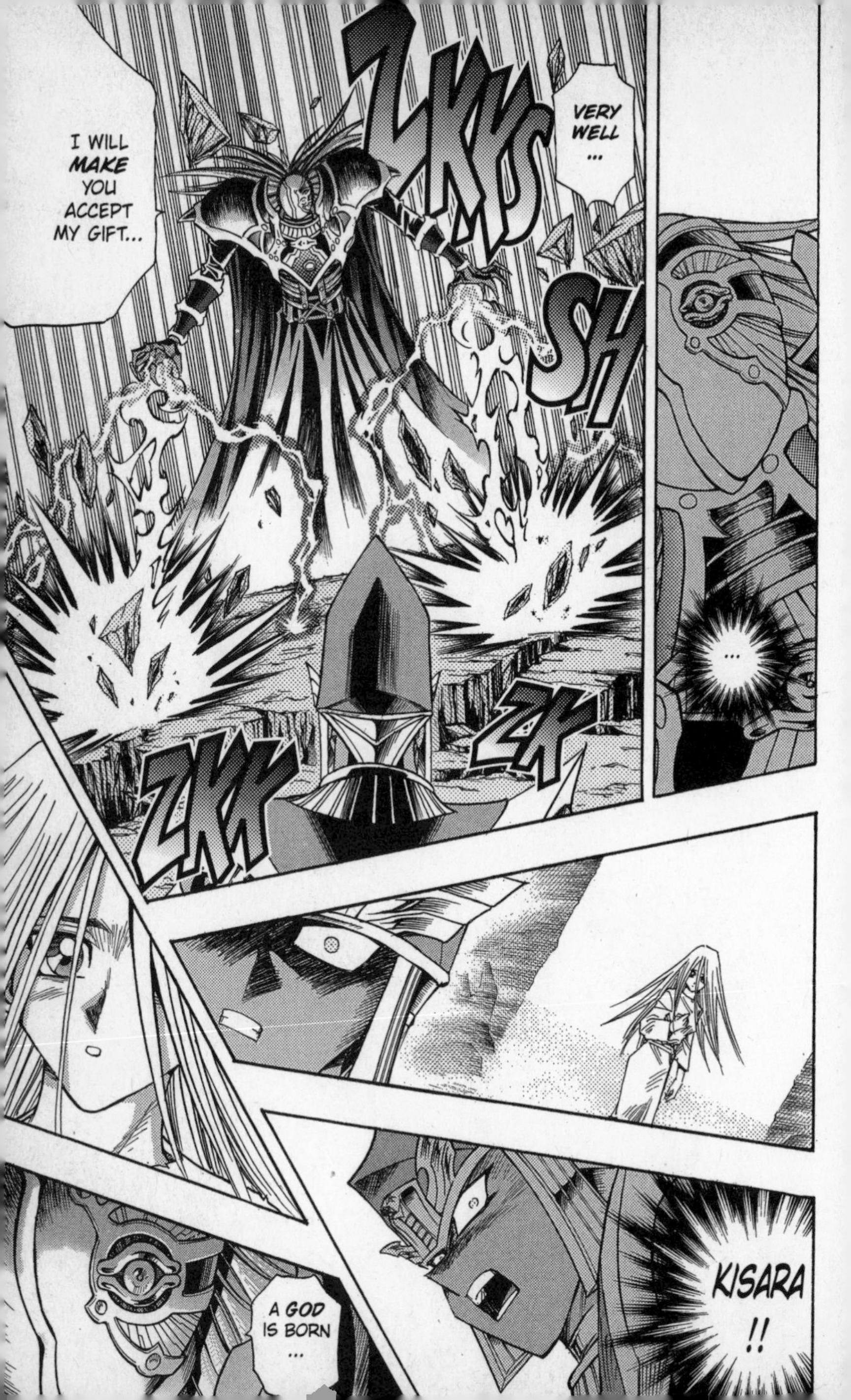
...
VERY WELL ...
ZKYS
I WILL MAKE YOU ACCEPT MY GIFT...
SH
ZK
ZKK
KISARA !!
A GOD IS BORN ...

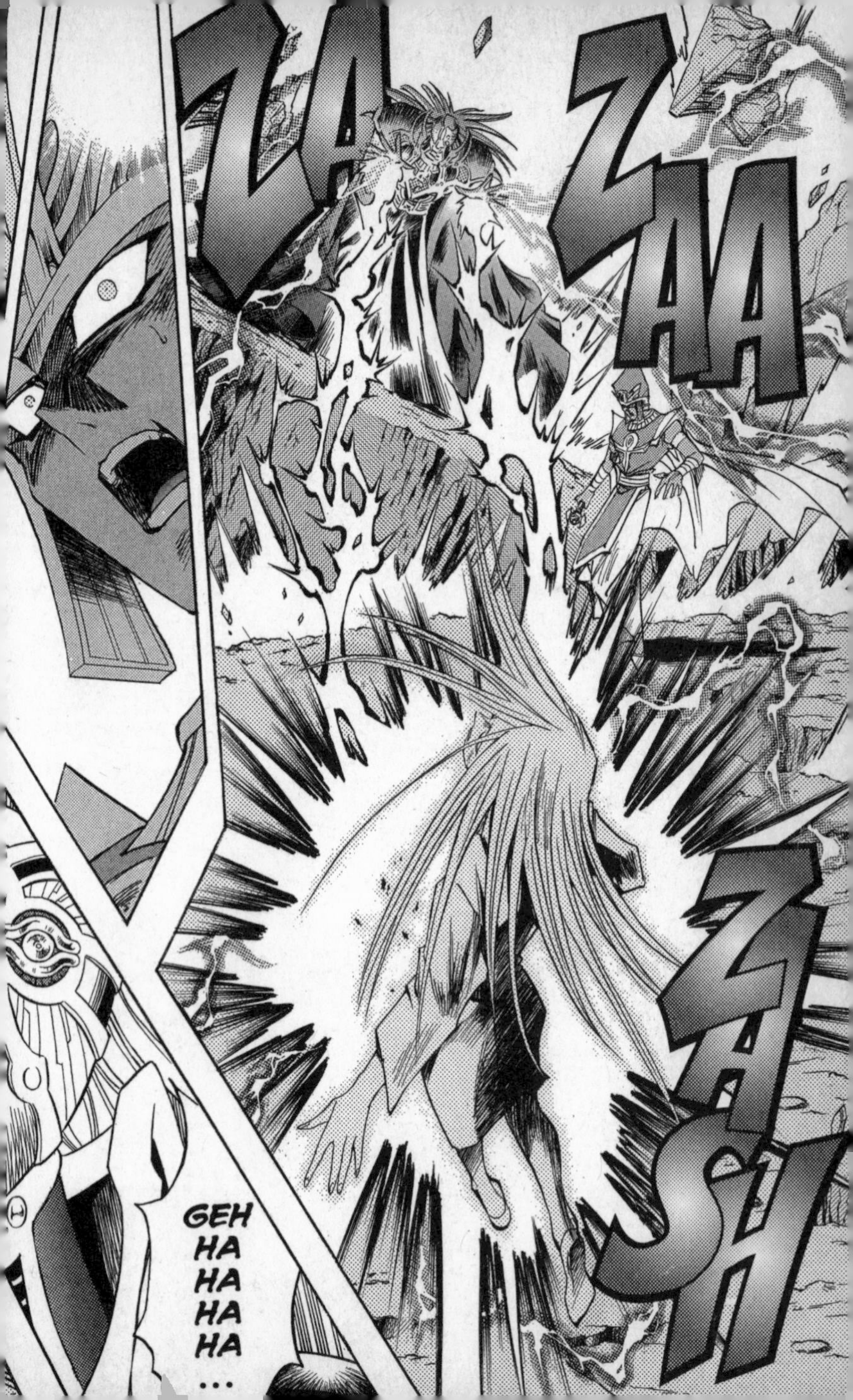
ZA ZAA
ZAZASH
GEH HA HA HA HA...

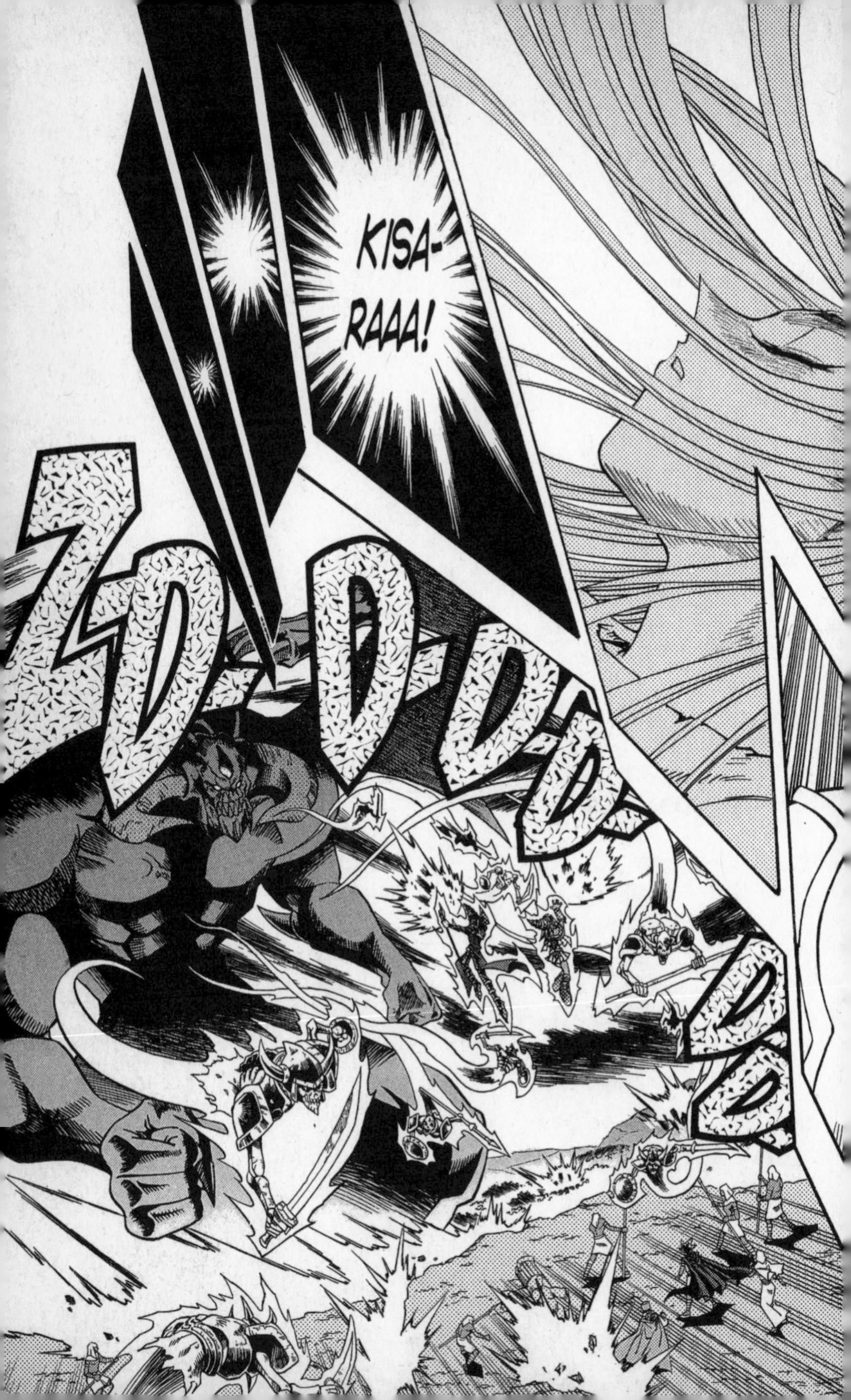
KISA-
RAAA!
ZDDDDDDDD

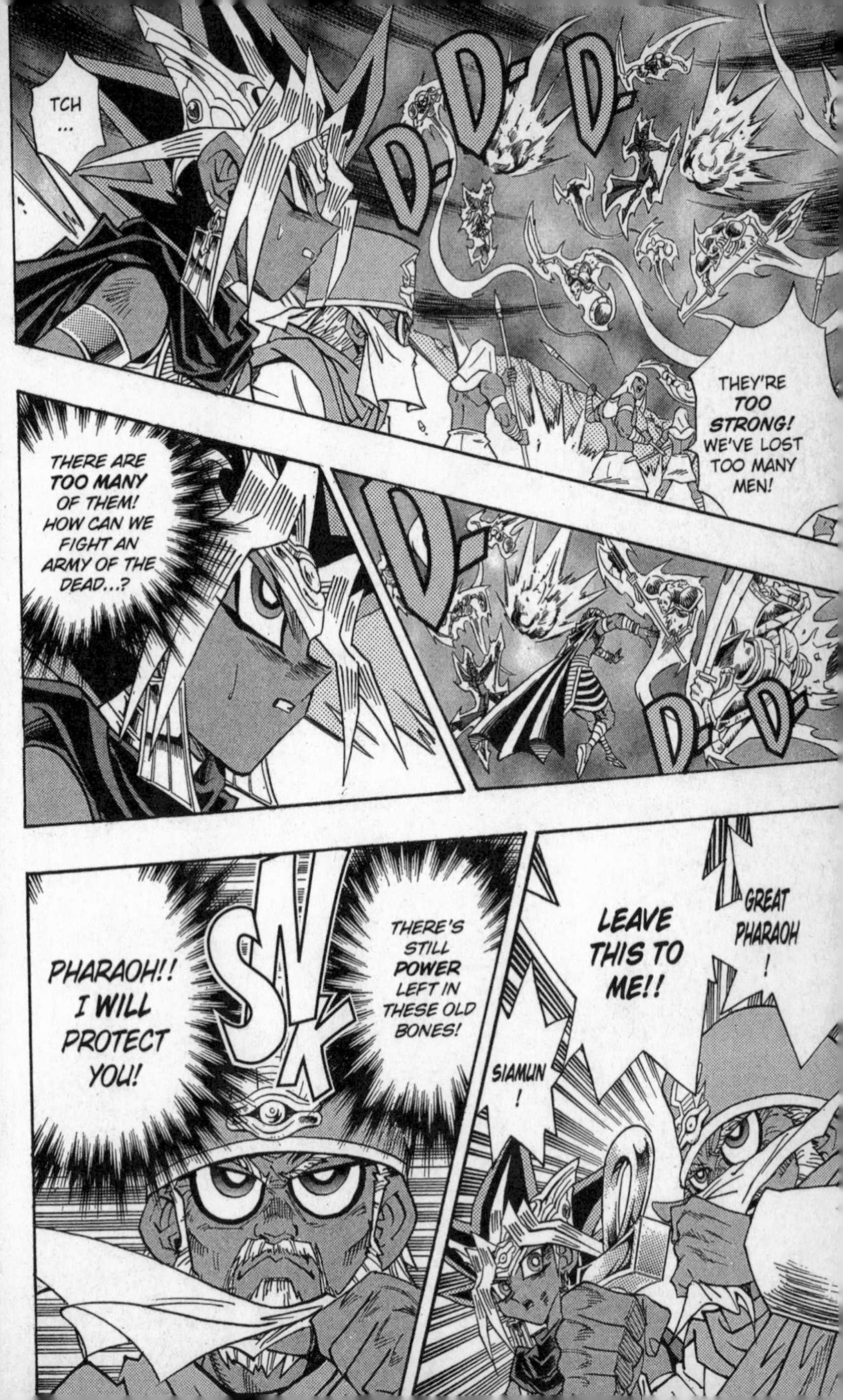
D-D-D-D
THEY'RE TOO STRONG! WE'VE LOST TOO MANY MEN!
TCH ...
D-D-D-D
THERE ARE TOO MANY OF THEM! HOW CAN WE FIGHT AN ARMY OF THE DEAD...?
GREAT PHARAOH!
LEAVE THIS TO ME!!
SIAMUN!
THERE'S STILL POWER LEFT IN THESE OLD BONES!
SK
PHARAOH!! I WILL PROTECT YOU!

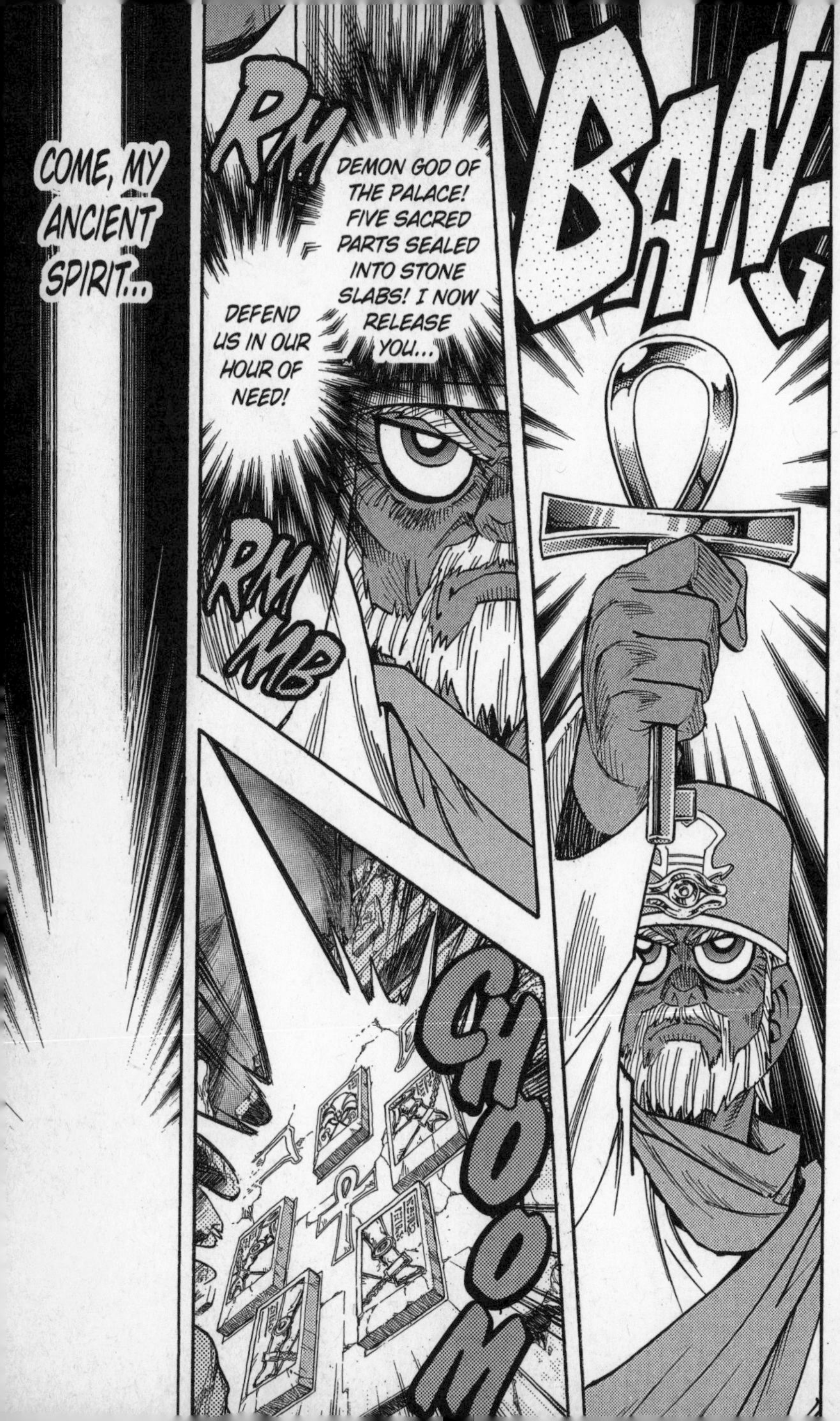
BANG
RM
DEMON GOD OF THE PALACE! FIVE SACRED PARTS SEALED INTO STONE SLABS! I NOW RELEASE YOU...
DEFEND US IN OUR HOUR OF NEED!
RMMB
CHOOOM
COME, MY ANCIENT SPIRIT...

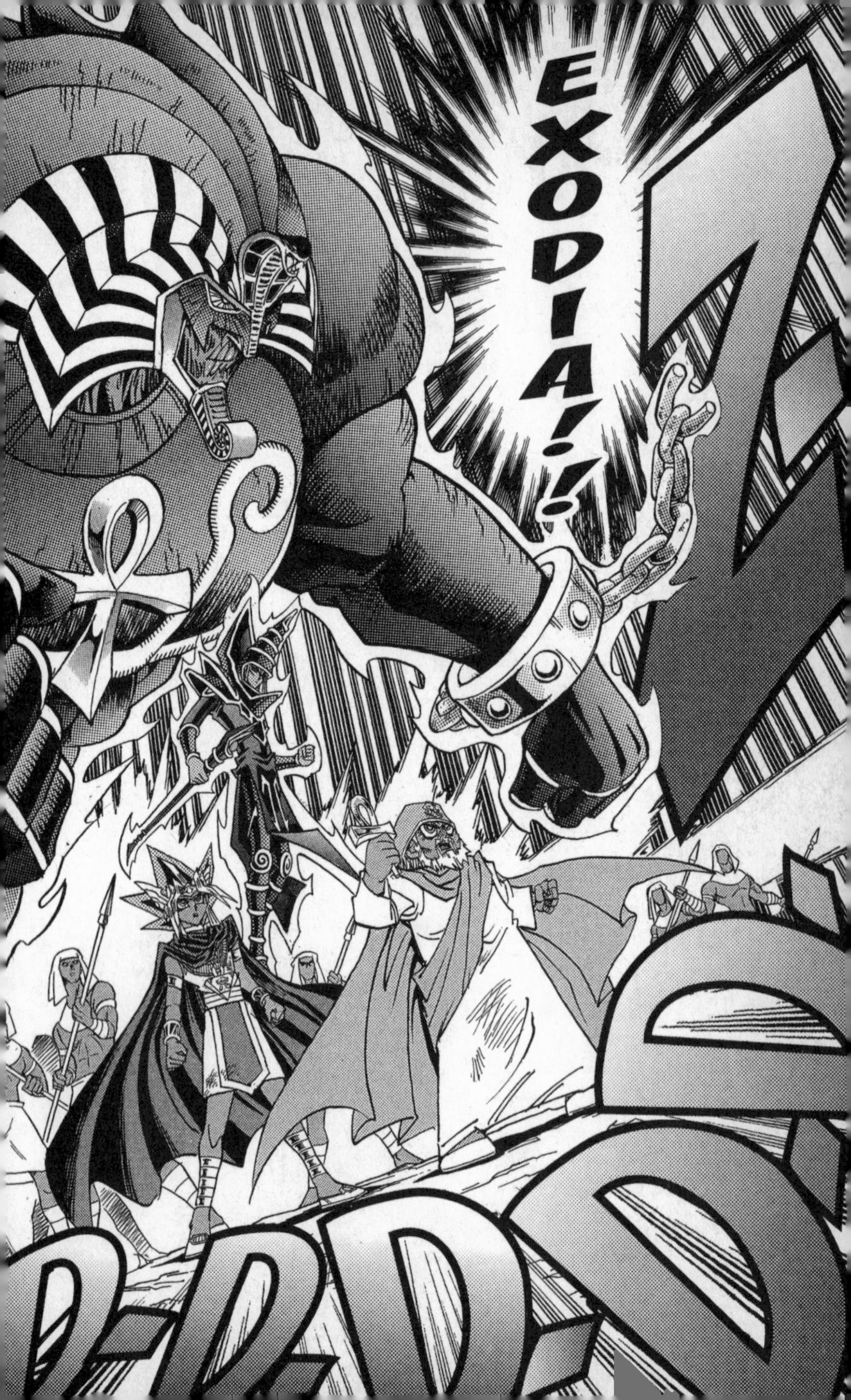
EXODIA!!

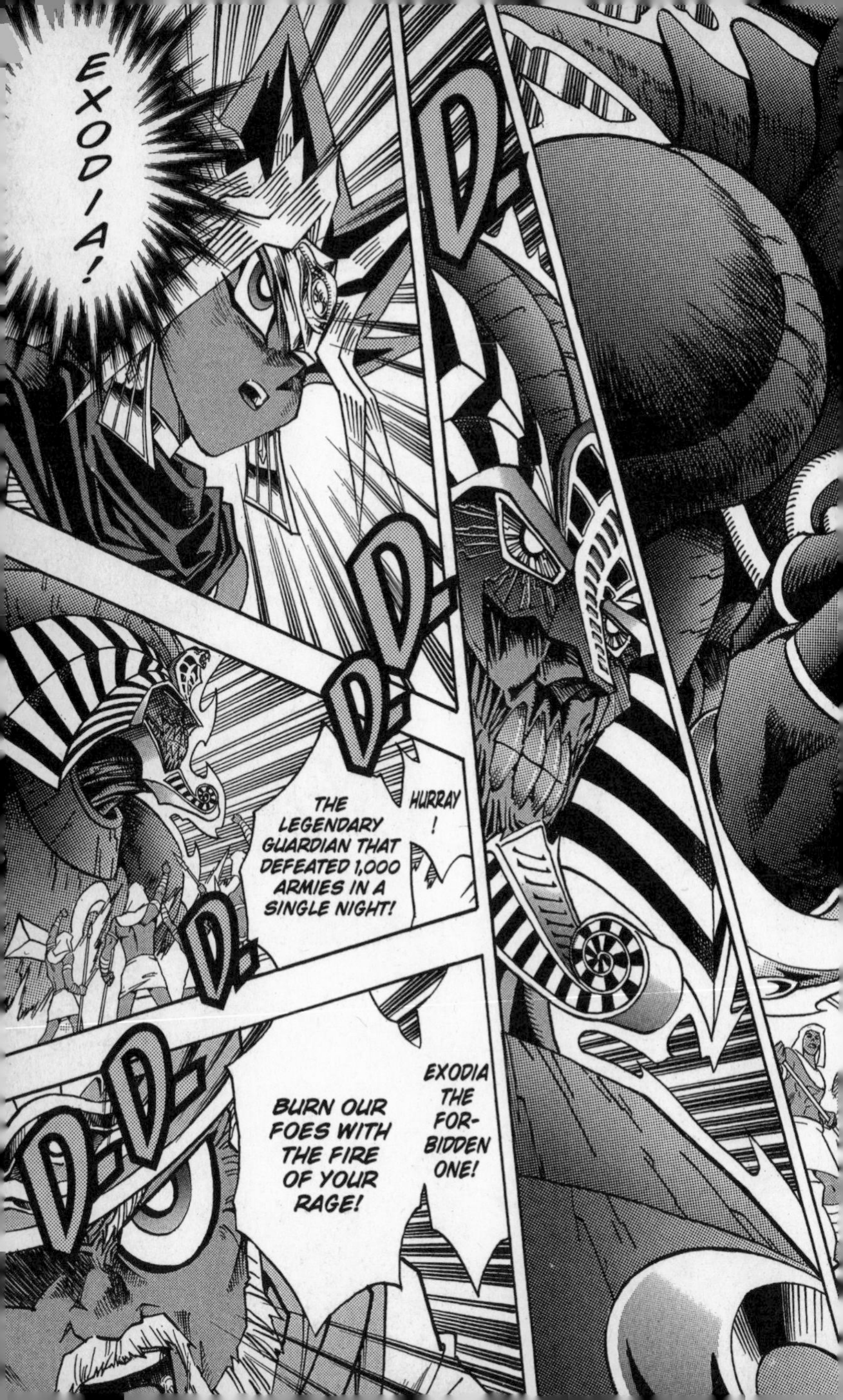
EXODIA!
HURRAY!
THE LEGENDARY GUARDIAN THAT DEFEATED 1,000 ARMIES IN A SINGLE NIGHT!
EXODIA THE FOR-BIDDEN ONE!
BURN OUR FOES WITH THE FIRE OF YOUR RAGE!

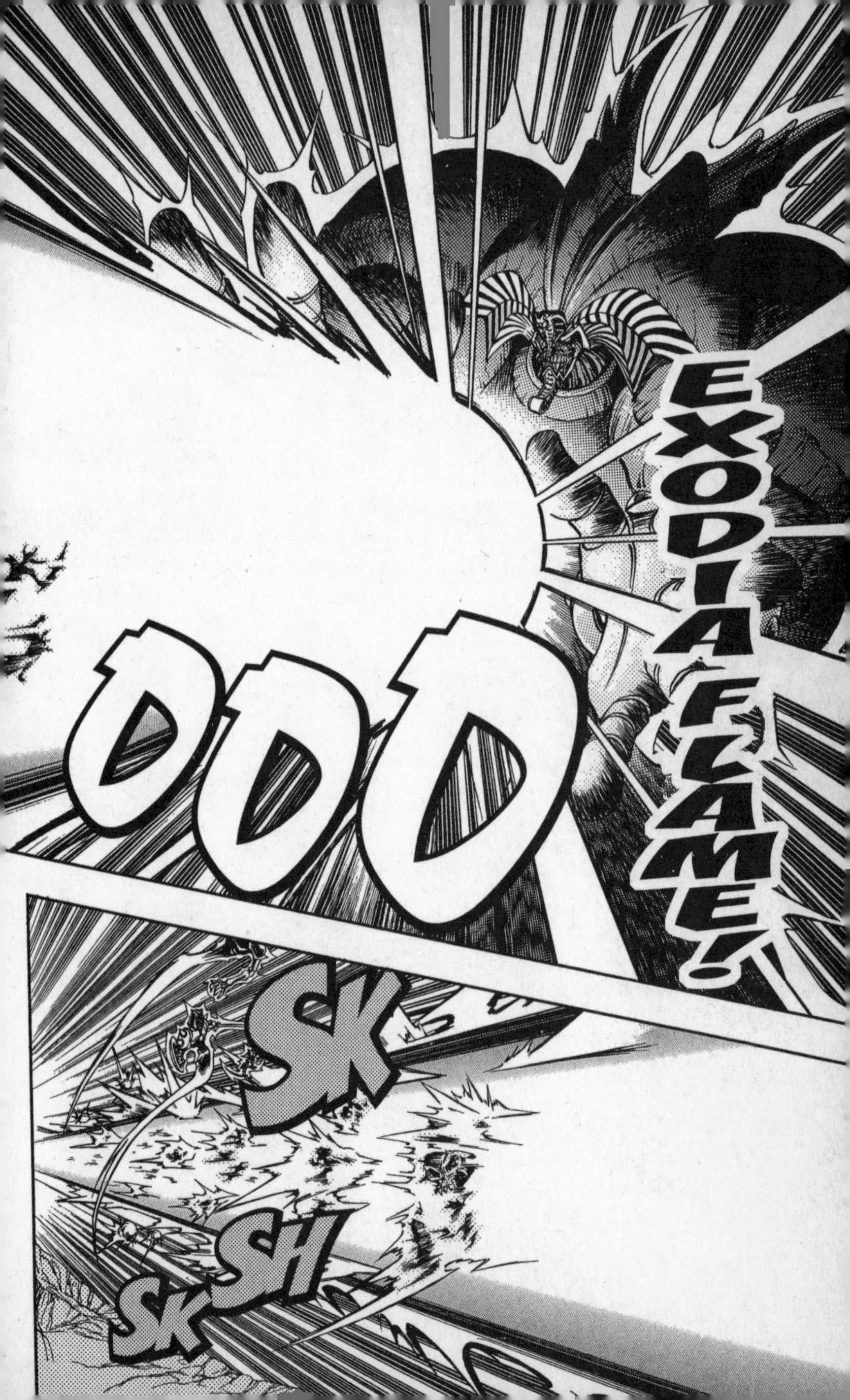
EXODIA FLAME!
DDD
SK
SKSH

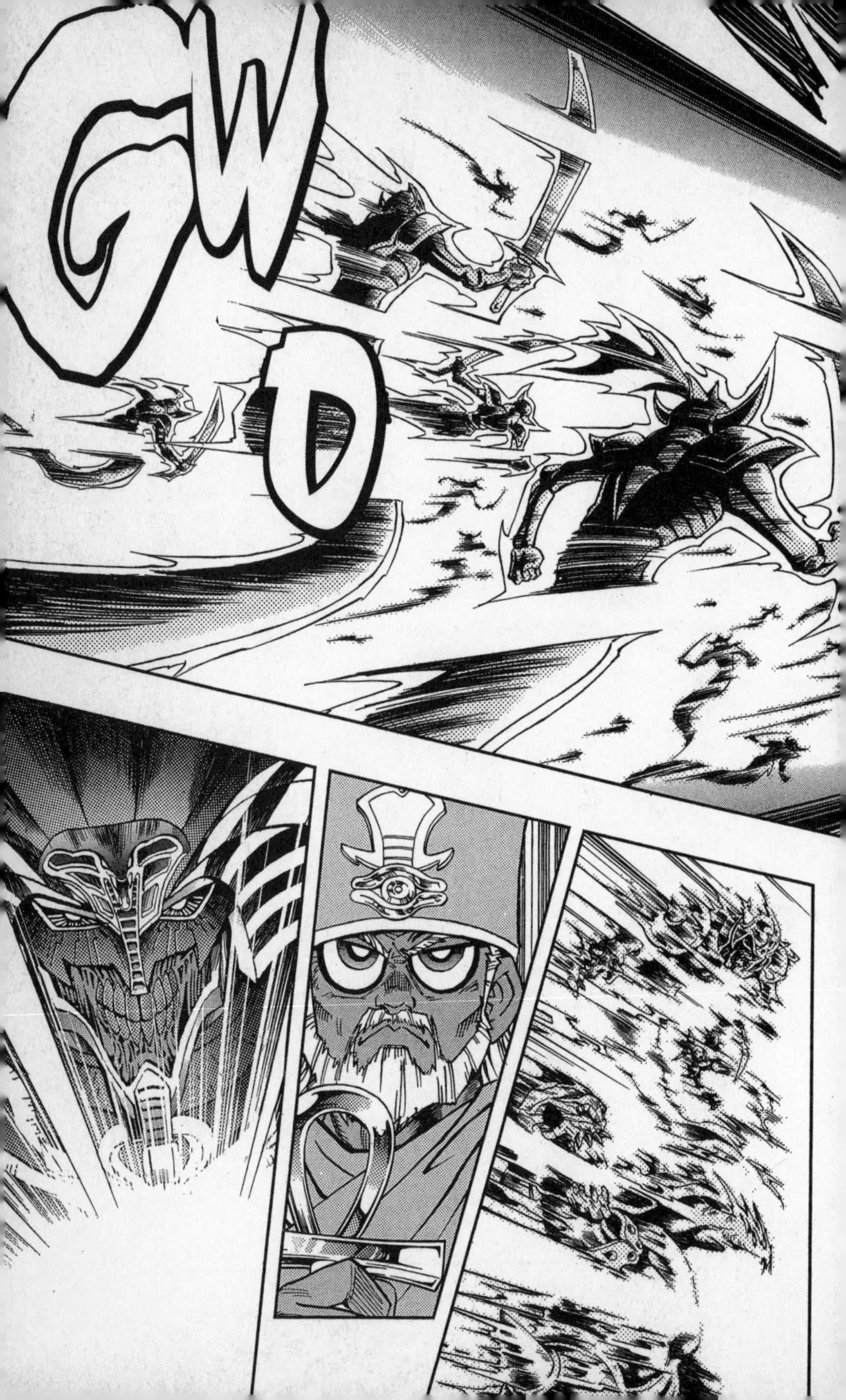
GW
D

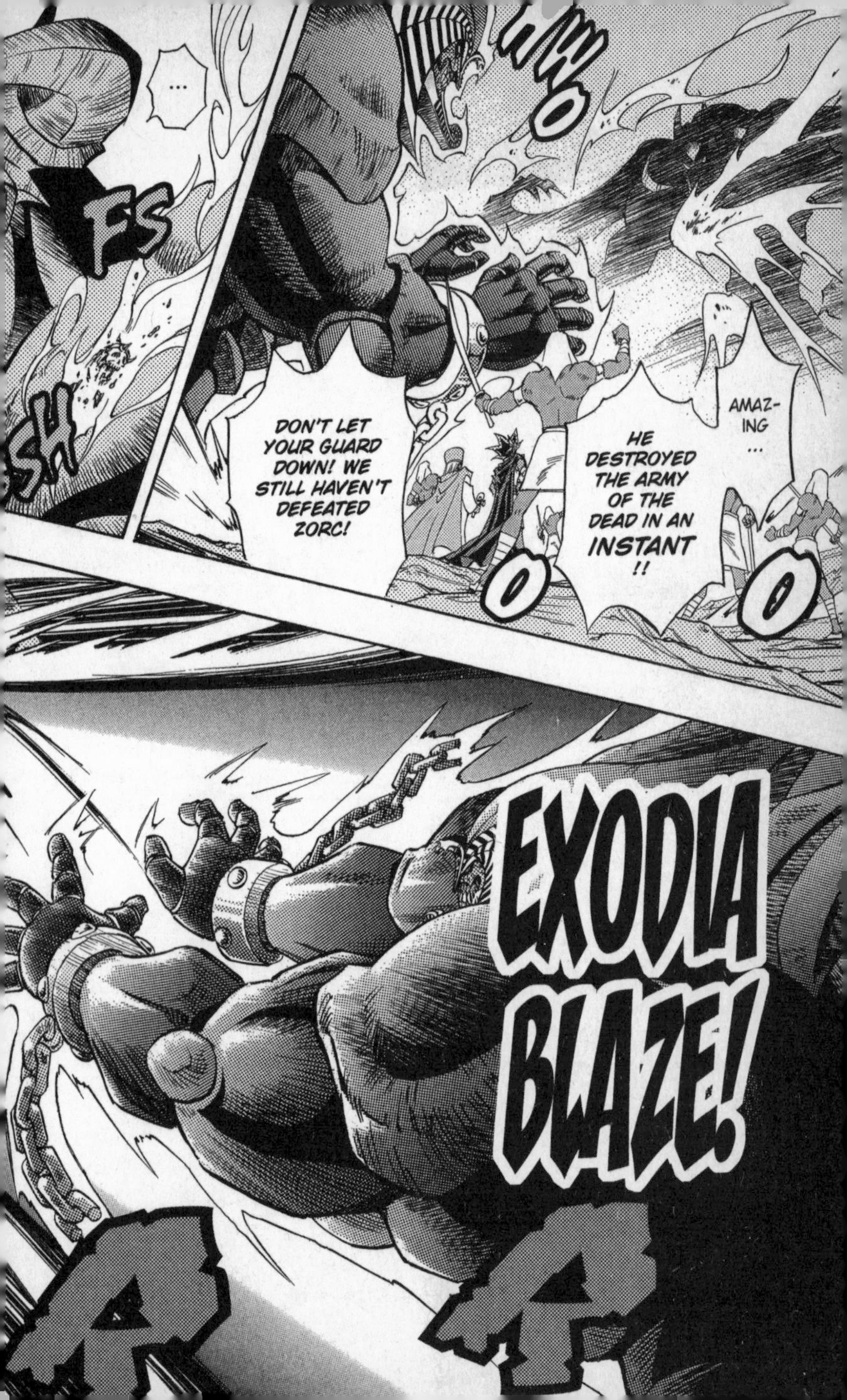

WHO
AMAZ-
ING
...
HE DESTROYED THE ARMY OF THE DEAD IN AN INSTANT !!
O
O
DON'T LET YOUR GUARD DOWN! WE STILL HAVEN'T DEFEATED ZORC!
...
FSSH
EXODIA BLAZE!

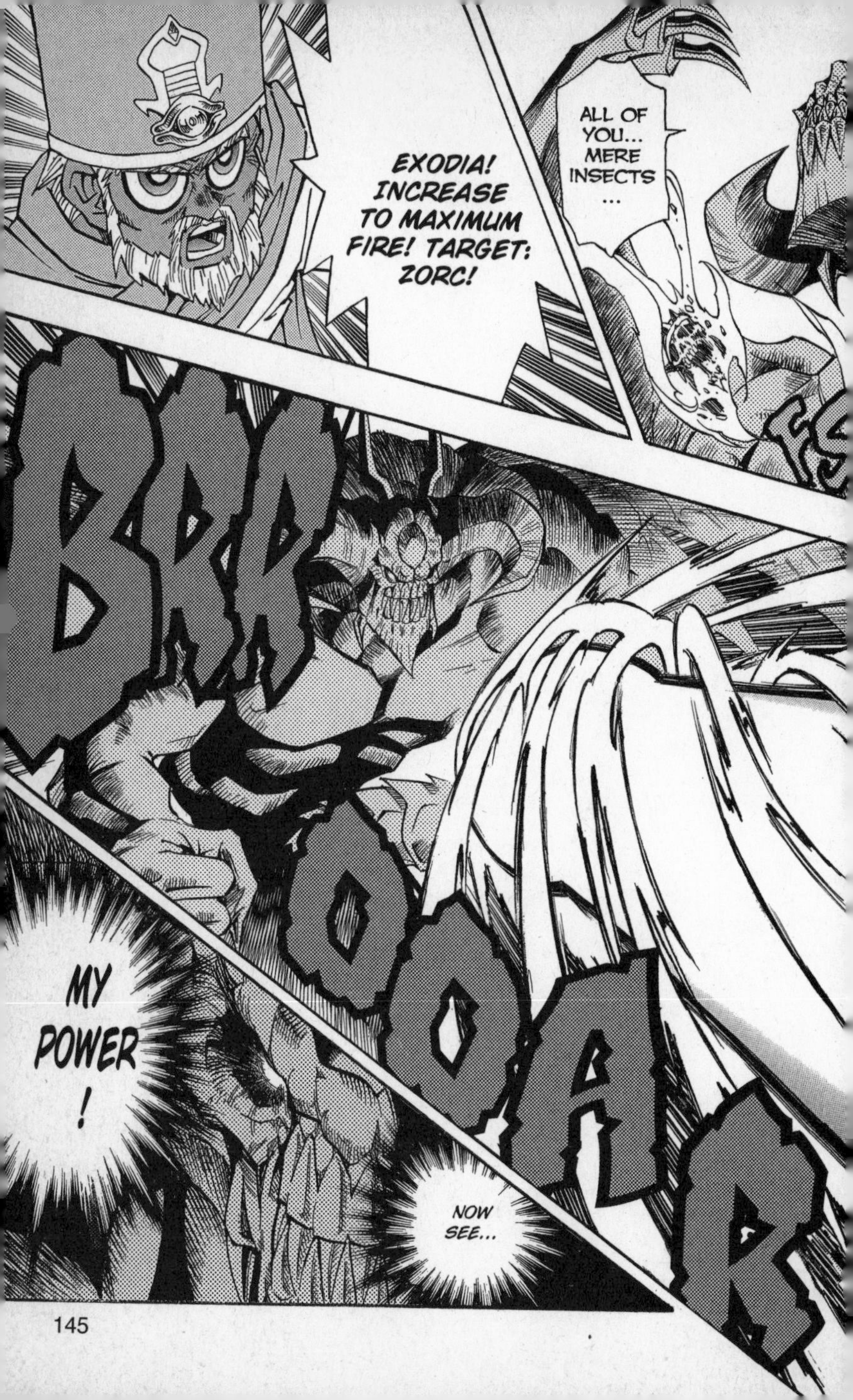
ALL OF YOU... MERE INSECTS ...
EXODIA! INCREASE TO MAXIMUM FIRE! TARGET: ZORC!
BRROOAR
NOW SEE...
MY POWER !

Duel 53: The Light of the Soul!

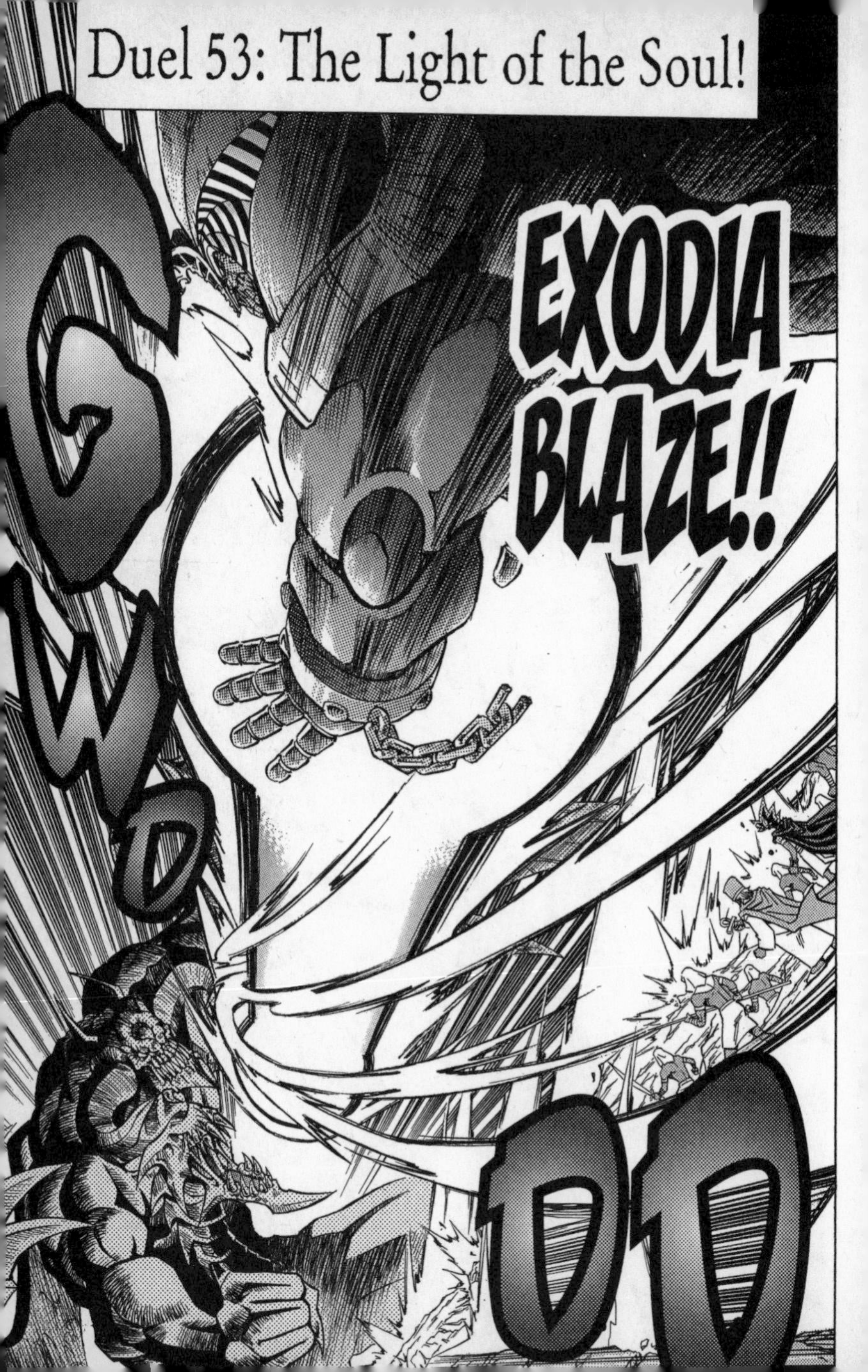
EXODIA BLAZE!!

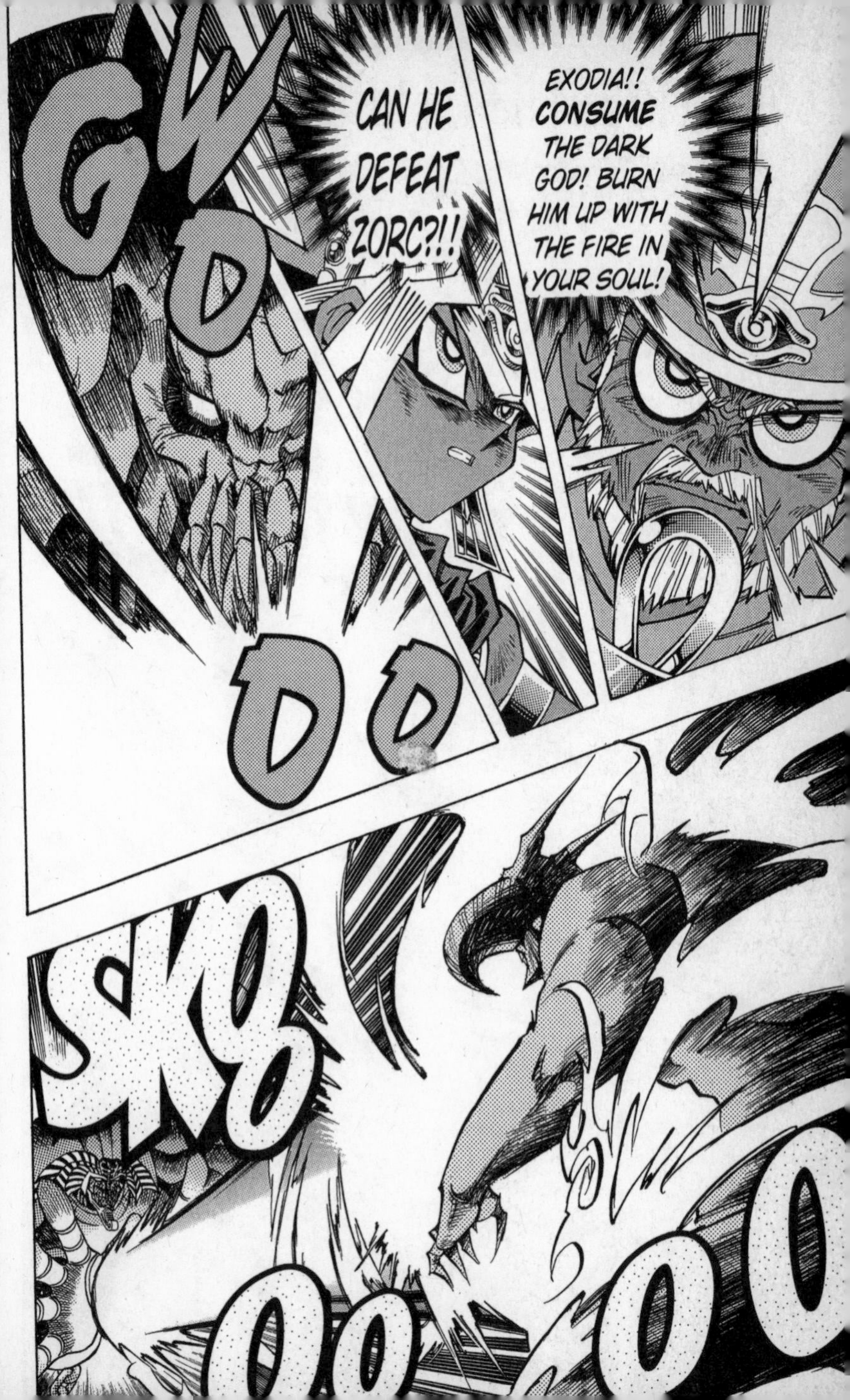
EXODIA!! CONSUME THE DARK GOD! BURN HIM UP WITH THE FIRE IN YOUR SOUL!
CAN HE DEFEAT ZORC?!!
GWOOO

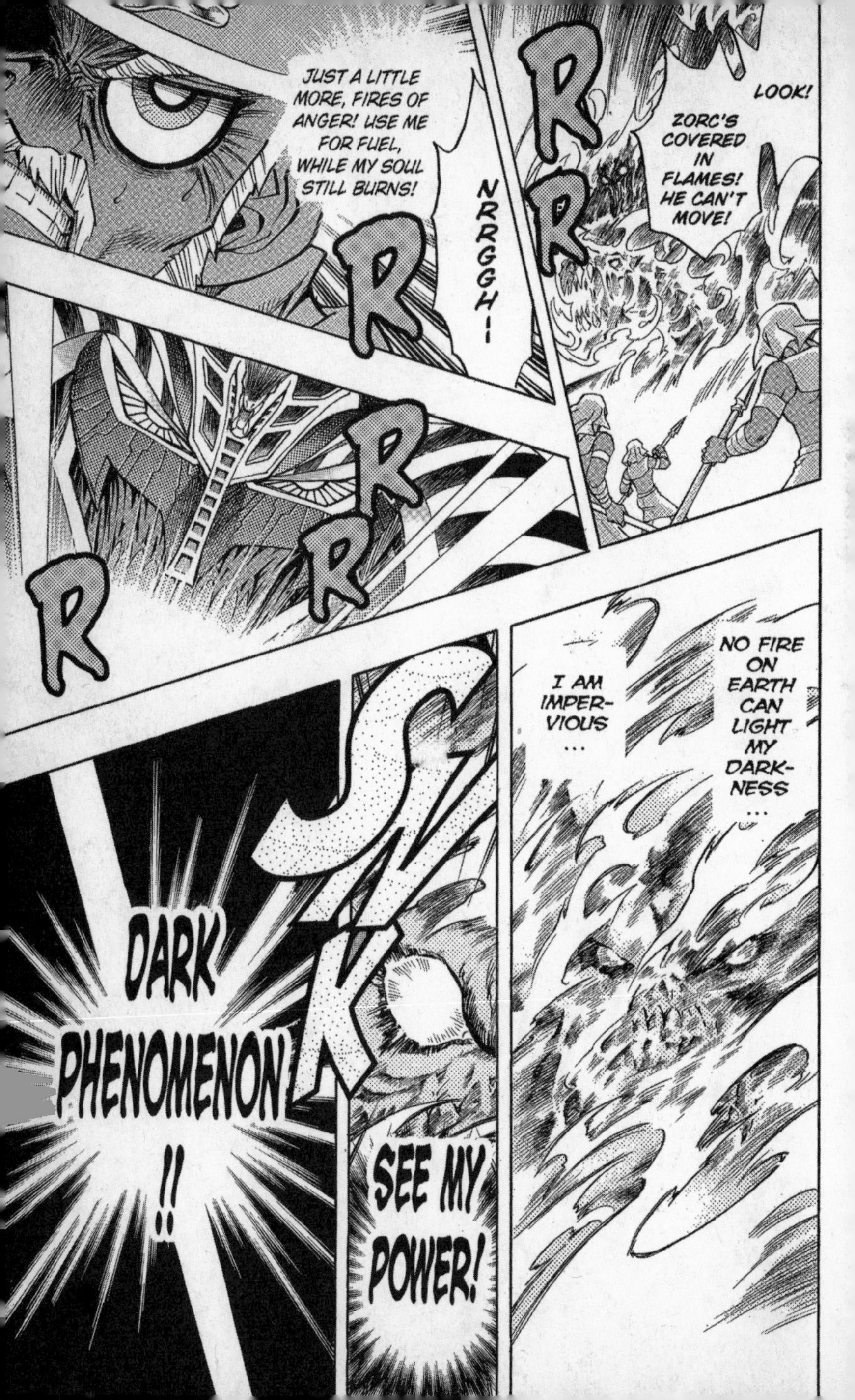
LOOK!
ZORC'S COVERED IN FLAMES! HE CAN'T MOVE!
R
R
JUST A LITTLE MORE, FIRES OF ANGER! USE ME FOR FUEL, WHILE MY SOUL STILL BURNS!
NRRGGH!!
R
R
R
R
NO FIRE ON EARTH CAN LIGHT MY DARKNESS...
I AM IMPERVIOUS...
SEE MY POWER!
DARK PHENOMENON!!

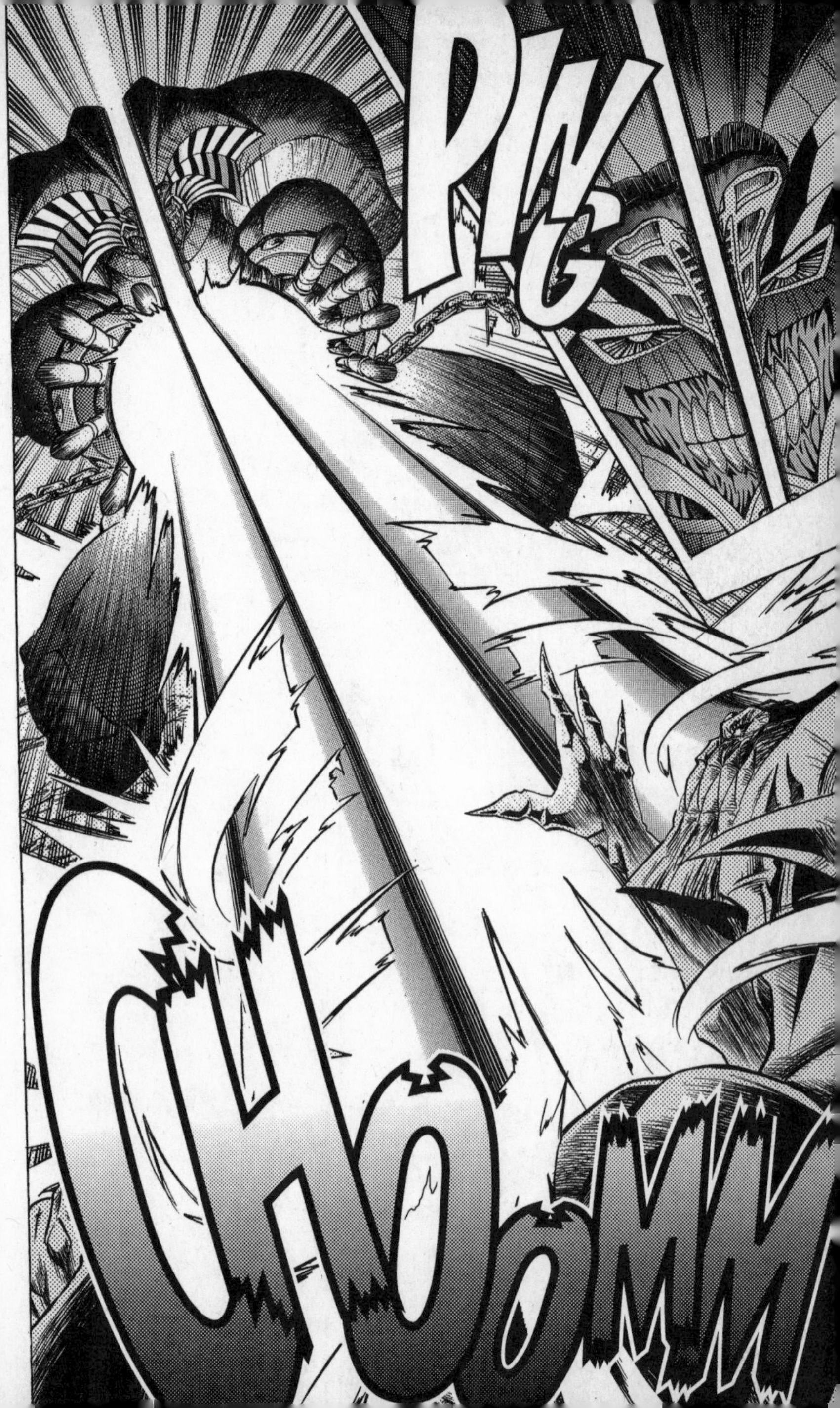
PING
CHOOMM

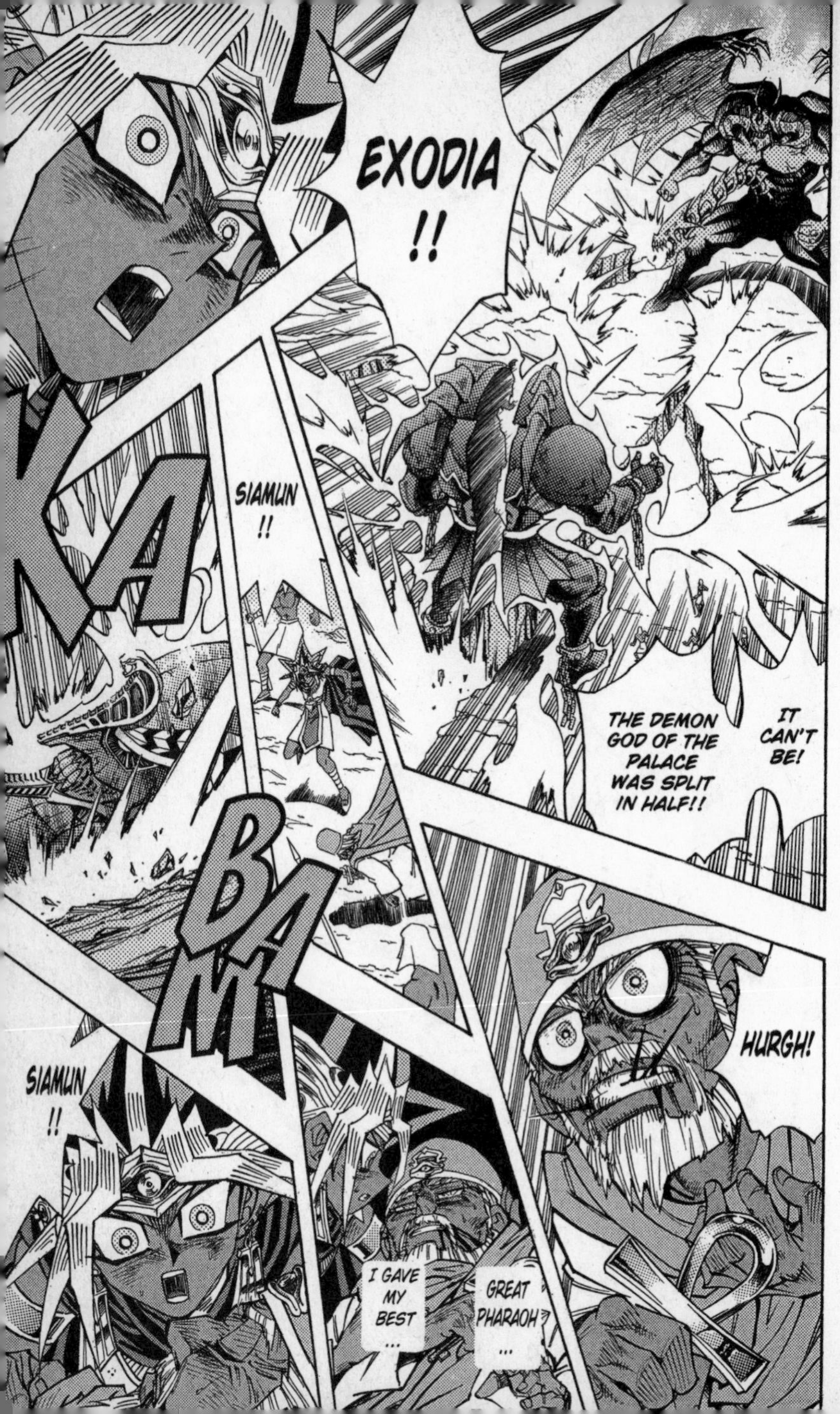
EXODIA !!
IT CAN'T BE!
THE DEMON GOD OF THE PALACE WAS SPLIT IN HALF!!
KA
SIAMUN !!
BAM
HURGH!
GREAT PHARAOH ...
I GAVE MY BEST ...
SIAMUN !!

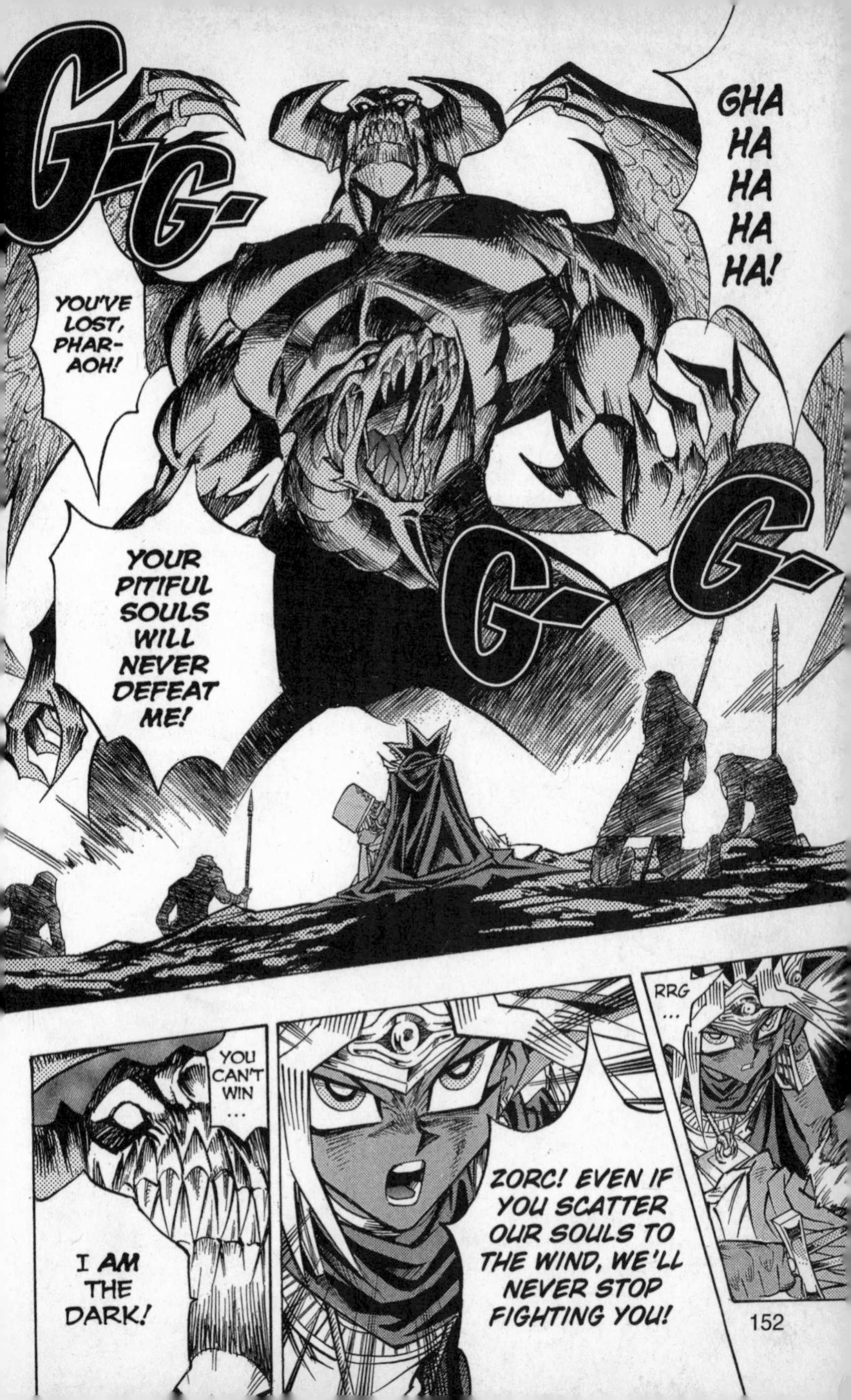

GHA HA HA HA HA!
G-G-
YOU'VE LOST, PHARAOH!
G-G-
YOUR PITIFUL SOULS WILL NEVER DEFEAT ME!
RRG...
ZORC! EVEN IF YOU SCATTER OUR SOULS TO THE WIND, WE'LL NEVER STOP FIGHTING YOU!
YOU CAN'T WIN...
I AM THE DARK!

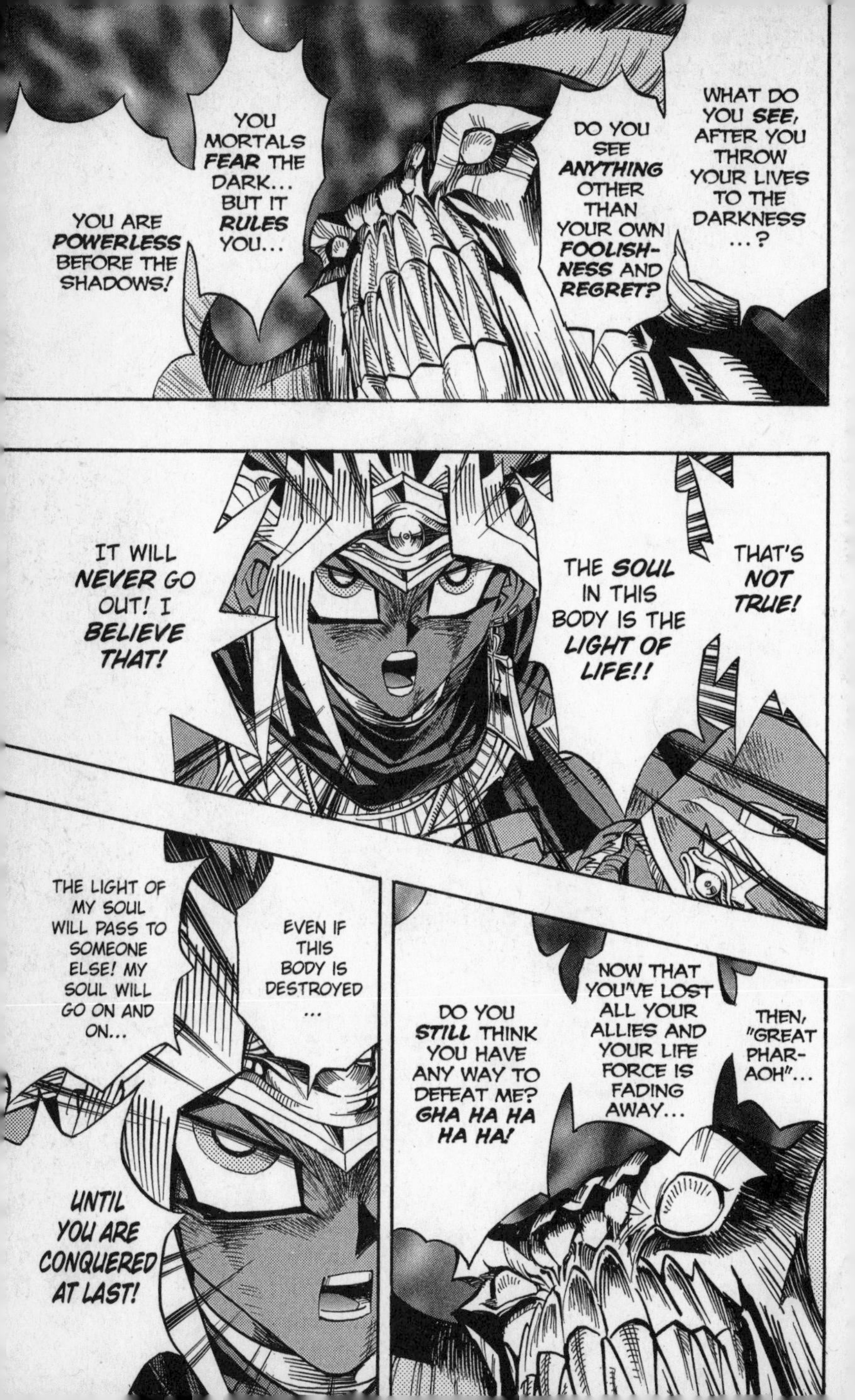
WHAT DO YOU SEE, AFTER YOU THROW YOUR LIVES TO THE DARKNESS ...?
DO YOU SEE ANYTHING OTHER THAN YOUR OWN FOOLISHNESS AND REGRET?
YOU MORTALS FEAR THE DARK... BUT IT RULES YOU...
YOU ARE POWERLESS BEFORE THE SHADOWS!
THAT'S NOT TRUE!
THE SOUL IN THIS BODY IS THE LIGHT OF LIFE!!
IT WILL NEVER GO OUT! I BELIEVE THAT!
THEN, "GREAT PHARAOH"...
NOW THAT YOU'VE LOST ALL YOUR ALLIES AND YOUR LIFE FORCE IS FADING AWAY...
DO YOU STILL THINK YOU HAVE ANY WAY TO DEFEAT ME? GHA HA HA HA HA!
EVEN IF THIS BODY IS DESTROYED ...
THE LIGHT OF MY SOUL WILL PASS TO SOMEONE ELSE! MY SOUL WILL GO ON AND ON...
UNTIL YOU ARE CONQUERED AT LAST!

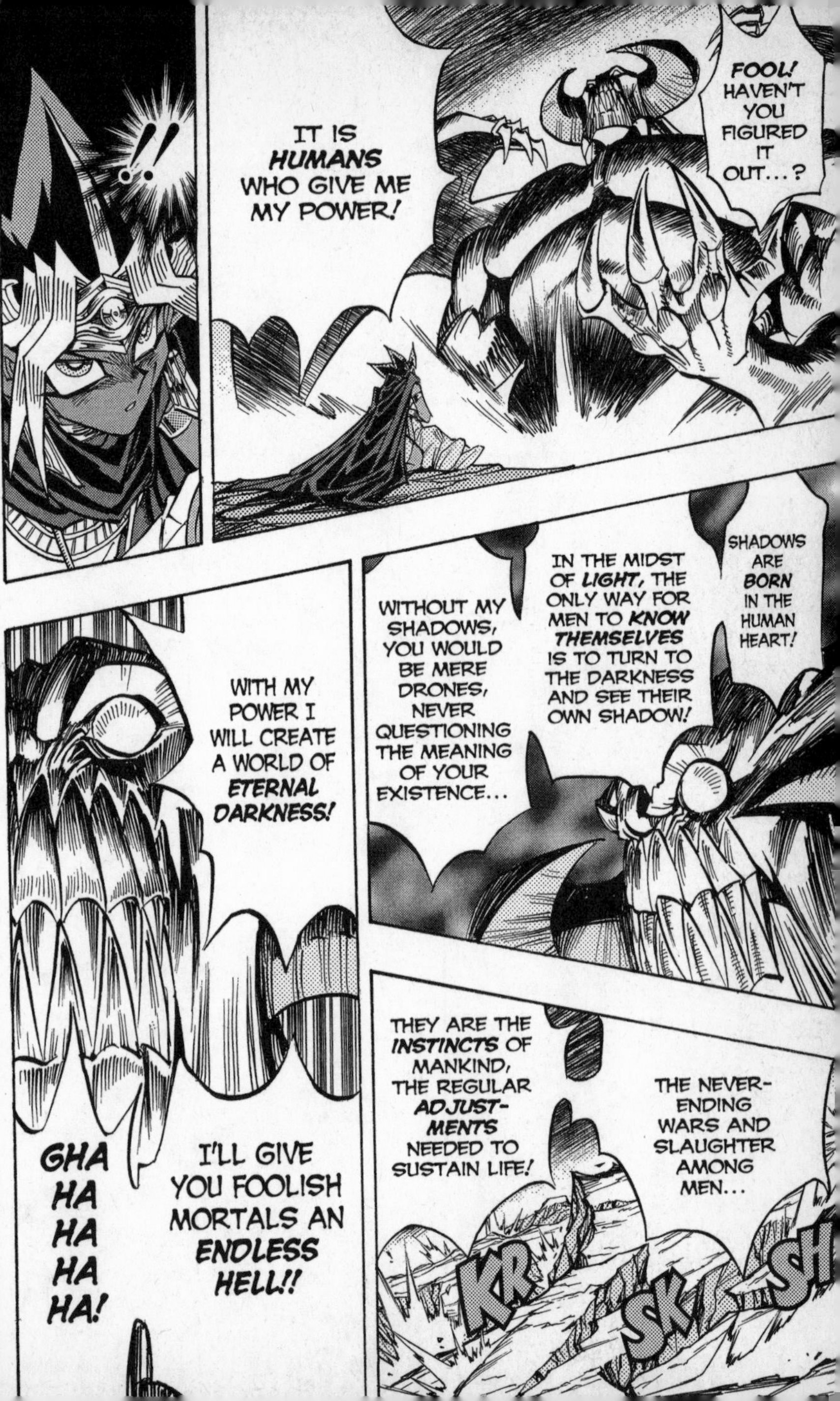
FOOL! HAVEN'T YOU FIGURED IT OUT...?
IT IS HUMANS WHO GIVE ME MY POWER!
!!
SHADOWS ARE BORN IN THE HUMAN HEART!
IN THE MIDST OF LIGHT, THE ONLY WAY FOR MEN TO KNOW THEMSELVES IS TO TURN TO THE DARKNESS AND SEE THEIR OWN SHADOW!
WITHOUT MY SHADOWS, YOU WOULD BE MERE DRONES, NEVER QUESTIONING THE MEANING OF YOUR EXISTENCE...
THE NEVER-ENDING WARS AND SLAUGHTER AMONG MEN...
THEY ARE THE INSTINCTS OF MANKIND, THE REGULAR ADJUSTMENTS NEEDED TO SUSTAIN LIFE!
SH
SK
KR
WITH MY POWER I WILL CREATE A WORLD OF ETERNAL DARKNESS!
I'LL GIVE YOU FOOLISH MORTALS AN ENDLESS HELL!!
GHA HA HA HA HA HA!

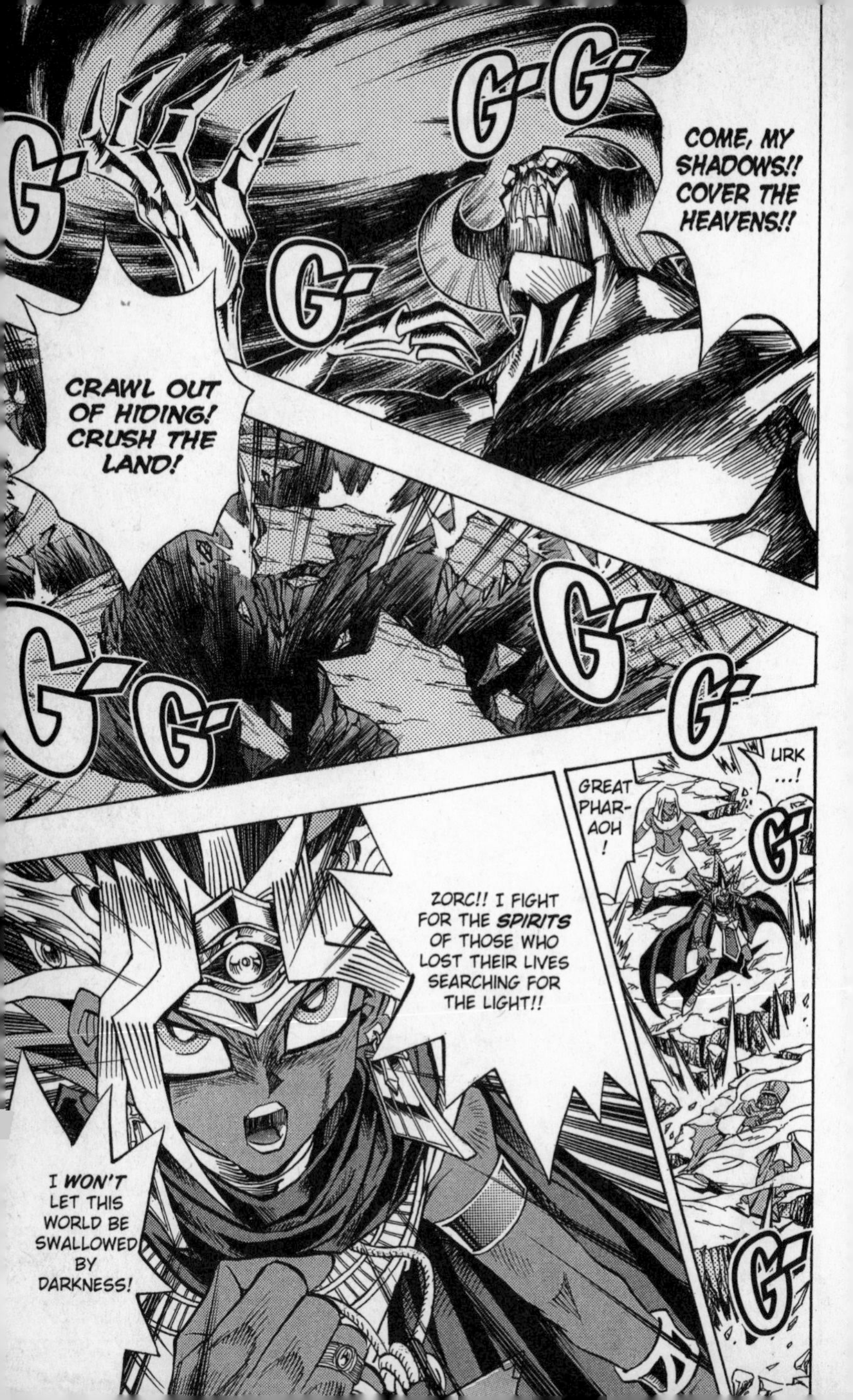

G-G-
COME, MY SHADOWS!! COVER THE HEAVENS!!
G-
G-
CRAWL OUT OF HIDING! CRUSH THE LAND!
G-
G-
G-G-
URK ...!
GREAT PHAR-AOH!
G-
G-
ZORC!! I FIGHT FOR THE *SPIRITS* OF THOSE WHO LOST THEIR LIVES SEARCHING FOR THE LIGHT!!
I *WON'T* LET THIS WORLD BE SWALLOWED BY DARKNESS!

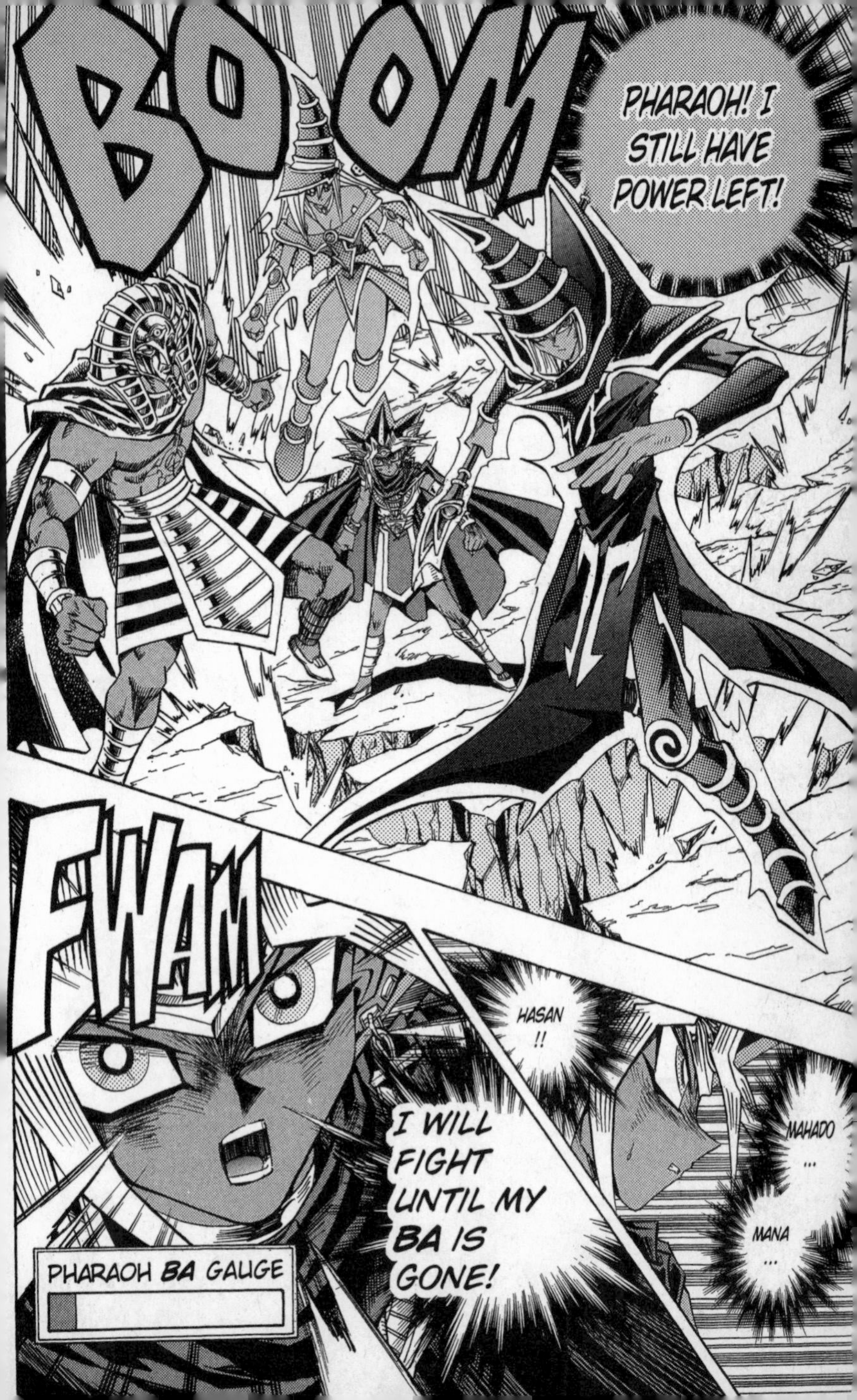
BOOM
PHARAOH! I STILL HAVE POWER LEFT!
HASAN !!
MAHADO ...
MANA ...
FWAM
I WILL FIGHT UNTIL MY BA IS GONE!
PHARAOH BA GAUGE

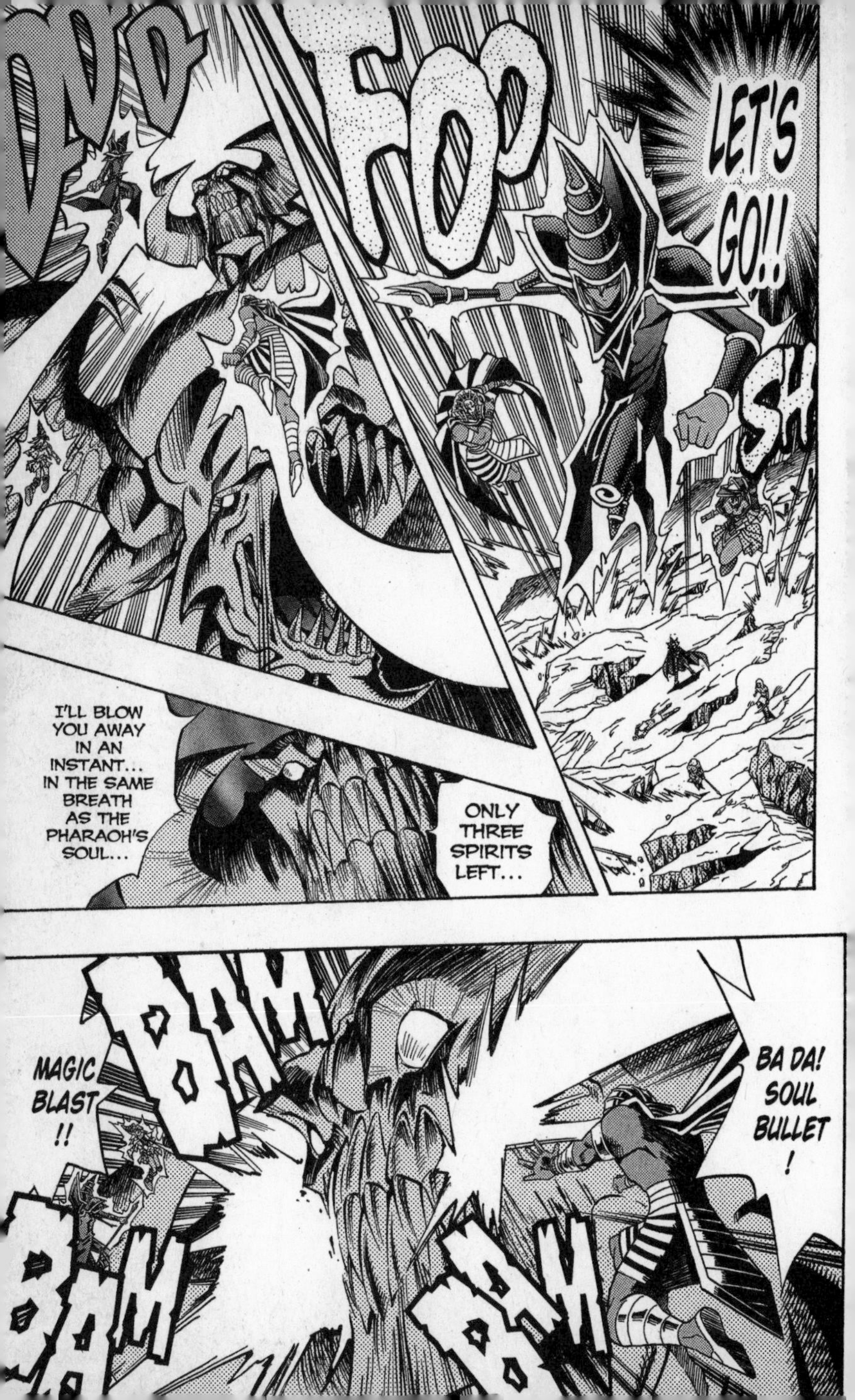
LET'S GO!!
ONLY THREE SPIRITS LEFT...
I'LL BLOW YOU AWAY IN AN INSTANT... IN THE SAME BREATH AS THE PHARAOH'S SOUL...
BA DA! SOUL BULLET!
BAM
MAGIC BLAST!!
BAM
BAM

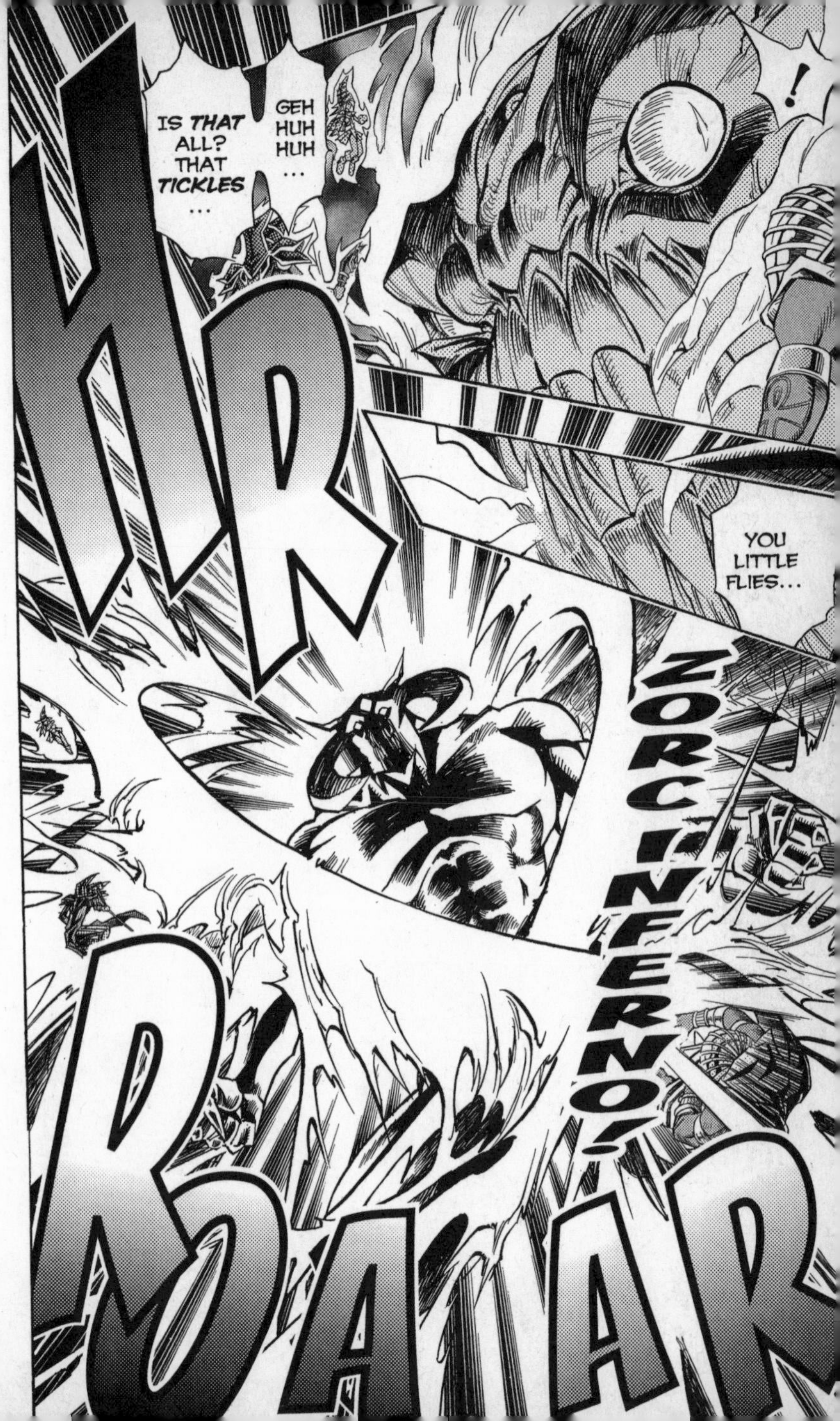
!
GEH HUH HUH ...
IS *THAT* ALL? THAT *TICKLES* ...
YOU LITTLE FLIES...
ZORC INFERNO!!

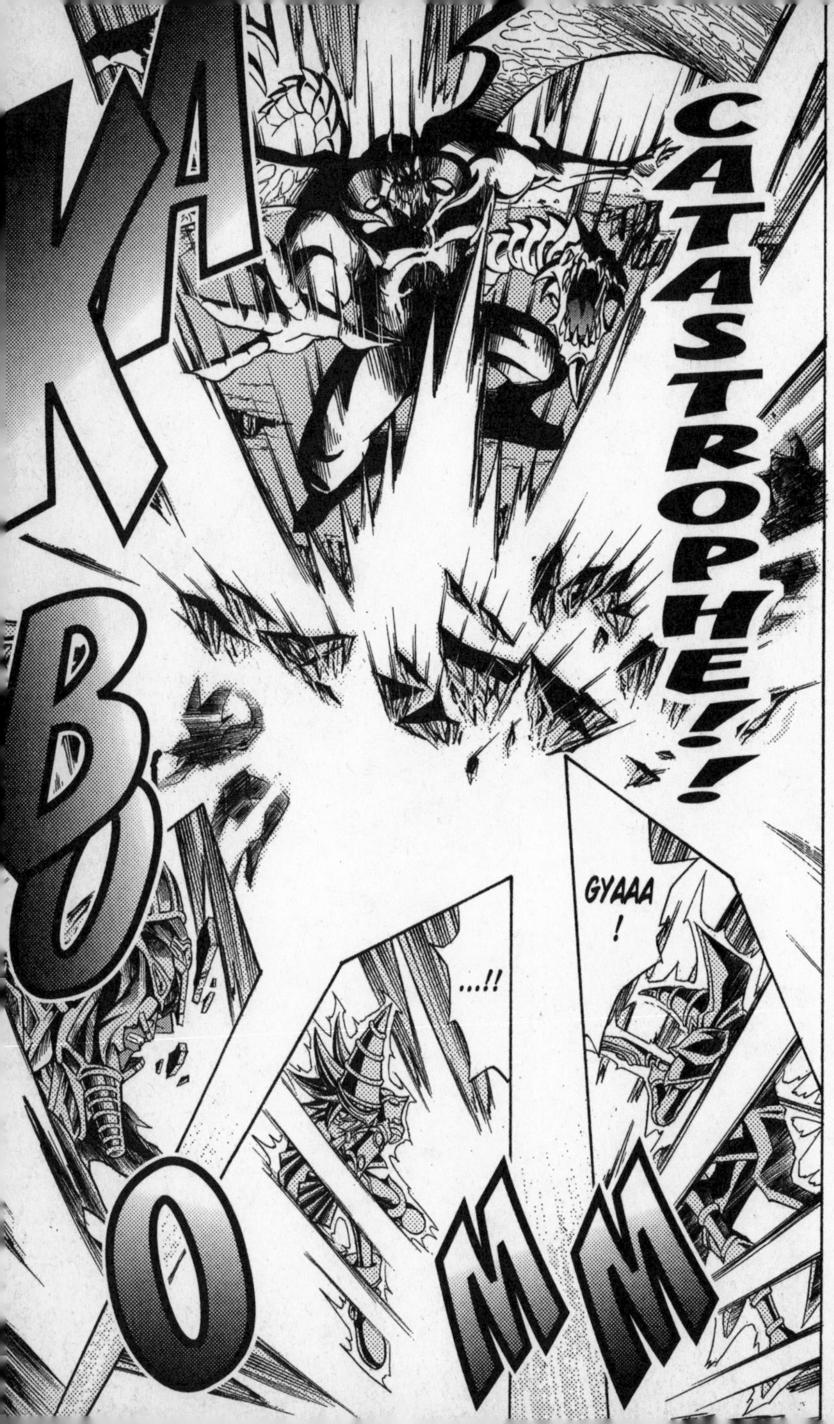
CATASTROPHE!!
ZABOOMM
GYAAA!
...!!

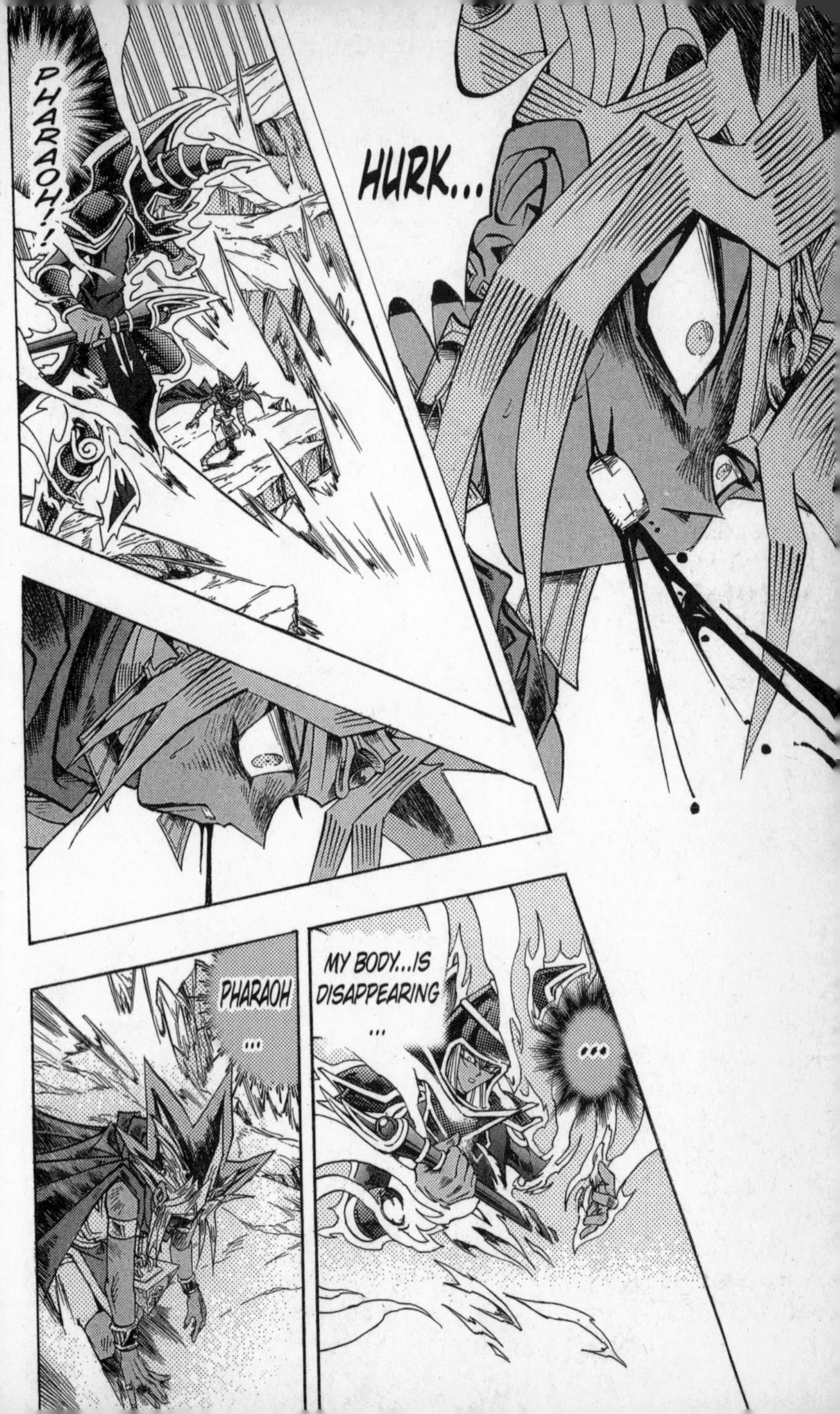
HURK...
PHARAOH!!
MY BODY...IS DISAPPEARING ...
...
PHARAOH ...

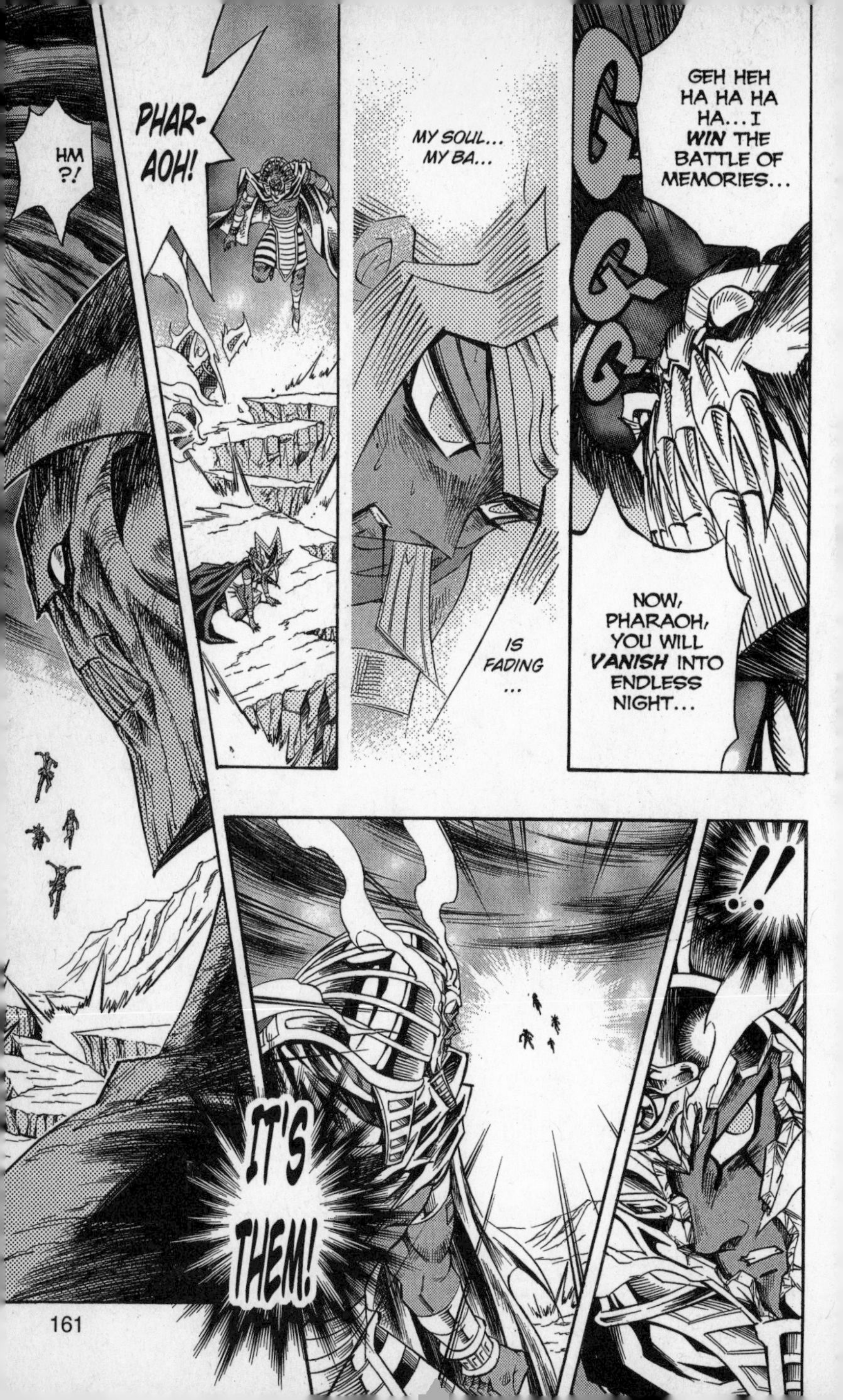
G G G G
GEH HEH HA HA HA HA... I **WIN** THE BATTLE OF MEMORIES...
NOW, PHARAOH, YOU WILL **VANISH** INTO ENDLESS NIGHT...
MY SOUL... MY BA...
IS FADING ...
PHAR-AOH!
!!
IT'S THEM!
HM ?!

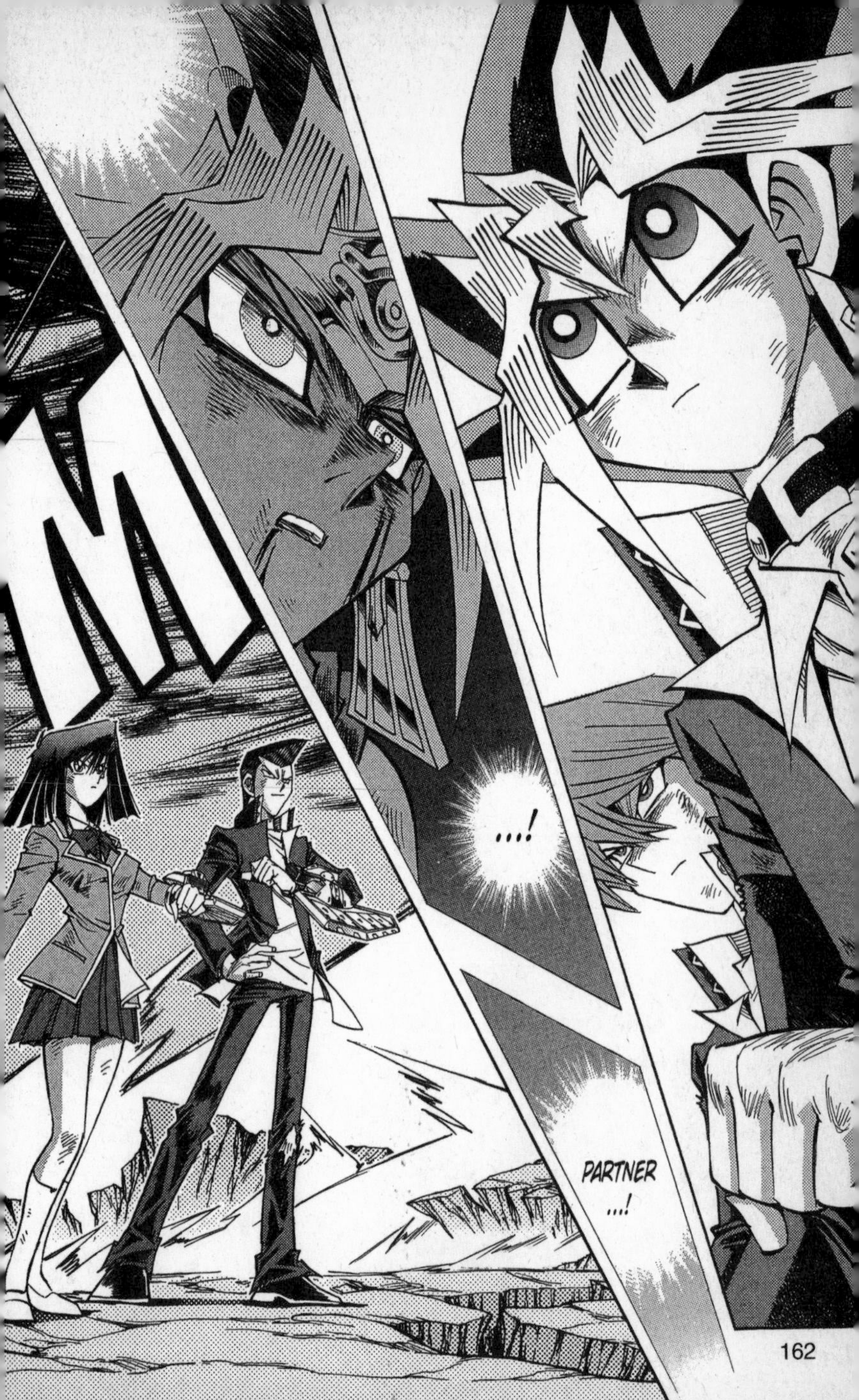
...!
PARTNER ...!

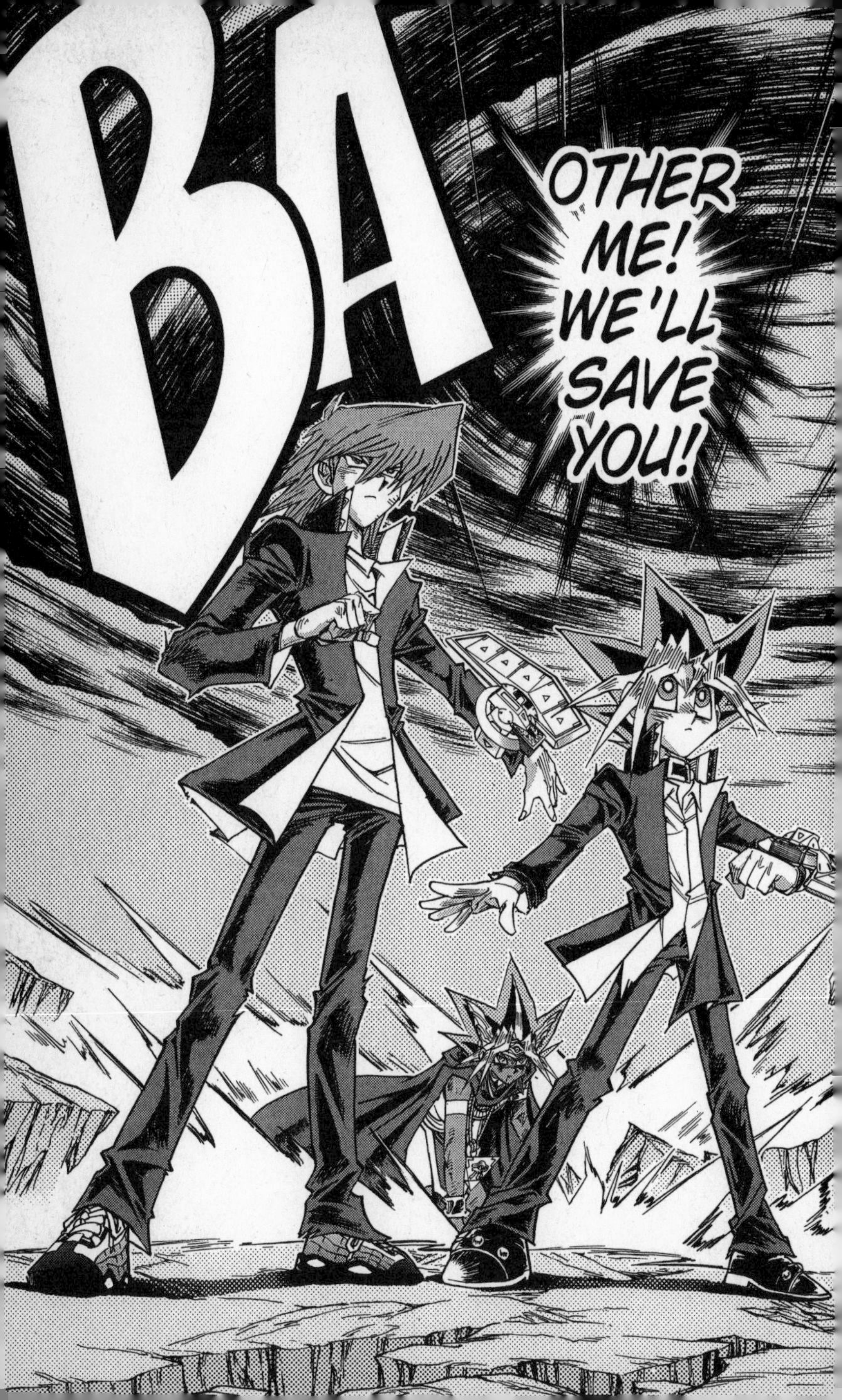
BA
OTHER ME! WE'LL SAVE YOU!

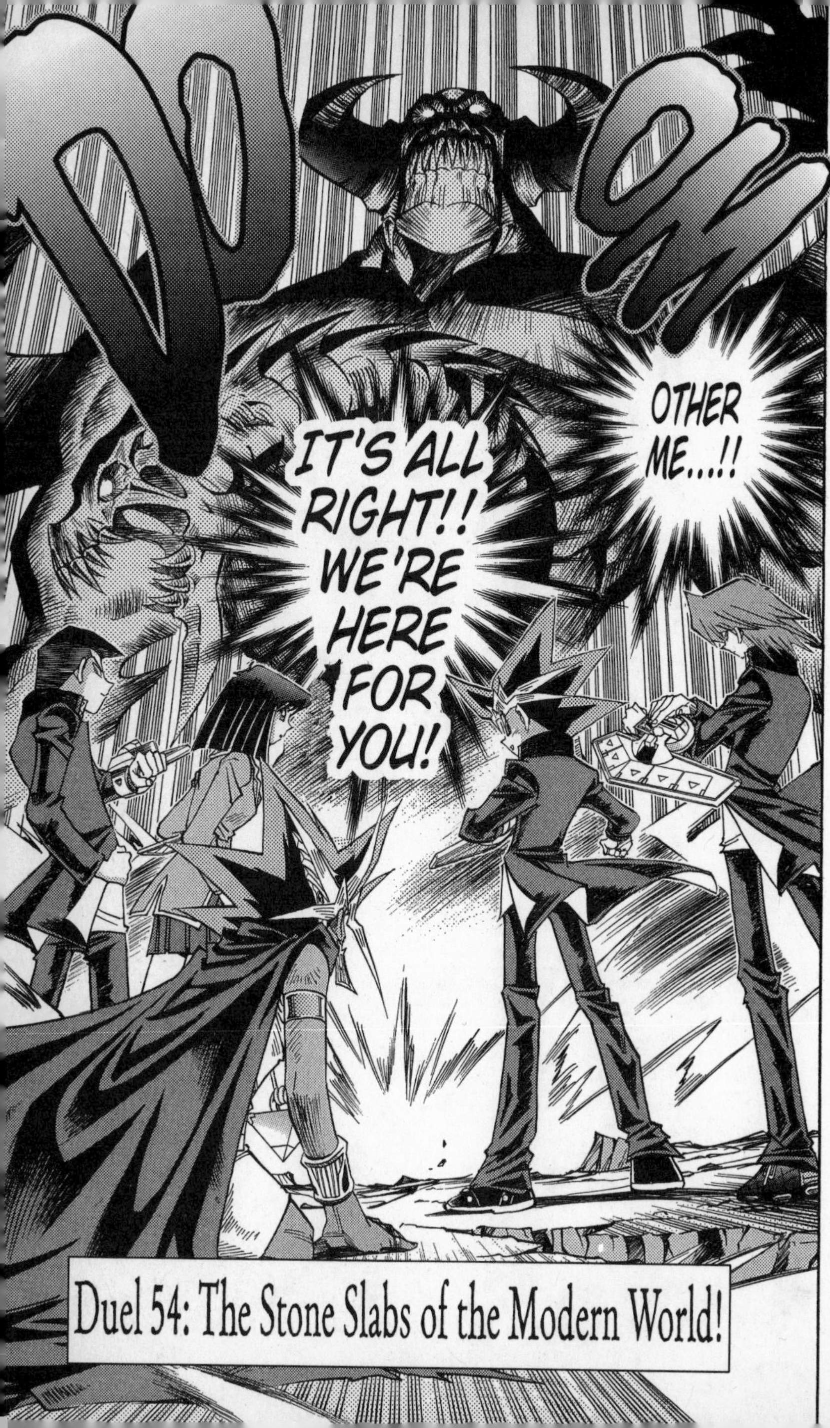
OTHER ME...!!
IT'S ALL RIGHT!! WE'RE HERE FOR YOU!

Duel 54: The Stone Slabs of the Modern World!

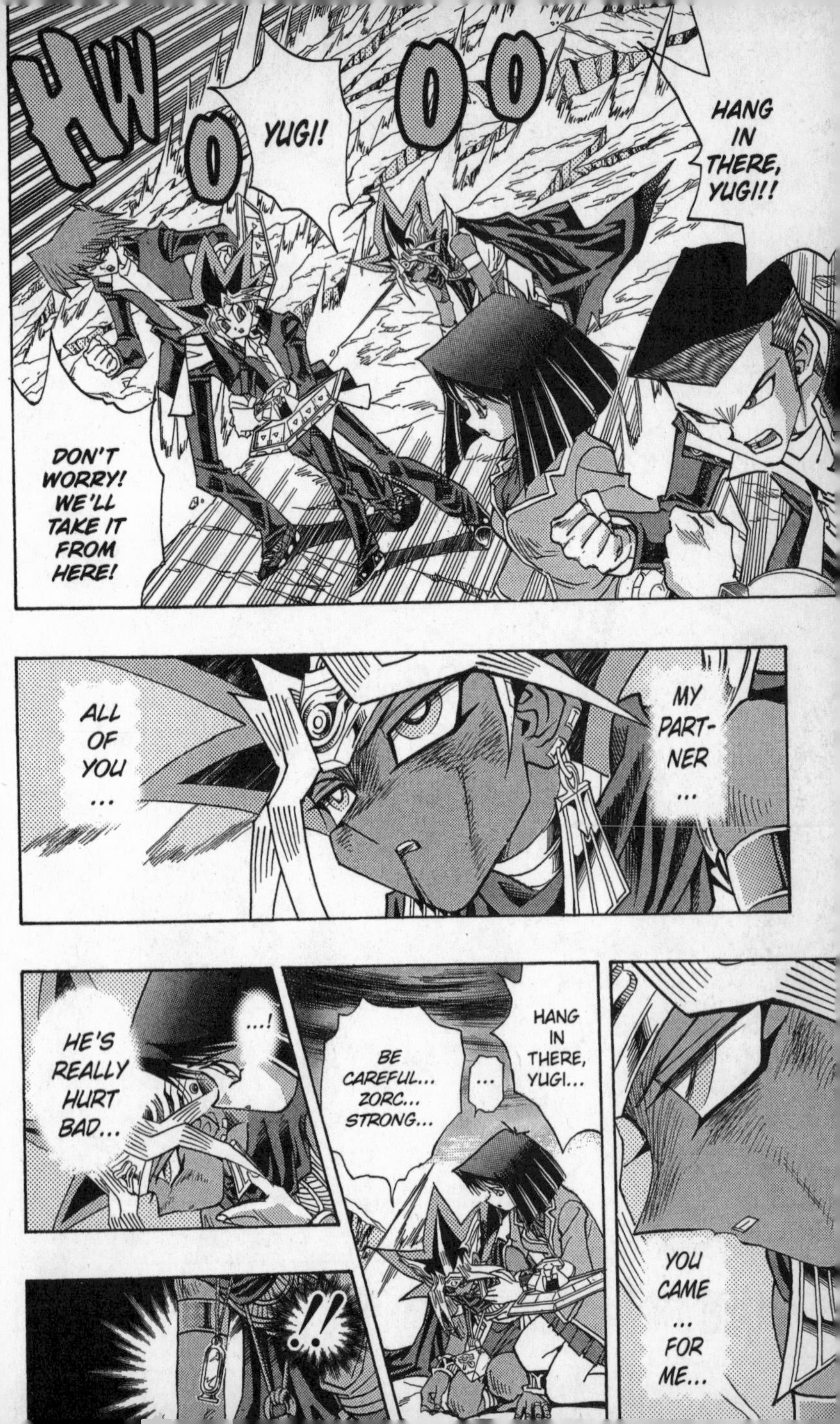
HANG IN THERE, YUGI!!
HWOOOO
YUGI!
DON'T WORRY! WE'LL TAKE IT FROM HERE!
MY PART-NER ...
ALL OF YOU ...
YOU CAME ... FOR ME...
HANG IN THERE, YUGI...
...
BE CAREFUL... ZORC... STRONG...
...!
HE'S REALLY HURT BAD...
!!

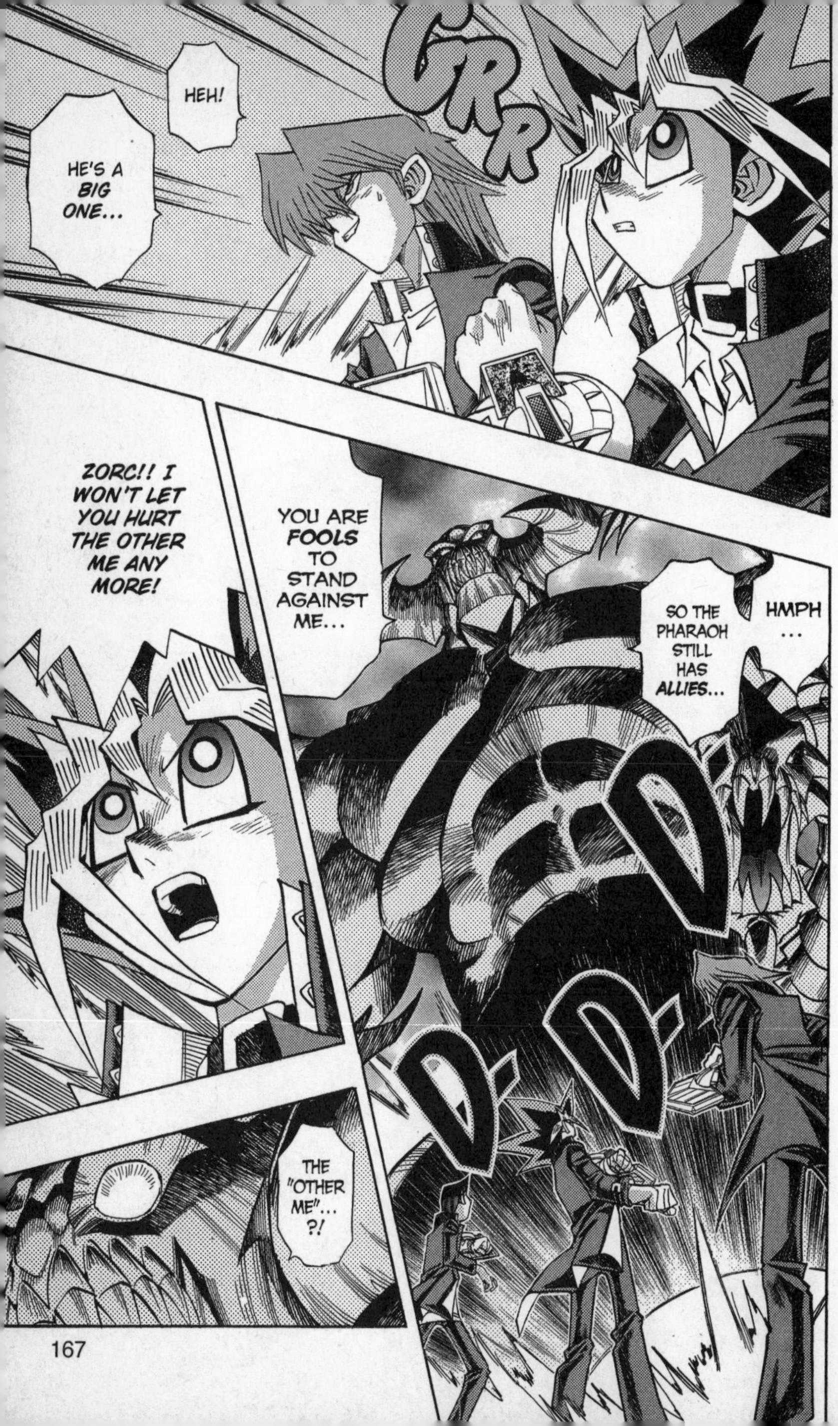
GRR
HEH!
HE'S A BIG ONE...
HMPH...
SO THE PHARAOH STILL HAS ALLIES...
YOU ARE FOOLS TO STAND AGAINST ME...
ZORC!! I WON'T LET YOU HURT THE OTHER ME ANY MORE!
THE "OTHER ME"... ?!

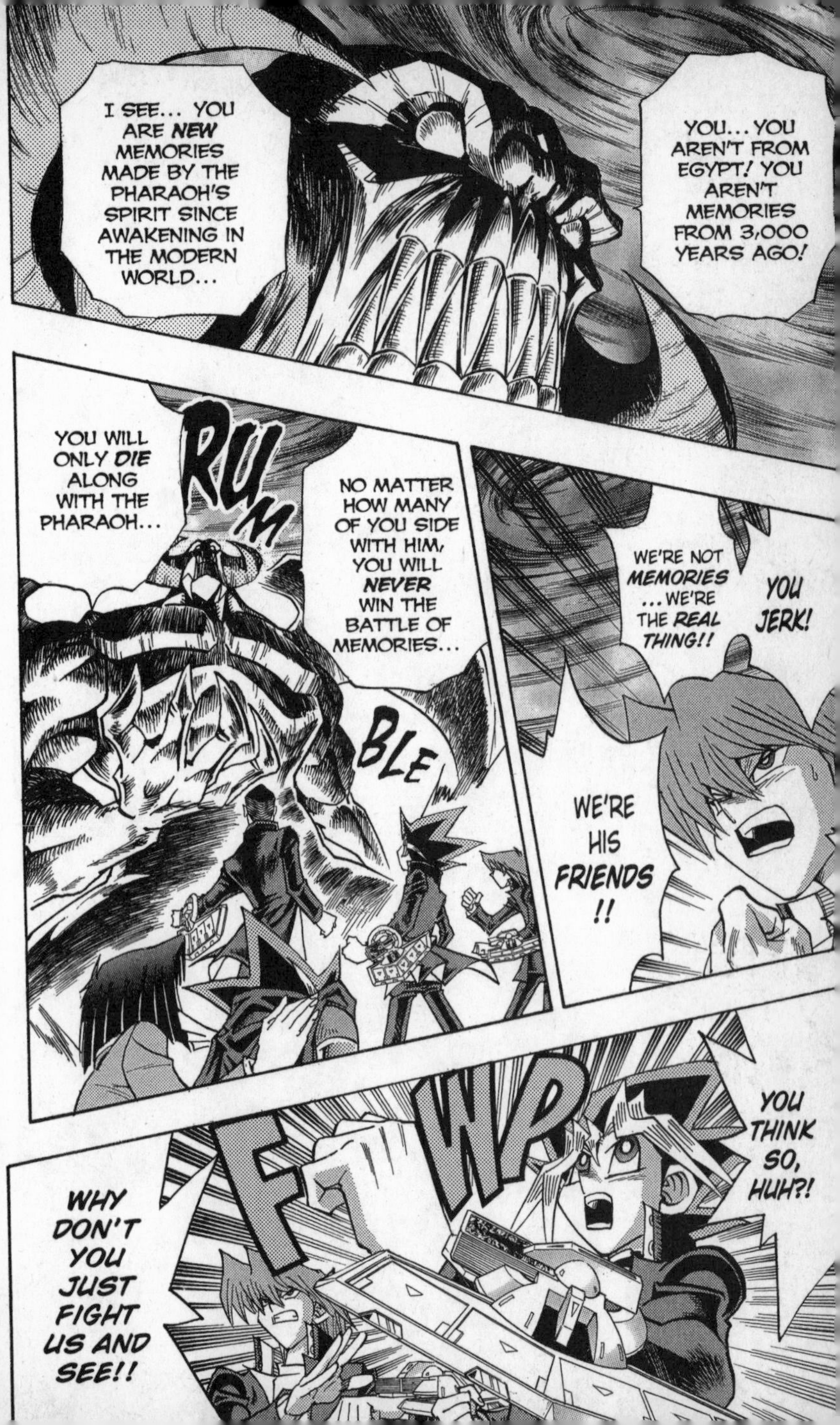
YOU... YOU AREN'T FROM EGYPT! YOU AREN'T MEMORIES FROM 3,000 YEARS AGO!
I SEE... YOU ARE NEW MEMORIES MADE BY THE PHARAOH'S SPIRIT SINCE AWAKENING IN THE MODERN WORLD...
YOU JERK!
WE'RE NOT MEMORIES ...WE'RE THE REAL THING!!
WE'RE HIS FRIENDS !!
RUMBLE
NO MATTER HOW MANY OF YOU SIDE WITH HIM, YOU WILL NEVER WIN THE BATTLE OF MEMORIES...
YOU WILL ONLY DIE ALONG WITH THE PHARAOH...
YOU THINK SO, HUH?!
FWP
WHY DON'T YOU JUST FIGHT US AND SEE!!

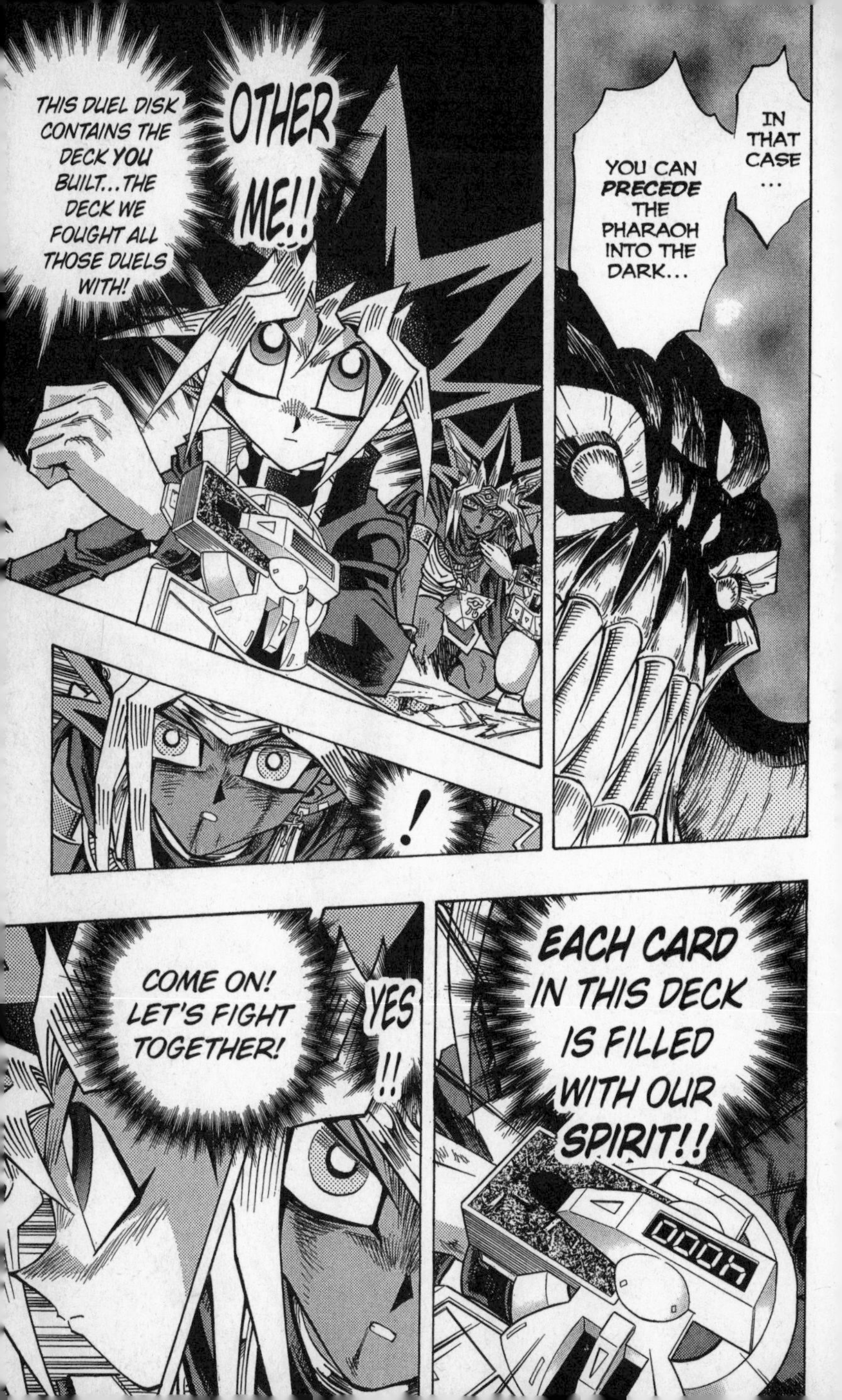
IN THAT CASE...
YOU CAN PRECEDE THE PHARAOH INTO THE DARK...
OTHER ME!!
THIS DUEL DISK CONTAINS THE DECK YOU BUILT...THE DECK WE FOUGHT ALL THOSE DUELS WITH!
!
EACH CARD IN THIS DECK IS FILLED WITH OUR SPIRIT!!
YES!!
COME ON! LET'S FIGHT TOGETHER!

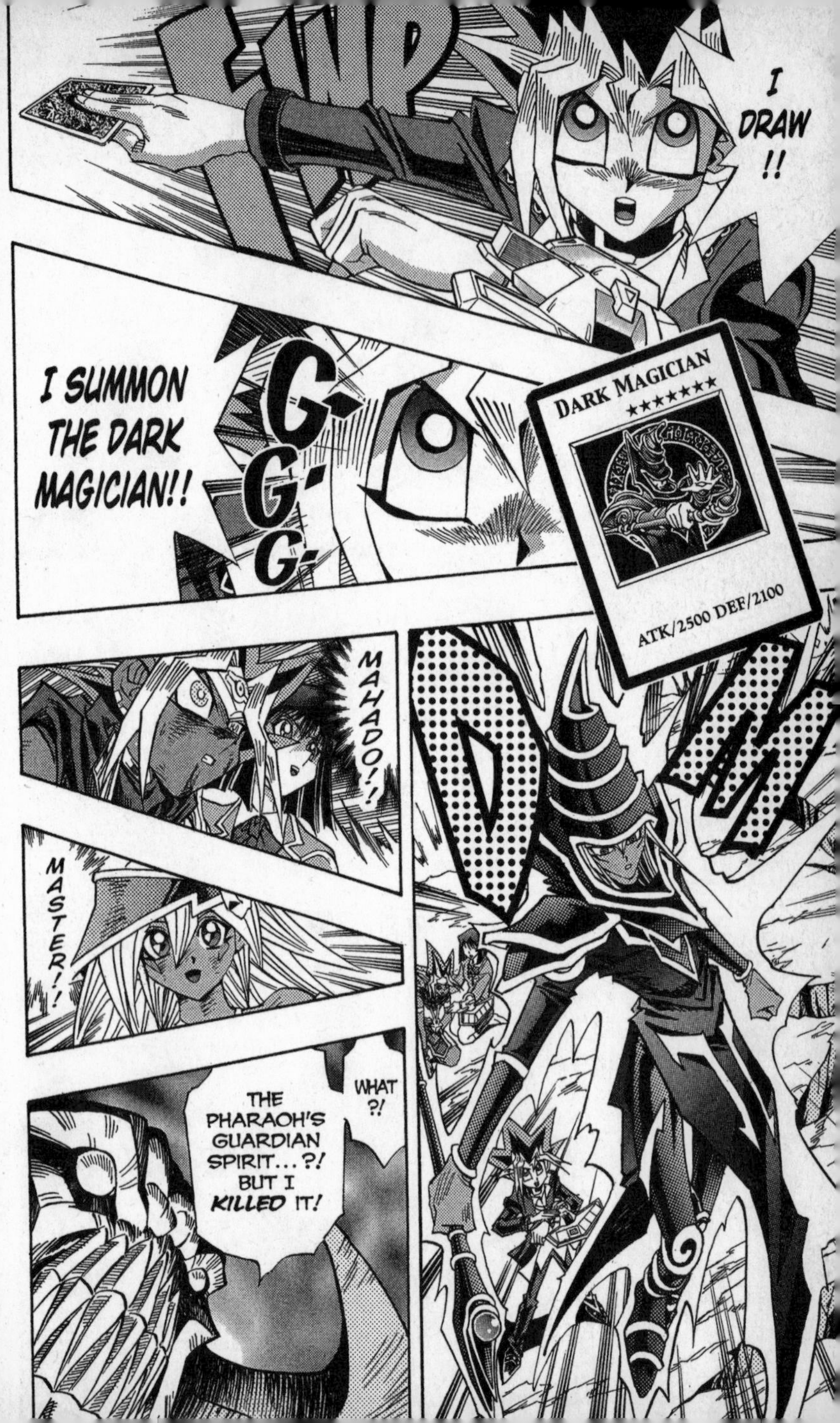
I DRAW!!
I SUMMON THE DARK MAGICIAN!!
G-G-G-
DARK MAGICIAN
★★★★★★★
ATK/2500 DEF/2100
MAHADO!!
MASTER!!
WHAT?!
THE PHARAOH'S GUARDIAN SPIRIT...?! BUT I *KILLED* IT!

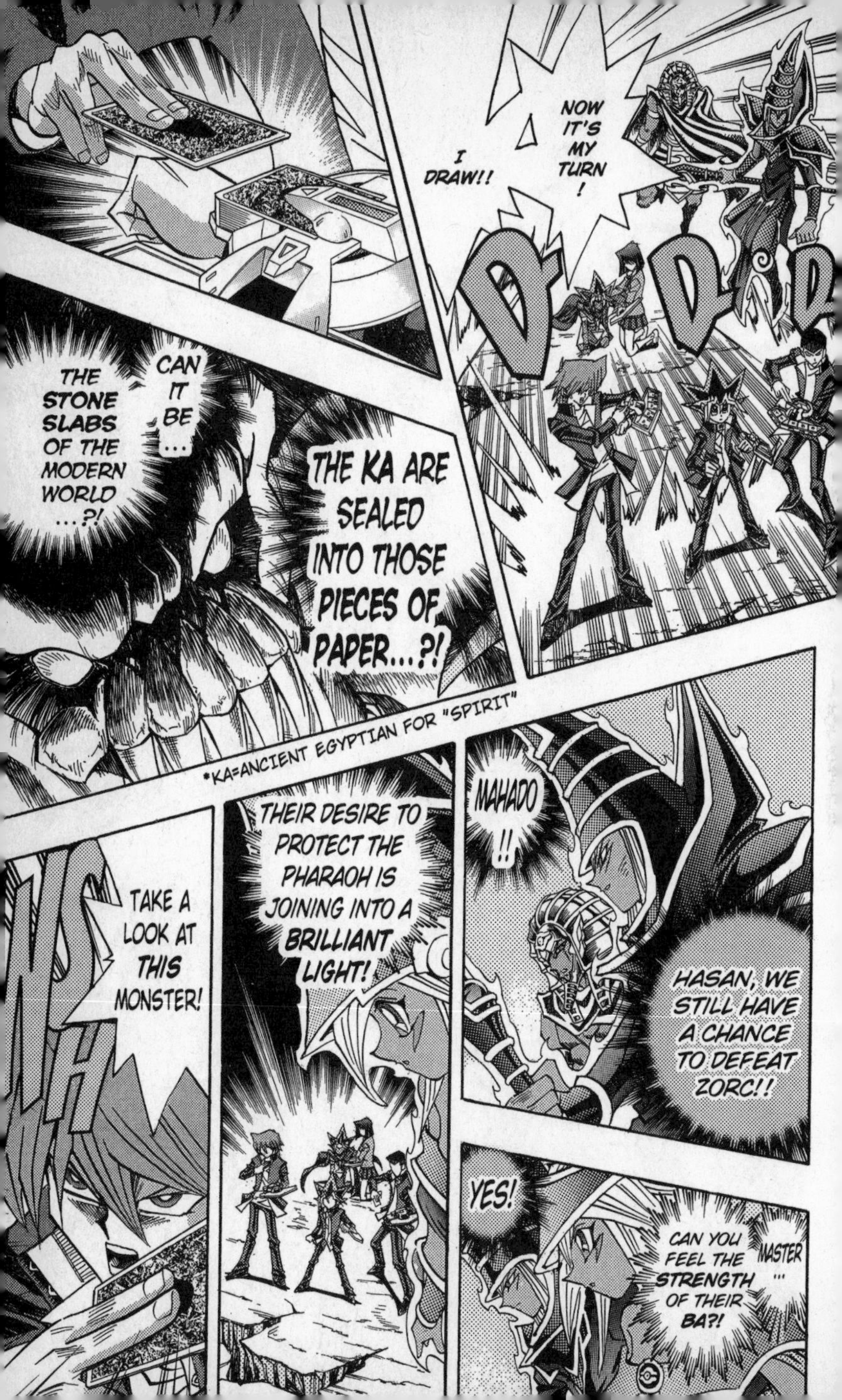

NOW IT'S MY TURN!
I DRAW!!
CAN IT BE...
THE STONE SLABS OF THE MODERN WORLD...?!
THE KA ARE SEALED INTO THOSE PIECES OF PAPER...?!
*KA=ANCIENT EGYPTIAN FOR "SPIRIT"
MAHADO!!
HASAN, WE STILL HAVE A CHANCE TO DEFEAT ZORC!!
YES!
MASTER...
CAN YOU FEEL THE STRENGTH OF THEIR BA?!
THEIR DESIRE TO PROTECT THE PHARAOH IS JOINING INTO A BRILLIANT LIGHT!
TAKE A LOOK AT THIS MONSTER!

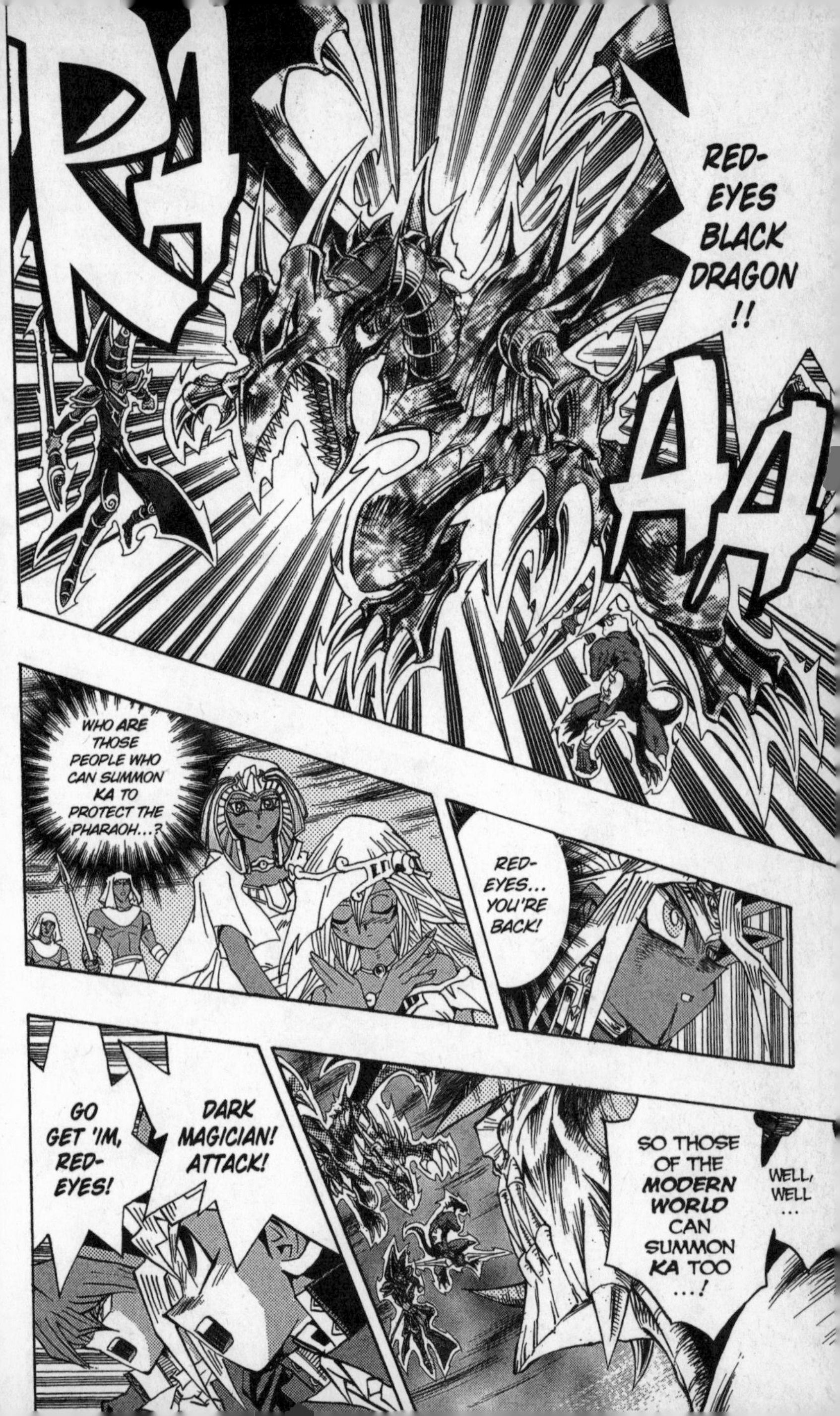
RED-EYES BLACK DRAGON!!
RED-EYES... YOU'RE BACK!
WHO ARE THOSE PEOPLE WHO CAN SUMMON KA TO PROTECT THE PHARAOH...?
WELL, WELL...
SO THOSE OF THE MODERN WORLD CAN SUMMON KA TOO...!
DARK MAGICIAN! ATTACK!
GO GET 'IM, RED-EYES!

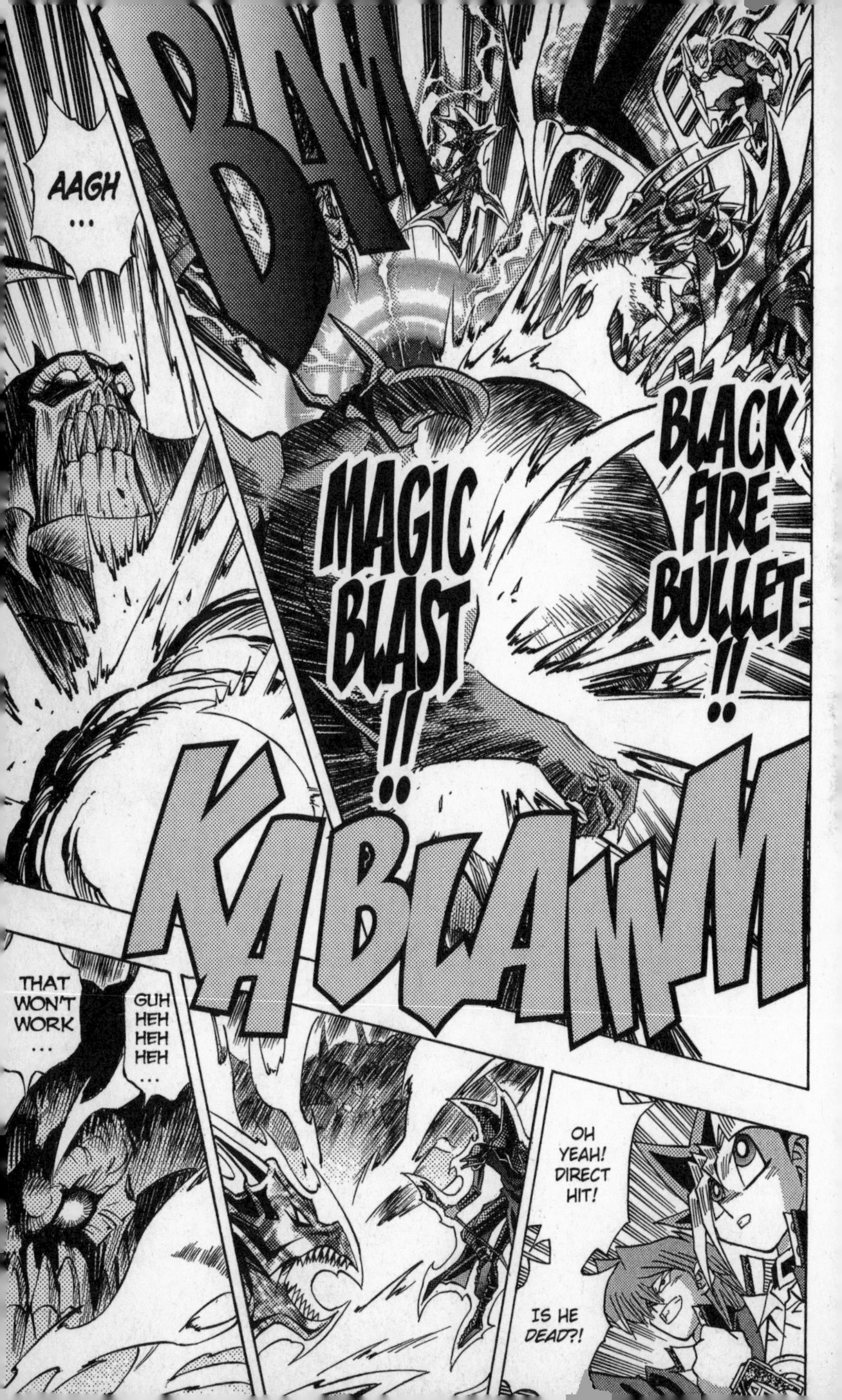
BAM
BLACK FIRE BULLET!!
MAGIC BLAST!!
KABLAMM
AAGH...
OH YEAH! DIRECT HIT!
IS HE DEAD?!
GUH HEH HEH HEH...
THAT WON'T WORK...

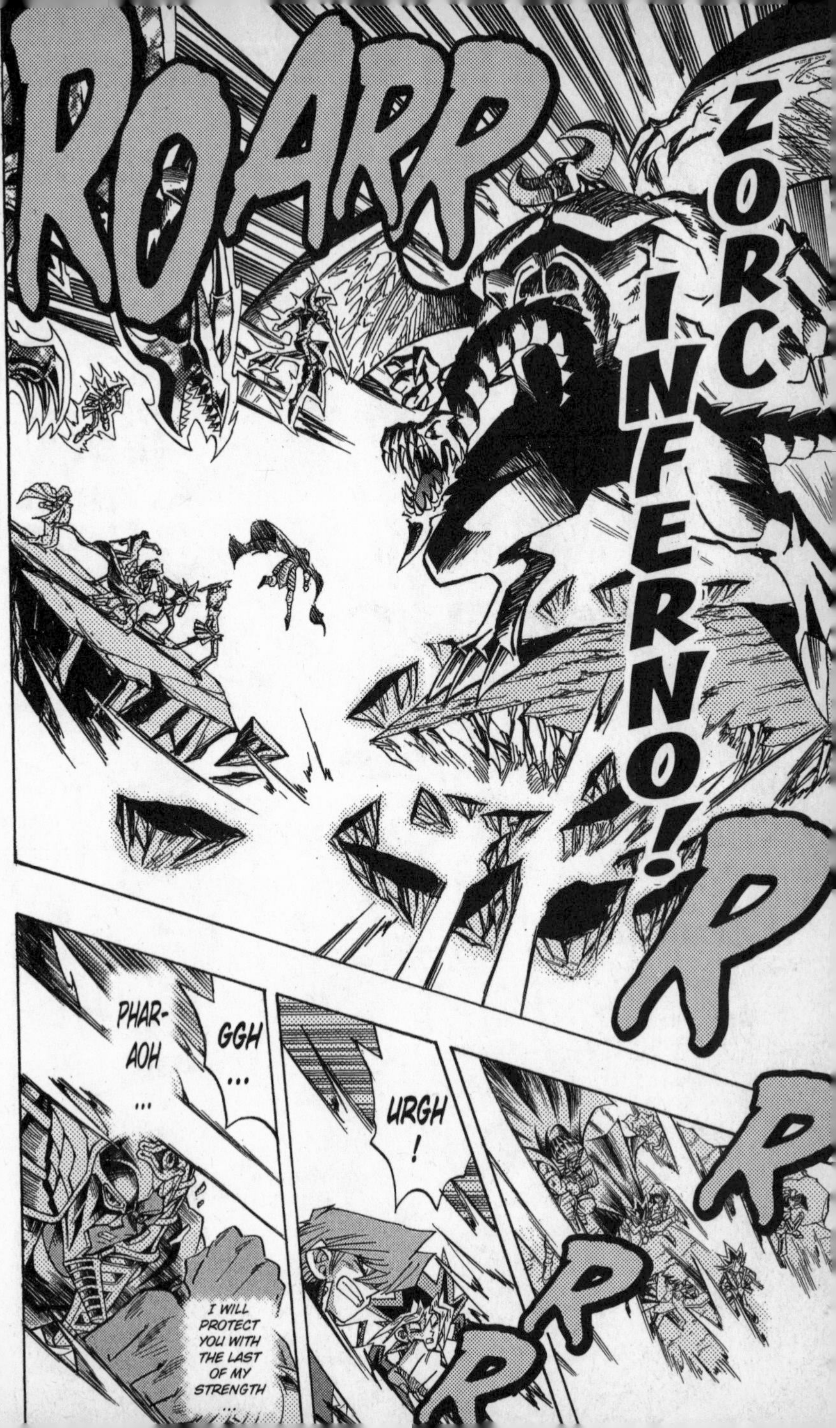
ROARR
ZORC INFERNO!
RRRR
URGH!
GGH...
PHAR-AOH...
I WILL PROTECT YOU WITH THE LAST OF MY STRENGTH...

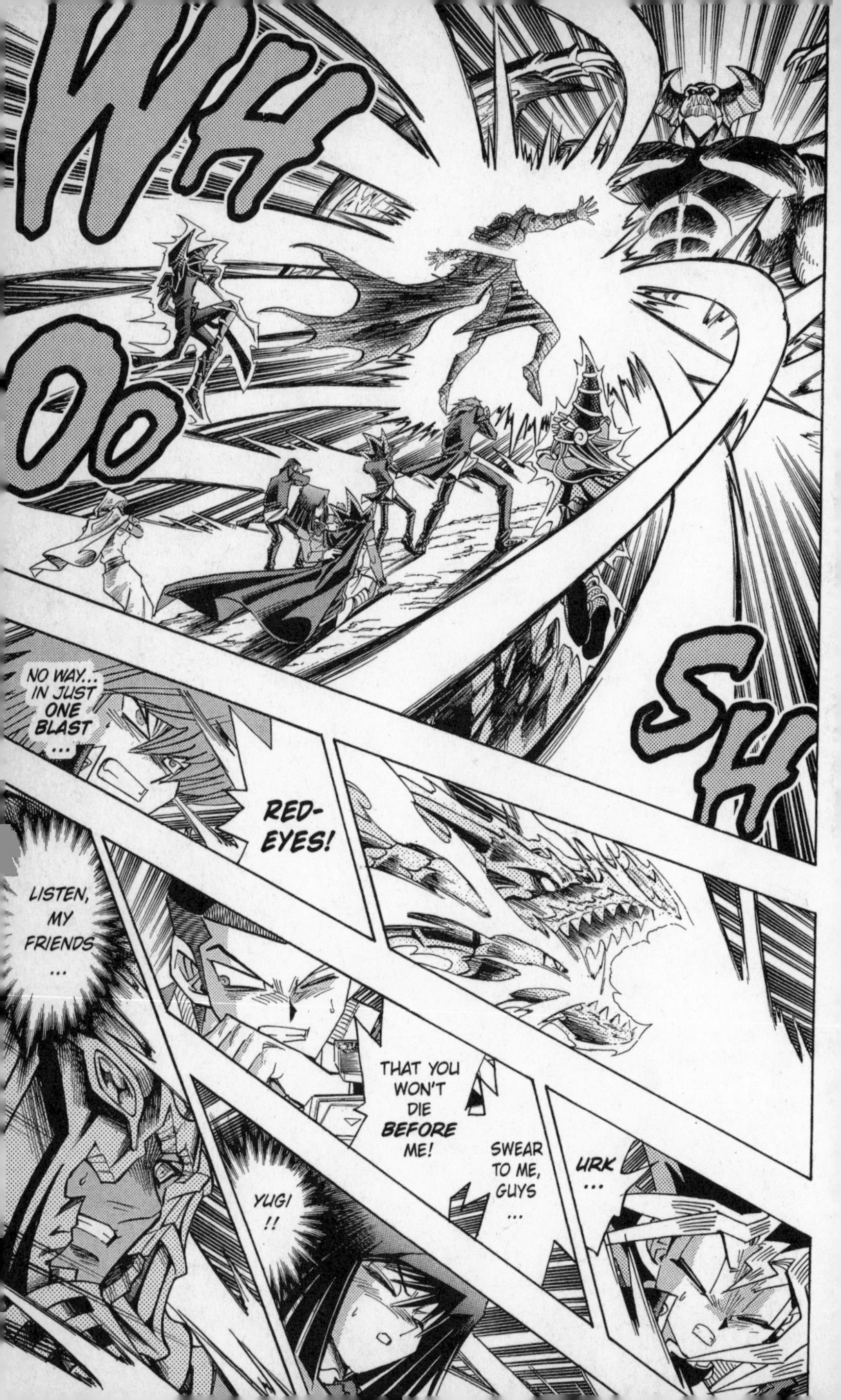

WHOOSH
RED-EYES!
NO WAY... IN JUST ONE BLAST...
LISTEN, MY FRIENDS...
URK...
SWEAR TO ME, GUYS...
THAT YOU WON'T DIE **BEFORE** ME!
YUGI!!

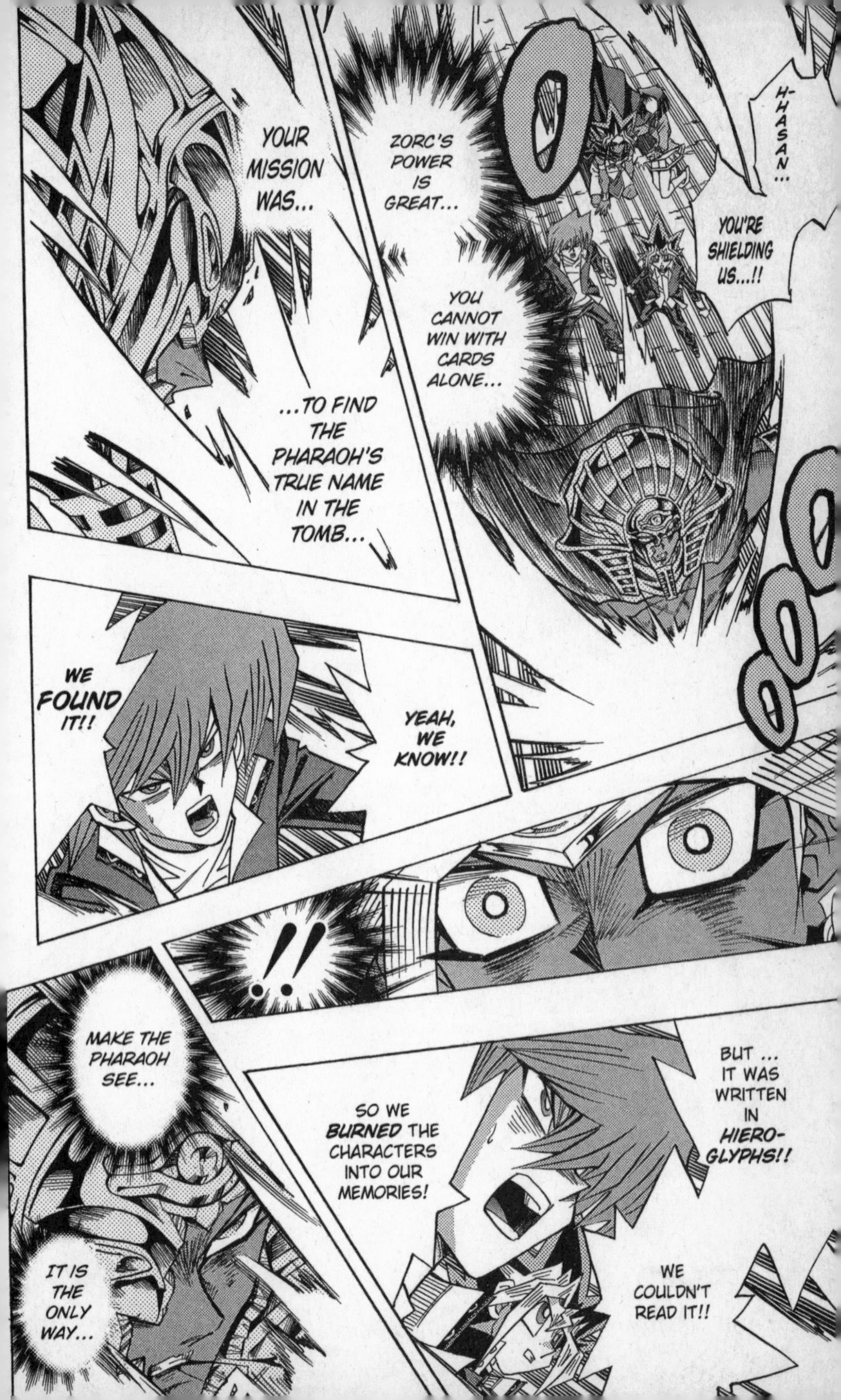
H-HASAN...
YOU'RE SHIELDING US...!!
ZORC'S POWER IS GREAT...
YOU CANNOT WIN WITH CARDS ALONE...
YOUR MISSION WAS...
...TO FIND THE PHARAOH'S TRUE NAME IN THE TOMB...
WE FOUND IT!!
YEAH, WE KNOW!!
!!
BUT ... IT WAS WRITTEN IN HIERO-GLYPHS!!
WE COULDN'T READ IT!!
SO WE BURNED THE CHARACTERS INTO OUR MEMORIES!
MAKE THE PHARAOH SEE...
IT IS THE ONLY WAY...

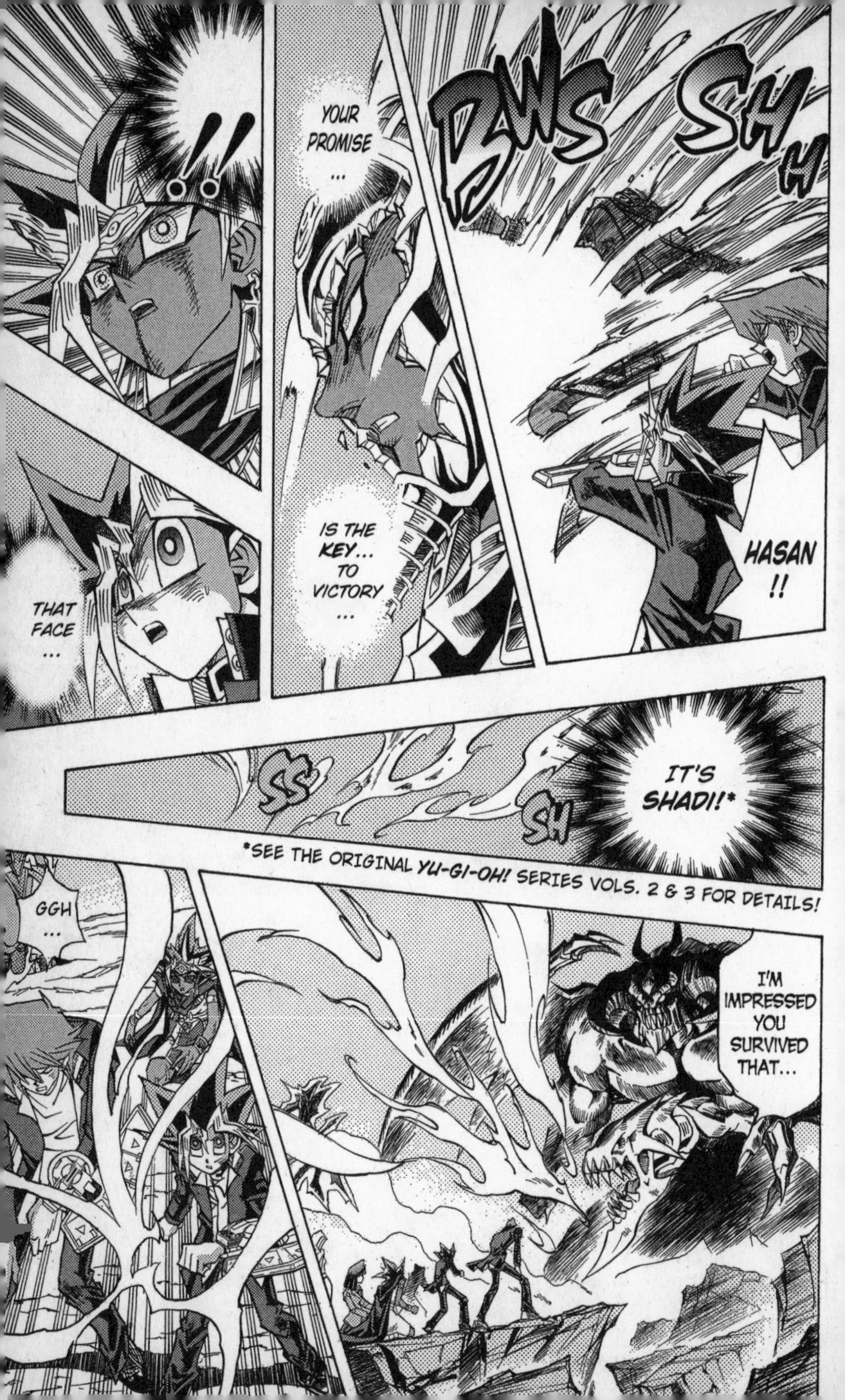
SHH
HASAN !!
YOUR PROMISE ...
IS THE KEY... TO VICTORY ...
!!
THAT FACE ...
IT'S SHADI!*
SH
SS
*SEE THE ORIGINAL YU-GI-OH! SERIES VOLS. 2 & 3 FOR DETAILS!
I'M IMPRESSED YOU SURVIVED THAT...
GGH ...

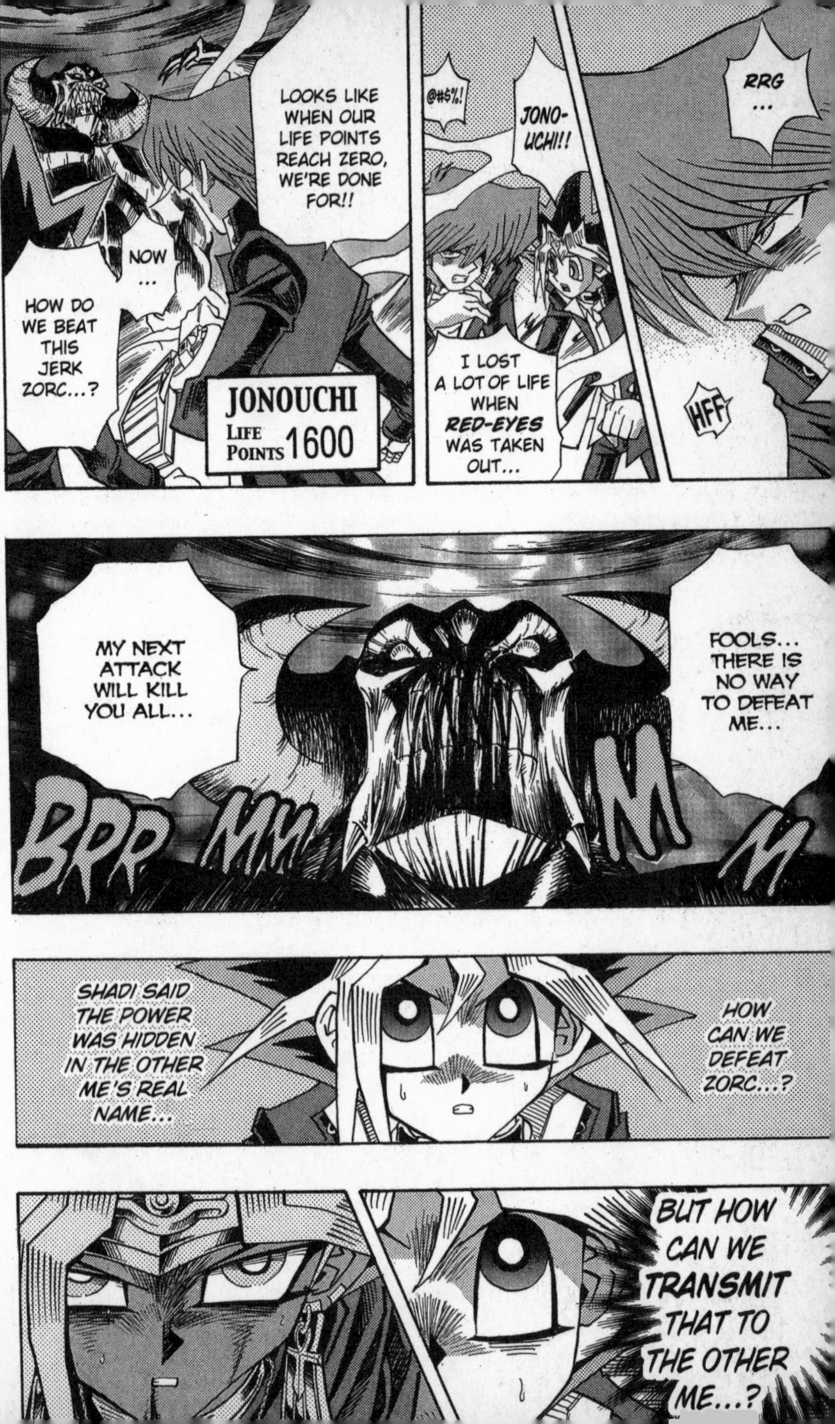
RRG ...
HFF
JONO-UCHI!!
@#$%!
I LOST A LOT OF LIFE WHEN RED-EYES WAS TAKEN OUT...
LOOKS LIKE WHEN OUR LIFE POINTS REACH ZERO, WE'RE DONE FOR!!
NOW ...
HOW DO WE BEAT THIS JERK ZORC...?
JONOUCHI LIFE POINTS 1600
FOOLS... THERE IS NO WAY TO DEFEAT ME...
MY NEXT ATTACK WILL KILL YOU ALL...
BRR MMMMMM
HOW CAN WE DEFEAT ZORC...?
SHADI SAID THE POWER WAS HIDDEN IN THE OTHER ME'S REAL NAME...
BUT HOW CAN WE TRANSMIT THAT TO THE OTHER ME...?

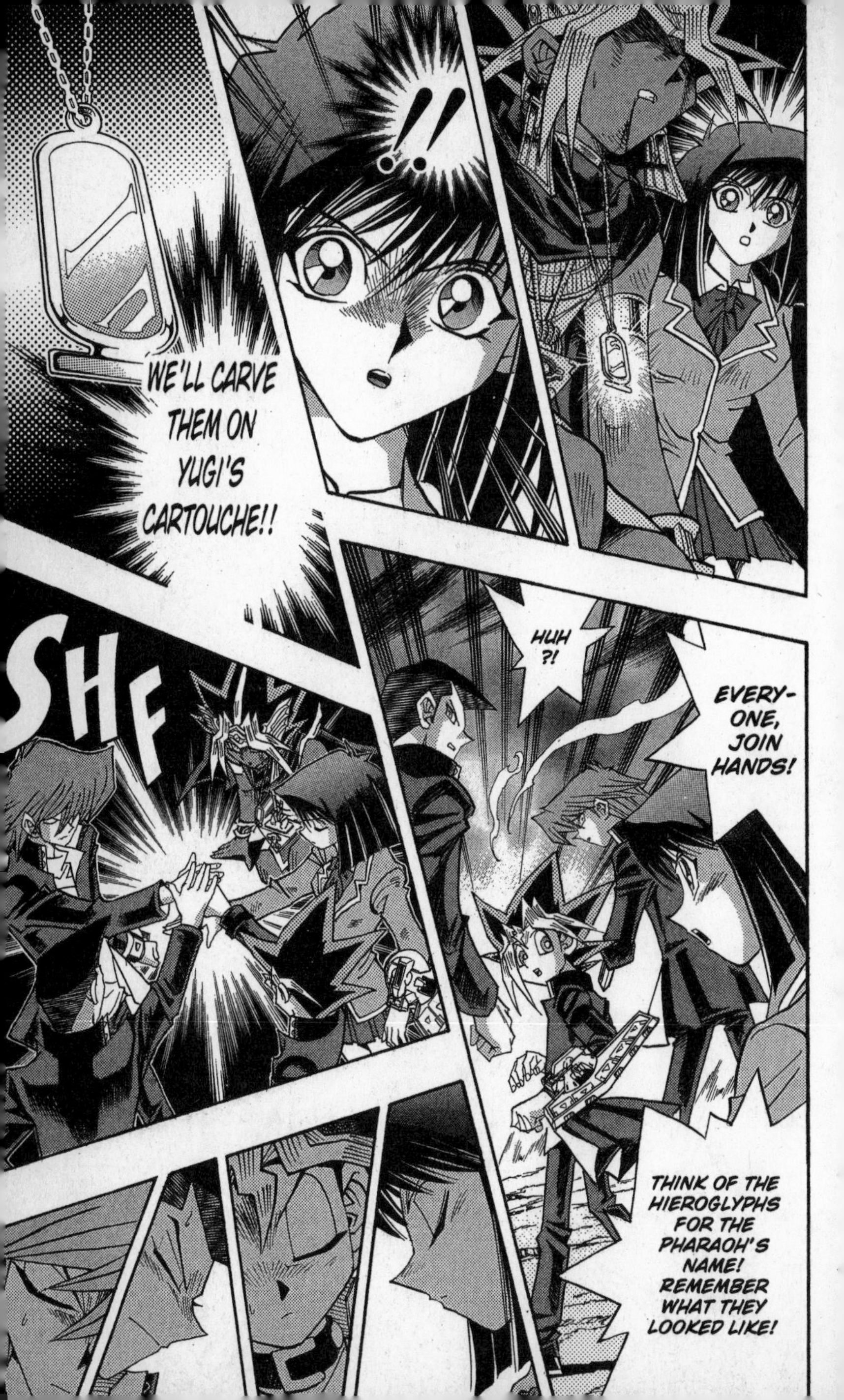
!!
WE'LL CARVE THEM ON YUGI'S CARTOUCHE!!
HUH ?!
EVERY-ONE, JOIN HANDS!
THINK OF THE HIEROGLYPHS FOR THE PHARAOH'S NAME! REMEMBER WHAT THEY LOOKED LIKE!
SHF

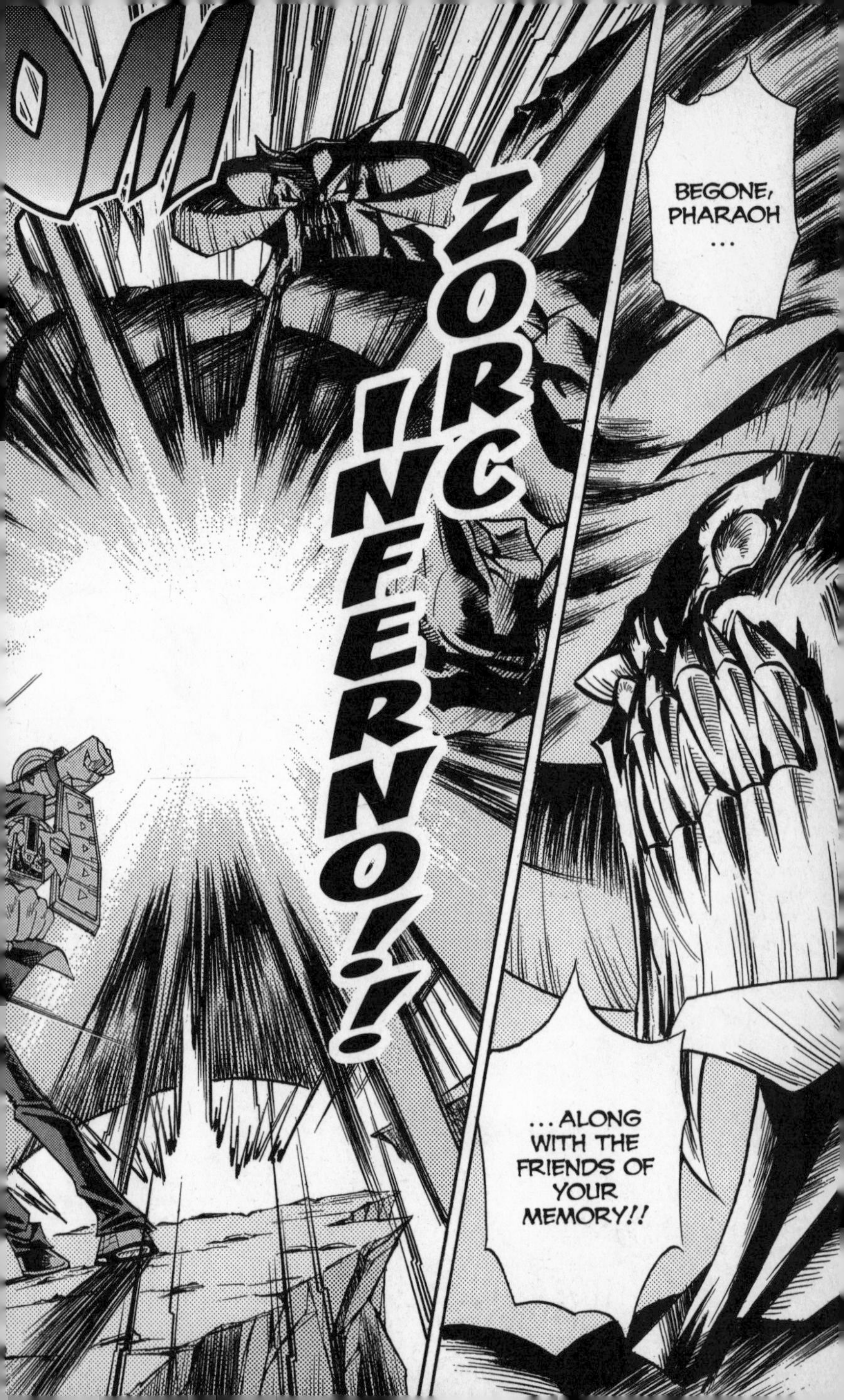
BEGONE, PHARAOH ...
ZORC INFERNO!!
...ALONG WITH THE FRIENDS OF YOUR MEMORY!!
OM

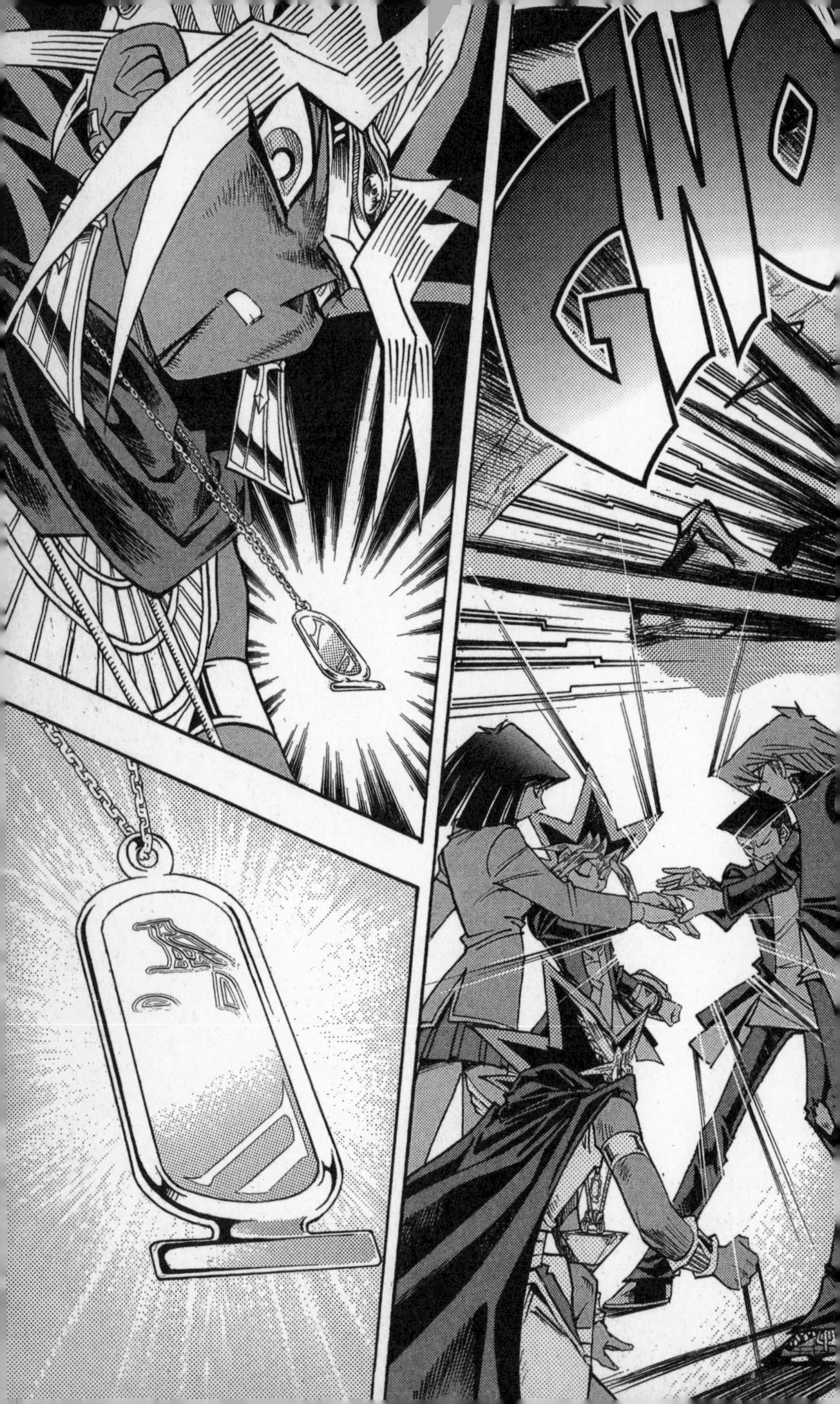

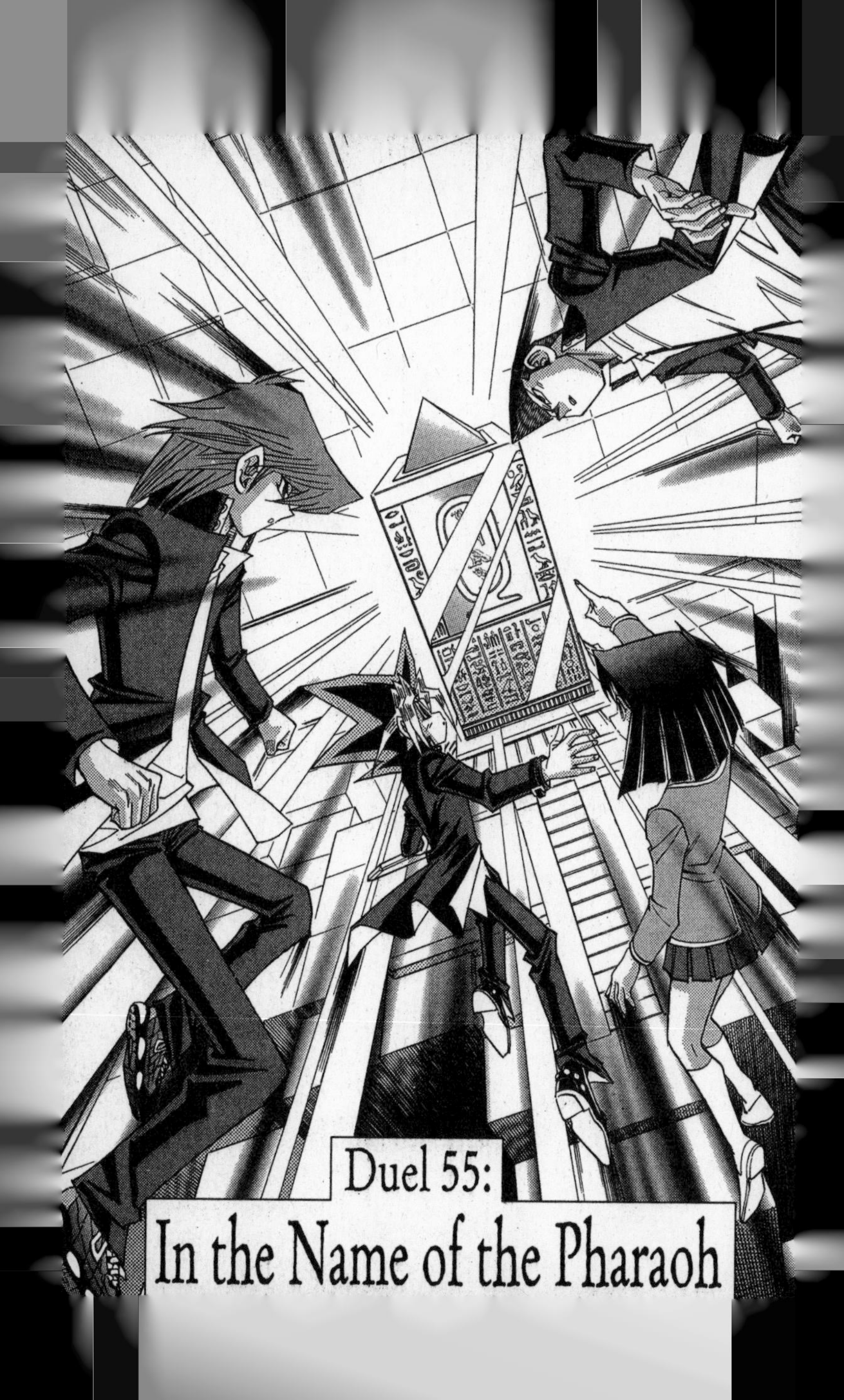
Duel 55:
In the Name of the Pharaoh

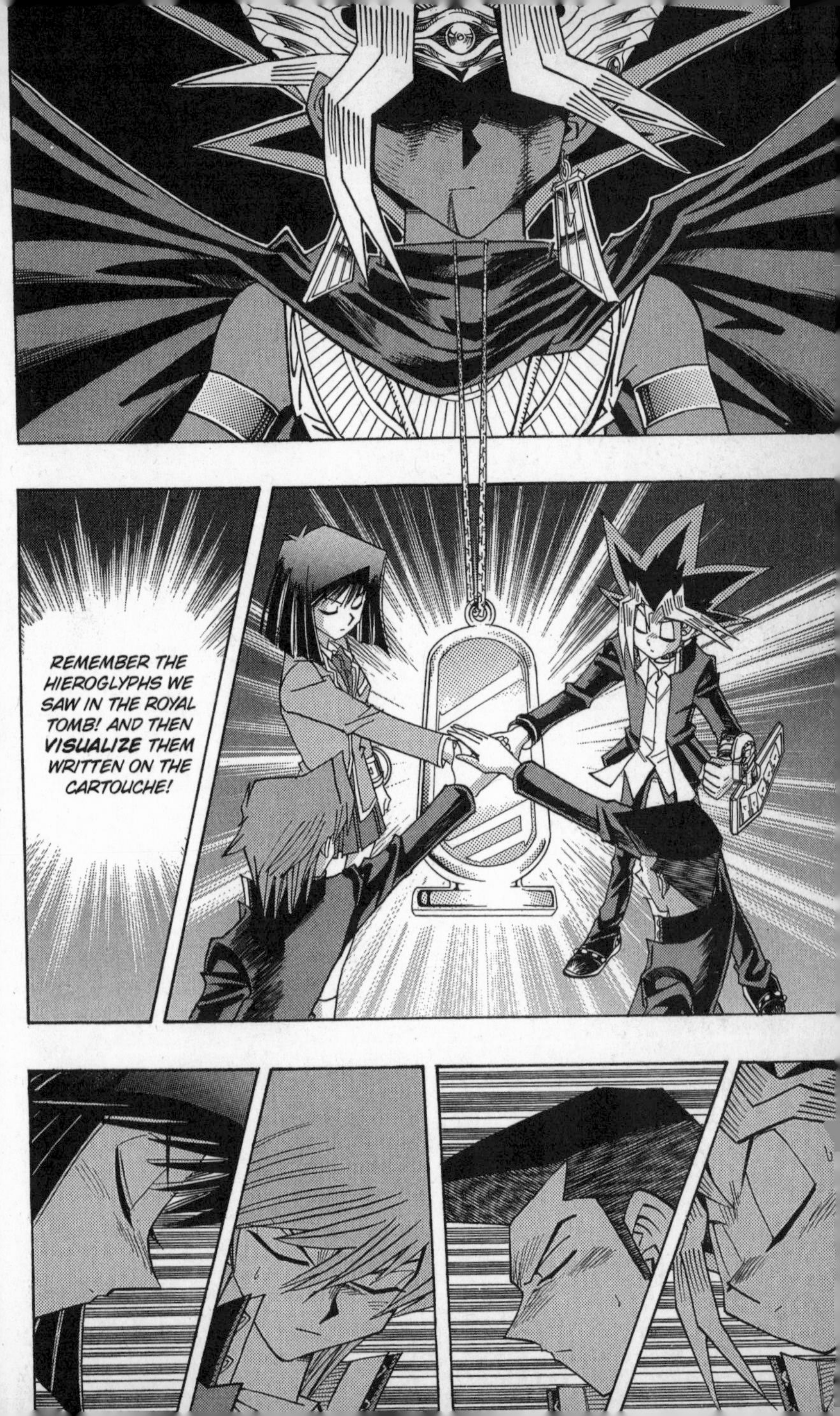
REMEMBER THE HIEROGLYPHS WE SAW IN THE ROYAL TOMB! AND THEN **VISUALIZE** THEM WRITTEN ON THE CARTOUCHE!

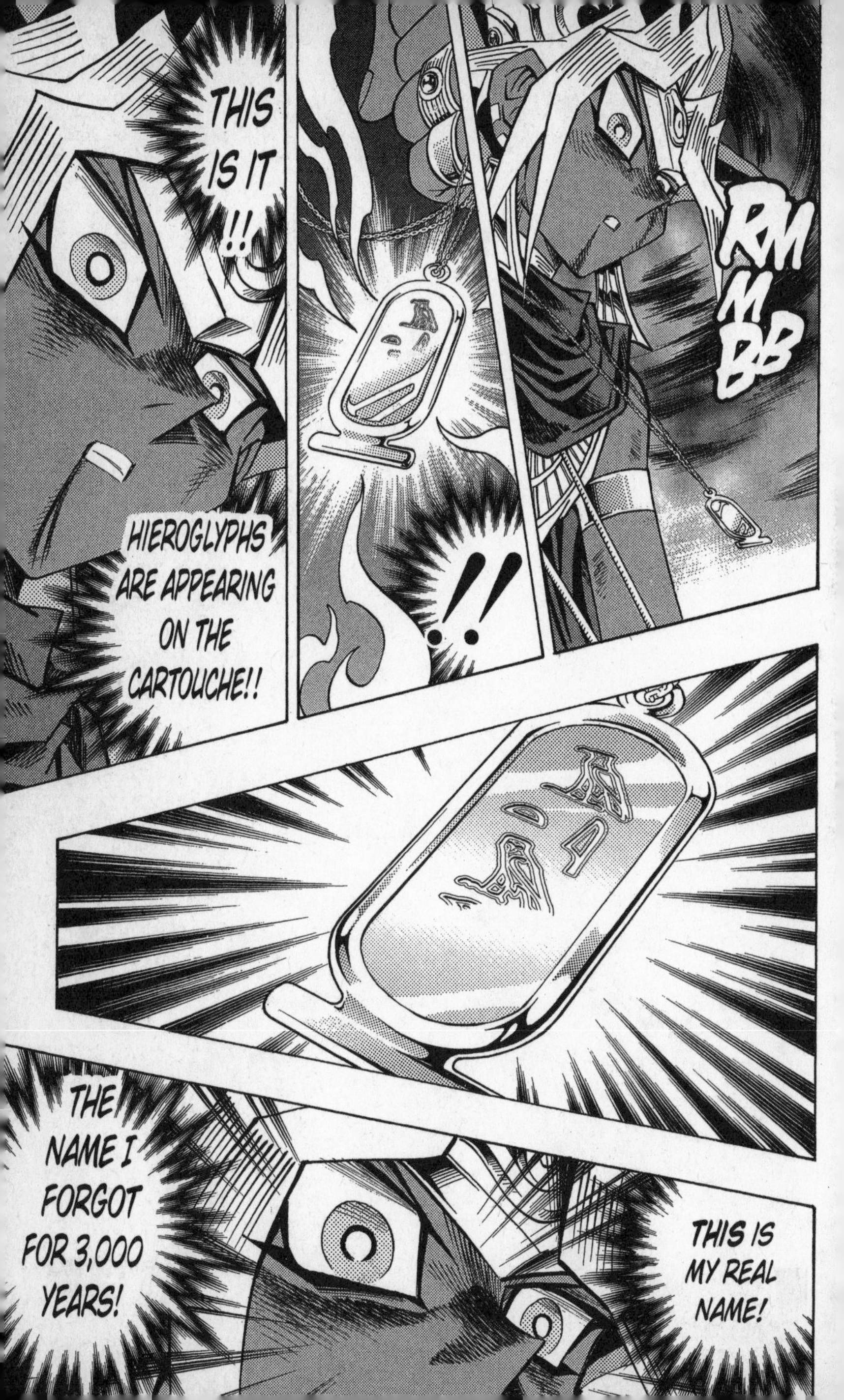
RMMBB
!!
THIS IS IT!!
HIEROGLYPHS ARE APPEARING ON THE CARTOUCHE!!
THIS IS MY REAL NAME!
THE NAME I FORGOT FOR 3,000 YEARS!

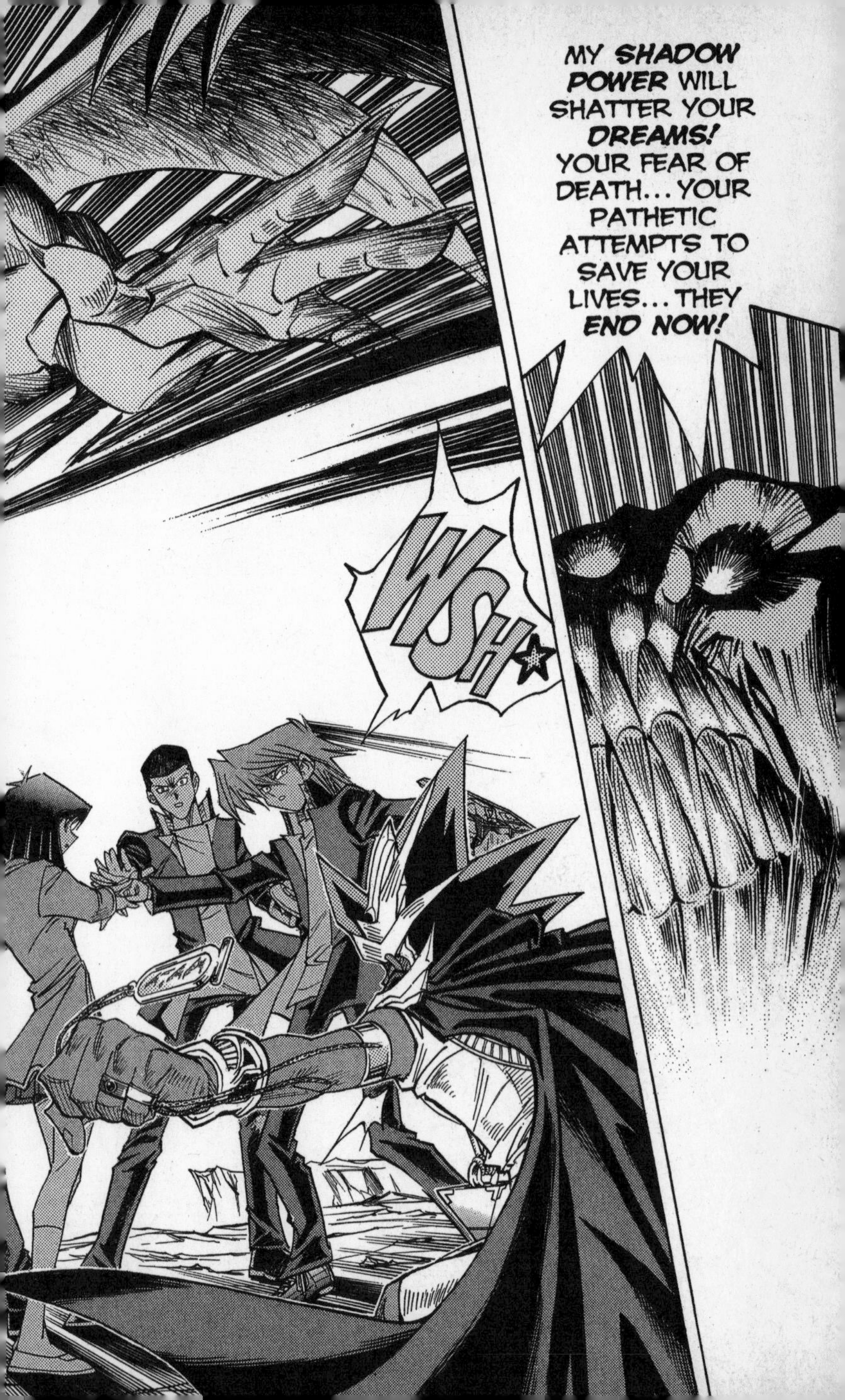
MY SHADOW POWER WILL SHATTER YOUR DREAMS! YOUR FEAR OF DEATH... YOUR PATHETIC ATTEMPTS TO SAVE YOUR LIVES... THEY END NOW!
WSH☆

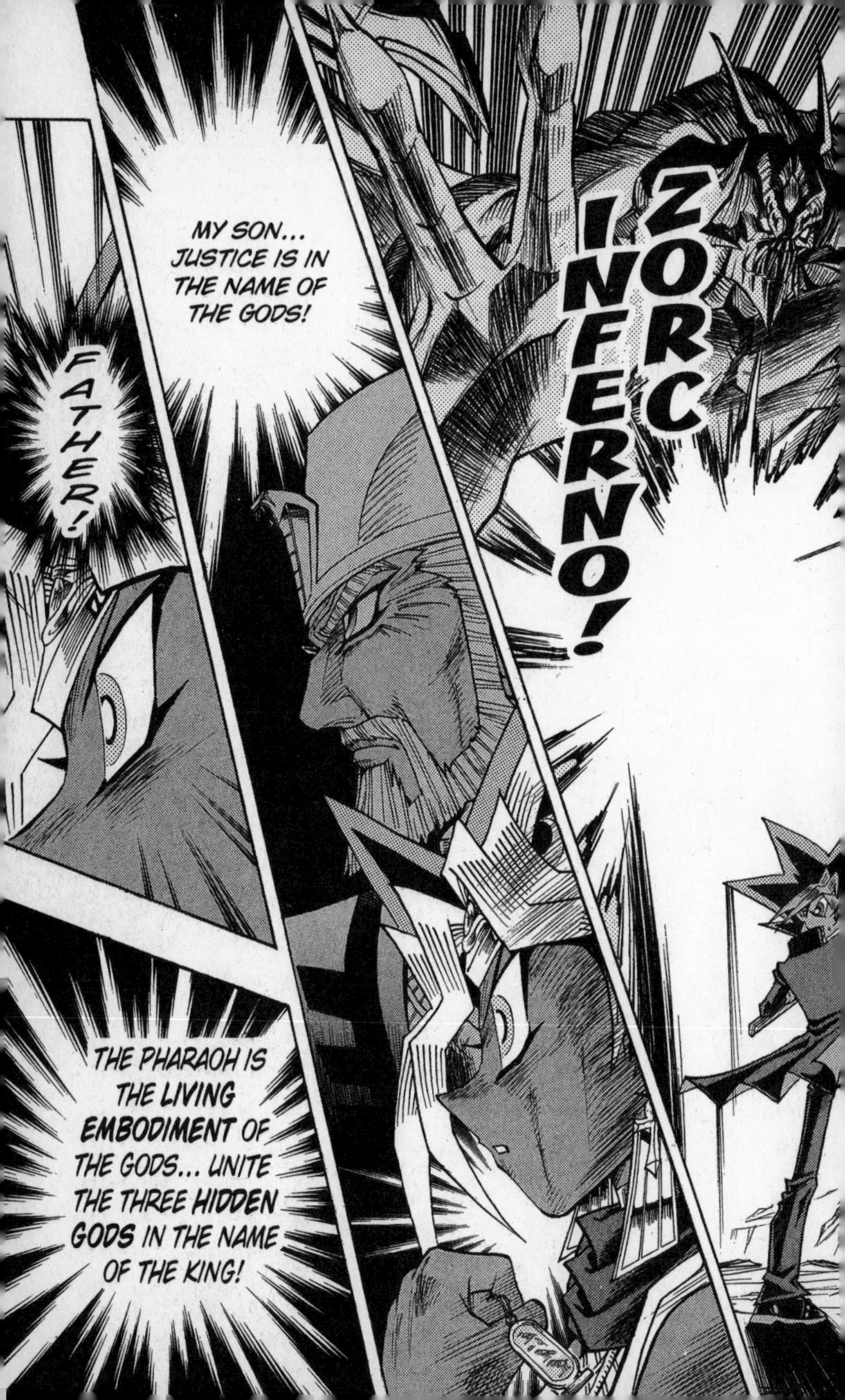
ZORC INFERNO!
MY SON... JUSTICE IS IN THE NAME OF THE GODS!
FATHER!
THE PHARAOH IS THE LIVING EMBODIMENT OF THE GODS... UNITE THE THREE HIDDEN GODS IN THE NAME OF THE KING!

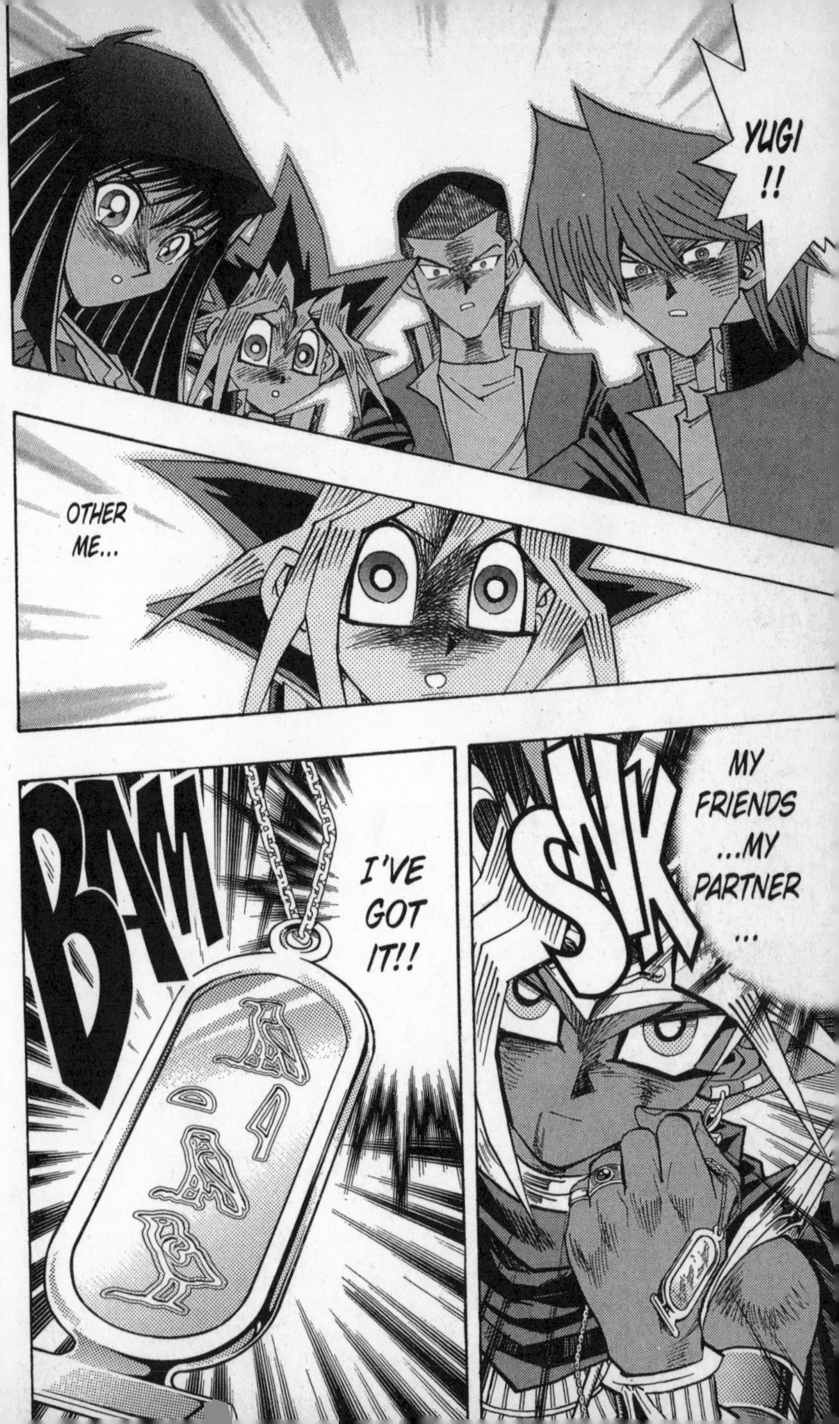
YUGI !!
OTHER ME...
SNK
MY FRIENDS ...MY PARTNER ...
BAM
I'VE GOT IT!!

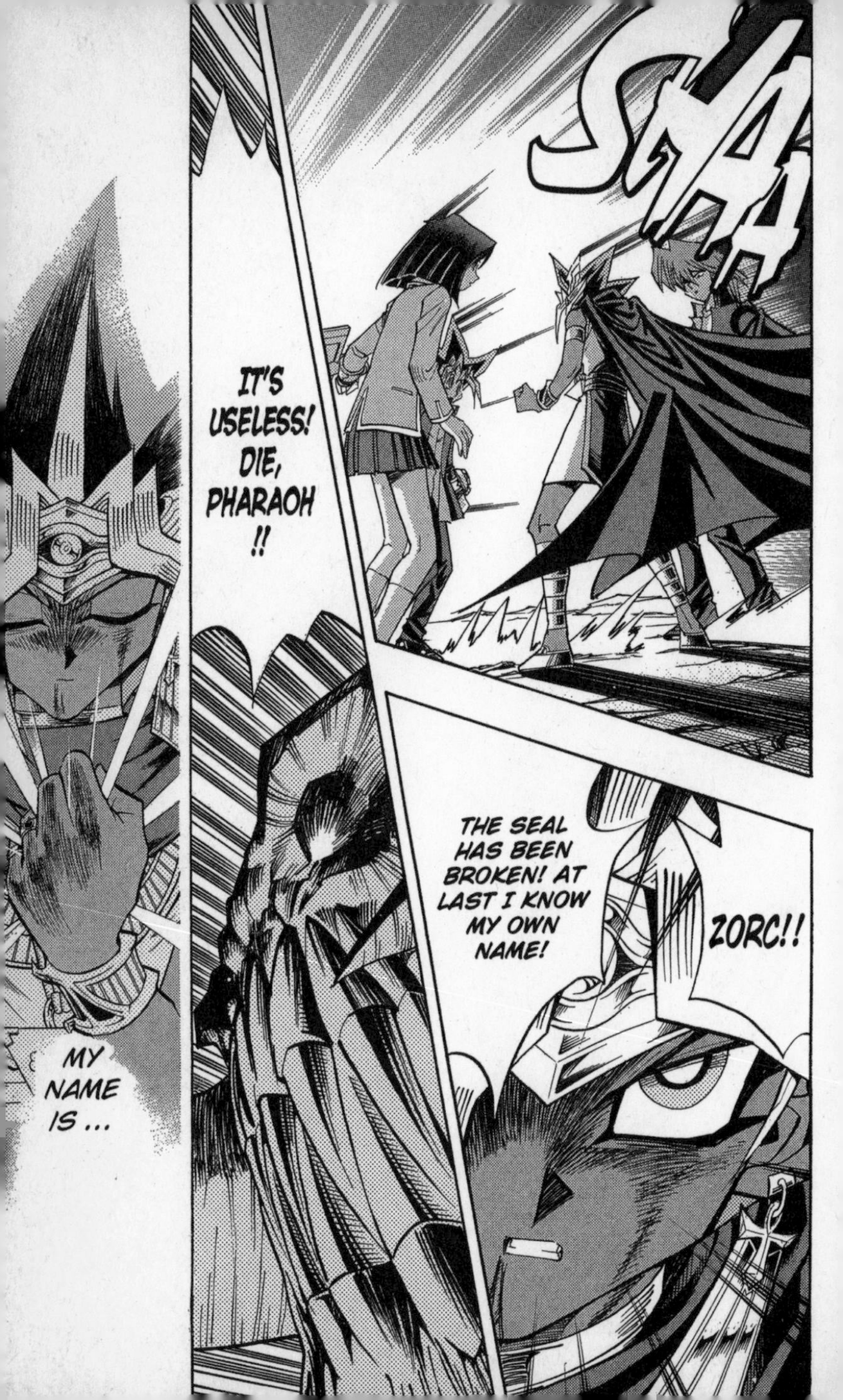
SHA
IT'S USELESS! DIE, PHARAOH!!
THE SEAL HAS BEEN BROKEN! AT LAST I KNOW MY OWN NAME!
ZORC!!
MY NAME IS ...

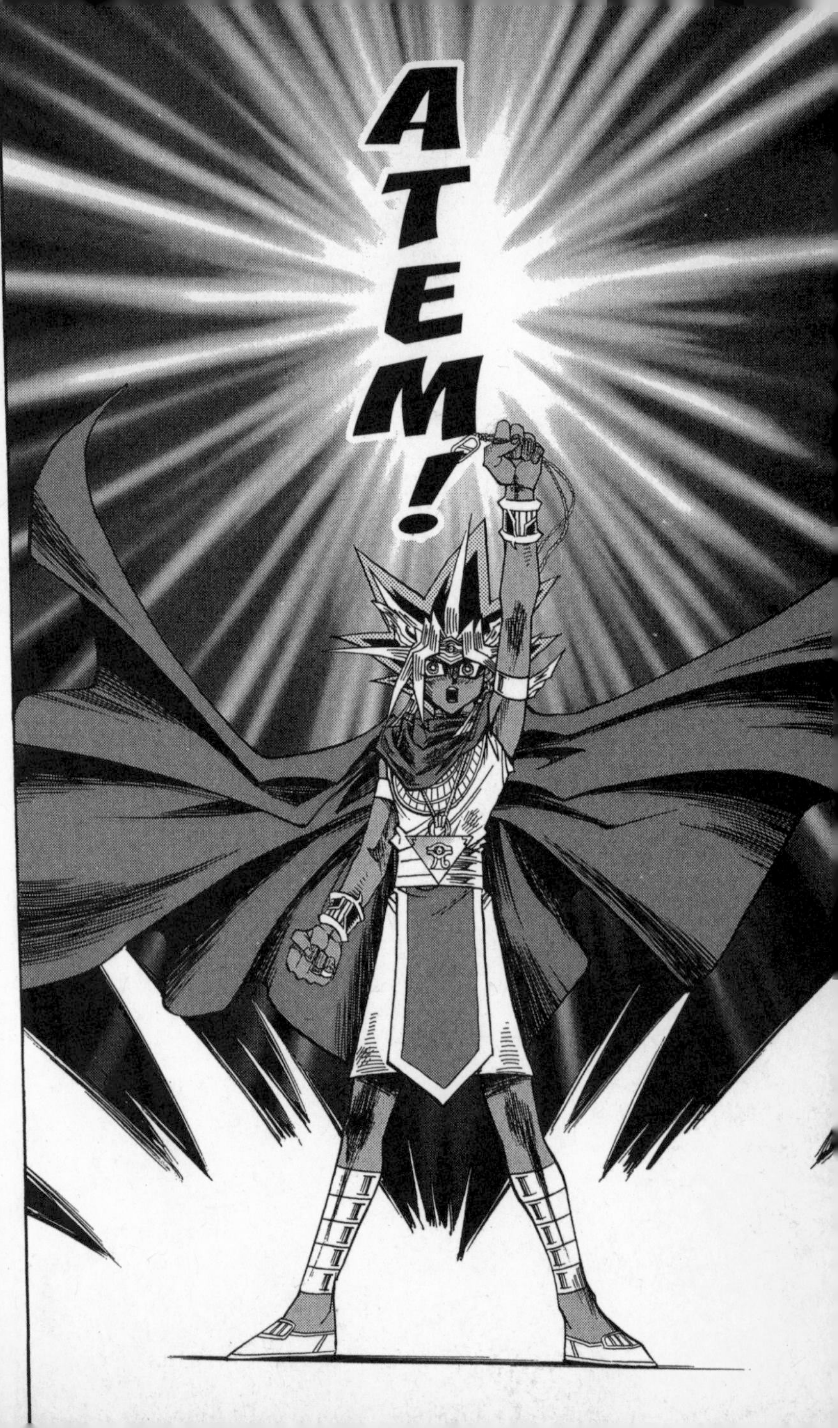
ATEM!

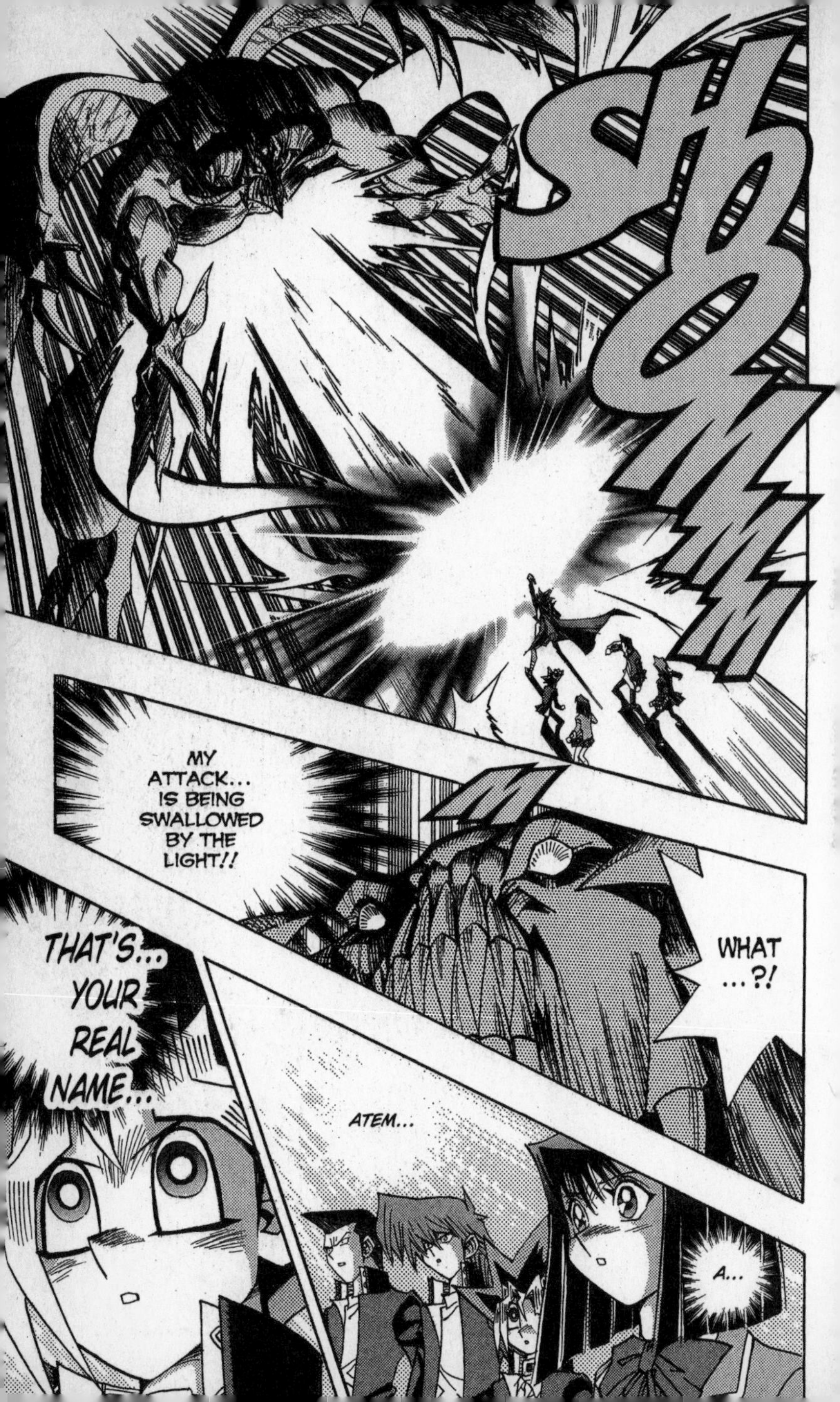
MY ATTACK... IS BEING SWALLOWED BY THE LIGHT!!
WHAT ...?!
A...
ATEM...
THAT'S... YOUR REAL NAME...

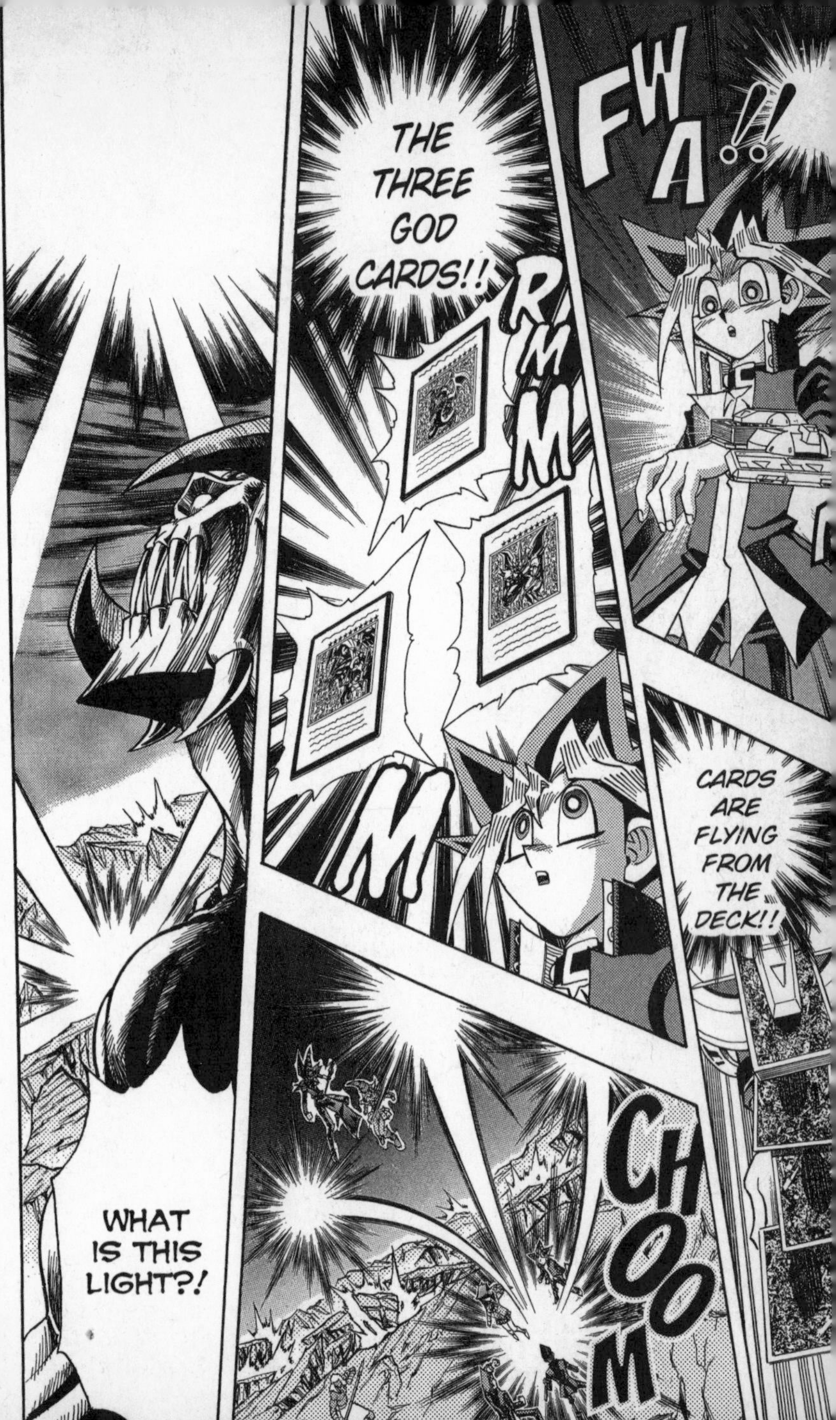
FWA!!
THE THREE GOD CARDS!!
RMMMM
CARDS ARE FLYING FROM THE DECK!!
CHOOOM
WHAT IS THIS LIGHT?!

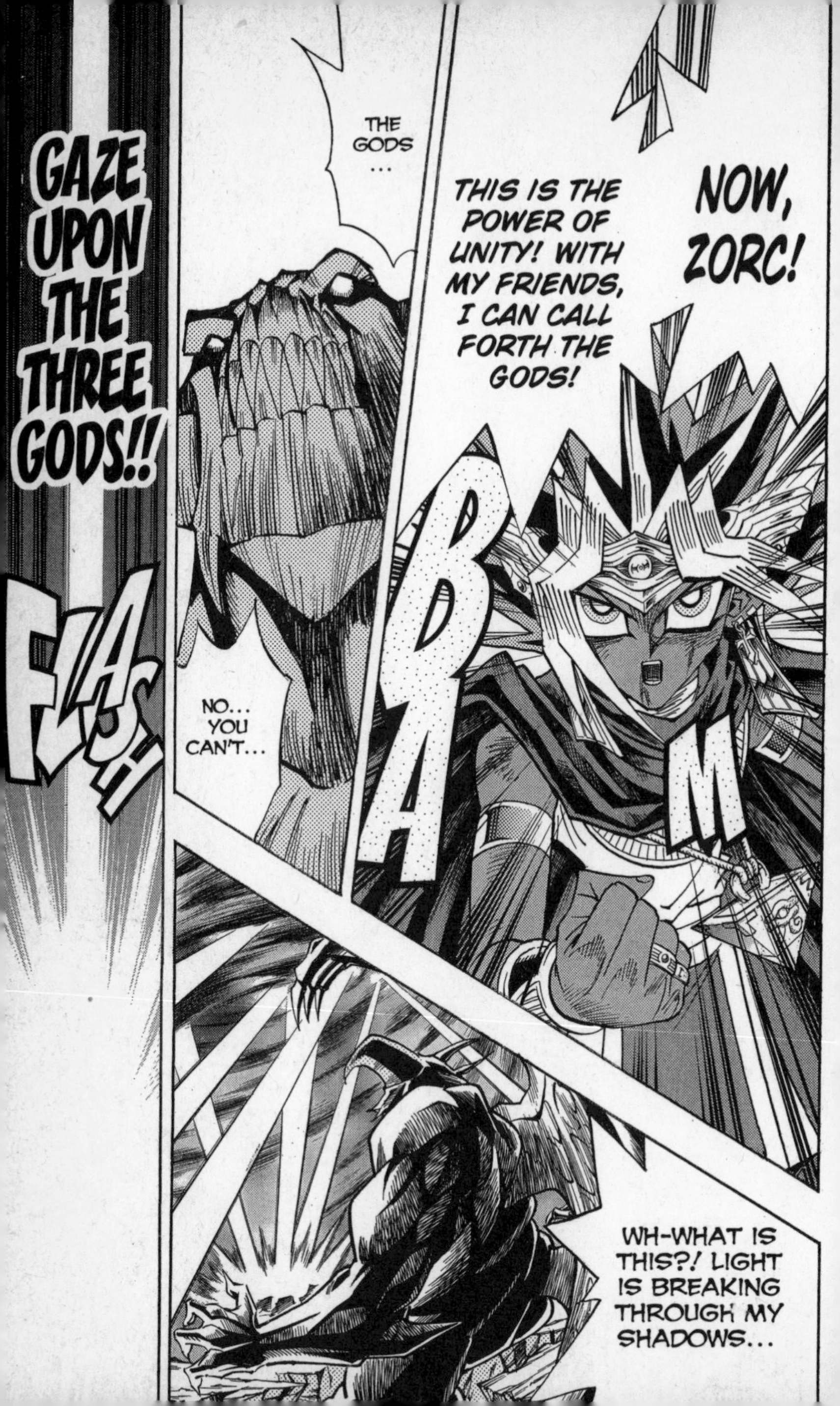
NOW, ZORC!
THIS IS THE POWER OF UNITY! WITH MY FRIENDS, I CAN CALL FORTH THE GODS!
BAM
THE GODS...
NO... YOU CAN'T...
WH-WHAT IS THIS?! LIGHT IS BREAKING THROUGH MY SHADOWS...
GAZE UPON THE THREE GODS!!
FLASH!!

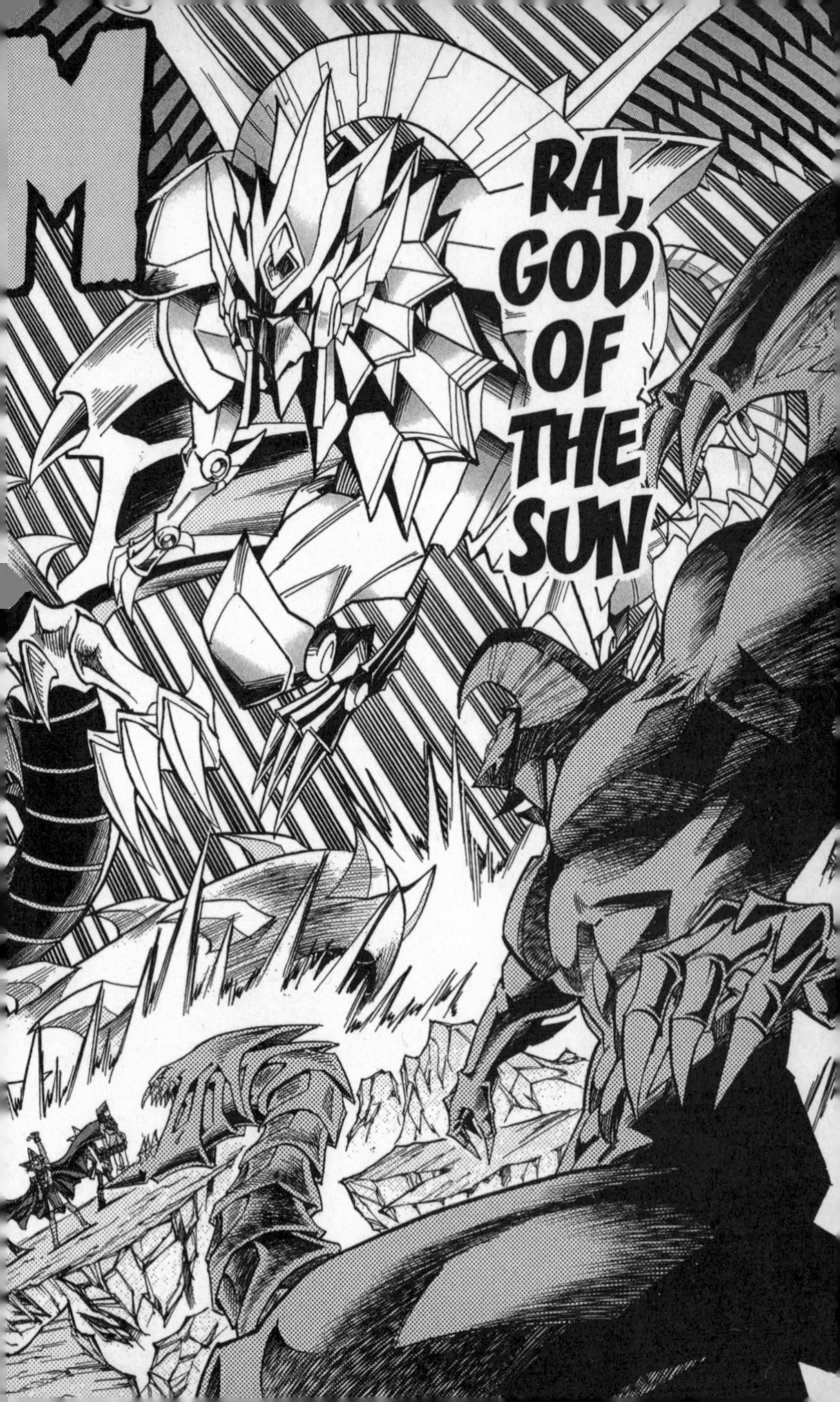

RA, GOD OF THE SUN

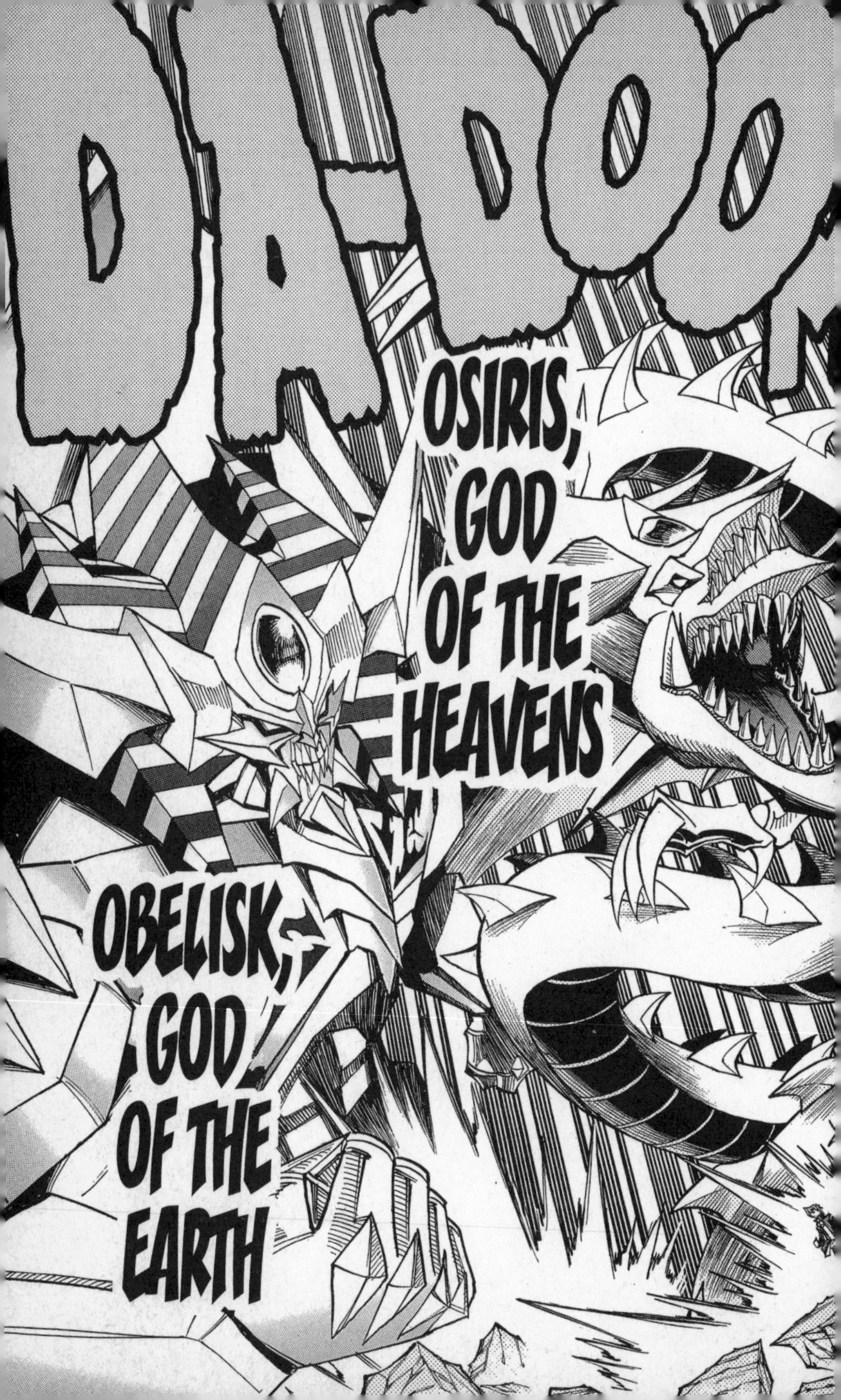
DA-DOOM
OSIRIS, GOD OF THE HEAVENS
OBELISK, GOD OF THE EARTH

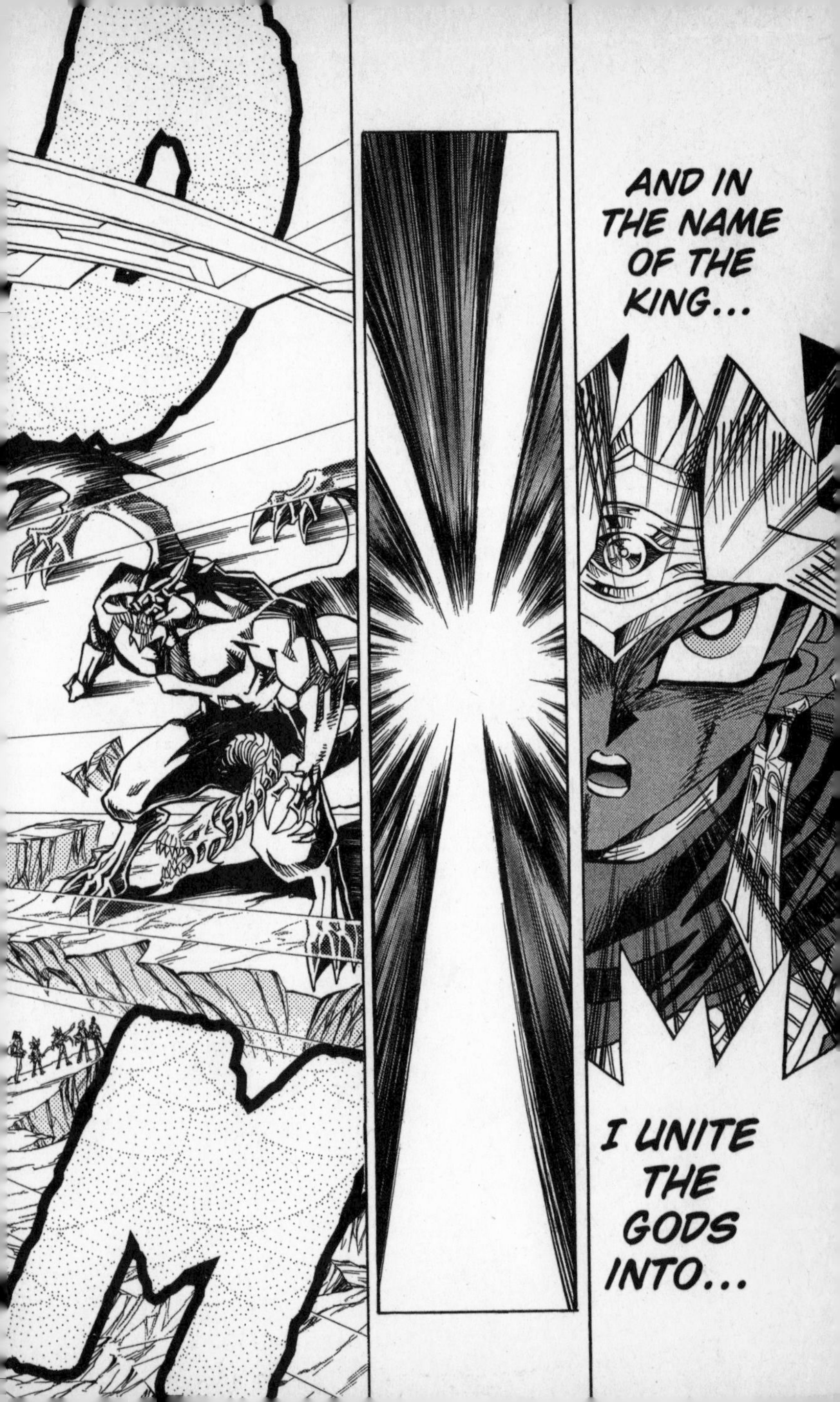
AND IN THE NAME OF THE KING...
I UNITE THE GODS INTO...

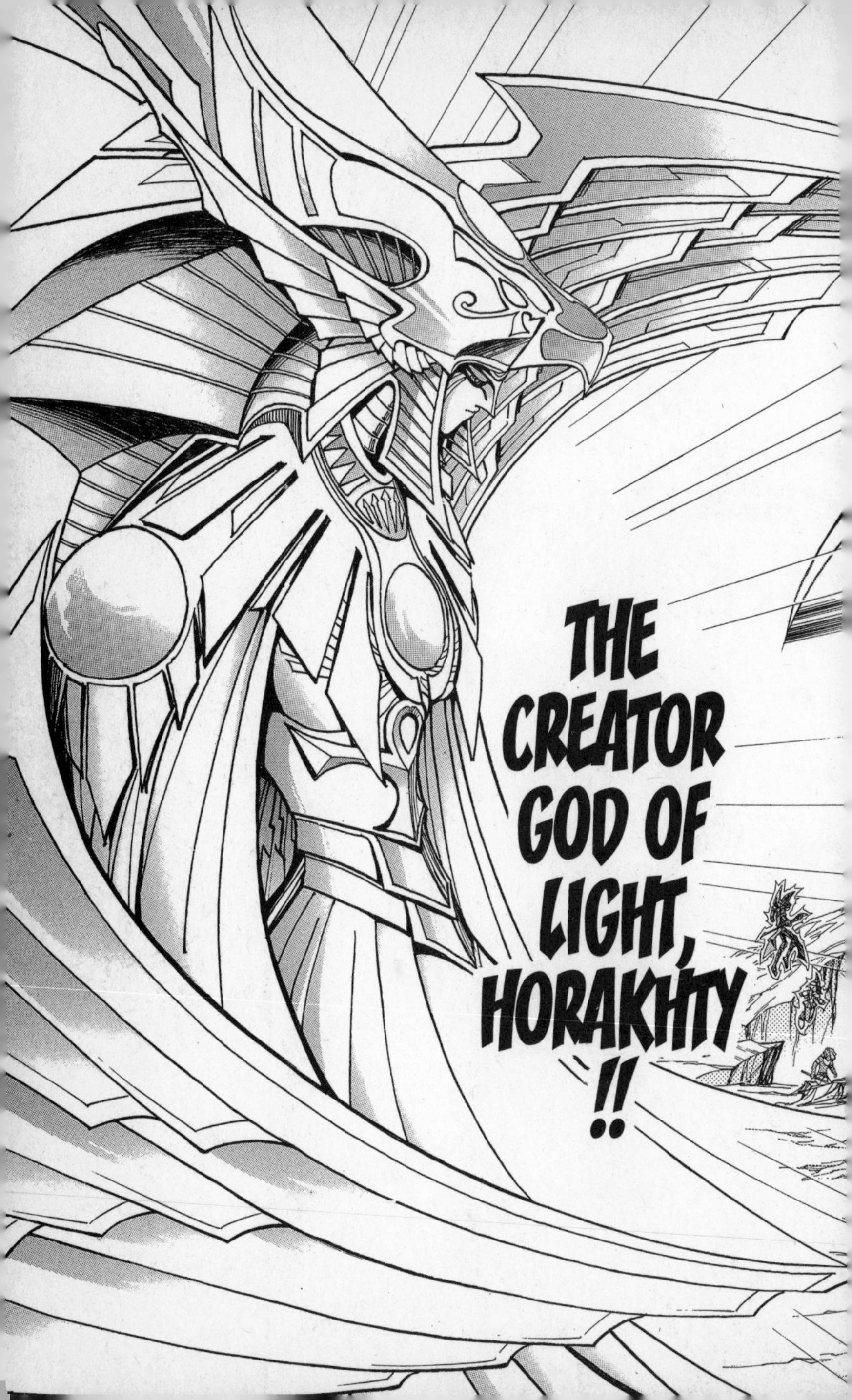
THE CREATOR GOD OF LIGHT, HORAKHTY!!

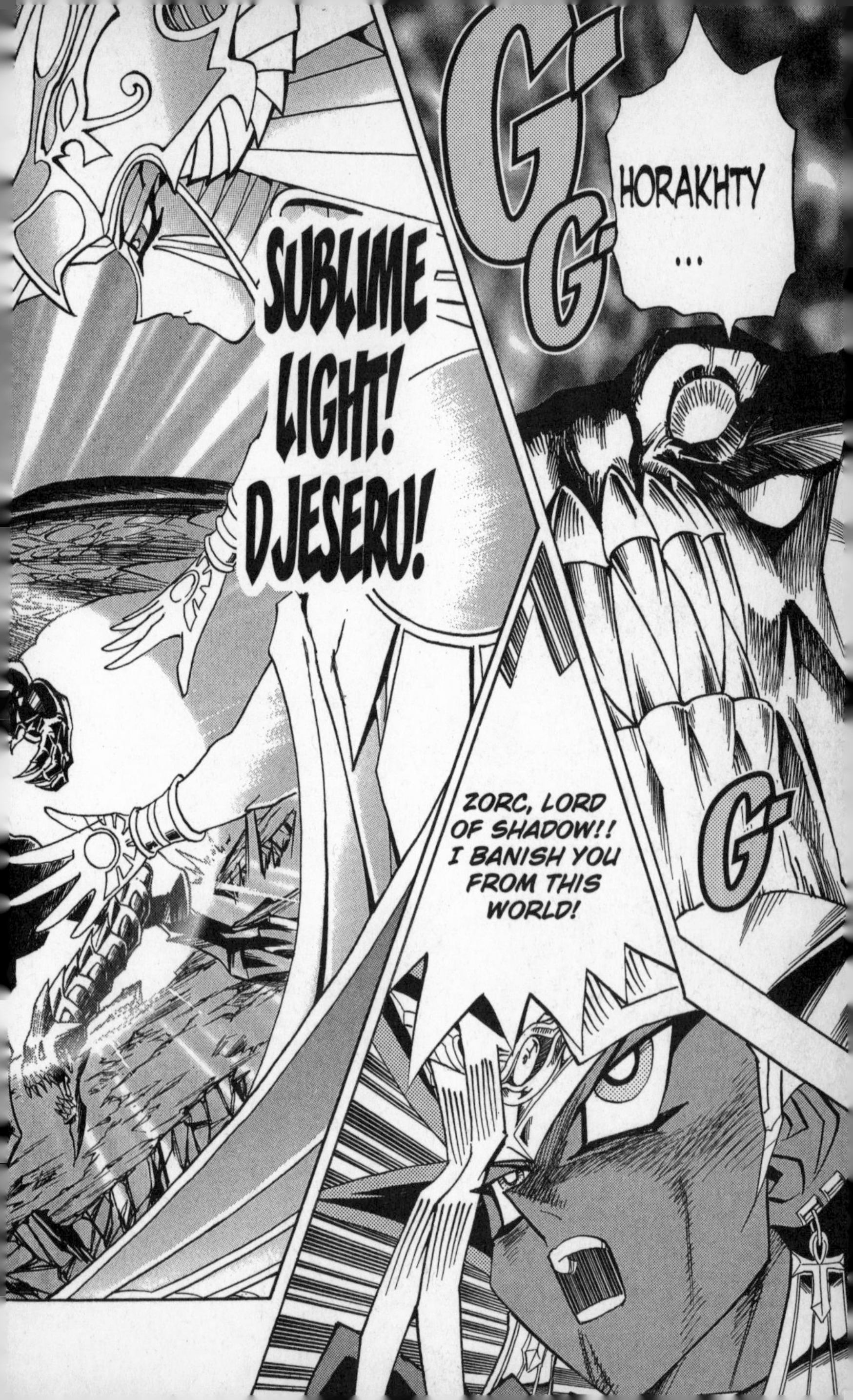
GG
HORAKHTY ...
G
ZORC, LORD OF SHADOW!! I BANISH YOU FROM THIS WORLD!
SUBLIME LIGHT! DJESERU!

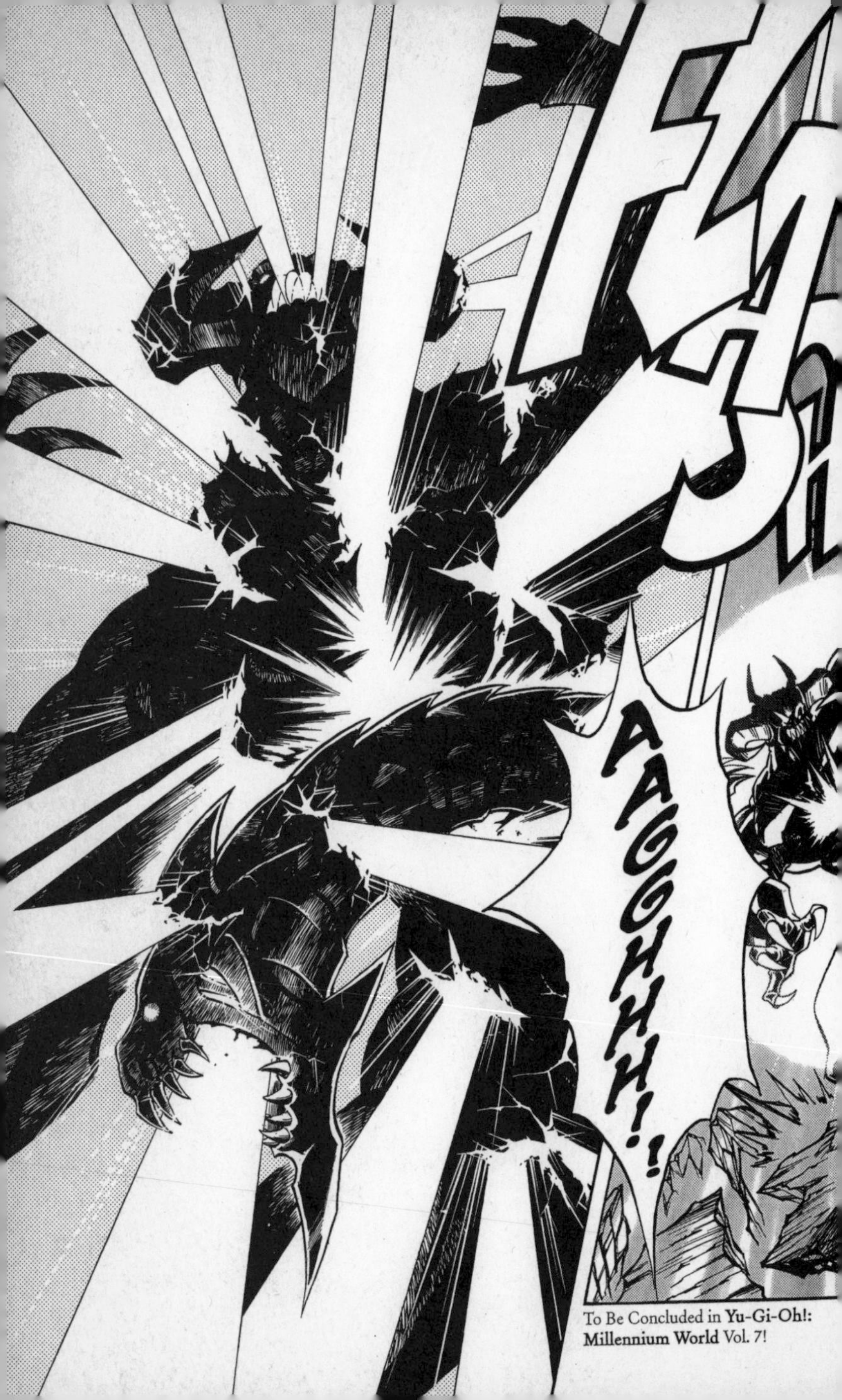
AAGGHHH!!

To Be Concluded in **Yu-Gi-Oh!: Millennium World** Vol. 7!

IN THE NEXT VOLUME...

In the illusionary Millennium World, the forces of good and evil clash for the last time. But can evil ever be truly conquered? Back in the modern world, the heroes must go on a journey to the real Egypt, where Yu-Gi-Oh—the pharaoh—must face his final destination. But first, he will have to defeat his toughest opponent...himself!

AVAILABLE FEBRUARY 2008!

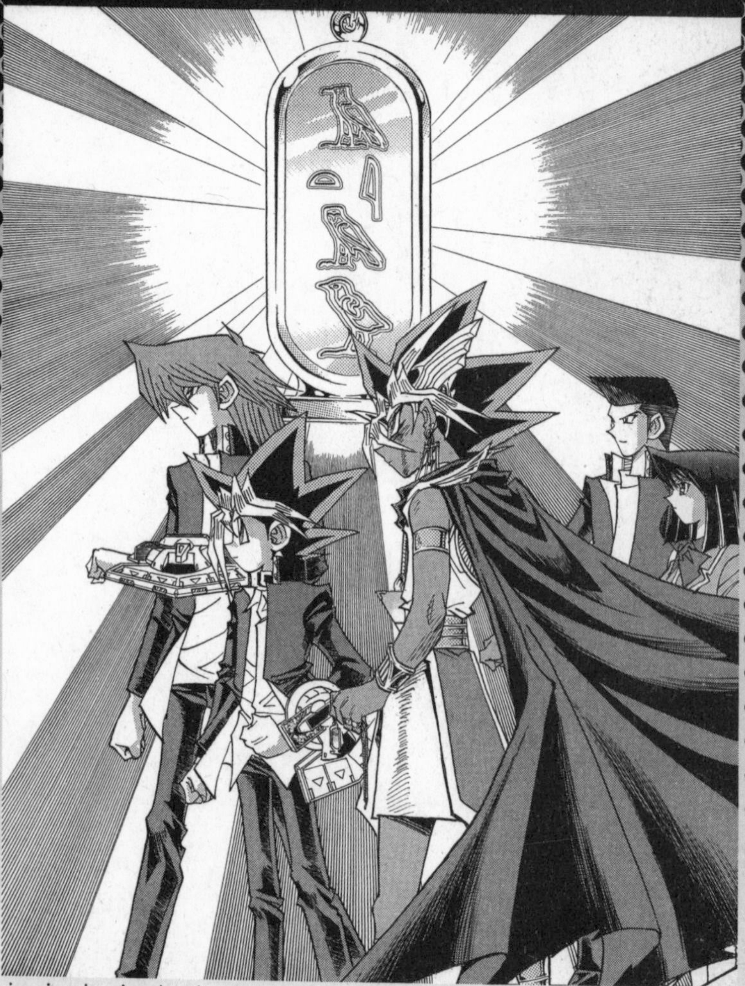

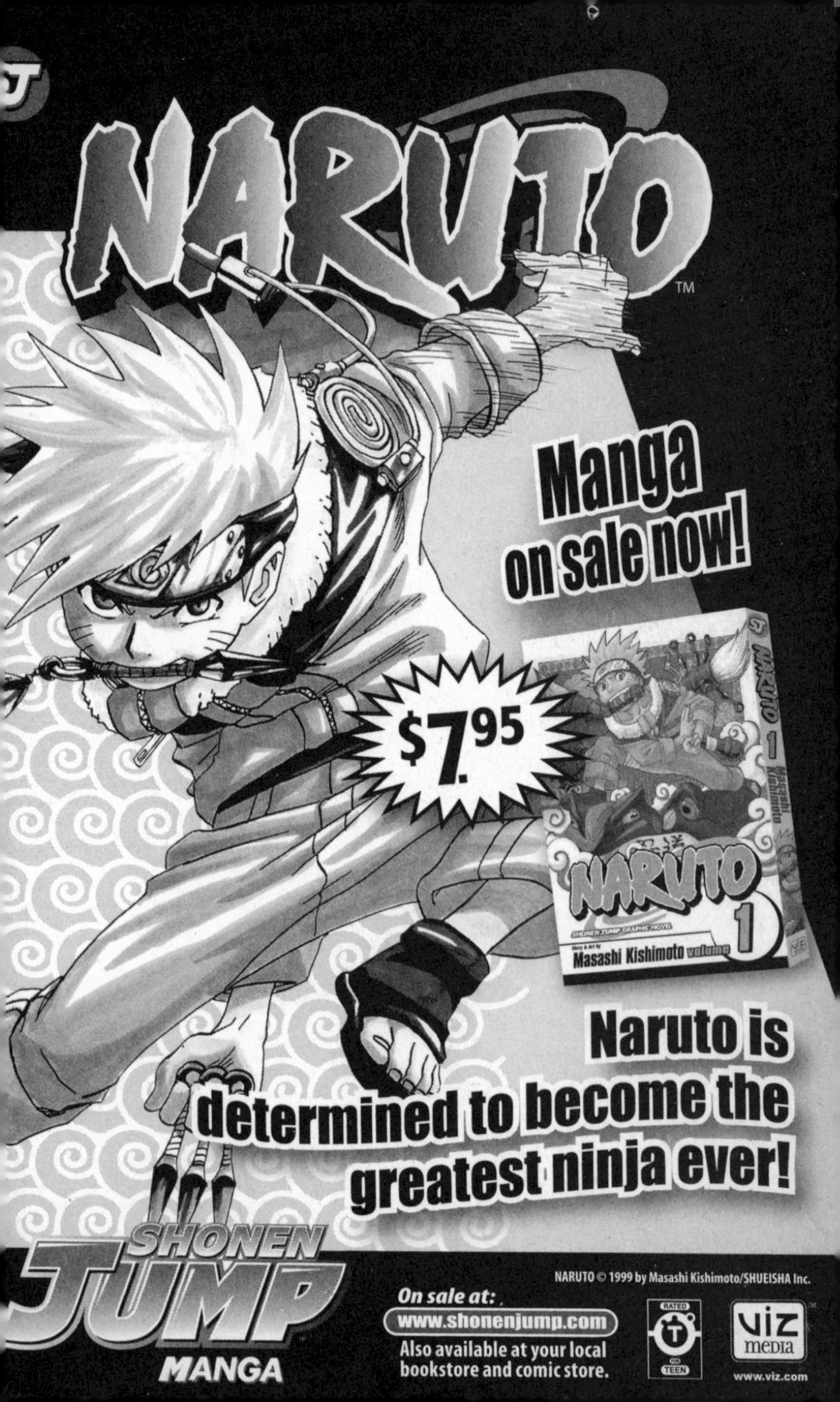
NARUTO™
Manga on sale now!
$7.95
NARUTO 1
SHONEN JUMP GRAPHIC NOVEL
Story & Art by Masashi Kishimoto volume 1
Naruto is determined to become the greatest ninja ever!
SHONEN JUMP MANGA
NARUTO © 1999 by Masashi Kishimoto/SHUEISHA Inc.
On sale at:
www.shonenjump.com
Also available at your local bookstore and comic store.
RATED T FOR TEEN
viz media
www.viz.com

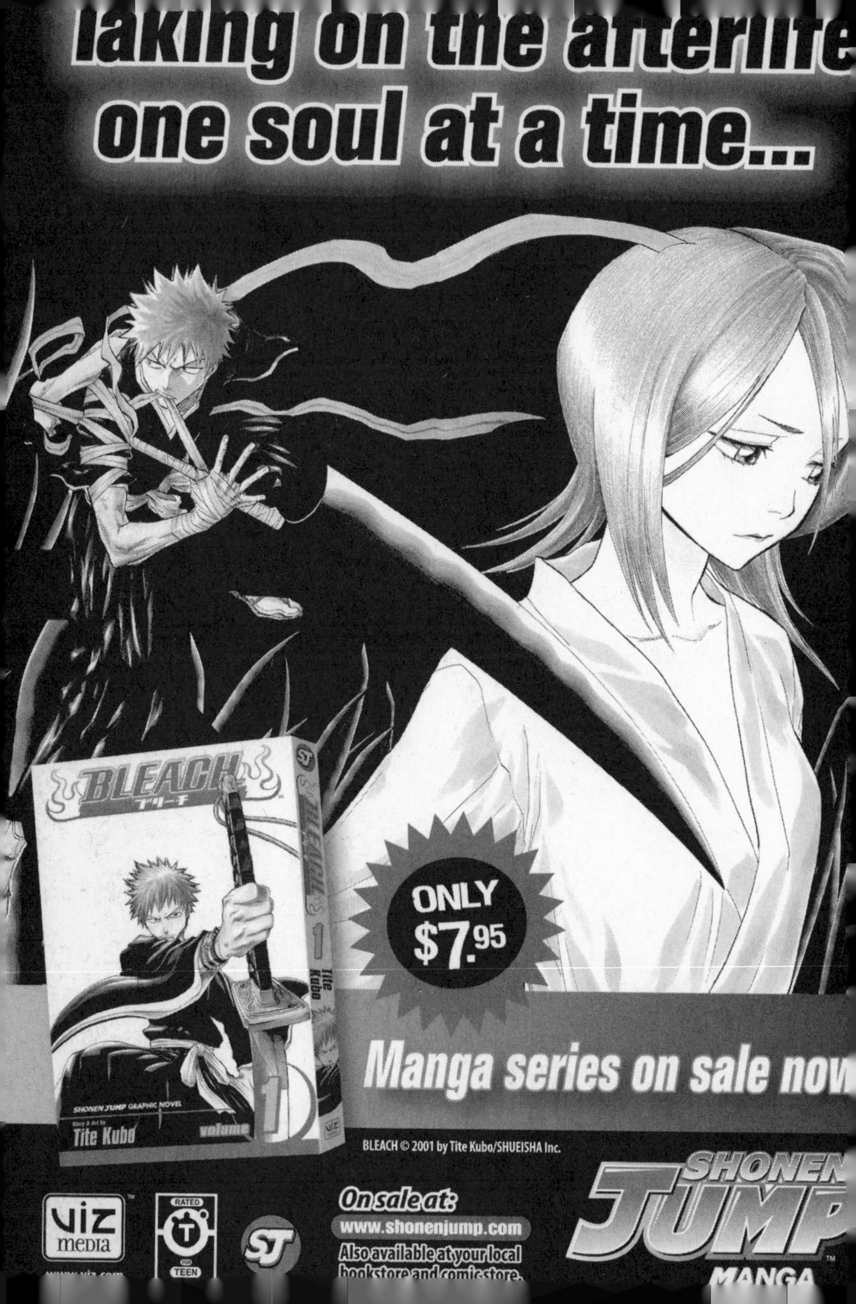

Taking on the afterlife
one soul at a time...
BLEACH
ブリーチ
SHONEN JUMP GRAPHIC NOVEL
Tite Kubo
volume 1
ONLY $7.95
Manga series on sale now
BLEACH © 2001 by Tite Kubo/SHUEISHA Inc.
viz media
RATED T FOR TEEN
SJ
On sale at:
www.shonenjump.com
Also available at your local bookstore and comic store.
SHONEN JUMP
MANGA

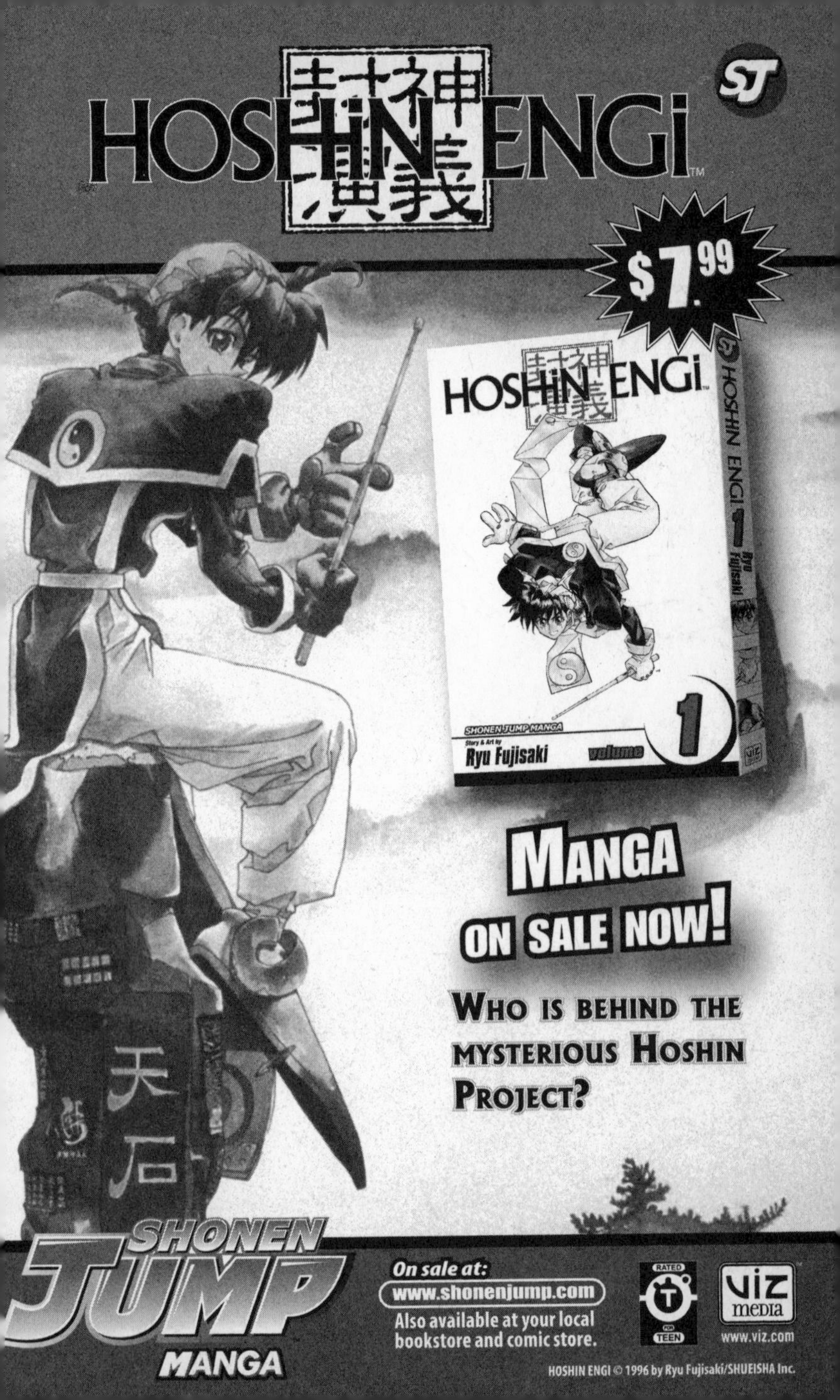
SJ
HOSHIN ENGI™
$7.99
SJ HOSHIN ENGI 1 Ryu Fujisaki
HOSHIN ENGI
SHONEN JUMP MANGA
Story & Art by
Ryu Fujisaki
volume 1
MANGA
ON SALE NOW!
WHO IS BEHIND THE MYSTERIOUS HOSHIN PROJECT?
SHONEN JUMP MANGA
On sale at:
www.shonenjump.com
Also available at your local bookstore and comic store.
RATED T FOR TEEN
VIZ media
www.viz.com
HOSHIN ENGI © 1996 by Ryu Fujisaki/SHUEISHA Inc.

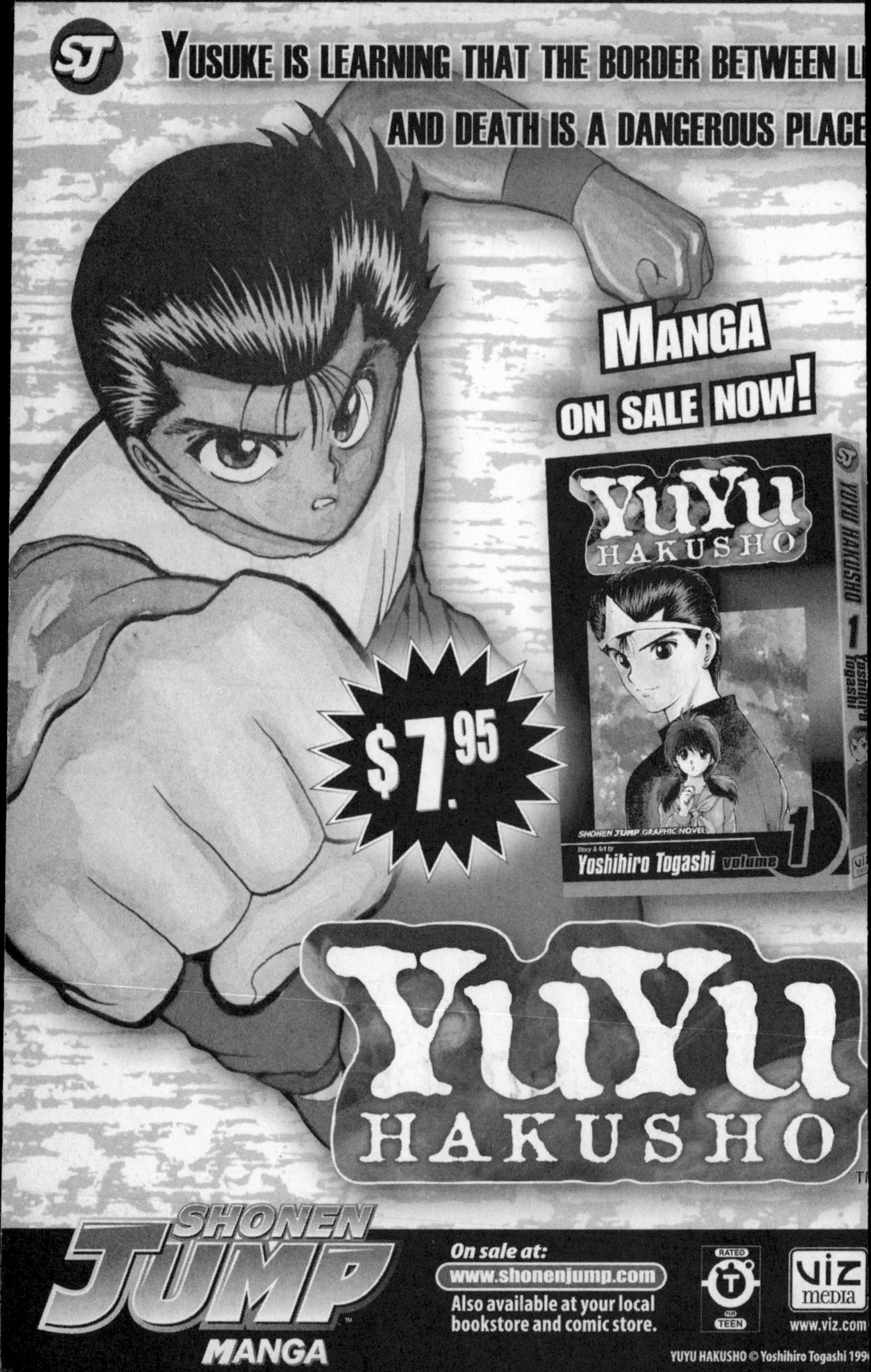
YUSUKE IS LEARNING THAT THE BORDER BETWEEN L
AND DEATH IS A DANGEROUS PLACE
MANGA
ON SALE NOW!
YUYU HAKUSHO
1
SHONEN JUMP GRAPHIC NOVEL
Yoshihiro Togashi volume 1
$7.95
YUYU HAKUSHO
SHONEN JUMP MANGA
On sale at:
www.shonenjump.com
Also available at your local bookstore and comic store.
RATED T TEEN
viz media
www.viz.com
YUYU HAKUSHO © Yoshihiro Togashi 199